FOOD AS AN IDOL

The Types, Causes, Consequences, Conquering, and Prevention of Disordered Eating

Other Books by Pamela K. Orgeron:

The ABC's of Life for Children and Adults: Short Stories, Essays, and Poems Promoting Christian Concepts (Xulon Press, 2003)

The New ABC's of Life for Children and Adults: Short Stories, Essays, and Poems Promoting Christian Concepts (ABC's Ministries, 2016)

We Survived Sexual Abuse! You Can Too! Personal Stories of Sexual Abuse Survivors with Information about Sexual Abuse Prevention, Effects, and Recovery (ABC's Ministries, 2016)

Food as an Idol: Finding Freedom from Disordered Eating (ABC's Ministries, 2017)

A Legacy to Remember: "Recollections of a Common Man" (ABC's Ministries, 2018)

***

FOOD AS AN IDOL

The Types, Causes, Consequences, Conquering, and Prevention of Disordered Eating

Written & Edited by:
Pamela K. Orgeron
M.A., Ed.S., BCCC, ACLC

ABC's Ministries
Nashville, TN

Table of Contents

Contents Continued

Contents Continued

Contents Continued

Figures

Tables

***

Preface

The best-selling book for ABC's Ministries, *Food as an Idol: Finding Freedom from Disordered Eating* published in 2017 offers hope and practical methods to overcoming and preventing disordered eating. This book is an adapted version of that book intended to reach a broader audience, especially classroom educators.

The first book entitled *Food as an Idol* was born out of the author's own struggle with food and body image issues throughout her childhood and young adult years. Like the first book entitled *Food as an Idol*, this book also includes sections on the types, causes, consequences, and conquering of disordered eating. To give book purchasers a better understanding of the contents of the book, the subtitle has been changed to *The Types, Causes, Consequences, Conquering, and Prevention of Disordered Eating*.

According to the author, the key points in overcoming and finding freedom from disordered eating that is stressed within *Food as an Idol* is to recognize both over and under eating as a symptom of something missing deeper within the heart of an individual and that disordered eating is a barrier between his or her relationship with God. Not until one discovers the roots of disordered eating and surrenders his or her appetites to God can one find true freedom and deliverance from disordered eating.

The section in both books of most importance to the author is information concerning the prevention of disordered eating. For example, often parents unintentionally set children up for eating disorders by using food as rewards and punishment. Such unhealthy practices of parents are covered within both editions of the book, as well as ways that schools and churches can help fight the obesity and disordered eating epidemic in America and around the world.

How is *Food as an Idol: The Types, Causes Consequences, Conquering, and Prevention of Disordered Eating* different from the first book? Intending this edition to be suitable as a textbook, the author has added an index and, at the end of each chapter a list of Key Terms and Questions for Reflection. Additionally, with the increasing number of sexual abuse scandals being reported in the news, the author thinks she would be remiss to not include more information linking sexual abuse and disordered eating. Thus, a revised edition of an article entitled "Linking Disordered Eating with Sexual Abuse" published by the author on her blog has been added to the Special Topics section.

***

Acknowledgments

This book evolved out of the applied project, *Exploration Linking Self-Reported Disordered Eating and Wellness in Undergraduate Health Students* (Morehead State University, 2009), which I completed to receive my Education Specialist degree. I gratefully acknowledge the guidance and assistance of my committee members for the project: Chairperson Dr. Lola Jean Aagaard-Boram, Dr. Dean W. Owen, Jr., and Dr. Beverly McCauley Klecker in being able to complete the project. Dr. Aagaard continues to remain an encourager and friend today.

In other aspects the roots to *Food as an Idol* stem from my own struggle with food and body image issues throughout my childhood and early adult years. I want to acknowledge the various psychologists and other therapists who walked along side me on my journey to healing. Among them are Dr. Douglas Vaughan and Dr. Kathryn Sherrod.

More recently, I would be amiss not to mention others who have encouraged me in the revision process of *Food as an Idol*. These individuals or groups who have influenced the development of this book include:

- The leaders and participants of the Author Learning Center at Westbow Press's Website
- Kim Avery and the members of her online group, Christian Coaches & Entrepreneurs Community
- Members of my home church, The Donelson Fellowship, Nashville, TN
- Members of Flourish, an online community for women that I recently joined
- And, lastly, but not least my husband, Milton J. Orgeron.

My biggest thanks go to God who ultimately healed and delivered me from those earlier struggles with food and body image issues. No doubt, God provided me with the talent, skill, and other resources to bring this book to fruition. I also appreciated the guidance of the Holy Spirit in writing and making decisions regarding the publication of this book.

Pamela K. Orgeron
March 25, 2019

***

Introduction

What is meant by the title *Food as an Idol*? To grasp the full meaning of the title, one must first understand the meaning and purpose of food and the meaning of the term, "idol". *Miller-Keane Encyclopedia and Dictionary of Medicine, Nursing, and Allied Health,* Seventh Edition (2003) defines food as "a nourishing substance that is eaten or otherwise taken into the body to sustain life, provide energy, or promote growth". (Food section, ¶ *1)*

What does God say about food? Physical hunger is the only biblical reason for eating (Shamblin, 1997; Arterburn & Mintle, 2004). Furthermore, for individuals practicing disordered eating to focus on satisfying or denying physical hunger to meet certain standards of physical beauty is a sin. Orgeron concludes this based on Matthew 6:25, where Christians are instructed not to worry about what they will eat, drink, or wear. For more Scriptures related to the misuse of food, see Appendix A. The most common term used in Scripture for having food as an idol is referred to as "gluttony". According to Bowers (2015), gluttony is "food worship displayed in both excessive eating and in pharisaical avoidance." (p. 76)

In the book, *Food as an Idol* Pamela K. Orgeron, the Author and Editor, a Board Certified Christian Counselor and an Advanced Christian Life Coach uses the term "gluttony" synonymously with "disordered eating", with the exception of the lowest point marked on the disordered eating continuum. The lowest point on the continuum is normal, healthy eating.

In *We Survived Sexual Abuse! You Can Too!* (2016, ABC's Ministries) Orgeron defines disordered eating:

> *Disordered eating defined. What is disordered eating? Orgeron explains disordered eating as being on a continuum where persons who do not display dieting, bingeing, purging, or other eating disorder behaviors are on the lower end. Persons hospitalized with clinically diagnosed eating disorders identified in the Diagnostic and Statistical Manual of Mental Disorders, Fifth Edition (DSM-V), published by the American Psychiatric Association (APA) (2013) fall on the upper end. Figure 1 below, Disordered Eating Continuum, illustrates classifications along this continuum, according to Vohs, Heatherton, and Herrin (2001), ranging from the nondieter to persons with clinical eating disorders identified in the DSM-V. (Orgeron, 2016, pp. 69-70)*

Figure 1: Disordered Eating Continuum

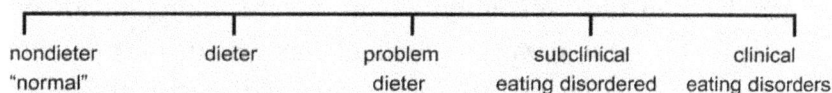

nondieter	dieter	problem	subclinical	clinical
"normal"		dieter	eating disordered	eating disorders

For a better understanding of gluttony as a sin, one might compare using food to using other God-given blessings, such as sex and money. Sex within the confines of a marriage between a man and his wife, a woman is both appropriate and healthy. Yet when lust takes over, and sex exists outside the marriage bed, sex becomes sinful. Likewise, money in and of itself is not evil. In Scripture, Paul wrote to Timothy, "For the love of money is a root of all *kinds of* evil, for which some have strayed from the faith in their greediness, and pierced themselves through with many sorrows." (1 Timothy 6:10) Just as sex and money used with healthy, biblical attitudes in appropriate ways is not sinful, neither is food. However, when we allow food, sex, money, or anything else to take priority over obeying God we are sinning and missing the best He has to offer us.

What is an idol? "Perhaps the best definition of an idol is something we ourselves make into a god. It does not have to be a statue or a tree. It can be anything that stands between us and God or something we substitute for God." (Youngblood, Bruce, & Harrison, 1995, ¶ 5) In Philippians 3:17-19, Paul warns Christians not to make food their god:

> *[17] Brethren, join in following my example, and note those who so walk, as you have us for a pattern. [18] For many walk, of whom I have told you often, and now tell you even weeping, that they are the enemies of the cross of Christ: [19] whose end is destruction, whose god is their belly, and whose glory is in their shame—who set their mind on earthly things. (NKJV)*

Homme (2000) reported that with disordered eating, "The positive attributes of our position in Christ are replaced by the eating-disordered distortions with their need to *perform, please,* or *control.* Eating-disordered behaviors (for example, restricting, bingeing, and purging) are typically a cover for these underlying problems." (p. 241)

When does food become an idol? Piper (December 17, 2015) listed four indicators that an individual is practicing gluttony:

1. A person becomes apathetic to the ill effects that food and his or her use of food is doing to the body.
2. A person becomes apathetic to the way he/she stewards his/her money purchasing wrong/unhealthy foods unwisely.
3. A person uses food for comfort to escape problems.
4. A person fails to see God's purpose for food. He or she no longer experiences pleasing God as the priority in life but he or she substitutes food for God.

> *For those who do not know or understand God, or who fear a relationship with him, food can seem the safer choice. This, however, places food in the position of an idol, as a created thing taking the place and position that rightly belongs to the Creator of all. "Do not worship any other god, for the Lord, whose name is Jealous, is a jealous God" (Exodus 34:14). (Jantz, 2010, p. 211)*

In *Food as an Idol: Finding Freedom from Disordered Eating* Orgeron combines her education with her life experience as a recovered bulimic to compile a book that will be helpful to others struggling with disordered eating issues and help in the prevention of disordered eating in today's world. Additionally, clinicians will find *Food as an Idol* helpful in working with clients who display disordered eating.

Orgeron divided *Food as an Idol* into six sections. Orgeron discusses the *types, causes, consequences,* and ways of *conquering* disordered eating in Sections 1-4, respectively. In Section Five of *Food as an Idol* she includes information on and suggestions for the *prevention* of disordered eating. In Section Six: Special Topics, Orgeron takes a closer look at disordered eating in athletes, adolescents, pregnancy, higher education, males, and in the church. Additionally, in the Special Topics section, Orgeron explores the link between disordered eating and sexual abuse.

The subtitle to this book, *Finding Freedom from Disordered Eating* contrasts with the title. The title *Food as an Idol* states the problem, while the subtitle *Finding Freedom from Disordered Eating* points to the solution. Orgeron believes that by writing this book others reading this book will find the freedom she found from disordered eating through Jesus Christ and His Word.

Pamela K. Orgeron, Author & Editor
Written 2017

Section 1: Types of Disordered Eating

Chapter 1: What About Dieting?

Most people experience disordered eating at some point in their life. To review what was shared in the Introduction disordered eating lies on a continuum between healthy normal eating and clinically diagnosed eating disorders. Classifications along this continuum, according to Vohs et al. (2001) include nondieter, dieter, problem dieter, subclinical eating disordered, and clinical eating disordered, who display symptoms identified in the Diagnostic and Statistical Manual of Mental Disorders, Fifth Edition, published by the American Psychiatric Association (APA, 2013). Anything outside of healthy normal eating is considered disordered eating. Common examples would be unhealthy fad diets promoted by the media.

Flot (2002) explained that where an individual lies on the continuum of disordered eating fluctuates over time as behaviors related to eating and exercise change. "In reality, most people probably find themselves somewhere in the middle of this continuum" (Flot, p. 1)

As a graduate student, Owens (2004b) investigated whether dieting is healthy. If dieting were found unhealthy, Owens also researched what is the best alternative to dieting? To answer these questions, one must first ask what a diet is. Looking at the broader definition of diet, "food or feed habitually eaten or provided: The rabbits were fed a diet of carrots and lettuce." (diet, n.d., definition 5), one can see that we are all on a diet. Consider the following statistics:

- Collectively our nation spends more than $40 billion dollars annually on dieting and diet related products (NEDA, 2005).
- Although individuals may lose weight by dieting, 95% of dieters gain the lost weight and more back within five years (Kratina, King, & Hayes, 1996, 1999, 2002).
- The number of Americans overweight continues to increase. National Center of Health Statistics (NCHS, 2017) reported 66.3% of adults in the United States are overweight (32.2% are obese). In children and adolescents, according to the Centers for Disease Control and Prevention (CDC, 2017). 17% are overweight.

With the statistics above reflecting the large amount of money spent on dieting yet an increasing number of persons overweight, Orgeron (2004b) concluded a problem exists that needs to be addressed. Furthermore, Orgeron has experienced problems related to weight and body image. Thus, her interest in disordered eating developed.

Do diets work? Kratina et al. (1996, 1999, 2002), NEDA (2002), Lobue and Marcus (1999), and McGraw (2003) stressed that diets do not work. Kratina et al. and NEDA reported multiple reasons for giving up dieting. The biggest reason pointed out is that dieting can lead to more serious eating disorders and is dangerous for personal physical health. Among the physical problems reported by NEDA that can result from dieting is malnutrition, electrolyte imbalances, fainting, less muscle strength and endurance, and loss of hair. Kratina et al. give other reasons for not dieting:

- Diets can be expensive.
- Dieters are boring to others when they focus on diet talk.

- Diets will not make a person beautiful or sexy, contrary to images portrayed by the media.
- Diets can lead to a fear of food.
- Diets rob participants of their energy.

Goldberg (2017, May) reported, "Those that have hit 'rock bottom' in the trenches of the diet world often realize, after gaining the weight back, that diets do not work." (¶ 2) Each time dieters participate in this roller coaster; they gain more weight and can cause additional harm to their bodies. How does one break the roller coaster of dieting cycle? Goldberg offers the following tips:

- Avoid reading and even looking at publications that focus on appearance and/or food. Find other hobbies to read about, such as decorating, music, or traveling.
- Avoid discussions about dieting, food, and appearance.
- Find a hobby or interest to develop the mind and take one's thoughts off of dieting.
- Change one's focus from belittling oneself to caring for self. Among the important parts of self-care listed by Goldberg include getting sufficient sleep, concentrating on mental health, and establishing appropriate healthy boundaries in relationships. Orgeron would add to that list eating healthy and getting regular exercise.

Diets to avoid. Put simply, fad diets are "bad" diets that should be avoided. Common diets to avoid cited by WebMD (2016), Hartel (n.d.), and Fetters (2017) include the HCG diet, the baby food diet, and the cabbage soup diet. WebMD and Fetters both cited the cotton ball diet, the tapeworm diet, the raw food diet, and the cookie diet. Hartel and Fetters listed the grapefruit diet and the blood-type diet as diets to avoid. Other unhealthy diets to avoid: the Twinkie diet, ear stapling diet, apple cider vinegar diet, cigarette diet, and the caffeine diet (WebMD); paleo diet, cleansing and "detox" diets, dukan diet, and very-low-calorie diet or fasting (Hartel); alkaline diets, the werewolf diet, the five-bite diet, the master cleanse/lemonade diet, and the sleeping beauty diet (Fetters). The previously mentioned diets may help an individual lose weight quickly; but are only temporary fixes; in the long run, these fad diets hurt more than they help. What makes these diets unhealthy? How does one tell if a diet is a "bad" diet to avoid? Robin Steagall, RD, nutrition communications manager for the Calorie Control Council, as cited by Strange (2006), reported, "A fad diet:

- *Doesn't include the variety of foods necessary for good health and/or doesn't teach good eating habits.*
- *Claims you can "trick" the body's metabolism into wasting calories or energy.*
- *Makes dramatic claims for fast and easy weight loss."* (Strange, Recognizing the fads section, ¶ 1)

Orgeron chose not to report the details of the "bad" diets listed in this section to protect those who are struggling with food issues from not getting any new unhealthy ideas regarding how to lose weight. Her advice—if anyone asks whether you'd like to try one of these diet, DON'T. Just say, "No"!!

Healthy diet options. Are all diets unhealthy? Mayo Clinic Staff (2016d) reported two ways healthy diets can be illustrated are through plate or pyramid designs. To exemplify a plate design,

MyPlate* illustrated as Figure 2 below is what the U.S. Department of Agriculture (2017) uses to promote healthy eating to the public. (Mayo Clinic Staff, 2016d)

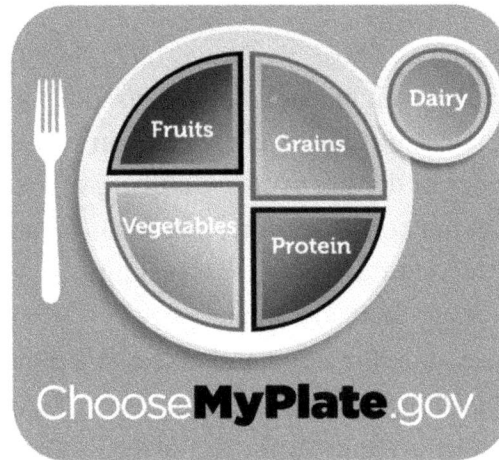

Figure 2: *Illustration adapted April 18, 2017 from https://www.choosemyplate.gov/

To reach and maintain one's optimum health, MyPlate requires individuals to focus on eating foods in moderation, eating an assortment of food, and eating foods with nutritional value.

Another standout among the healthy diets is the *real* Mayo Clinic Diet. Zelman (2016) reported the real Mayo Clinic Diet, as opposed to a phony version that also exists, "is a scientifically sound, healthy approach to long-term weight management." (The Mayo Clinic Diet: What it is section, ¶ 4) The food pyramid to this diet, much like the Food Guide Pyramid of the U.S. government, recommends a well-balanced assortment of healthy foods, according to Zelman.

Examples of pyramid design diets familiar to Orgeron mentioned by Mayo Clinic Staff (2016d) include the Mediterranean and the vegetarian diets. Other pyramid diets listed by Mayo Clinic Staff are the Asian and Latin American diets. The Mediterranean diet is defined by Mayo Clinic Staff (2017a) as "a healthy eating plan based on typical foods and recipes of Mediterranean-style cooking." (¶ 1) The pyramid design for this diet (Gunnars, 2012-2017) is illustrated in Figure 3 below:

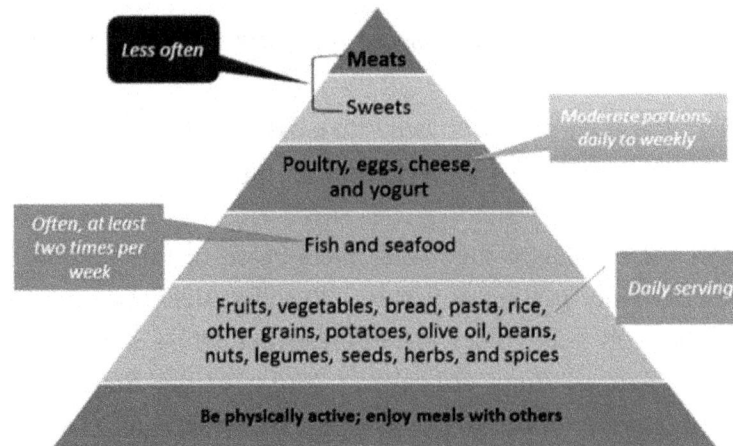

Figure 3: *Illustration adapted April 19, 2017 from https://authoritynutrition.com/mediterranean-diet-meal-plan/

According to Gunnars, "Numerous studies have now shown that the Mediterranean diet can cause weight loss and help prevent heart attacks, strokes, type 2 diabetes and premature death." (¶ 3)

The pyramid diet that Orgeron has tried and prefers is the vegetarian diet. The name would imply a diet where only vegetables grown on the land would be eaten. However, vegetarian diets, as reported by the Mayo Clinic Staff (2016e) come in a variety of assortments, including the following:

- *Lacto-vegetarian* diets exclude meat, fish, poultry and eggs, as well as foods that contain them. Dairy products, such as milk, cheese, yogurt and butter, are included.
- *Ovo-vegetarian* diets exclude meat, poultry, seafood and dairy products, but allow eggs.
- *Lacto-ovo vegetarian* diets exclude meat, fish and poultry, but allow dairy products and eggs.
- *Pescatarian* diets exclude meat and poultry, dairy, and eggs, but allow fish.
- *Pollotarian* diets exclude meat, dairy and fish, but allow poultry.
- *Vegan* diets exclude meat, poultry, fish, eggs and dairy products — and foods that contain these products. (Types of vegetarian diets section, ¶ 2)

Health benefits to vegetarian diets, according to Mayo Clinic Staff (2016e), include "reducing your risk of heart disease, diabetes and some cancers." (¶ 1)

One diet that Orgeron previously knew little about is called the Maker's Diet. Developed by Jordan S. Rubin, the Maker's Diet "is based on the theory of a 'biblically correct diet and lifestyle,' including modest portions of whole foods from sources consumed in as close to a natural (unrefined and unprocessed) state as possible." (Strange, 2006, Eating From the Bible section, ¶ 1) The diet has also become known as the Bible Diet, according to *Wikipedia*, The Free Encyclopedia (2016). Rubin (2004) reported,

The Creator didn't design our bodies to operate at optimum levels on junk food, fast food, or prepackaged foods prepared in microwave ovens. His laws that govern our entire human nature, including our health, bring consequences when violated, whether or not we accept the fact that they are still in place. (Rubin, p. 31)

Dreher (1999-2014) reported seven keys that Rubin believes will enable an individual to develop and maintain a healthy lifestyle. These keys include eating healthy; taking nutritional supplements, such as cod liver oil and fish oil; practicing high levels of cleanliness; conditioning one's body by getting regular exercise and with body therapies, such as adequate sleep and sunlight; lessen environmental toxins; managing emotions appropriately (e.g.: offering forgiveness when needed); and, finding and living out one's purpose in life.

A dietician from Northwestern Memorial Hospital's Wellness Institute, Chicago, Victoria Shanta-Retelny, RD, as cited by WebMD (2004), critiqued The Maker's Diet: "The basic premise of The Maker's Diet, which is a '40-day health experience that will change your life forever,' begs skepticism." (Nutritionists

Sound Off section, ¶ 5) Other concerns she voiced about the diet include its focus on one day weekly fasts and recommending unhealthy supplements, such as coconut oil.

Another nutritionist Ruth Kava, Ph.D., R.D. Director of Nutrition, American Council on Science and Health, New York also had concerns. She told WebMD (2004),

> *I don't know of any data that suggests that organic is better than other produce, but it's more expensive. 'Organic' and 'natural' have that 'good-for-you buzz,' but there are a lot of natural poisons and carcinogens, so that part of this marketing ploy does not get me too excited. (Nutritionists Sound Off section, ¶ 1)*

Orgeron understands these concerns and believes the diet is too expensive and not practical for the general population. She agrees with the response of Shanta-Retelny to the question whether any population existed where they might benefit from using the Maker's Diet: "Since this diet is based (in part) on kosher practices, it may be better for a strict Orthodox Jewish population, who may practice holistic living, but I would not recommend it to the general population." (¶ 11)

Regardless of what diet an individual chooses to follow, Orgeron recommends consulting with a physician and making sure the diet follows the elements of a healthy eating plan:

> *Whether in pyramid or plate form, most healthy eating plans emphasize the following:*
> - *Eating more plant foods, including fruits, vegetables and whole grains*
> - *Choosing lean protein from a variety of sources*
> - *Limiting sweets and salt*
> - *Controlling portion sizes*
> - *Being physically active (Mayo Clinic Staff, 2016c, Basic Principles of a Healthy Diet section, ¶ 4)*

Healthy alternatives to "dieting". Katrina et al. (1996, 1999, 2002), LoBue and Marcus (1999), and McGraw (2003) presented alternatives to dieting. The nondiet approach of Katrina et al. encourages on demand eating where persons eat only when they are physiologically hungry. Furthermore, any food a person wants to eat is acceptable. Like Katrina et al., LoBue and Marcus encourage these practices. Additionally, LoBue and Marcus recommend that individuals not base their self-worth on weight or appearance and that they find a support person or group.

McGraw's (2003) solution to achieving and maintaining a healthy weight encompasses seven keys that result in permanent weight management. The first key presented by McGraw is to eliminate self-defeating, negative thoughts and to believe that you can succeed. Key Two involves learning to overcome emotional eating and to deal with unresolved past triggers that trigger overeating. Creating a no-fail environment is Key Three. A no-fail environment promotes external control. For example, McGraw requires participants in his programs to not bring problematic/binge foods into their homes. Key Four in McGraw's plan teaches participants to recognize personal eating habits, assess what needs to be changed, and then make the choice to change.

In Key Five McGraw (2003) advocates a healthy selection of foods that he calls High-Response Cost, High-Yield Food Plan. High-response cost foods require more effort to prepare and eat and the calorie payoff is low. An example is raw broccoli. On the contrary, an example of a low-response cost food would be a sour cream-and-bean burrito purchased at a fast food restaurant.

McGraw (2003) promotes regular, intentional exercise as Key Six to permanent weight management. According to McGraw, exercise must be a priority to be successful at achieving and maintaining optimum health. McGraw's last key to permanent weight management involves having relationships that support a healthy lifestyle and behavioral changes.

> "Exercise must be a priority to be successful at achieving and maintaining optimum health."

In summary, Orgeron believes that to maintain optimum health one must avoid temporary "bad" or fad diets and live a permanent healthy lifestyle. A healthy lifestyle includes eating a healthy diet, getting adequate exercise, sufficient sleep, and having healthy relationships with both friends and family.

***

Chapter 1: What About Dieting?

Key Terms/Concepts

DE continuum
Diet
Disordered eating
Healthy eating plan
High-response cost food
Lacto-ovo vegetarian diet
Lacto-vegetarian diet
Low-response cost food
Maker's Diet
Mediterranean diet
No-fail environment

Nondiet approach
Overweight
Ovo-vegetarian diet
Pescatarian diet
Plate diet
Pollotarian diet
Pyramid diet
Vegan diet
Vegetarian diet

Questions for Reflection:

1. Do diets work? Are all diets healthy?
2. What makes a diet healthy?
3. According to researchers, what is the biggest reason "dieting" is unhealthy?
4. According to NEDA, what are physical problems that can result from unhealthy dieting?
5. What diets should be avoided?
6. Distinguish between a plate diet and a pyramid design diet.
7. What are the different types of vegetarian diets, and what are the differences among the various vegetarian diets?
8. What are the seven keys to developing and maintaining a healthy lifestyle, according to the Maker's Diet? Why doesn't the author recommend this diet?
9. What are the elements of a healthy eating plan, according to Mayo Clinic Staff?
10. What is the premise of the nondiet approach to eating?
11. What are McGraw's seven keys to achieving and maintaining a healthy weight? Explain why each key is important.
12. What does Orgeron believe one must do to maintain optimum health? What makes up a healthy lifestyle?

***

Chapter 2: Classifications of Eating Disorders

"Eating disorders are extreme cases of disordered eating." (Kelty Eating Disorders, 2017, ¶ 3) Orgeron believes one good way to distinguish between disordered eating and eating disorders is to remember "all eating disorders are disordered eating; but, not all disordered eating is an eating disorder". In this chapter the feeding and eating disorders classified in the *Diagnostic and Statistical Manual of Mental Disorders*, Fifth Edition (DSM-5) published in 2013 by the American Psychiatric Association (APA) will be discussed briefly. The APA (2013) described the feeding and eating disorders as being "characterized by a persistent disturbance of eating or eating-related behavior that results in the altered consumption or absorption of food and that significantly impairs physical health or psychosocial functioning." (p. 329)

DSM-5 Official Classifications

Anorexia Nervosa

"The diagnosis of anorexia nervosa overrides bulimia nervosa." (Turner & Hersen, 1997, p. 466) Diagnostic criteria in the DSM-5 for anorexia include refusing to maintain the minimally healthy body weight for age and height; fearing weight gain, even though underweight; being disturbed by one's body weight or shape, being influenced by body weight or shape on self-evaluation, or denying the seriousness of the current low body weight. A person with anorexia may have one of two subtypes. Persons with the restricting type of anorexia starve their bodies without binging or purging over the prior 3 months. Binge-eating/purging type anorexia nervosa is diagnosed when the person regularly engages in binge-eating or purging behavior over the last 3 months during the present episode of anorexia.

Severity level classifications. Rather than using traditional height/weight charts, the severity level classifications are based on body mass index (BMI). Dictionary.com (n.d.) defines BMI as, "an index for assessing overweight and underweight, obtained by dividing body weight in kilograms by height in meters squared: a measure of 25 or more is considered overweight." The severity levels for anorexia, as reported by APA (2013), are:

- *Mild: BMI $\geq$ 17 kg/m^2*
- *Moderate: BMI 16—16.99 kg/m^2*
- *Severe: BMI 15—15.99 kg/m^2*
- *Extreme: BMI < 15 kg/m^2* (p. 339)

> **"The biggest threat to individuals with anorexia is suicide."**

Anorexia—not to be taken lightly. Dennis (2016) reported "approximately .5% of the U.S. population will suffer from Anorexia Nervosa." (AACC, p. 37) The biggest threat to individuals with anorexia is suicide. According to Dennis, "up to 50% of deaths with anorexics are suicide." AACC reported, "Sudden cardiac death is the second most common cause of death in Anorexia Nervosa patients." (p. 37)

Avoidant/Restrictive Food Intake Disorder

To be diagnosed with avoidant/restrictive food intake disorder (ARFID), a person must avoid or restrict the quantity of food eaten, as characterized by malnutrition and low energy linked with at least one of the following:

1. *Significant weight loss (or failure to achieve expected weight gain or faltering growth in children).*
2. *Significant nutritional deficiency.*
3. *Dependence on enteral feeding or oral nutritional supplements.*
4. *Marked interference with psychosocial functioning. (APA, 2013, p. 334)*

Other criteria to meet a diagnosis of ARFID are: the problem is not the result of a lack of food or a culturally appropriate custom; the behaviors cannot be attributed to a diagnosis of anorexia or bulimia; there's no disruption in a person's body weight or shape; and the symptoms are not attributable to a medical condition or other mental illness.

What causes ARFID? "Anecdotally, clinicians report that avoidance of eating may be rooted in traumatic experiences related to consuming food, such as a personal or witnessed episode of choking, gagging, or vomiting." (Belak, 2016, March 21, Etiology section, ¶ 1) Other causes reported by Belak are: experiencing chronic gastrointestinal problems or having unpleasant sensations when met with food.

Belak (2016, March 21) reported contrary to anorexia and bulimia, ARFID seems to develop at an earlier age, and also affects more males than either anorexia or bulimia. Additionally, long-term prognosis for individuals with ARFID is not available yet: although, early detection is beneficial.

Binge-Eating Disorder

Binge-eating disorder criteria are:
- Reoccurring incidents of binge eating. A person on a binge is described as eating, in a short time span an amount of food that is definitely more than other people would eat during a similar time span and under similar circumstances. The individual also must have lost his or her sense of control over what and the quantity of food eaten.
- The eating binges are associated with at least three of the following:
  - Eating faster than usual
  - Eating beyond fullness

- o Eating large quantities of food when not physically hungry
- o Eating privately due to embarrassment over the quantity one is eating
- o Feeling disgusted, depressed, or guilty after one overeats.
- The binge eating results in marked distress.
- The binge eating occurs at least once weekly for 3 months.
- The symptoms do not meet the criteria for anorexia or bulimia.

Statistics. "Binge-eating often begins in the late teens or early 20's." (AACC, 2016, p. 18) Binge foods usually have a high caloric content and are of the type and texture to facilitate being eaten quickly as inconspicuously as possible or in secret. Turner and Hersen (1997) reported about studies by Mitchell, Pyle, and Eckert (1981). In these studies subjects recorded what they ate during a binge. These studies revealed that the average number of calories eaten per binge was 3, 415 with a range of 1,200 to 11,500 calories. The same studies reported an average duration of 1.18 hours per binge with a range of 15 minutes to 8 hours (Turner & Hersen). Statistics related to binge-eating reported by Stellato (2015) are

- ☐ *1 in 5 patients who binge will consume approx. 5,000 calories in a "typical" episode.*
- ☐ *1 in 10 patients who binge will consume approx. 6,000 calories in a "typical" episode.*
- ☐ *3,415 calories is the average amount consumed per binge.*
- ☐ *20-40% of individuals participating in a weight control program are reported to binge.*
- ☐ *The average duration of a binge is 78 minutes.*
- ☐ *Most people who binge also diet.*
- ☐ *BED is the most common ED.*
- ☐ *BED affects 2% of the population.*
- ☐ *It is estimated that 8% of people who are obese also have BED, some estimates are as high as 20% (Statistics section).*

Severity level classifications. The severity levels for BED, according to the APA (2013) are based on the number of times a person binges each week. They are:
- **Mild**—1 to 3 incidents weekly
- **Moderate**—average 4 to 7 incidents weekly
- **Severe**—average 8 to 13 incidents weekly
- **Extreme**—average at least 14 incidents weekly

Common myths. Craigen (2017) reported eight common myths, or misconceptions in society that pertain to BED. These myths are:
1. Myth: "Binge eating disorder isn't a big deal." (¶ 6) Fact: With the highest incidence rate of all the eating disorders in America, BED is a very serious condition that can lead to increased risks for health issues (e.g.: heart, cholesterol, and blood pressure problems) and other psychological

issues (e.g.: depression, low self-esteem, anxiety) and that requires immediate treatment from professionals.

2. Myth: "Binge eating disorder is the same as overeating." (¶ 7) Fact: Though BED and overeating are often used interchangeably, the two terms have distinct meanings. There's a difference between occasionally eating extra servings of your favorite food (overeating), and losing control of what one eats a minimum of once weekly (BED). BED episodes also are accompanied by strong feelings of regret and embarrassment.

3. Myth: "Binge eating disorder impacts only overweight individuals." (¶ 8) Fact: BED affects people with all types of body shapes and sizes.

4. Myth: "There's an easy fix for binge eating disorder – just eat less." (¶ 9) Fact: That's false because the roots to BED are emotional in nature. Until the emotions that trigger the binges are dealt with (not always an easy process), healing from BED will not happen.

5. Myth: "Weight loss or dieting will stop you from binge eating." (¶ 10) Fact: The opposite is true. Trying to lose weight and dieting are often the catalysts to BED.

6. Myth: "Binge eating disorder only involves high-fat food." (¶ 11) Fact: The type of foods people binge on varies with each individual. Some persons may binge on fats while others binge on carbohydrates.

7. Myth: "Binge eating disorder only affects adults." (¶ 12) Fact: BED affects about 1.6% of children ages 6 thru 18 years of age.

8. Myth: "Binge eating disorder only impacts women." (¶ 13) Fact: It is estimated that men comprise about 33-50% of BED diagnoses.

Bulimia Nervosa

To be diagnosed with Bulimia Nervosa, an individual must present with the following symptoms:

* "Recurrent episodes of binge eating." (APA, p. 345) As with binge-eating disorder, a person on a binge is described as eating, in a short time span an amount of food that is definitely more than other people would eat during a similar time span and under similar circumstances. The individual also must have lost his or her sense of control over what and the quantity of food eaten.

* Recurrent use of self-induced vomiting; laxatives; diuretics, enemas, or other medications; fasting or exercise to prevent weight gain.

* The eating binges and compensatory behaviors both occur at least once weekly and for a period of 3 consecutive months.

* The person's body shape and weight determines his or her self-evaluation.

* The behaviors do not happen exclusively during incidents of anorexia.

    Severity level classifications. The severity levels for bulimia, according to the APA (2013), are based on the number of times a person purges each week. They are:

- **Mild**—1 to 3 incidents weekly
- **Moderate**—average 4 to 7 incidents weekly

- **Severe**—average 8 to 13 incidents weekly
- **Extreme**—average at least 14 incidents weekly.

Concerns of bulimia. Mintle (2016) reported bulimia occurs more often than anorexia; yet is not as noticeable due to the fact that purging done by most persons with bulimia enables them to maintain a normal weight appearing as a healthy eater. Dennis (2016) listed the health concerns of the person with bulimia. Among those concerns, but not exclusive, are cardiovascular problems; electrolyte imbalances; 30% of bulimics will experience amenorrhea, losing their period; gastrointestinal problems, one of the most severely damaged systems in a person with bulimia; weakened musculoskeletal system; dermatologic problems, including discolored skin, loss of hair, and broken blood vessels (around face/eyes); seizures caused by electrolyte imbalances; and dental problems.

Other Specified Feeding or Eating Disorder

Other specified feeding or eating disorders refers to

> *presentations in which symptoms characteristic of a feeding or eating disorder that cause clinically significant distress or impairment in social, occupational, or other important areas of functioning predominate but do not meet the full criteria for any of the disorders in the feeding and eating disorders diagnostic class.* (APA, 2013, p. 353)

Examples of such disorders include atypical anorexia; bulimia or binge-eating disorders with limited time span and/or of low rates of recurrence; and purging disorder without binging. Another disorder fitting into this category that Orgeron has researched before and finds intriguing is night eating syndrome.

Night-eating syndrome is characterized by eating most of one's food after dinner hour but before breakfast. The person is aware of and remembers the eating. Behavior patterns of night-eating syndrome produce guilt and shame, and cause sleep disturbances. Contrary to binge eating behavior done in relatively shorter episodes, persons with night-eating syndrome eat continuously during the evening hours and may wake up at night to eat. Additionally, the symptoms are not better attributed to another mental illness, a medical condition, or as a side effect of medication.

Pica

The primary feature of pica is eating one or more nonnutritive substances persistently for a period of at least 1 month. The substances eaten vary with age. Infants and younger children generally eat paint, plaster, string, hair or cloth while older children may prefer animal droppings, sand, insects, leaves, or pebbles. Teenagers and adults may consume clay or soil.

Additional criteria to meet the diagnosis of pica include: the eating behavior is considered inappropriate to the person's developmental level and the eating behavior is not considered normal sanctioned behavior in the person's culture. Additionally, if the eating behavior is associated with another mental illness, such as mental retardation, pervasive developmental disorder, or schizophrenia, the behavior is significantly severe to warrant independent clinical attention.

Rumination Disorder

The primary symptom of rumination disorder is repeatedly regurgitating and rechewing food. This behavior must exist for a period of at least 1 month following a period of normal functioning, and must not be caused by esophageal reflux or another associated gastrointestinal medical condition.

Unspecified Feeding or Eating Disorder

Like other specified feeding or eating disorders, unspecified feeding or eating disorder refers to

> *presentations in which symptoms characteristic of a feeding or eating disorder that cause clinically significant distress or impairment in social, occupational, or other important areas of functioning predominate but do not meet the full criteria for any of the disorders in the feeding and eating disorders diagnostic class.* (APA, 2013, p. 354)

Distinguishing the two disorders, unspecified feeding or eating disorder is where the clinician decides not to give the reason that the symptoms fail to meet another feeding or eating disorder. This includes situations, such as in an emergency room setting, where there is inadequate information to give a diagnosis.

Other Related Cases

In prior research Orgeron remembers specific disorders or syndromes that are related to feeding and eating disorders. She feels she would be amiss to not include them in *Food as an Idol*.

Muscle Dysmorphia

Muscle dysmorphia (bigorexia). Formerly classified as an ED-NOS in earlier editions of the DSM, individuals with muscle dysmorphia, the opposite of anorexia, obsess about being too thin; when in reality they may be big with well-developed muscles. Persons with this disorder abuse exercise and steroids to build what they feel are inadequate muscles. The APA (2013) now classifies muscle dysmorphia as a type of body dysmorphic disorder, included in the obsessive-compulsive and related disorders section of the DSM-5.

Nocturnal Sleep-Related Eating Disorder

Nocturnal sleep-related eating disorder, in spite of its name, is thought to be more of a sleep disorder where people have episodes of eating in a state somewhere between being awake and asleep, usually sleepwalking. Mayo Clinic Staff (2014) reported, "The person has impaired consciousness while preparing food and eating it, with little or no memory of these actions the next morning. A sleep-related eating disorder can cause dangerous use of kitchen appliances or injury from eating something toxic." (Definition section, ¶ 1-2) Persons with this disorder sometimes eat unusual combinations of food or non-food items, such as soap they have sliced like they would slice cheese. Mayo Clinic Staff reports a person with this disorder usually eats foods that are high in carbohydrates and fat. However, some persons with this disorder have reported eating coffee grounds, frozen foodstuff, and cigarette butts.

Gourmand Syndrome.

A rare eating disorder with an organic cause is Gourmand syndrome, according to research (Bramen, 2011; Regard & Landis, 1997; *Uher* & Treasure, 2005; Wikipedia, 2017c). First recognized by Regard and Landis, Gourmand syndrome is defined as "a rare, *benign* condition that sometimes occurs in people who sustain injuries to the right *frontal lobe*. These people develop a new, post-injury passion for *gourmet* food." (Wikipedia, ¶ 1) In these cases a person's entire being becomes obsessed with gourmet food. According to Regard and Landis, as cited by Wikipedia, "The most famous case of gourmand syndrome developed in a Swiss stroke patient. After his release from the hospital he immediately quit his job as a political journalist and took up the profession of food critiquing." (Wikipedia, ¶ 2) Bramen reported, "There is also the potential for consequences more serious than career changes; sometimes the obsession is severe enough to lead to an eating disorder such as bulimia." (¶ 5)

Uher and Treasure (2005) conducted a research study linking localized brain damage with the etiology of eating disorders. This study supported the research of Regard & Landis (1997). Uher and Treasure concluded, "Implication of frontotemporal circuits is consistent with functional neuroimaging research in eating disorders and with benign changes in eating, such as the gourmand syndrome. Therefore, we conclude that evidence favours cortical mechanisms in the genesis of eating disorders over hypothalamic ones." (p. 856)

Prader-Willi Syndrome

Prader–Willi syndrome (PWS) is defined as "a *genetic disorder* due to loss of function of specific genes.[3] In *newborns* symptoms include *weak* muscles, poor feeding, and slow development. In childhood the person becomes constantly hungry which often leads to *obesity* and *type 2 diabetes*." (Wikipedia, 2017d, ¶ 1) While the root cause of most disordered eating has a psychosomatic origin, disordered eating from PWS occurs because the physiological brakes controlling appetite and hunger are defective. The Prader-Willi Syndrome Association (2016a) reports,

> *Prader-Willi syndrome (PWS) is the most common known genetic cause of life-threatening obesity in children. Although the cause is complex, it results from an abnormality on the 15th chromosome. It occurs in males and females equally and in all races. Prevalence estimates have ranged from 1:8,000 to 1:25,000 with the most likely figure being 1:15,000. (¶ 1)*

Signs that one's baby may have this syndrome are hypotonia (poor muscle development); poor sucking reflex due to lower muscle tone; distinct facial appearance; in general appears tired and unresponsive; and underdeveloped genitals. As the child ages, possible indicators of PWS include constant food cravings with rapid weight gain; hypogonadism (underproduction of sex hormones); problems with the endocrine system; mental retardation; speech and motor problems; and behavior and sleep disorders. (Mayo Clinic Staff, 2017b) For more information on PWS, Orgeron recommends visiting the Prader-Willi Syndrome Association (2016b) Website.

Is Obesity an Eating Disorder?

Is obesity an eating disorder? Obesity alone is not sufficient evidence to diagnose a person with an eating disorder. Multiple factors, including genetic and biological factors, contribute to the growing number of obese persons in society. Thus, the APA (2013) does not include obesity in the DSM-5 as an ED. However, overlapping patterns do exist between obesity, anorexia, and bulimia. These overlapping patterns were illustrated by Comer (2001, p. 327), and are depicted in Figure 4:

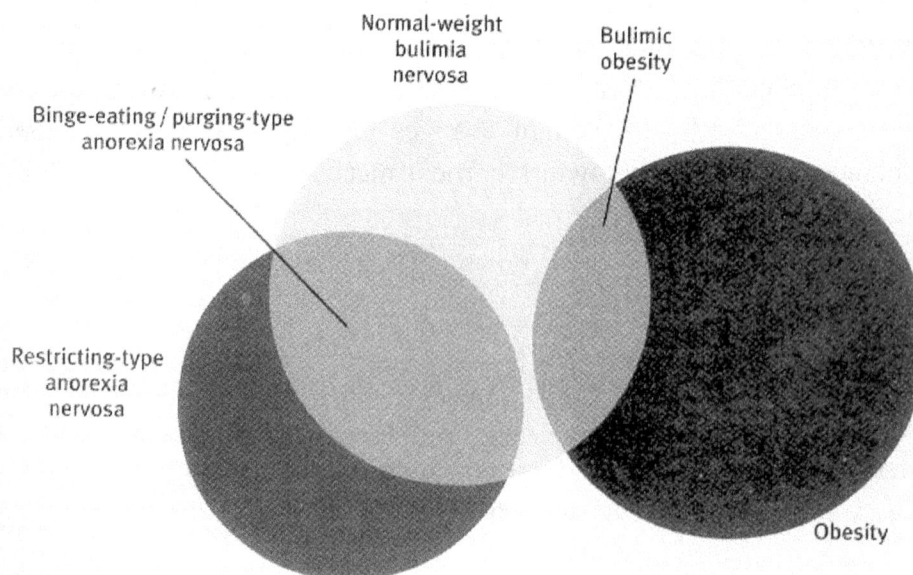

Figure 4: Overlapping Patterns—Anorexia, Bulimia, & Obesity

Because of the strong link between obesity and eating disorders, Orgeron has chosen to devote the next chapter to overweight and obesity.

Before closing this chapter, Orgeron wants to remind others that there is no shame in having any of the eating or feeding disorders, or syndromes discussed in the chapter. The shame comes when one chooses to live in denial and not seek professional help for overcoming or learning how to best manage the disorders.

***

Chapter 2: Classifications of Eating Disorders

Key Terms/Concepts

Anorexia nervosa
Avoidant/restrictive food intake disorder
Binge eating disorder
Body mass index
Bulimia nervosa
DSM-5
Gourmand syndrome

Muscle dysmorphia
Night-eating syndrome
Other specified feeding or eating disorder
Pica
Prader-Willi syndrome
Rumination disorder
Unspecified feeding or eating disorder

Questions for Reflection:

1. What are the classifications of eating disorders, according to the DSM-5?
2. What are the criteria for diagnosing anorexia? What are the severity levels?
3. Define body mass index.
4. What is the biggest threat to individuals with anorexia?
5. What are the criteria for diagnosing avoidant/restrictive food intake disorder?
6. Distinguish between binge eating disorder and bulimia nervosa.
7. What are common myths related to BED?
8. Is BED easily treated?
9. What are the concerns of persons with bulimia?
10. What is other specified feeding or eating disorders?
11. Describe night-eating syndrome.
12. What is the primary feature of pica?
13. What is rumination disorder?
14. Contrast muscle dysmorphia with anorexia.
15. What is nocturnal sleep-related eating disorder?
16. What causes Gourmand syndrome?
17. Distinguish the etiology of Prader-Willi syndrome with the more commonly known types of disordered eating.
18. Is obesity an eating disorder?

***

Chapter 3: Overweight and Obesity

Overweight and obesity, "also known as adiposity" (NIH, 2017a), is defined by the WHO (2016) as "abnormal or excessive fat accumulation that may impair health." (What are overweight and obesity? section, ¶ 1) However, Orgeron finds the definitions distinguishing between overweight and obesity given by National Institute of Diabetes and Digestive and Kidney Diseases Health Information Center (NIDDK) (2012) more precise. The NIDDK definitions are: "**Overweight** refers to an excess amount of body weight that may come from muscles, bone, fat, and water. [NIH, 1998]" and "**Obesity** refers to an excess amount of body fat. [NIH, 1998]" (NIDDK, About overweight and obesity section, ¶ 1)

Is Being Overweight Always Bad?

Introduction

What causes a person to be overweight? According to the WHO (2016), the most common cause is an energy imbalance where an individual is eating more calories than what is being used by one's body. Simply stated, when one eats too much, those extra calories turn into fat.

Since body weight comes from fat, muscles, organs, bones, fluids, and skin, does it matter what makes up the weight measured on the scales? A common misconception is that muscle weighs more than fat. This is a myth.

The truth is that when placed on a scale, one pound of fat is going to weigh the same as one pound of muscle – just like one pound of bricks is going to weigh the same as one pound of feathers. Where the confusion comes in is that muscle and fat differ in density (muscle is about 18% more dense than fat) and one pound of muscle occupies less space (volume) than one pound of fat.

So yes, muscle seems to weigh more because there is a difference in the volume between the two. When a cubic inch of muscle and a cubic inch of fat are measured, the cubic inch of muscle will weigh more. As you add compact muscle mass to the body, body weight may increase. However, pound for pound, muscle and fat weigh the same and when tracking progress of a fitness program, it is very important to look at all markers of improvement, and not just the numbers on the scale. (Regan, 2013, True or false: Muscle weighs more than fat? section, ¶ 2)

BMI versus Body Fat Percentage

What is body mass index (BMI)? BMI is commonly used to determine one's health status. MedicineNet (2016) gave the following definition:

> BMI is a person's weight in kilograms (kg) divided by his or her height in meters squared. The National Institutes of Health (NIH) now defines normal weight, overweight, and obesity according to BMI rather than the traditional height/weight charts. Overweight is a BMI of 27.3 or more for women and 27.8 or more for men. Obesity is a BMI of 30 or more for either sex (about 30 pounds overweight). A very muscular person might have a high BMI without health risks. (¶ 1)

What is Body Fat Percentage? Wikipedia (2017a) defines body fat percentage (BFP) as "the total mass of *fat* divided by total *body mass*; body fat includes essential body fat and storage body fat." (¶ 1) Essential fat is the fat surrounding the organs that one must have to live.

The debate. Research (Casey, 2003; Moore, 2013; Regan, 2013; Yun, n.d.) indicates a debate exists among scholars whether BMI or BFP is the most accurate measurement to use. Why? Because, "BMI does not distinguish fat from muscle." (Casey, Are you at risk? section, ¶ 6). Casey reported,

> In September 2000, the American Journal of Clinical Nutrition published a study showing that body-fat percentage may be a better measure of your risk of weight-related diseases than BMI. Steven Heymsfield, MD, director of the Obesity Research Center at St. Luke's Roosevelt Hospital in New York, and his colleagues evaluated more than 1,600 people from diverse ethnic backgrounds. Researchers took body-fat measurements and studied how their body fat related to disease risk. (Are you at risk? section, ¶ 4)

Heymsfield said, as cited by Casey, "BMI is a broad, general measure of risk. Body-fat assessment is much more specific to your actual fat content and thus provides a more accurate picture." (Are you at risk? section, ¶ 7)

Gallagher et al. (2000) reported,

> Some individuals who are overweight are not overfat (e.g., bodybuilders). Others have BMIs within the normal range and yet have a high percentage of their body weight as fat. Although these misclassified persons are uncommon relative to the population as a whole [NIH, 1998], the question arises as to how they might be evaluated correctly according to body fatness. Moreover, screening and retention of military recruits [Institute of Medicine, 1998; Sharp, Nindle, Westphal, Friedl, 1994], policemen, firemen[Gledhill, & Jamnik, 1992], and other workers in whom high fitness levels are required are often based on BMI standards and in some cases on a second tier body fat evaluation [Institute of Medicine, 1998]. (p. 694)

Orgeron thinks when you consider the benefits to having more lean muscle as opposed to the health risks of having more body fat the debate is understandable. Let's look at those differences, as cited by Regan (2013), in Table 1:

Table 1: Muscle Mass Pros versus More Body Fat Cons

Muscle Mass Advantages	Health Risks to More Body Fat
□ boost your metabolic efficiency □ better your balance and mobility □ build a leaner physique □ create metabolic reserve in times of traumas such as (car accidents and burns) □ enhance strength, stability, power and endurance □ improve insulin sensitivity and blood glucose control □ increase energy and vitality □ raise your confidence □ reduce your risk of injury □ strengthen athletic performance (Benefits of having more lean muscle mass section, ¶ 2)	□ cardiovascular disease □ cancer □ diabetes □ high blood pressure □ liver and kidney disease □ osteoarthritis □ pregnancy issues □ sleep apnea □ stroke (Body composition and fat percentage section, ¶ 2)

Physical health risks are not the only ill effects of carrying extra body fat. Other negative effects may come in the form of depression or self-esteem problems and facing prejudice or discrimination at work and from others in society. (Kirby, 2004)

Orgeron does not know the answer to the debate question. She suspects more research is required. However, what she does know is that she does not depend solely on the number on the scales and her BMI measurement to monitor progress while striving for optimum health and wellness. One way she has used to assess her progress towards better health is with keeping a journal to chart her body weight and measurements. She found that even though the scales might not change but her measurements were smaller, she was encouraged. Before and after pictures also can reflect one's progress, along with the old fashion method of asking oneself, "Do my clothes fit better? Are they looser?" Doctors also can help monitor one's progress to better health through measuring blood pressure, heart rate, muscle strength, etc.

What about Obesity?

Introduction

Obesity defined. Traditionally, obesity was defined as when an individual is greater than 20% of his or her ideal body weight. Ideal weight considered the age, build, height, and sex of a person. More recently, obesity has been defined as having a BMI of at least 30. Extreme obesity is diagnosed when the BMI is over 40, according to Christensen and Hainline (2016).

Statistics. Obesity is now an epidemic in the United States, according to the Centers for Disease Control & Prevention (CDC, 2015b) and Christensen & Hainline (2016). Ogden, Carroll, Fryar, and Flegal (2015) reported the latest statistics on obesity determined from information gathered in the 2011-2014 *National Health and Nutrition Examination Survey*. The main points in the report by Ogden et al. (2015) are:

- Approximately 36.5% adults were obese; 17% children.
- By sex, more women than men were obese; 38.3% and 34.3%, respectively.
- By age, middle-age adults had the highest prevalence rate of obesity (40.2%) followed by older adults (37%). Young adults had the lowest prevalence rate with 32.3%.
- By race, according to the CDC (2016b) from highest to lowest the rates were Non-Hispanic blacks (48.1%); Hispanics (42.5%); non-Hispanic whites (34.5%); and non-Hispanic Asians (11.7%).

Overweight and obesity are not just problems in the United States, but worldwide, according to the WHO (2016). Latest statistics the WHO reports are:

- *Worldwide obesity has more than doubled since 1980.*
- *In 2014, more than 1.9 billion adults, 18 years and older, were overweight. Of these over 600 million were obese.*
- *39% of adults aged 18 years and over were overweight in 2014, and 13% were obese.*
- *Most of the world's population live in countries where overweight and obesity kills more people than underweight.*
- *41 million children under the age of 5 were overweight or obese in 2014.* (Key Facts section)

Causes of Obesity

Just as the etiology of eating disorders is multifactorial, the causes of obesity differ with each individual. The CDC (2016a), Christensen & Hainline (2016), the NIH (2017b), and WHO (2016) discussed the possible causes of obesity. They include:

Brain damage. Hypothalamic obesity, named so because of an injury to the hypothalamus, "is thought to arise from overeating due to poor regulation of satiety and hunger." (Christensen & Hainline, 2016, Head trauma may be a factor in obesity section, ¶ 1) This type of obesity, according to

Christensen and Hainline, has been found in children with brain tumors and some cases where a child has had surgery or radiation.

Orgeron wonders whether hypothalamic obesity would be an appropriate diagnosis for an unnamed friend whom she will give the pseudonym Barbie to share her tragedy. Here's Barbie's story: About 25 years ago when Orgeron first met Barbie, Barbie was tall, thin, intelligent, and full of energy. She worked as an engineer. She and Barbie became friends fast. Then Barbie had an accident that resulted in a Traumatic Brain Injury (TBI). After the TBI, Barbie started having cognitive problems that resulted in her having to quit her job. Orgeron moved away temporarily not seeing Barbie for a number of years. When Orgeron returned, she was shocked to see how much weight Barbie had gained. When Orgeron spoke with Barbie about the situation, Barbie told her that she really can't tell when she's hungry, and that she also forgets that she has eaten. Since Barbie lives alone with no one to keep her accountable, she continues to gain weight. Orgeron gets frustrated at times not knowing how to help Barbie; but, the two remain friends.

Chromosomal abnormalities. Chromosomal conditions, such as Down's syndrome, Klinefelter syndrome, and Turner syndrome also increase the chances of an individual developing a problem with overweight or obesity, according to Christensen and Hainline (2016). These disorders will not be discussed here.

Endocrine disorders. Imbalances in hormones or tumors related to the endocrine system can be the root cause of overweight and obesity in some individuals. NIH (2017b) lists threes possible causes to overweight and obesity related to the endocrine system. These are:

- **Hypothyroidism.** People with this condition have low levels of *thyroid hormones.* These low levels are associated with decreased *metabolism* and weight gain, even when food intake is reduced. People with hypothyroidism also produce less body heat, have a lower body temperature, and do not efficiently use stored fat for energy.
- **Cushing's syndrome.** People with this condition have high levels of *glucocorticoids,* such as *cortisol,* in the blood. High cortisol levels make the body feel like it is under *chronic* stress. As a result, people have an increase in appetite and the body will store more fat. Cushing's syndrome may develop after taking certain medicines or because the body naturally makes too much cortisol.
- **Tumors.** Some tumors, such as craneopharingioma, can cause severe obesity because the tumors develop near parts of the brain that control hunger. (Endocrine disorders section, ¶ 2)

Environmental factors. CDC (2016a), Christensen & Hainline (2016), and WHO (2016) mentioned environmental factors as a reason for the obesity epidemic. One example would be the easy access to unhealthy fast foods. Another example would be an individual choosing to ride a bus somewhere rather than walking due to unavailable sidewalks and walking paths.

Genetic syndromes. The CDC (2016a), Christensen and Hainline (2016), and the NIH (2017b) gave genetic syndromes contributing to the obesity epidemic. Among them are "Prader-Willi syndrome,

Albright hereditary osteodystrophy, Alstrom syndrome, Bardet-Biedi syndrome, Borjeson-Forssman-Lehmann syndrome, Cohen syndrome and fragile X syndrome." (Christensen & Hainline, ¶ 10) Prader-Willi syndrome was discussed in Chapter 2 and will not be discussed here. What about the rest of the genetic syndromes? Let's look at them briefly.

> **Albright's hereditary osteodystrophy** is a syndrome with a wide range of manifestations including short stature, obesity, round face, subcutaneous (under the skin) ossifications (gradual replacement of cartilage by bone), and characteristic shortening and widening of the bones in the hands and feet (brachydactyly). The features of Albright's hereditary osteodystrophy are associated with resistance to parathyroid hormone (pseudohypoparathyroidism) and to other hormones (thyroid-stimulation hormone, in particular). This *autosomal dominantly* inherited condition is caused by mutations in the *GNAS* gene. Treatment consists of calcium and vitamin D supplements. (Genetic and Rare Diseases Information Center, 2012, Summary section, ¶ 1)

"Alstrom Syndrome is a rare genetic disease that affects many parts of the body. Alstrom Syndrome is named for a Swedish doctor, *Carl-Henry Alstrom*, who first described it in 1959." (Alstrom Syndrome International, 2014, ¶ 1) According to Christensen and Hainline (2016), obesity usually occurs before a child is 5 years old and escalates with age.

Bardet Biedi syndrome (BBS) is another rare genetic defect with symptoms that may include obesity, extra fingers or toes, retinal degeneration, among other abnormalities. With over 20 genes linked to BBS, the root cause is a cilia defect. Cilia are tiny hair like organelles that are crucial to cellular communication. Thus, BBS is classified as a ciliopathy. (Bardet Biedi Syndrome Family Association, n.d.)

Like BBS, Börjeson-Forssman-Lehmann syndrome (BFLS) also is a very rare diagnosis caused from a genetic mutation. Besides obesity, other characteristics of the disorder are intellectual debility, failure of the sex organs to produce the normal level of sex hormones, unique facial features, and seizures. (National Organization for Rare Disorders, 2016)

"Cohen syndrome is a very rare genetic disorder characterized by infantile hypotonia (a weakening of the skeletal muscles), childhood obesity and several malformations." (The Gale Group, 2002, Definition section, ¶ 1) Babies born with Cohen syndrome usually have low birth weights. However, according to The Gale Group, about 70% of those diagnosed with Cohen syndrome develop "Truncal obesity, or the abnormal deposition of fat around the mid-section of the body." (Physical appearance section, ¶ 2)

Fragile X syndrome (FXS), according to the National Fragile X Foundation (1998-2017), can be described as follows:

> *Fragile X syndrome (FXS) is a genetic condition that causes intellectual disability, behavioral and learning challenges and various physical characteristics. Though FXS occurs in both genders, males are more frequently affected than females, and generally with greater severity.*

Life expectancy is not affected in people with FXS because there are usually no life-threatening health concerns associated with the condition. (¶ 1)

Christensen and Hainline (2016) reported that a subset of cases of FXS present differently than the usual presentation. "These individuals have a full, round face, small and broad hands/feet, areas of more darkly colored skin (hyperpigmentation), and obesity. . . . Fragile X analysis is widely available and should be considered in cases of childhood obesity." (Fragile X syndrome section, ¶ 3)

Medication side effects. CDC (2016A) and NIH (2017b) report weight gain and obesity may be due to the side effects of certain prescription medicines, such as steroids and certain antidepressants. Orgeron recommends consulting with a doctor or pharmacist if experiencing weight gain while taking medication. Ask the doctor or pharmacist whether other medications exist to treat the situation that would not cause weight gain.

Unhealthy behavior patterns. Overconsumption of food and/or the lack of exercise explain some cases of obesity. WHO (2016) reports the major cause of obesity is the energy imbalance created when one overeats without getting enough exercise. This is due to people eating more high fat food while having more sedentary lifestyles than years ago before the computer generation and public transportation existed. People got more exercise then.

Psychosocial factors. While most people know overeating, underactivity, and genetics contribute to the high rates of obesity, Rutters (2015) reports there are three psychosocial factors that affect obesity. These factors are stress, inadequate sleep, and what Rutters refers to as "social jetlag". Rutters defined stress as anything that a person sees as a threat, whether "real" or "imagined". Wardle, Chida, Gibson, Whitaker, and Steptoe (2011) conducted a meta-analysis of studies that linked psychosocial stress and adiposity. They concluded "psychosocial stress is a risk factor for weight gain but effects are very small. Variability across studies indicates there are moderating variables to be elucidated." (p. 771) Rutters reported weight gain from stress can result from the behavioral pathway of overeating due to the stress or from the endocrine pathway of higher cortisol levels created from the stress that leads to weight gain.

A psychosocial factor of adiposity that is not as well-known is sleep. Weight gain and not enough sleep are linked, according to research (Cappuccio, Taggart, Kandala, Currie, Peile, Stranges et al., 2008; Chaput, Després, Bouchard, & Tremblay, 2007, 2011; Friedman, 2016; Lumeng, Somashekar, Appugliese, Kaciroti, Corwyn, & Bradley, 2007; Magee, Caputi, & Iverson, 2014; Magee, & Hale, 2012; Patel & Hu, 2008; Rutters, 2015; Taheri, Lin, Austin, Young, & Mignot, 2004; Taveras, Rifas-Shiman, Oken, Gunderson, & Gillman, 2008).

The first indicator linking sleep with adiposity is ecological in nature. "Studies have shown that in the past 50 years, we went from sleeping about 8.5 a night to sleeping only 7 or less. This happened at around the same time period as the obesity epidemic." (Rutters, 2015, Sleep section, ¶ 2) Additionally, studies (Cappuccio et al., 2008; Chaput et al., 2007, 2011; Magee et al., 2014; Rutters, Nieuwenhuizen, Lemmens, Born, & Westerterp-Plantenga, 2009; Taheri et al., 2004; Taveras et al., 2008) reveal that "short sleep" increases the likelihood of adiposity. Rutters (2015) reported

In addition to sleep quantity, sleep quality is also important. In two large studies in which we subjected people to nights of disturbed sleep, we woke them every hour or every 2 hours and saw that indeed, the energy balance was disturbed and the endocrine factors involved in weight regulation were altered. [Gonnissen, Hursel, Rutters, Martens, & Westerterp-Plantenga, 2013; Hursel, Gonnissen, Rutters, Martens, & Westerterp-Plantenga, 2013; Rutters, Gerver, Nieuwenhuizen, Verhoef, & Westerterp-Plantenga, 2010] (Sleep section, ¶ 5)

Sleep is very important. Not only are inadequate and poor quality sleep factors in adiposity but it can also lead to depression, which also can be a precursor to weight gain. Orgeron experienced this in her journey. When she was unable to sleep, she used to get depressed. Then she would often turn to eating food for comfort, which led to weight gain.

Another less known factor that can lead to weight gain is what Rutters (2015) refers to as social jetlag, which simply refers to the difference between an individual's internal sleep rhythm and his or her external sleep rhythm dictated by the environment.

For example, let's say I am a night owl. I produce and am at my best in the evening. Some people are really early birds and get up at the crack of dawn. But when society puts you in a situation where you are not an early bird but you still have to be at work at 7 AM, then a dysregulation between the two rhythms happens, which we call "social jetlag." During the weekends, when I don't have to work and am left to live on my own rhythm, I end up producing a mini-jetlag when I switch back to society's rhythm. After every weekend, when I return to work, I have a mini-jetlag of a few hours. (Social Jetlag section, ¶ 4)

A study by Garaulet and Gómez-Abellán (2013), as cited by Rutters (2015), showed that social jetlag is linked to higher BMIs. Rutters also reported, "In one of my own studies, I showed that it is indeed associated with changes in behavior—people become less active. There are also changes in endocrinology, so people have a higher HPA axis." (Roenneberg, Allebrandt, Merrow, & Vetter, 2012; Rutters, Lemmens, Adam, et al., 2014) HPA axis refers to communications among the hypothalamus, pituitary, and adrenal glands.

Consequences of Obesity

The same consequences of having extra fat cited by Regan (2013) mentioned previously apply to the obese but with a greater risk. Sassi (2016) reported, "At any time an obese person incurs at least 30% higher medical expenditures than someone of a healthy weight." (¶ 1) Because of the seriousness of obesity with it being life-threatening, Orgeron will list here again for review the risks cited by Regan:

- cardiovascular disease
- cancer
- diabetes
- high blood pressure

    ☐   liver and kidney disease
    ☐   osteoarthritis
    ☐   pregnancy issues
    ☐   sleep apnea
    ☐   stroke (Body composition and fat percentage section, ¶ 2)

Other consequences of being obese reported by CDC (2016a) include:

- Higher mortality rate from any cause
- Abnormal cholesterol and triglyceride levels
- Gallbladder disease
- Breathing problems
- Poorer quality of life
- Psychiatric disorders (e.g.: depression, anxiety)
- Body pain
- Trouble functioning physically

Not only are there the individual risks to being obese, CDC discussed how the economy and society take a hard hit from those who are obese. Obese employees typically have lower productivity, more absenteeism, in addition to premature disability and an earlier death brought on by the poor health caused from obesity. With obesity preventable, if not manageable, Orgeron is concerned about these negative consequences placed on society and wants to help motivate the obese to take steps to minimize the costs to society—another reason for writing *Food as an Idol.*

The Prevention and Reduction of Obesity

Whether you want to avoid gaining weight or are already overweight or obese, preventing new weight gain is possible. Orgeron also knows from first-had experience that whatever one does to lose weight, one has to continue to do to keep the weight off. Obesity prevention is similar to ED prevention, which will be covered more thoroughly in another section of *Food as an Idol.* However, Orgeron would like to share treatment strategies specific to the obese here.

Both healthy individual choices and societal support are necessary to overcome obesity, according to research (CDC, 2009, 2015b, 2017; Crevar, 2013; Mayo Clinic Staff, 2015, WHO, 2016; WikiHow, n.d.). In her research Orgeron noted the following common individual tactics required to combat obesity:

- Eat only healthy foods in *moderation.*
- Start MOVING! If you can only walk two steps today, then tomorrow you may be able to walk more. Small steps are better than no progress or not trying.
- Avoid stress. WikiHow (n.d.) reported,

Some people also react to stress by stress eating, which is consuming foods to soothe emotions and alleviate stress.[3] Unfortunately, any relief gained by stress eating is temporary, meaning you may continue to stress eat. In addition, the long-term health effects of coping with stress with food far outweigh the momentary comfort it may provide. (Fostering your emotional health section, ¶ 2)

- Be positive. Practice positive self-talk. For Christians, a great verse that Orgeron recommends is Philippians 4:13—"I can do all things through Christ who strengthens me."
- Have a plan, and stick to the plan. Mayo Clinic Staff (2015) reports, "Sticking to your healthy-weight plan during the week, on the weekends, and amidst vacation and holidays as much as possible increases your chances of long-term success." (Be consistent section, ¶ 6)

Personal responsibility can only go so far without having access to the tools necessary for a healthy lifestyle. Overcoming obesity demands the support of family, friends, and society. How can the family help? First, quit enabling the unhealthy behaviors of the obese. For example, I have known at least three obese individuals who knew they were obese. Instead of trying to help themselves, they sat around in front of the television or whatever demanding that family members bring them something to eat. This ought not to be. I told one such individual, "You know where the kitchen is. If you want something, get up and get it yourself." That might sound cruel to some people but family members of the obese need to establish and maintain healthier boundaries to help motivate the obese on their journey to a healthier life. Friends should do likewise.

At the societal level it is important to support individuals in following the recommendations above, through sustained implementation of evidence based and population based policies that make regular physical activity and healthier dietary choices available, affordable and easily accessible to everyone, particularly to the poorest individuals. An example of such a policy is a tax on sugar sweetened beverages. (WHO, 2016, How can overweight and obesity be reduced? section, ¶ 3)

In concluding this section, Orgeron would like to address the negative stigma in society against the obese. Yes, a large majority of obesity cases might have been due to laziness or poor personal choices. Such cases might have been prevented given healthier choices by the individual and/or access to a healthier environment promoting a healthier lifestyle. On the other hand, for example, genetic abnormalities are not a choice. No one asked to be born with chromosomal or genetic flaws. That's why society needs to be more careful about judging the obese. Obesity is NOT always a choice! In such cases, Orgeron recommends these individuals seek professional intervention to know how to best manage the situation.

***

Chapter 3: Overweight and Obesity

Key Terms/Concepts

Adiposity

Albright's hereditary osteodystrophy

Alstrom syndrome

Bardet Biedi syndrome (BBS)

Body fat percentage (BFP)

Body mass index (BMI)

Body weight

Börjeson-Forssman-Lehmann syndrome (BFLS)

Cohen syndrome

Cushing's syndrome

Fragile X syndrome

Hypothalamic obesity

Hypothyroidism

Muscle mass

Obesity

Overweight

Positive self-talk

Social jetlag

Questions for Reflection:

1. Is being overweight always bad?
2. What causes a person to be overweight?
3. What composes a person's body weight?
4. Distinguish between BMI and BFP.
5. What are the advantages of muscle mass?
6. Identify the health risks to having excess body fat.
7. What are possible causes of obesity?
8. What genetic syndromes contribute to the obesity epidemic?
9. According to the World Health Organization, what is the major cause of obesity?
10. According to Rutters, what are three psychosocial factors that affect obesity?
11. What are the links between adiposity and sleep deprivation?
12. Why is sleep important?
13. What are possible consequences of being obese?
14. How are the economy and society affected by those who are obese?
15. What are five common methods of combating obesity according to research?
16. How can families help the obese?
17. Discuss the negative stigma society has against the obese.
18. Is obesity always a choice? Why or why not?

***

Treat the obese with respect. Only God knows their entire "story". Don't be prejudiced.

***

Romans 14:10:
[10]But why do you judge your brother? Or why do you show contempt for your brother? For we shall all stand before the judgment seat of Christ.

Section 2:
Causes of
Disordered Eating

Chapter 4: Etiology of Disordered Eating

What causes people to resort to gluttony, or disordered eating? The cause, also known as the etiology, of disordered eating is multifaceted. In this chapter, Orgeron discusses individual, family, sociocultural, biological, and spiritual factors that can contribute to the development of disordered eating.

Individual Factors

Personal history of dieting. Orgeron knows from research and from personal experience that diets do not work. "Dieting is the perfect environment to cultivate a deeper love for food." (Shamblin, 1997, p. 30) Consider the following statistics:

> *Nearly 65 percent of dieters return to their pre-dieting weight within three years, according to Gary Foster, Ph.D., clinical director of the Weight and Eating Disorders Program at the University of Pennsylvania. The statistics for dieters who lose weight rapidly, according to Wellsphere, a website sponsored by Stanford University, is worse. Only 5 percent of people who lose weight on a crash diet will keep the weight off. Crash diets include any unhealthy diet, from severe calorie-restriction diets to diets that consist of only a few kinds of foods.* (O'Meara, November 17, 2015, Rebound Dieting Section, ¶ 1)

Comer (2001) points out that with the large number of diets and diet pills on the market; almost no evidence supports the notion that dieting can produce long-term weight loss. In fact, contrarily, studies show the rebound effect, which is gaining weight back after losing. These diet rebounds may lead to dysfunctional eating patterns, especially binge eating, according to research by Venditti et al. (1996), as cited by Comer. From a cohort study of adolescent health in Victoria, Australia, Patton (1999) concluded, "dieting is the most important predictor of new eating disorders." (p. 1) Results from this study suggested that females who dieted more strictly were 18 times more likely to develop an eating disorder than non-dieters. Moderate female dieters were five times more likely to develop an eating disorder than the non-dieters were.

For more information about dieting, see chapter 6 entitled "The Solution to Disordered Eating: Do Diets Work?" The article is an updated edition of a paper Owens (2004) wrote while in graduate school.

Food as a drug. Similar to alcohol with an alcoholic, food also may be an addictive agent in the life of an individual. Minirth, Meier, Hemfelt, and Sneed (1990, p. 60) give six-steps in the downward spiral of developing an addiction. Figure 5 depicts this process.

Figure 5: The Addictive Cycle

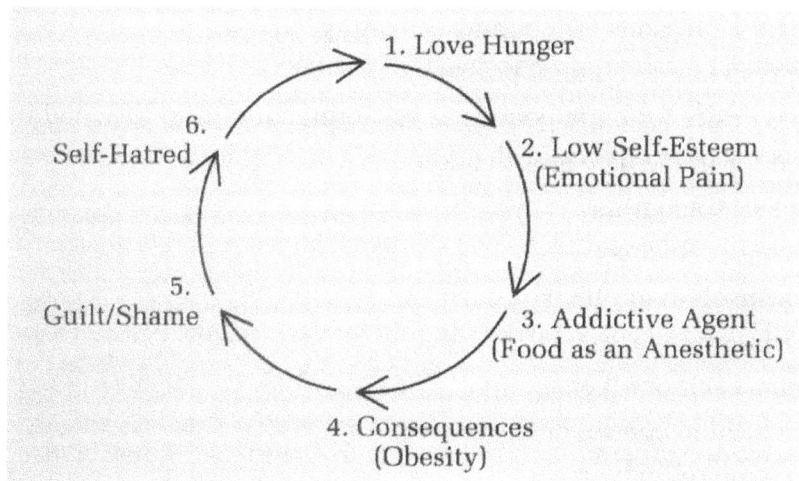

Arterburn and Felton (2001) described "addiction as idolatry . . . . The worship aspect of addiction is easily seen in the lives of most addicts." (p. 91) Arterburn and Felton reported a common element among all addicts is that they worship the process and the outcome. They exemplified this concept through the following story of someone addicted to food:

An extremely overweight friend of mine would not stop eating excessively, even for the sake of his family. He loved food and had some with him most of the time. He could go hours during the day without touching food, but when he was home in the evenings, he spent most of his time eating—a reward for his hard work. It compensated for his deprivation as a child. He lived to eat.

It didn't matter that he embarrassed his children. It was insignificant that his cholesterol level shot up into dangerous levels. He didn't react when his wife threatened to leave if he refused to lose weight. Food was too much a portion of his life to do without. He was always thinking about what to eat next. While he was eating, nothing mattered but how good he felt. No follower of any religion had a more devoted member than this man who served the god of food. (pp. 91-92)

When does eating become an addiction?

Enjoying good food and looking forward to an excellent meal is certainly not a bad thing, in fact it is part of a quality life. But if we find ourselves obsessively thinking about our next meal, eating faster than those around us choosing certain places to go solely for the food, and placing ourselves at risk with extremes in weight, then our obsession with eating is dysfunctional and addictive and ultimately creates health and body image problems. (DeGoede, 1998, p. 65)

"The compulsive overeater may be a few pounds or a few hundred pounds overweight. The issue is not how much the person weights, but rather his or her reasons for eating." (Minirth et al., 1990, p. 13) Minirth et al. share 12 reasons for compulsive eating:

- Compulsive response to cultural pressures
- Subconscious desire for extra pounds as self-protection from love and intimacy
- To fill a need for immediate gratification
- To use food as a tranquilizer
- To avoid facing problems
- To punish themselves or others
- To relieve depression or stress
- To rebel against self or others
- To express a need to control circumstances
- Faulty perception of body image
- Learned emotional feelings about food
- To satisfy love hunger.

Schwartz and Gay (1996) used existing research linking sexual abuse and disordered eating, along with information from their clinical experience, to compile a table of the functions, or purposes that eating disorder symptoms can serve. Appendix B lists the "Adaptive Function of Eating Disorder Symptoms" (Schwartz & Gay, p. 95).

Poor body image. NEDA (2016i) reports "People with negative body image have a greater likelihood of developing an eating disorder and are more likely to suffer from feelings of depression, isolation, low self-esteem, and obsessions with weight loss." (Body Image and Eating Disorders Section, ¶ 1) Results of studies by Fabian and Thompson (1989) and by Brown, Cash, and Lewis (1989) support the NEDA report.

Attention Deficit Hyperactivity Disorder (ADHD). The Emily Program (2017, July 11) reported research has revealed that EDs and ADHD share common indicators; for examples, attention deficit, hyperactivity, and impulsivity. The results of one such study (Ferre, Cambra, Ovejero, & Basurte-Villamor (2017) revealed "Patients diagnosed with ED who also had symptoms suggestive of ADHD presented a higher number and severity of eating disorder symptoms, greater motor and cognitive impulsivity, increased dysfunction and a poorer quality of life." (Abstract, Results section)

While studies describing the link between ADHD and eating disorders are limited, earlier studies have shown children diagnosed with ADHD exhibit more abnormal eating behaviors than children not having ADHD. Additionally, persons diagnosed with ADHD are at three times a greater risk of developing an ED than those persons without ADHD. Thus, "a diagnosis of ADHD is a crucial component to consider in eating disorder treatment, as many of the symptoms that accompany this attention deficit disorder may exacerbate or prompt disordered eating. (Emily Program, 2017, July 11, ¶ 1).

Family Factors

Prior abuse. Past sexual abuse in families is a contributing factor for sexual abuse. According to Mintle (2016), the rates of sexual abuse in females with BN have been conveyed as high as 35% in some studies. A number of researchers support the link between eating disorders and abuse. Among these studies are:

- Beckman and Burns (1990)
- Conners and Morse (1993)
- Folsom, et al. (1993)
- Kinzl, Traweger, Guenther, and Biebl (1994)
- Schwartz and Cohn (1996)
- Tripp and Petrie (2001)
- Vanderlinden and Vandereycken (1993)
- Waller (1991, 1993)

Jantz (2014) indicated that the past abuse linked to eating disorders does not have to be only sexual in nature. He reported:

> *Often at the core of every eating disorder, and many disordered eating patterns, lies some sort of abuse or abusive situation—verbal, emotional, physical, sexual abuse, or a combination of these. When this abuse is added to a family situation where perfectionism and high expectations are the order of the day, food becomes your coping mechanism, your way of masking the real pain in your life. (¶ 1)*

Jantz (2010) reported at least 80% of individuals with disordered eating indicate some form of past and/or current abuse in their life.

Solomon (2017) reported that eating disorders and PTSD commonly coexist. According to a National Women's Study, as cited by Solomon, "among people with bulimia nervosa, 37% met the criteria for PTSD at some point during their lifetimes. Across studies, people with eating disorders are found to have higher than average rates of PTSD." (¶ 3) In such cases, PTSD can act as an obstacle to ED recovery.

> *Many professionals who treat eating disorders recognize that untreated PTSD may be a missing link in long-term recovery. This could be in part because of how the symptoms of the eating disorder can function to help reduce or minimize, for a short time, the symptoms of PTSD. (¶ 4)*

"EDs have been described as a direct reaction to trauma (Dawson, Rhodes, & Touyz, 2014)." (Henretty, n.d., ¶ 4) Why? Are there benefits of EDs in traumatized individuals?

> *Possibly the most widely acknowledged benefit of EDs for individuals who have experienced trauma is that of emotion regulation. ED behaviors—whether restricting, binging, or purging— often are used as distress tolerance or a way to "deaden the pain" (Lord, Reiboldt, Gonitzke,*

Parker, & Peterson, 2016, p. 5). They have been described as a way to release anger, to escape the feelings the [sic] arise during boredom, to channel negative feelings away from thoughts of trauma to the safer ED (Jeppson, Richards, Hardman, & Granley, 2003); to self-soothe and provide pleasure or a sense of well-being (Lord et al., 2016; Jeppson et al., 2003), to fill emotional emptiness with food (Jeppson et al., 2003), to preoccupy the mind (Jeppson et al., 2003), and to dissociate (Lamoureux & Bottorff, 2005). (Henretty, n.d., Eating Disorders As a Response to Trauma section, ¶ 1)

Whether the ED behaviors led to being overweight or underweight, especially prominent among clients who have past sexual trauma, EDs can be an attempt to avoid being sexually attractive. For clients diagnosed with AN, preventing the developmental process, the development of amenorrhea, and keeping a child-like physique can be either a deliberate or unintentional means of self-protection. With anorexia clients specifically, a desire to become unnoticeable exists. Likewise, in today's world that overrates being thin, binge behaviors resulting in added pounds may also act as a protective shield to put distance between self and others. (Jeppson et al., 2003, as cited by Henretty, n.d.)

ED behaviors can also be used as a form of self-punishment reacting to false guilt and low self-esteem (Moulding, 2015) that resulted from trauma. "Along those lines, ED behaviors could be considered a relatively socially acceptable form of self-harm or a 'slow suicide' (Jeppson et al., 2003, p. 121), and an intentional way to self-sabotage (Lord et al., 2016)." (Henretty, n.d., Eating Disorders As a Response to Trauma section, ¶ 3)

Childhood trauma often results in a sense of losing control. As a result, an ED may be an effort to reestablish that control. EDs have been labeled as

providing a sense of security or certainty (Weaver, Wuest, & Ciliska, 2005); a sense of power (Jeppson et al., 2003; Lamoureux & Bottorff, 2005); a way to feel independent (Jeppson et al., 2003); and a way to rebel, resist, or oppose (Jeppson et al., 2003). Especially relevant for survivors of physical and sexual trauma, EDs have been described as a way of regaining control or regaining ownership of the body, and as a way of distancing oneself from the body (Dawson et al., 2014). (Henretty, n.d., Eating Disorders As a Response to Trauma section, ¶ 4)

While trauma steals an individual's voice, or any choice in what happened, an ED may also be an effort to communicate with others (Weaver et al., 2005, as cited by Henretty). The ED can reflect the internal pain that is being felt by the client. On the other hand, AN especially "in today's thin-obsessed culture can be an attempt to portray to others 'I'm perfect' or at least 'I'm ok' (Moulding, 2015; Jeppson et al., 2003). EDs have also been utilized as a way to punish others (Weaver et al., 2005)." (Henretty, Eating Disorders As a Response to Trauma section, ¶ 5)

Koenig (2017, June 29) reported that emotional eating resulting from traumatic experiences comes from one of two emotional states, hyperarousal or dissociation. Dorland's Medical Dictionary, as cited by Bailey (2013), reported hyperarousal, also known as the "fight or flight" response, is defined as "a state of increased psychological and physiological tension marked by such effects as reduced pain tolerance, anxiety, exaggeration of startle responses, insomnia, fatigue and accentuation of personality traits." (¶ 1)

Dissociation (2017), according to dictionary.com, in psychiatry is defined as "the splitting off of a group of mental processes from the main body of consciousness, as in amnesia or certain forms of hysteria." According to International Society for Study of Trauma and Dissociation (ISSTD, 2004-2015), "[t]there are five main ways in which the dissociation of psychological processes changes the way a person experiences living: depersonalization, derealization, amnesia, identity confusion, and identity alteration." (What is dissociation? Section, ¶ 3)

Dysfunctional parenting.   Family environment plays a key role in the occurrence of eating disorders.   Children learn false beliefs and emotional feelings about food from their parents and extended families.   Parental commands such as "Clean up your plate," and "you eat too much" cause children to mistrust their natural appetites (DeGoede & Drews, 1998).   Orgeron herself often received the "Clean up your plate" message, as others reminded her of all the starving children in Africa.

Dysfunctional eating attitudes and behaviors also are learned when parents model chronic dieting, excessive exercising to lose weight, and eating too much without getting any exercise.   Minirth et al. (1990) consider the environment around the dinner table important in determining whether an individual develops an eating disorder.   Unhealthy emotional feelings learned from families of origin may stem from:

➢ Experiencing family meals as a battleground.   Is the atmosphere at the dinner table a shooting gallery?   Do family members overeat?   These are crucial questions to consider when assessing the etiology of an eating disorder.

➢ "You must eat" syndrome.   One case described by Minirth et al. involved a female adult who recalled her mother forcing her to sit at the table for hours when she failed to eat everything on her plate.   When the woman as a young child wanted to rebel, she also received the powerful, hypnotic message: "You must eat."

➢ Using food as a comforter, as a reward or as part of celebration rituals.   Most true food addicts, similar to the alcoholic, eat for comfort when they feel bad and overeat at celebrations.   Every individual with an eating disorder has trigger foods and situations that may result in an uncontrollable "rush".   Minirth et al. report sugar and chocolate as the most popular trigger foods.   Trigger situations may include family gatherings, parties, award banquets, grocery shopping, the smell of food, and for some individuals just driving past a fast food restaurant.

➢ Overeating to please others. Dr. Meier shared his own experience here of how he grew up eating to please his mother:

> I grew up in a German home. My mother was a wonderful cook, and still is, at age eighty, a wonderful cook. And, like good old-world eaters, we put butter on everything. Sometimes I used to food my butter rather than butter my food. (p. 32)

He added that his eating to please his mother became a type of codependency.

Sociocultural Factors

Messages from the media. NEDA (2016f) and Mintle (2016) recognize the power of the media, advertising and celebrity spotlights in the development of eating disorders. Statistics reported by NEDA that support this theory of etiology include:

- *Over 80% of Americans watch television daily. On average, these people watch over three hours per day.*
- *American children engage in increasing amounts of media use, a trend fueled largely by the growing availability of internet access through phones and laptops. On a typical day, 8 – 18-year-olds are engaged with some form of media about 7.5 hours. Most of this time is spent watching television, though children play video games more than an hour per day and are on their computers for more than an hour per day. Even media aimed at elementary school age children, such as animated cartoons and children's videos, emphasize the importance of being attractive. Sexually objectified images of girls and women in advertisements are most likely to appear in men's magazines. Yet the second most common source of such images is the advertisements in teen magazines directed at adolescent girls.* (We live in a media-saturated world and do not control the message Section, ¶ 1)

Results from one study reported by Owens (2002) of 4,294 television commercials show that 1 out of every 3.8 commercials portray an "attractiveness message". These messages tell viewers what is considered attractive and unappealing. Researchers from this study estimate that the average adolescent views over 5,260 of these messages per year.

A second study that offers evidence linking watching television with the development of disordered eating was reported by The Gale Group (1999), as cited by Owens (2002) and by Goode (May 20, 1999). This study by Harvard anthropologist Anne Becker assessed the affect that the arrival of television had on the Fiji Islands. Survey results reported that 38 months after Western television shows were introduced in Fiji via satellite the number of teenage girls who vomited to control their weight increased fivefold, along with an increase in abnormal attitudes toward eating. Prior to the introduction of television, Fijian women were not bothered by the fact that four-fifths of them were overweight by American standards. Traditionally, Fijians valued larger proportions and were more concerned about being too thin than too fat. (Owens)

> 1 Samuel 16:7
>
> . . . For the Lord does not see as man sees; [a] for man looks at the outward appearance, but the LORD looks at the heart."

Mintle (2016) discussed how unrealistic it is for anyone to try to model after media images, which have often been airbrushed. She reported only about .02% of the general population meets the weight standards of these "Supermodels".

Prejudice against obesity. Comer (2001) reports that anguish associated with being obese goes far beyond the physical health problems.   Obese individuals are often discriminated against in seeking admission to college, employment, and promotions. Adults are not alone in their prejudice against the obese. In one study cited by Comer where preschoolers were given a choice between a chubby and a thin rag doll, the thin rag doll was preferred.   In light of this prejudice against obesity, the number of eating disorders is increasing and the age that individuals develop eating disorder symptoms is becoming younger.

Biological Factors

Biological and biochemical factors also are being studied as contributing causes to eating disorders. According to National Alliance for the Mentally Ill (2001), as cited by Owens (2002), one study conducted by researchers from Utrecht University Medical Center in Utrecht, the Netherlands found variations in the chemical sequence of the agouti-related protein (AGRP) gene that helps to regulate a person's sense of hunger. The AGRP gene reduces the activity of the melanocortin-4 receptor in the brain. Subjects in this study were 100 people diagnosed with anorexia compared with 244 healthy individuals.

Comer (2001) offers data that supports a biological origin to eating disorders. He reports that relatives of individuals with eating disorders are six times more prone to develop the same eating disorder than other individuals in general. Additionally, many individuals with eating disorders have been found with low levels of serotonin activity.

Regarding anorexia specifically, Blair (2013) reports on studies linking brain function and anorexia. These studies report weaker connections in the brain of those diagnosed with anorexia. Blair points out that the brain dysfunction can be structural or functional in nature.

Biological theories also stem from the weight set point theory. According to Thompson, Muhlheim, and Farrar (1997/2014), each individual is biologically and genetically determined to weigh within a certain weight range.   Theorists who support set point theory maintain that the body is programmed to maintain the set point weight.

> *Scientists estimate that the average person has a set point range of about ten to twenty pounds, meaning at any given time, there is a ten-to-twenty-pound range at which your body will be comfortable and not resist attempts to change.* (Thompson, et al., ¶ 3)

Metabolism slows down when one goes under his or her body's set point while metabolism is increased if one's weight goes above the set point. No test exists to determine one's set point. Only by listening to the hunger cues of one's body, by eating healthy and exercising moderately will one reach his or her body's set point, which differs individually.

Spiritual Factors

At its root, disordered eating is a spiritual problem (Dennis, 2016; Mintle, 2016; Pitman, 2016). Orgeron too believes there is a spiritual basis to disordered eating that may result from factors such as unconfessed sin, unforgiveness towards self and/or an abuser, and even as a natural consequence of The Fall reported in Genesis of The Holy Bible.

Pitman (2016) believes spiritual and emotional factors are the root cause of disordered eating.

> *Rather than embracing a disease model, I believe eating disorders and disordered eating are emotionally based coping strategies, shaped by early development and some form of loss. At their heart, they're an intelligent attempt – grounded in a deep, if misunderstood love of the self – to soothe and care for spiritual, psychological and emotional pain. It is this spiritual and emotional pain that is the true cause of the eating disorder, what comes out sideways in food. (¶ 2-3)*

Mintle (2016) discussed how spiritual issues may be instrumental in the development of eating disorders. She gave three spiritual factors that can lead to an eating disorder, including an inaccurate perception of Who God is, not seeing oneself in God's eyes, and projecting attitudes and behaviors of earthly parents onto God.

Orgeron advocates spiritual roots as the ultimate source of DE. She believes there are four truths in Scripture that individuals with disordered eating do not understand fully. These include:

1.   For Christians, our body is God's temple:

> *Corinthians 3:16-17:[16] Do you not know that you are the temple of God and that the Spirit of God dwells in you? [17] If anyone defiles the temple of God, God will destroy him. For the temple of God is holy, which temple you are.*

Additionally, Corinthians 6:19-20 refers to the body as God's temple. Verse 20 tells us to glorify, or honor God in both our body and spirit. The behaviors, such as starving and stuffing, which are associated with disordered eating, do not glorify God.

2.   Outward beauty is temporary. God's love is eternal.

> *Proverbs 31:30: Charm is deceitful and beauty is passing, But a woman who fears the* LORD, *she shall be praised.*

Not only is beauty temporary; but standards of what is considered beauty change over time. In earlier centuries, being heavier was more acceptable than being thin. Being heavier was a sign of wealth and status. In today's society, being thin and staying in style is equated with beauty. Who should set the standard for one's beauty? Orgeron believes when individuals stray from God's standards of beauty to follow after the world's standards, they are setting themselves up for disordered eating.

> *What does our loving heavenly Father have to say about our bodies and real beauty? Check out these Scriptures:*
> - *Genesis 1:27 – You were made in the image of God.*
> - *Psalm 8 – In the whole wonderful universe, He gives you a place of honor.*

- *Proverbs 31:30 – Outward appearances don't matter as much as what's inside.*
- *Zephaniah 3:17 – The God of the universe takes delight in YOU!*
- *Romans 5:8 – God loves you enough to send His Son to die for you.*
- *1 Peter 3:3 – How you look is not what really makes you beautiful.* (Focus on the Family, 1997-2017, Nothing But the Truth section, ¶ 1)

3.   Our bodies are good (Psalm 139:14). Consider the entire Psalm 139. According to Focus on the Family (1997-2017),

> *The author of that poem knew that the human body is among God's most miraculous creations. He thanked God for carefully forming out bodies even before birth – for creating us each unique and incredibly special. If God created our bodies, then they are **good**!* (Nothing But the Truth Section, ¶ 2)

4.   Forgiveness is a must!! (Ephesians 4:32; Matthew 6:14-15; Colossians 3:13) "We need to forgive others in order to be free from our pasts and to prevent Satan from taking advantage of us." (Anderson, Zuehlke, & Zuehlke, 2000, p. 396) Paul wrote in 2 Corinthians 2:10-11, "[10] Now whom you forgive anything, I also *forgive*. For if indeed I have forgiven anything, I have forgiven that one[a] for your sakes in the presence of Christ, [11]lest Satan should take advantage of us; for we are not ignorant of his devices." Henry (1997) reported, "Satan has many plans to deceive, and knows how to make a bad use of our mistakes." (p. 1120)

> ### Ephesians 4:26-27
>
> [26]"'Be angry, and do not sin:' do not let the sun go down on your wrath, [27] nor give place to the devil."

For those persons with DE associated with past abuse or past wrongs, the abuser must let go of any anger and find forgiveness in his or her heart towards the perpetrator or offender. Otherwise, the anger will turn to bitterness, which will eat the person up inside, resulting in stress that can be manifested in overeating, undereating, and physical symptoms.

Not only is forgiving others important; but, forgiving oneself for past mistakes and any damage done to our bodies from DE also is crucial to finding freedom from disordered eating. "To forgive yourself is to accept God's cleansing and forgiveness." (Anderson et al., 2000, p. 397)

Before one can offer forgiveness to self or others, one must understand what forgiveness is and is not. Here are a few main points to remember about forgiveness:

- "Forgiveness is *not forgetting*." (Anderson et al., 2000, p. 397) Based on Hebrews 10:17, "[17] *then He adds,* "Their sins and their lawless deeds I will remember no more."[a], some people think forgiveness is equated to forgetting. That's not true. If that isn't the truth, what is the truth?

> *God, being omniscient, cannot forget. To remember our sins 'no more' means that God will never use the past against us (See Psalm 103:12). Forgetting may be the result of forgiveness,*

but it is never the means of forgiveness. When we bring up the past against others, we are saying that we have not forgiven them. (Anderson, et al., p. 397)

- Forgiveness doesn't automatically happen. It's a decision, a choice we make and can only do through the power of the Holy Spirit living in us.
- Some people think by forgiving they are letting the offender "off the hook". In the flesh, they often want vengeance. But God tells us in Romans 12:19, "… "Vengeance *is* Mine, I will repay"…." By forgiving an offender, we are not saying that what the person did is okay but that we will not seek vengeance. God will take care of that: Galatians 6:7—"Do not be deceived, God is not mocked; for **what**ever a man **sow**s, that he will also **reap**."
- You forgive others for your sake, not for the offender. "Your need to forgive is not an issue between you and the offender; *it is between you and God.*" (Anderson, et al., p. 398)
- Forgiveness isn't a feeling. Don't procrastinate in forgiving *"until you feel like forgiving; you will never get there.* Feelings take time to heal after the choice to forgive is made and Satan has lost his foothold (see Ephesians 4:26-27). *Freedom is what will be gained, not a feeling."* (Anderson, et al., p. 398)

Now that we understand what encompasses forgiveness, we can offer forgiveness. How is this done? Is confronting the offender necessary? No, one need not communicate with the offender directly to offer forgiveness. In some instances, that would be impossible, for example, if the offender is deceased or his or her whereabouts unknown. Forgiveness does not equate reconciliation. In some situations, a direct confrontation expecting reconciliation would only make matters worse leading to more pain in one or both parties. Thus, Orgeron suggests one way that she was able to forgive past offenders. She wrote letters to the individuals, expressing how she felt offended and that she was choosing to forgive the wrongs against her. Orgeron does not recommend mailing such letters.

Anderson, et al. (2000) recommended another way. They recommend those offended pray the following prayer for each offender in one's life:

Lord,

     I forgive _____ for (verbally share every hurt and pain the Lord brings to your mind, and how it made you feel).

After you have forgiven every person for every painful memory, finish this step by praying the following:

Lord,

     I release to you all these people and my right to seek revenge. I choose not to hold on to my bitterness and anger, and I ask you to heal my damaged emotions. In Jesus' name, I pray. Amen. (p. 399)

***

Chapter 4: Etiology of Disordered Eating

Key Terms/Concepts

Addictive cycle   Rebound effect
Food as a drug   Weight set point theory

Questions for Reflection:

1. What four factors contribute to developing disordered eating?
2. According to Patton, what is the biggest predictor of an ED developing?
3. List the six elements of the addictive cycle.
4. What do addiction and idolatry have in common?
5. When does eating become an addiction?
6. According to Minirth et al., what are twelve suggested reasons people eat compulsively?
7. What are some examples of adaptive functions of eating disorder symptoms?
8. What is the link between EDs and ADHD?
9. What are two common family factors contributing to DE? How so?
10. What are the benefits of EDs in traumatized individuals?
11. Do you agree that ED behaviors can be a form of self-protection in persons with past sexual abuse? Why or why not?
12. According to Minirth et al., where can unhealthy emotional feelings towards food stem from?
13. What sociocultural messages can contribute to the development of DE?
14. How is watching television linked to the development of DE?
15. Explain the weight set point theory.
16. How can DE be a spiritual problem?
17. According to Mintle, what are three spiritual factors that can lead to an eating disorder?
18. According to Orgeron, what are four spiritual truths that persons with DE often misunderstand?
19. In the lives of persons with DE, why is forgiveness important?
20. Describe the attributes of forgiveness. What does forgiveness not equate to?

***

1 Corinthians 6:19-20:

[19] Or do you not know that your body is the temple of the Holy Spirit *who is* in you, whom you have from God, and you are not your own?[20] For you were bought at a price; therefore glorify God in your body and in your spirit, which are God's.

Section 3:
Consequences of
Disordered Eating

Chapter 5: Consequences of Disordered Eating

The cost in the quality of life of the person with an eating disorder is high. Eating disorders are not merely "fads" or "phases" that individuals go through. People do not simply "catch" an eating disorder. Eating disorders are serious, potentially life-threatening conditions that affect health, productivity, and relationships. A person's emotional and physical well-being is damaged from eating disorders and often results in unfulfilled dreams and unrealized potentials.

Physical Consequences

Vredevelt, Newman, Beverly, and Minirth (1992) outlined the physical effects of eating disorders in alphabetical order:

- amenorrhea
- blood cell functioning
- cardiovascular complications
- digestive problems
- erosion of tooth enamel
- forgetfulness
- glandular functioning
- hypoglycemia
- impulse control disorder
- judgment
- musculoskeletal problems
- other physical problems
- renal problems
- seizures
- vision impairment
- weight
- x ray abnormalities

Amenorrhea. Amenorrhea is the abnormal absence of the menstrual cycle. Females with bulimia tend to have irregular periods while females with anorexia often skip three or more consecutive periods.

Blood cell functioning. Either low or high blood sugar levels may occur. Low blood sugar or hypoglycemia may occur after a binge intake of high calorie, simple sugar foods. Symptoms include fatigue, feelings of anxiety, dizziness, and headaches. Low blood sugar suggests kidney or liver problems and can lead to neurological and mental deterioration. An elevated blood sugar can result in diabetes, liver and kidney malfunctions, and circulatory and immune system problems. Anemia brought on by poor nutrition also can occur in persons with eating disorders.

Cardiovascular complications. "Perhaps the most dangerous medical complications of all" (Vredevelt et al., 1992, p. 36) are the cardiovascular complications. According to the International Eating Disorder Referral Organization, as cited by Owens (2002), serious heart problems, such as cardiac arrhythmia, bad circulation, or heart attack, can result from electrolyte imbalances (especially potassium deficiency), dehydration, malnutrition, abnormal blood pressure, extreme orthostatic hypotension and hormonal imbalances, which often occur, in individuals with eating disorders.

Digestive problems. Problems of the digestive system that can develop in a person with an ED include reflux disorders, Barrett's esophagus, Mallory-Weiss tear, gastric rupture, pancreatitis, peptic ulcers, and bowel dysfunction. Esophageal reflux/acid reflux disorders where partially digested items in the stomach, mixed with acid and enzymes, regurgitate into the esophagus can damage the esophagus, larynx, and lungs. Reflux disorders also increase the risk of developing cancer in the esophagus and voice box. Esophageal reflux can develop into Barrett's esophagus that is associated with cancer of the esophagus. Mallory-Weiss tear is a tear of the gastroesophageal junction associated with vomiting. Gastric ruptures where the stomach suddenly erodes, tears, or ruptures also may develop in persons with eating disorders. Pancreatitis and peptic ulcers also are at increased risk in individuals with eating disorders. The functioning of the bowels of an individual with an eating disorder may increase or decrease. Cramps, bloating, constipation, diarrhea, or incontinence may occur with eating disorders. (International Eating Disorder Referral Organization, as cited by Owens, 2002)

Dental health effects. Anorexia and bulimia profoundly affect the teeth and gums. Possible dental consequences of these disorders include:

- tooth decay, with possible tooth loss
- enamel erosion on the "tongue side" of the teeth, resulting from too much stomach acid
- worn-away enamel that causes fillings to appear raised and teeth look dark
- bone loss due to osteoporosis
- biting surfaces of the top teeth develop jagged edges
- altered bite
- bleeding gums and burning tongue
- chronic sore throat with problems swallowing
- dry mouth from decreased salivary flow and swollen glands; cracked lips
- inflamed esophagus
- abnormally sensitive and sore teeth, mouth, throat, tongue, gums, and salivary glands
- enlarged parotid glands
- abnormal jaw alignment. (NEDA, 2016b; Remuda Ranch, 2014a)

Central nervous system mental processes. Malnutrition resulting from eating disorders affects the brain and the central nervous system, which can cause slower mental processing, incoherent talking, forgetfulness, and delirium. Permanent brain damage may result if left untreated.

The thyroid gland in a person with an eating disorder may begin to function abnormally. This may cause lowered body temperature, dry skin, brittle nails, decreased reflexes, and mild fluid retention.

Musculoskeletal problems. Patients with eating disorders may develop muscle spasms, pain, atrophy, osteopenia, and osteoporosis. According to the International Eating Disorder Referral Organization, as cited by Owens (2002), a calcium and/or vitamin D deficiency cause Osteopenia which is a below normal bone mass that leads to osteoporosis, a thinning of the bones that predisposes a person to bone fractures.

Miscellaneous health issues. Other physical problems associated with eating disorders are edema, loss of head hair, insomnia, infertility, pregnancy problems, and broken blood vessels in the face, bags under the eyes, fainting spells, hyperactivity, TMJ "Syndrome", and lanugo. Lanugo is the soft, downy hair a person with anorexia gets on the face, back and arms as a defense to keep warm.

Renal problems. Complications with the kidneys sometimes occur in individuals with eating disorders. "If the body weight gets low enough—fifty pounds or so, and Dr. Minirth has seen patients at this weight—the kidneys will shut down. The person then goes into kidney failure and dies." (Vredevelt et al., 1992, p. 44)

Seizures. Individuals with anorexia and bulimia may be at a higher risk of seizures due to dehydration. Seizures may also result from chronic malnutrition and a shortage of oxygen in the brain. (Eating Disorder Referral and Information Center, 2017)

Vision impairment. Eatingdisordersonline.com (2016) reported about vision impairment that can occur with disordered eating. They reported impaired night vision due to malnutrition and low vitamin A may result, Additionally, blurred vision can occur.

The Parent's Guide to Eating Disorders by Marcia Herrin, EdD, MPH, RD and Nancy Matsumoto, as cited by Eatingdisordersonline.com (2016), reported other forms of vision impairment exist, such as blood vessels bursting in an eye. Burst blood vessels in eye cause redness and are likely due to vomiting and increased eye pressure caused from vomiting. If the vomiting is severe enough, retinal detachment, requiring surgery to reattach, occurs. Petechiae, "a minute, round, nonraised hemorrhage in the skin or in a mucous or serous membrane," (Dictionary.com, 2017) occurs if the vomiting has been induced forcefully.

Weight. A word of caution to those who screen individuals for DE, eating disorders cannot be diagnosed based on weight and appearance alone. Eating Disorder Referral and Information Center (2017) reported

> *Sometimes those suffering with Anorexia and Bulimia do not appear underweight – some may be of "average" weight, some may be slightly overweight, variations can be anywhere from extremely underweight to extremely overweight. The outward appearance of a person suffering with an eating disorder does not dictate the amount of physical danger they are in, nor does is determine the severity of emotional conflict they are enduring.* (Medical Issues: General, Physical Dangers Section, ¶ 1)

Thus, Orgeron encourages physicians and other clinicians to consider an eating disorder as the underlying cause when diagnosing the above medical issues. On the other hand, an eating disorder may not be the root of a weight problem. Weight problems may result from genetic problems, abnormal metabolism, illness, unhealthy lifestyle patterns, and emotional problems. Determining the root cause of unhealthy weight is crucial to finding the right treatment and healing.

X ray abnormalities. Bowden, Kilburn-Toppin, and Scoffings (2013) reported that radiologists are crucial in identifying and monitoring treatment of eating disorders. Bowden et al. (2013) reported radiologists "review the radiologic findings that may be seen in patients with eating disorders, with examples of complications involving each organ system." (p. 1172) Table 2 on the next page shows information retrieved from "Table 2 Spectrum of Medical Complications Arising from Eating Disorders" (Bowden et al., p. 1173).

> **"Determining the root cause of unhealthy weight is crucial to finding the right treatment and healing."**

Table 2: Spectrum of Medical Complications Arising from Eating Disorders

Organ System	Complications
Musculoskeletal	Osteopenia, osteoporosis, insufficiency fractures, marrow atrophy, premature fatty bone marrow conversion, skeletal myopathy, diffuse soft-tissue emphysema
Gastrointestinal	Esophageal tears, gastric dilatation or rupture, delayed gastric emptying, intestinal atony, constipation, cathartic colon, SMA syndrome, acute pancreatitis, hepatic steatosis, cholesterol gallstones
Respiratory	Aspiration pneumonia, lung abscesses, wasting of respiratory muscles, emphysema, spontaneous pneumothorax, pneumomediastinum
Cardiovascular	Pericardial effusion, heart failure, mitral valve prolapse, ipecac-associated cardiomyopathy, refeeding cardiomyopathy
Gynecologic	Anovulation, amenorrhea, delayed onset of puberty
Neurologic	Brain volume loss, osmotic myelinolysis, WE, seizures, peripheral neuropathy, stroke (after mitral valve prolapse), subacute combined degeneration of the cord
Endocrine	Growth retardation, estrogen deficiency, sustained hypercortisolism, electrolyte disturbances

Note.—SMA = superior mesenteric artery, WE = Wernicke encephalopathy.

Psychosocial Consequences

Self-injury. Carcieri (2015) reports that many individuals diagnosed with eating disorders engage in the act of self-injury. Similar to the dysfunctional eating, self-mutilation is a way to cope with, block out, and release pent up feelings and emotions. Orgeron recalls a former co-worker diagnosed with AN. This individual used razor blades to cut both her arms, at times to the point of endangering her life. According to Levenkron (1998), cutting one's skin is a common behavior in individuals diagnosed with anorexia. Self-mutilators meet the following criteria:

> Similar to the dysfunctional eating, self-mutilation is a way to cope with, block out, and release pent up feelings and emotions.

➢ Persistent cutting or burning of one's skin.
➢ Immediately prior to the act of self-mutilation, stress is experienced.
➢ Physical pain and relaxation, gratification, pleasant feelings, and numbness are experienced simultaneously.
➢ Individuals who self-mutilate try to hide scars, blood, and other evidence of their behavior because of a sense of embarrassment and fear of social stigma.

Co-morbidity. Baker (2003) reported eating problems and obsessive-compulsive personality share similar characteristics, including perfectionism, a need to control, indecisiveness, inflexibility, and emotional distance. This link may explain why statistics reveal individuals with EDs have higher incidents of compulsive spending, stealing, and sexual promiscuity.

Eating disorders are also often associated with mood disorders, anxiety disorders, and personality disorders. Bulimia nervosa may be particularly associated with substance abuse problems. Anorexia nervosa is often associated with obsessive-compulsive symptoms. The scope of related problems associated with eating disorders highlights the need for prompt treatment and intervention." (Eating Disorder Referral and Information Center, Psychosocial Section, ¶ 1)

***

Matthew 22:36-39:

36 "Teacher, which *is* the great commandment in the law?"

37 Jesus said to him, "'You shall love the LORD **your God with all your heart, with all your soul, and with all your mind.'[a]**

38 This is *the* first and great commandment.

39 And *the* second *is* like it: *'You shall love your neighbor as yourself.'*[b]

***

Question for Reflection: How can you love your neighbor if you can't love yourself?

Chapter 5: Consequences of Disordered Eating

Key Terms/Concepts

Amenorrhea
Barrett's esophagus   Mallory-Weiss tear
Esophageal reflux/acid reflux disorders   Malnutrition
Gastric rupture   Osteoporosis
Hypoglycemia   Pancreatitis
Lanugo   Petechiae

Questions for Reflection:

1. What are possible physical consequences of DE?
2. What are symptoms of hypoglycemia?
3. What are possible consequences of low blood sugar?
4. According to Vredevelt et al., what may be the most dangerous medical problems resulting from DE?
5. What problems can develop in the digestive system as a result of an ED?
6. How can the bowel functioning of an individual diagnosed with an ED be affected?
7. What are possible dental health consequences of having an ED?
8. How does malnutrition affect the body?
9. What are possible symptoms of a malfunctioning thyroid gland?
10. What musculoskeletal problems can result in persons with EDs?
11. What may cause persons with EDs to be at a higher risk for having seizures?
12. Can eating disorders be diagnosed on weight alone?
13. Why is finding the root cause of unhealthy weight important?
14. What are possible psychosocial consequences of DE?
15. Why do individuals diagnosed with EDs self-injure?
16. What are the characteristics of a self-mutilator?
17. According to Baker, what characteristics do DE and obsessive-compulsive personality share?
18. What other mental disorders are often associated with DE behaviors?

***

10 COMMANDMENTS OF SELF LOVE

1. I SHALL LOVINGLY ACCEPT MYSELF AS I AM RIGHT NOW.

2. I SHALL APPRECIATE ALL THE BEAUTY THAT MAKES ME WHO I AM.

3. I SHALL REGULARLY GIVE THANKS FOR ALL OF MY BLESSINGS.

4. I SHALL TRUST IN MY ABILITY TO TAKE CARE OF MYSELF.

5. I SHALL NOT CRITICIZE MYSELF.

6. I SHALL NOT CRITICIZE OTHERS.

7. I SHALL FORGIVE MYSELF WHEN I MAKE A MISTAKE.

8. I SHALL BE KIND TO OTHERS, WITHOUT SACRIFICING MY OWN NEEDS.

9. I SHALL TAKE RESPONSIBILITY FOR MY LIFE.

10. I SHALL LOVE MYSELF TO THE BEST OF MY ABILITY.

ambitionperfection.tumblr.com

Section 4:
Conquering
Disordered Eating

Chapter 6: Treatment of Eating Disorders

Introduction

The wide scope of effects brought on by eating disorders demands that treatment and recovery is multifaceted, often involving both medical and psychiatric interventions. Treatment options include medication; nutrition therapy; exercise; individual, family, and group counseling/psychotherapy; Expressive Therapy, including activities such as art, music, dance/movement, and writing; and, most recently, equine therapy. Each case is different and must be assessed as such to determine whether inpatient, outpatient, individual, family, or group treatment is needed for optimum recovery. More important than the medical and psychiatric interventions is spiritual healing, which will be covered separately in Chapter 11.

Before anyone with an ED can receive treatment, they must first break through denial, especially if trauma exists in the person's past. They must realize they need help and want help for treatment to be effective. Sometimes, when a person persists in denial, interventions from parents, professionals, and others may be necessary. What can you do if you recognize someone in this situation?

Solomon (2017) offered five suggestions to help someone with ED and PTSD symptoms. They are:

1. If you and the person share the same traumatic past experience, realize you too may have been affected by the event. Even if you did not experience the trauma, you can experience PTSD through what is known as *vicarious traumatization*. "This means that if your loved one has shared details of the event, you might develop your own symptoms." (¶ 6) If this happens, don't put off getting help for yourself.

2. Encourage the person to get professional help.

3. Use active listening to be supportive. Don't blame or shame. Avoid being a "rescuer". Just listen attentively with a compassionate ear.

4. Talk with the person about how you might help them on the road to healing.

5. Have your own support system. Also don't neglect other important relationships you have and always practice self-care. Don't allow yourself to become enmeshed in the other person's problems.

EDs can be very effective, yet deadly, maladaptive ways of dealing with PTSD and any existing stress. Therefore, besides trauma-focused work, treating patients diagnosed with an ED who have a history of trauma need to recognize the ED benefits and identify alternative, healthy means of "regulating emotion, tolerating stress, protecting and caring for the self, placing blame, feeling empowered and in control, and/or communicating with others." (Henretty, n.d., A Word on Treatment section, ¶ 1). For clients who are vitamin deficient, symptoms are not likely to abate short of weight restoration. Irrespective of perceived nutrition, the health problems of EDs must be checked.

Treatment for EDs falls into a continuum from low to high structure; thus, if a patient is not making progress in outpatient therapy, clinicians should consider a higher level-of-care—intensive outpatient, partial hospitalization, or residential treatment—at an ED treatment center that also specializes in the treatment of trauma. (Henretty, n.d., A Word On Treatment section, ¶ 1).

The Road to Recovery

Assessment

The assessment process to determine whether a person has an ED should include both a thorough physical examination and a complete family and individual history of eating behaviors and other related disorders. Additionally, patients may be given one or more available tests used in the screening process.

Eating Attitudes Test (EAT-26). EAT-26 (2009-2017) reports that this test developed by Dr. David Garner is probably the most popular measure of symptoms and issues related to eating disorders. This test is included as Appendix C and may be taken on line at http://www.eat-26.com/.

On-line testing. The website psychcentral.com (Grohol, 1995-2017) offers free online screening tests for eating disorders. These tests include Binge Eating Disorder Quiz; Eating Disorder Screening Test; a new Do I Have an Eating Disorder? Quiz; and the EAT-26 mentioned previously. Cambridge Eating Disorder Center (2017) and Screening for Mental Health, Inc. (SMH) partnered to offer a free online screening tool for eating disorders.

Pharmacological Treatments

The use and effectiveness of treating individuals diagnosed with eating disorders using medication depends on the type of ED, such as AN, BN, or BED; and on whether co-existing diagnoses, such as depression, OCD, alcohol or substance abuse, anxiety disorders, PTSD and ADD, exist. Regarding pharmacological treatment for anorexia, Mayo Clinic Staff (2016a) and WebMD Staff (2017a) reported that no medications have been approved by the FDA as treatment for anorexia, as no medication used has been very effective. David T. Tharp M.D., M.Div., Medical Director and founder of Stonebriar Psychiatric Services (n.d.b) and a former "staff psychiatrist at the Remuda Ranch Center for Anorexia and Bulimia in Arizona, a treatment program for women with eating disorders and dual diagnoses," (Stonebriar Psychiatric Services, n.d.a, (¶ 2) reported in treating AN:

Some studies have found Periactin and other medications which stimulate appetite to be helpful. However, many of these young women already live with constant hunger, and the idea of a medicine that tries to "make them eat" is frequently terrifying for them. If depression is present, anti-depressants may be helpful if one understands that you cannot achieve full therapeutic benefit until there has been some weight restoration. Some of the newer "antipsychotic" medications have also been helpful in low doses, and it is felt that this is partly due to alleviating some of the body image anxiety and possibly some of the distortion, which at times almost seems to take on delusional proportions. (Tharp, 2006a, p. 2)

A study by Kaye et al. (2001) offers evidence that Prozac is effective in treating anorexia. Subjects of the study were 35 people with anorexia discharged from the hospital after regaining weight. Sixteen of the 35 patients received Prozac while the remaining 19 received a placebo. After a year of outpatient treatment, results showed that 10 of the 16 individuals treated with Prozac maintained a healthy body weight without relapsing, as compared to 3 of the 19 patients treated with placebo.

Bulimia pharmacological treatment. Mayo Clinic Staff (2016b) and WebMD Staff (2017b) report antidepressants in conjunction with psychotherapy are helpful in the treatment of BN. WebMD Staff report "Antidepressants, such as selective serotonin reuptake inhibitors (SSRIs) – including Prozac, Zoloft, Celexa and Lexapro – in combination with psychological therapies, are now a mainstay in bulimia therapy." (Medications for bulimia section, ¶ 1) However, Mayo Clinic Staff report Prozac is the only antidepressant approved by the FDA to treat bulimia.

BED Pharmacological Treatment. Tharp (2006b) reported:

There are a number of antidepressants, as well as some anti-obesity agents and anticonvulsants which have shown to be of some benefit with BED. However, these have generally not yet been approved for the treatment of BED by the FDA. These would include Meridia (sibutramine) and Xenical (orlistat) as anti-obesity agents, along with Topamax as one of the anticonvulsants that has at times been helpful. Fluoxetine (Prozac) in its higher dose ranges of 60-80 mg per day has frequently been helpful in reducing the frequency of binges and often with accompanying weight loss. Other medications in the SSRI group, such as the Zoloft, Celexa, and Luvox have shown similar trends. (p. 2)

Nutrition Therapy

Nutrition education and intervention, by a registered dietitian, is a key element of treating eating disorders, according to Ozier, Henry, and American Dietetic Association (2011). Ozier et al. (2011) notes the responsibilities of the dietician as assessing the nutritional status, knowledge base, motivation, and current eating and treatment plan; developing the nutrition section of the proposed treatment; implementing the treatment plan and supporting the patient in achieving his or her goals. The dietician continuously relates with the patient throughout the course of treatment and assists the primary medical provider with monitoring lab results, vital signs, and any physical symptoms related to malnutrition.

Exercise Therapy

Although concerns exist for using exercise to treat ED, especially in those individuals who are compulsive exercisers, Hausenblas, Cook, and Chittester (2008) concluded that exercise may be beneficial as an intervention for ED. Hausenblas et al. (2008) reported

Theoretical justification suggests that by improving physical fitness through regular healthy exercise, patients with ED may experience improved self-esteem, body image, and mood, as well as a reduction in the uncomfortable sensations of bloating and distention during eating [Fossati, 2004]. *Additionally, exercise promotes self-regulation. Therefore, exercise may reduce bodily tensions and negative mood and increase tolerance to everyday stress, which are all triggers for binging and purging* [Alpers & Tuschen-Caiffier, 2001]. (p. 44)

Psychotherapy

Another vital member of the treatment team for a person with an ED is a psychologist. Treatment procedures that are recommended by any one therapist will reflect his or her treatment philosophy, according to Freeman, Miller and Mizes (2000). In treating eating disorders psychologists often need to fill the role of educator as well as help the client deal with the broader problems that led to the disorder. Most professionals, according to The Something Fishy Website on Eating Disorders (1998-2017), adopt an eclectic approach that combines cognitive, behavioral, and psychodynamic models with family therapy and psychoeducation.

Cognitive-behaviorists presume the primary vehicle for permanent recovery is cognitive; although, they assume lasting change occurs at many levels, including behavioral, cognitive, and emotional. The goal of cognitive-behavioral therapists is to have the patient change overrated concepts about the desirability of thinness and to overcome fears about weight gain (Williamson & Netemeyer, 2000).

Cognitive techniques. Ridding the patient of self-defeating attitudes and beliefs that precipitated the disorder is the goal of cognitive therapists treating eating disorders. Old beliefs and attitudes are replaced with realistic, healthy ones.

The integrative cognitive therapy (ICT) treatment method for eating disorders proposed by Wonderlich, Peterson, Mitchell, and Crow (2000) differs from other cognitive and interpersonal models by placing a greater clinical emphasis on cultural factors, self-oriented cognition, interpersonal schemas, interpersonal relationship styles, and affect regulation. In this multifaceted treatment method, multitudes of strategies for overcoming eating disorders exist but the authors focus on three, which they consider crucial to recovery. The first goal of the ICT therapist is to promote behavioral change in food consumption, meal planning, and poor nutritional habits. This goal is accomplished through teaching clients about the maladaptive nature of dieting, the cultural factors that encourage it, and providing healthy alternatives to eating behaviors which can be implemented into the client's lifestyle. The second mechanism of change advocated by ICT is to modify the actual self-perception and improve self-esteem. Finally,

helping the patient to adopt an interpersonal stance that allows her to be interpersonally attached to others, but very much aware of boundaries and limits, is considered optimal. Helping the patient to identify and express her thoughts and feelings in relationships is considered an essential element to the healthy functioning of an autonomous self. (p. 279)

Behavioral therapy. Many hospital and day programs incorporate behavior therapy into their programs. This approach is tailored to the needs of each patient individually and involves the gradual increase in activities with weight gain or loss.

Psychodynamic models. Psychodynamic therapists focus on early experiences that may have contributed to the course of development in an ED. The goals of psychodynamic therapists include: understanding the different purposes that maintaining eating disordered symptoms serve for a client, improving the client's self-esteem, increasing the client's self-differentiation, improving the eating disorder symptomatology, and improving social functioning. Mechanisms of change that psychoanalysts use include corrective emotional experiences, making the unconscious conscious, gaining insight, and internalization (Fallon & Bunce, 2000).

Self psychology therapy is a psychoanalytic theory reported by Sands (2000) to treat eating disorders. Self psychology theory emphasizes the inner world of the patient. Sands separated "out four mechanisms of change offered either explicitly or implicitly by self-psychology over the years which, in their most simplified form, can be called forms of (1) internalization, (2) resumption of development, (3) desomatization, and (4) integration." (p. 203) Kohut (1971, 1977, 1984), as cited by Sands, describes the way clients change as "transmuting internalization process." (Sands, p. 203) For this process to be successful an empathic relationship must exist between the client and therapist, as the client internalizes behaviors, such as self-calming, learned from the therapist. The second method of change "resumption of development" "suggests that empathic understanding serves as a facilitating medium reinstating self-developmental processes." (Sands, p. 204)

As cited by dictionary.com, psychiatrists define somatization as "the conversion of anxiety into physical symptoms." (Somatization, n.d.) Using desomatization as a way to help clients change, the client learns to express emotions verbally rather than stuffing them to manifest in the form of physical symptoms.

As cited by dictionary.com, psychologists define integration as "the organization of the constituent elements of the personality into a coordinated, harmonious whole." (Integration, n.d.) According to Sands (2000), "it is the empathic responsiveness of the therapist which allows disowned domains of the self to become recognized, understood, and slowly integrated into the patient's central self-structure." (p. 205)

Psychoeducation. Treasure, Schmidt, and Troop (2000) view anorexia not just as a dieting disorder but also as a form of stress response to severe life events or problems. Initial treatment sessions focus on answering the questions "where is the patient at; where is she coming from and how can we help her move in the direction of sustained change?" (p. 284). Therapy goals include teaching the patient that the "cons" of maintaining anorexic behaviors outweigh the "pros". Self-esteem is monitored during the entire treatment process. The techniques of motivational interviewing are utilized, which requires the therapist to express empathy, develop discrepancy, avoid arguments, and roll with resistance and support self-efficacy.

Family Therapy

Bryant-Waugh (2000) described family therapy as an approach to treating eating disorders that integrates developmental psychology, Bowenian systems theory, and feminist ideology. Exploring the patient's developmental history and analyzing past patterns of response to life changes and stress manifest the influence of developmental psychology in this approach.

Bowenian therapists view therapy as an opportunity for people to learn more about themselves and their relationships, so that they can assume responsibility for their own problems. This is a process of active inquiry that helps family members get past blaming and fault finding in order to face and explore their own roles in family problems. Understanding, not action is the key to solving dysfunctional behavior. Treatment involves placing the problem in a multigenerational framework through a timeline and a genogram, lowering anxiety in the patient, increasing differentiation, and using process questions and relationship experiments. (Nichols & Schwartz, 2001, as cited by Owens, 2002)

For treating eating disorders, Giacomo and Antonietta (2000), as cited by Owens (2002), proposed the Elementary Pragmatic Model that evolved out of general systems theory and has a strong focus on family participation and intervention. This approach also embraces intensive, multidisciplinary Day Hospital treatment that includes psycho-education on eating disorders, group therapy, nutrition therapy, creativity groups, and physical rehabilitation.

Group therapy

"Group therapy is just as effective as individual therapy – for treating a wide range of symptoms – and … group participation offers a unique therapeutic advantage." (Rosenfeld, 2017, ¶ 3) The advantage is group members can identify with each other, they can learn from each other, and support one another. As members interact, group therapists also can offer insight to members on how to improve one's boundaries or communication skills. Furthermore, "Group therapy offers a cost-effective alternative to individual therapy, and group treatment allows access to a larger population of individuals, who might not otherwise receive care." (Rosenfeld, ¶ 5)

Equine therapy

Eating Disorder Hope (2012) defines equine therapy as

> *a form of psychotherapy in which horses are utilized as tools for a man or woman to develop greater self-understanding and assist in emotional growth. Equine Therapy is a form of animal assisted therapy, an aspect of mental health that acknowledges the bond between animals and humans in addition to the opportunity for emotional healing that can occur when a relationship is initiated between two species, such as human and horse.* (What is Equine Therapy? Section, ¶ 1)

According to Eating Disorder Hope (2012), "many eating disorder therapists and professionals recognize the benefits of equine therapy as a method of improving lives and refer patients to riding programs." (What is Equine Therapy? Section, ¶ 2)

"Founded in 1999, the Equine Assisted Growth and Learning Association (EAGALA) is the leading international nonprofit association for professionals incorporating horses to address mental health and personal development needs." (Welcome section, ¶ 1) The website of EAGALA (2009-2010) sites the goals and opportunities offered by the organization. Among these objectives and opportunities are training and certifying therapists in the field of Equine Assisted Psychotherapy (EAP); annual conferences; and providing educational, training, and support resources.   In addition, EAGALA offers a map and search options to find where their programs are located.

EAP patients learn about themselves when they participate in activities with horses and then discuss feelings and behavior patterns learned. Canopy Cove (2016) and Remuda Ranch (2014b, 2016, 2017a) are located in settings that allow them to utilize equine therapy as a part of the recovery process for patients. Horse care, grooming procedures, saddlery, and basic equitation (horseback riding) may be a part of eating disorder treatment for patients at Remuda Ranch. Research from Remuda Ranch indicates a number of benefits to EAP. These benefits include:

- Enhanced self-esteem
- Overcoming fears
- Impulse modulation
- Renewed self-efficacy
- Feelings of belonging
- Reaching out
- Improved body image awareness
- Self-acceptance
- Assertiveness
- Development of trust
- Outward direction of focus
- Improved communication skills
- Improved emotional awareness
- Improved emotional regulation
- Improved self-control
- Healing relationships
- Freedom from inhibitions
- Spiritual growth.

Expressive Creative Therapy

As a part of their multi-disciplinary treatment program, the staff of Remuda Ranch (2017b) offers expressive arts therapy as a component of treating eating disorders. Through expressive arts therapy patients explore their identities and problems using their personal creativity. Self-worth, self-concept, and a sense of individual purpose may be discovered using therapeutic music, dance/movement (DMT), art, and creative writing. Relationship systems also are examined through the expressive therapies. (Owens, 2002)

Remuda Ranch (2017b) lists the benefits to expressive arts therapy:

- *Patients share their perceptions and viewpoints that might otherwise be difficult to express through more traditional therapies.*
- *Promoting a sense of freedom allows patients to unearth and dissect their inner feelings during the healing process.*
- *Using images to express their feelings may be easier than conveying these feelings in words.* (Healing Through Art section, ¶ 1)

Music/DMT. According to Wennerstrand (2002), as cited by Owens (2002), research shows that many individuals with eating disorders have alexithymia, "defined as difficulty in putting feelings and fantasies into words (Zerbe, 1995)." (Wennerstrand, ¶ 2) Through DMT patients express that which cannot be expressed with words. Dance/movement therapy practiced by trained dance/movement therapists certified by The American Dance Therapy Association is a body-based therapy that combines interpersonal, object-relations theory, movement analysis, and dance technique.

Art/writing. Many researchers and practitioners recommend that persons recovering from eating disorders keep daily food journals and a journal to uncover and express both stuffed and current feelings. Orgeron has found journaling helps to release pent-up emotions, to discover one's trigger foods and situations, and to facilitate in positive self-talk. DeGoede and Drews (1998) recommend 15 to 20 minutes of journaling daily.

When you use your daily journal, allow yourself to write without worrying about grammar, sentence structure, or spelling: it doesn't even have to make sense. This is an exercise in beginning to get to know the "inside" you from the "outside" you. (DeGoede & Drews, p. 17)

Avoiding Relapse

Short of God's intervention with a miracle of deliverance (Orgeron, He delivered her.), relapses cannot be avoided completely but can only be faced through having a plan, according to research. (Arterburn & Mintle, 2004; Cipolia & Berman, 2015; Klimek, n.d.; Komosky, n.d.; Muhlheim, 2017; NEDA, 2016h) Disordered eating did not develop overnight nor will it be healed overnight. Recovery comes in stages, often with a few slips along the way. If not handled appropriately, these slips can lead to full blown relapse. What can one do to ward off relapse? First, having a relapse prevention plan is crucial to success in recovery. Additionally, those in recovery need to know the stages and signs of relapse to be able to help self-monitor potential situations that may lead to relapse.

Have a Plan

Keep doing what works. What helps and how much it helps one move forward in recovery will vary with each individual. Here are common practices that people in recovery can do:

- Keep eating regular healthy meals.
- Plan healthy meals and snacks.
- Shop wisely and consistently for healthy foods.
- Keep a food log.
- Review literature given out by one's professional clinicians. (Komosky, n.d.)
- Review one's journal entries. Orgeron found that reviewing her recovery notebook that included both literature from specialists and her journaling reminded her where she came from and how much she had progressed.
- Keep exercising regularly in moderation.
- Get plenty of sleep and rest.
- Practice self-care.
- Rely on God.
- Practice spiritual disciples. Arterburn and Mintle (2004) list the spiritual disciplines as "prayer, worship, confession, Bible study, giving, fasting, submission, service, and forgiving." (p. 233)

Avoid triggers. Triggers are those foods, places, or anything else that might tempt one to slip off the road to recovery. Triggers differ with each individual. Common triggers include:

- Being in a grocery store—if grocery shopping is a temptation, those in recovery should send someone else to the store, or take a friend along for accountability.
- Gyms—for those who used exercise to purge after a binge, going to a gym to work out may trigger bad memories and a slip.
- Mirrors—if looking in the mirror causes distress, one can remove the mirror or post positive messages, especially favorite Scriptures, on the mirror that promote positive thoughts when using the mirror.
- Scales—Klimek (n.d.) reported, "A scale is not a necessity to sustaining life, so a woman in recovery should not have one. It is that simple." (Looks For The Things that Help & Hurt Recovery, ¶ 4) Orgeron remembers hiding her bathroom scales for a season during her recovery from disordered eating. She measured her success by how her clothes fit.
- Fashion and mainstream magazines—Komosky (n.d.) reported that the airbrushed body images depicted in magazines "are, in fact, scientifically unattainable. There's zero need to attempt to live up to 'cultural standards' that simply don't exist in the real world." (¶ 3) Not to mention a lot of the nutritional advice and advertisements in magazines can be incorrect or misleading.

Muhlheim (2017) compiled a list of situational triggers for disordered eating. This list includes:

- *Stress and/or a busy schedule which makes planning meals difficult*
- *Becoming overwhelmed by feelings and emotions*
- *Loss of a family member, friend, etc.*

- *Marital, social or family problems*
- *Change in schedule (such as going on summer break) or a move (going away to school, etc.)*
- *Weight gain*
- *Dieting or any form or food restriction*
- *Missing a meal or snack*
- *Juice cleanses and detox efforts*
- *Being under the influence of a diet guru or overly health conscious person*
- *Having friends or family who diet*
- *Following any form or [sic] restrictive eating plan*
- *Being in unfamiliar food environments and/or having unrestricted access to food (at a buffet, holiday, or potluck for example)*
- *Getting weighed at the doctor*
- *Shopping for clothes*
- *Pregnancy*
- *Dating*
- *Others commenting on your weight*
- *Health problems. (¶ 3)*

One last possible trigger that Orgeron found reported in literature is using fitness trackers (Eikey & Reddy, 2017; Emily Program, 2017a), "those trendy apps people use to record things like steps, calories, and heart rate." (Emily Program, 2017a, ¶ 1). Eikey and Reddy (2017) concluded from a small study they conducted of women with DE that "While these apps can be beneficial to users, they can also have negative effects on users with eating disorder behaviors." (Abstract, ¶ 1)

The Emily Program (2017a) reported that Eikey and Reddy (2017) classified the ways in which the women used the apps unhealthily. These classifications include:

1. Using the apps obsessively
2. Striving for perfection in tracking food eaten
3. Dire awareness of numbers. One participant wrote, "I think it's definitely very triggering because you become obsessed with food, you look at food differently...That's protein, that's fat, that's carbs instead of like that's a chicken breast, that's peanut butter, that's a piece of bread." (Emily Program, ¶ 2)
4. Restricting
5. Manipulating the app to drop pounds quicker (e.g.: not reporting all their exercise when they over-exercised)
6. Compensatory actions (e.g.: not eating enough calories one day when they ate too many another day)
7. Using the app to circumvent undesirable emotions (e.g.: not reporting correctly everything that one eats on days they cheated).

Think permanent lifestyle change. In overcoming disordered eating the goal should be to make the positive changes made become a natural part of one's being. These changes become a part of a life-long pattern of making healthy choices for living well.

Stages of Relapse

Arterburn and Mintle (2004) discussed "the phases of relapse" (pp. 228-230). These phases or stages include complacency, confusion, compromise, and catastrophe.

Complacency. This is when those in recovery first let their guard down and neglect doing what they need to do, what they have been doing that has helped them move towards healing. During this stage people may think they no longer need help. Thus, they may relax their boundaries and even drop support groups or therapy that have been keys to their previous progress.

Confusion. Secondly, they become double-minded. Doubt is the dominant thought. They have doubts about the severity of their disordered eating or whether they need additional long-term treatment and support. Their recovery plan is put on the back burner with unhealthy and erratic choices made.

Compromise. During the phase of compromise, people revert to "using food to comfort and to fill emotional needs once again." (p. 229) Because they refuse to accept responsibility for their actions and pull further away from their support team, they are headed for disaster.

Catastrophe. At this stage, those who have backslidden into disordered eating have lost any and all previous feelings of control. "The main feeling at this stage is helplessness and hopelessness." (p. 230) "Backslidden individuals have gained a "significant amount of weight back, and there is no end in sight to that state of being." (p. 230)

Signs of Relapse

NEDA (2016h) reported warning signs to relapse. The following warning signs are adapted from NEDA's list:
- Constant thoughts about food, diet, or weight
- Lying to one's treatment providers
- Worrying one has lost control; overcompensating by striving to be perfect.
- Feeling there are no buffers to stress in one's life
- Feeling one has no purpose or goals in life.
- The primary goal has become to be attractive rather than eating and exercising for health.
- Believing one can't be happy without looking a certain way
- Seeing oneself at an unhealthy weigh
- Others indicate a person has a faulty self-perception.
- One compulsively weighs or looks in a mirror.
- Skipping meals; purging after eating
- Irritability
- Feeling guilt and shame over what one eats

- Avoiding activities where food is present
- Isolating oneself; eating in secret
- Looking down on others with a weight problem (projection).

What can one do to get back on track during a relapse? Cipolia and Berman (2015) shared seven tips to remember during a relapse:

1. Get professional support.
2. Talk with members of your support system (e.g.: family) to allow them to help you.
3. Remember you are not a failure. Relapses can make you stronger. Get back on track.
4. Remember your motives for recovery.
5. Remember you are worth taking care of, including enjoying life. Practice self-care, and find new hobbies to enjoy.
6. Reflect on the relapse to determine the trigger. Think about what you might do differently when faced with similar situations in the future.
7. Live in the present moment. Don't live in the past, or worry about the future. Each day offers a new beginning.

In closing the section on relapse, Orgeron wants to point out that though she believes our goal is to have a permanent healthy lifestyle, we want to remember as Muhlheim (2017) reported,

During the recovery process it is not always possible to avoid slips and relapses. Many people tend to be very hard on themselves if they do have a slip or relapse. It's important to remember that no one can recover perfectly. If you have a bad day, you can forgive yourself, put it behind you, and continue to move forward in your recovery. It is important to look back at the lapse to learn from it and at the same time, be compassionate and not beat yourself up. Lapses are a normal part of recovery and can actually be helpful in making recovery stronger. (¶ 6)

"While a relapse may feel demoralizing, or that everything you gained through recovery is gone, it's actually far from that. Relapses are often natural parts of the process. As they say, sometimes you need to take a step back to take two forward." (Cipolia & Berman, 2015, ¶ 3).

***

Chapter 6: Treatment of Eating Disorders

Key Terms/Concepts

Art therapy

Catastrophe

Complacency

Compromise

Confusion

Dance/movement therapy

Denial

Eating Attitudes Test

Equine therapy

Exercise therapy

Expressive creative therapy

Family therapy

Fitness trackers

Group therapy

Journaling

Music Therapy

Nutrition therapy

Periactin

Permanent healthy lifestyle

Psychotherapy

Prozac

Relapse

Relapse prevention plan

SSRI medications

Stages of relapse

Triggers

Vicarious traumatization

Writing therapy

Questions for Reflection:

1. According to Solomon, what are five ways one might help a person in denial with an eating disorder?

2. In assessing for an eating disorder, what must the assessment include?

3. What is probably the most popular measure of eating attitudes and symptoms?

4. Are medications effective in the treatment of individuals diagnosed with an eating disorder? If so, what medications have been found to be effective in the treatment of eating disorders?

5. According to the Mayo Clinic Staff and WebMD Staff, what is the best approach to treating bulimia?

6. What are the different approaches of psychotherapy that clinicians can use in treating eating disorders?

7. Discuss equine therapy and its benefits.

8. How are art and writing therapies beneficial to persons with eating disorders?

9. What are the signs and stages of relapse? And how does one avoid relapse?

10. What is the importance of persons with EDs avoiding triggers?

***

Philippians 3:13-14

[13] Brethren, I do not count myself to have apprehended; but one thing *I do,* forgetting those things which are behind and reaching forward to those things which are ahead, [14] I press toward the goal for the prize of the upward call of God in Christ Jesus.

Chapter 7: A Wholistic Model in Treating Disordered Eating

The wholistic, or "whole-person approach is not a quick fix. It is a long-term, life-changing strategy for recovery and healing." (Jantz, 2010, p. 2) Dr. Gregory Jantz founded The Center: A Place of Hope that utilizes a whole-person approach to treating disordered eating that is personalized to each individual's needs. This approach identifies mankind's intricate nature as individuals and shoots for fitness and balance in all areas of a person's life, including "emotional, intellectual, physical, relational, and spiritual." (Jantz, p. 2) An individual's emotions both influence and are affected by disordered eating. Old deep-seated emotions from past experiences can fuel disordered eating. For example, a young girl who has been sexually abused may begin to overeat to gain weight in a subconscious effort to protect herself where she thinks men will no longer find her attractive. The pain from the sexual abuse and the girl's fear of it happening again would be addressed in the whole-person approach.

With the whole-person approach of recovery from disordered eating, one's intellect must assist one's emotional self in healing by throwing out old false beliefs and incorporating new truths into one's being. "The whole-person goal is for the emotional and the intellectual selves to complement and support each other in healing and recovery." (Jantz, 2010, p. 4)

The physical self refers to how one's body functions. In treating disordered eating, doctors at The Center look at physical illnesses that may have been catalysts for one's developing DE.

> *We will also look at how your body can function in the future. Nutritional advances offer hope to support physical healing and return your body to optimum functioning. Each of us has the ability to appropriately nurture our own body, providing health and vitality.* (Jantz, 2010, p. 4)

Jantz noted addressing the physical consequences of disordered eating in addition to the emotional ramifications is crucial for recovery. Orgeron knows from her experience that the two facets of an individual, emotional and physical, go hand in hand and both elements take time and patience to heal.

The relational part of one's self refers to both former and current relationships. The relational self affects both the emotional and intellectual selves. Dysfunctional relationships may be one of the root causes of disordered eating. "The whole-person approach works to reestablish proper connections with others, mend past associations, and build healthy new relationships, including those involving appropriate sexual intimacy." (Jantz, 2010, p. 4)

The whole-person approach also encourages one to recognize and develop one's spiritual self. "The more you turn to a physical comfort like food, the less likely you are to turn to God for spiritual comfort." (Jantz, 2010, p. 26) Once discovered, the spiritual self adds hope, strength, and purpose to one's life. Furthermore, while the physical body perishes, the spiritual aspect lives forever. The obsession with controlling the body with food quenches the Holy Spirit's work within a person. By being connected with God and leaning on Him, healing is possible. Orgeron credits her relationship with

God as the most important asset that she had to overcome disordered eating and to remain free from the bondage of food addiction.

With disordered eating, "food has been removed from its God-designed context of food and nutrition for your body. Instead, it has moved into the realms of control, companionship, numbing, compensation, reward, self-righteousness, self-loathing, denial, pleasure." (Jantz, 2010, p. 34) These unhealthy motives for eating need to be replaced with eating for nutritional purposes only.

> Orgeron credits her relationship with God as the most important asset that she had to overcome disordered eating and to remain free from the bondage of food addiction.

Jantz (2010) described an ED as "a time bomb" (p. 17) about to explode. To defuse the bomb, one must break through denial to admit there's a problem. Jantz stressed,

Your self-destructive behavior did not come about for no reason. Most people who develop a severe eating disorder have had some history of abuse, and I encourage you to believe in what your past reveals. You must be determined to examine your past and accept the truth that is revealed. You must take the truth of your past and put it into perspective as an adult. (p. 97)

To remain in denial fuels the disordered eating and keeps one from experiencing the best life God has to offer.

> **2 Peter 2:22**
>
> 22 But it has happened to them according to the true proverb: "A dog returns to his own vomit,"[a] and, "a sow, having washed, to her wallowing in the mire."

What about relapse? Jantz (2010) warns those in recovery to expect relapse. While moving through recovery, some individuals "may want to 'recycle' back into old patterns. . . . Second Peter 2:22 says this tendency to return to destructive patterns is like a dog returning to its own vomit or a washed pig going back to wallowing in the mud." (p. 141)

What can one do to prepare for and ward against relapse? Jantz (2010) indicated that prayer is the best defense to prevent relapse. He suggested the following prayer:

Dear God, I've been existing in the stagnation of my disordered relationship with food, living from moment to moment in destructive obsession. I want to be free! I will reclaim the joy of faith in the future. Help me to see beyond today.

Thank you for helping me refocus my thoughts on the inward beauty of your creation. I will to see myself as someone lovely, valuable, and precious. Thank you for helping me love myself. (p. 142)

Like Jantz (2010), Orgeron believes it is crucial for individuals who practice disordered eating "to establish, regain, or strengthen a healthy relationship with God." (p. 208) Thus, Orgeron will devote the next chapter to discussing "A Spiritual Approach to Healing".

For more information on The Center or the ministry of Dr. Greg Jantz, visit their websites at https://www.aplaceofhope.com/ or http://www.drgregoryjantz.com/, respectively. The Center Staff may be reached through email, info@aplaceofhope.com; or by telephone at 888-771-5166 or 425-771-5166.

Chapter 7: A Wholistic Model in Treating Disordered Eating

Key Terms/Concepts

Denial   Relational self
Intellect   Spiritual self
Physical self   Wholistic model of treatment
Relapse

Questions for Reflection:

1. According to Jantz, what is the goal in using the wholistic approach in recovering from disordered eating?
2. Give an example of how old deep-seated emotions from past experiences can trigger disordered eating.
3. What is the role of the intellect in healing from disordered eating?
4. Why is looking at the physical self crucial to working with clients who have disordered eating?
5. What is meant by the relational part of one's self?
6. What are benefits to discovering one's spiritual self?
7. What is the only healthy reason for eating?
8. What is the outcome of a person with an ED remaining in denial?
9. According to Jantz, what is the best defense to prevent relapse?

***

Chapter 8: A Spiritual Approach to Healing

Overcoming disordered eating is probably one of the most difficult journeys one can face in life. Unlike alcohol, drugs, and other types of addictions where one can stop the behavior cold turkey and guard oneself from being in tempting situations, one must "eat to live". No one has to face the recovery journey alone,

> *Especially when God the creator of the universe is right there just waiting to help you. All you must do is ask. He will take your hand and walk alongside you through this time. Will it be easy? Once again ... no. God never promised any of His children that their lives would unfold without struggle or pain. What He did promise was that He would never, ever leave us or forsake us.*
>
> *And you know what? That's enough. Remember ... you can travel the recovery road the hard way, or the far easier way ... by making God your partner in the journey.* (Ekern, 2017b, Faith in the Recovery Journey from an Eating Disorder section, ¶s 3-4)

How does one make God their partner in overcoming disordered eating? First, one must come to know Jesus Christ as Lord and Savior. By following the steps outlined in Figure 6: The ABC's of Salvation, anyone can begin the journey to overcoming disordered eating with God as your strength and guide. Without repentance and coming to know Jesus as Lord and Savior, God will not hear the prayers of the lost world, unless the prayer is a prayer of repentance and surrender. Psalm 34:15 tells us that: "[15] The eyes of the Lord *are* on the righteous, And His *ears are open* to their cry." So does Psalm 66:18: "If I regard iniquity in my heart, The Lord will not hear."

What is repentance? Repentance can be defined as feeling so much regret or dissatisfaction in circumstances, as to change one's mind. Thus, the process of breaking through denial and, in time, of learning healthier behavior patterns is a form of repentance. For the person with disordered eating who has experienced abuse, the repentant behavior would move the survivor of abuse away from the abuse and the self-destructive or self-protective behavior patterns adopted early on to deal with the abuse. (Allender, 1990)

For those backsliders who once had a closer relationship with God, these individuals too can renew their walk with the Lord through repentance and rededication. 2 Chronicles 7:14 tells us, "if My people who are called by My name will humble themselves, and pray and seek My face, and turn from their wicked ways, then I will hear from heaven, and will forgive their sin and heal their land." This verse is often referred to as the prescription for revival. Revival begins in the heart of an individual with the Holy Spirit's calling, "Come home. Come back to Me, My child."

The **ABC**'s of Salvation

Admit that you are a sinner.

A
"^{23}for all have sinned and fall short of the glory of God,"
                                    Romans 3:23
"^{23}For the wages of sin *is* death, but the gift of God *is* eternal life in Christ Jesus our Lord."
                                    Romans 6:23
Believe in the Lord, Jesus Christ.

B
"^{16}For God so loved the world that He gave His only begotten Son, that whoever believes in Him should not perish but have everlasting life."
                                    John 3:16
Choose to confess and accept the gift of salvation.

C
"^{10}For with the heart one believes unto righteousness, and with the mouth confession is made unto salvation."
                                    Romans 10:10

Figure 6: The ABC's of Salvation

Gluttony in Scriptures

Gluttony is known as one of the seven deadly sins, along with pride, envy, anger (unrighteous), sloth, greed, and lust (Segal, 2015). Food, the object of gluttony, has existed since the days of Adam and Eve.

> *Food can heal. Food can sustain. But as we see in Genesis 2–3, food can also kill. After planting the man in the garden, God instructed him to eat from every tree—with one exception: the tree of the knowledge of good and evil. "[F]or," said God, "in the day that you eat of it you shall surely die." (Gen. 2:17) Tragically, Adam and Eve chose death over life in response to the serpent's scheme.* (Bowers, 2015, p. 73)

Bowers (2015) pointed out how Adam's and Eve's transgression, the first sin recorded in Scripture resulting in The Fall, stemmed from the appetite with inappropriate motives for eating the forbidden fruit. Genesis 3:6 tells us that—"[6] So when the woman saw that the tree *was* good for food, that it *was* pleasant to the eyes, and a tree desirable to make *one* wise, she took of its fruit and ate. She also gave to her husband with her, and he ate." "In the moment of temptation, the fruit embodied Eve's deepest cravings: cravings for pleasure, for beauty, for wisdom. Rather than satisfy these cravings within the boundaries of God's good design, Eve opened her mouth — and her heart — to rebellion." (Bowers, p. 74) Is not that like a lot of people today?

Bowers (2015) reported the dangers to gluttony. They include:

- Gluttony puts food in God's rightful place becoming an idol.
- Gluttony harms our relationships. For the overeater, while that person sits overeating, another person may go hungry. In today's world this might be exemplified at a church covered dish dinner where those at the front of the line overload their plates while those at the end of the line, get little, if anything to eat.
- Gluttony, a type of self-indulgence, sets individuals up to fall into other sinful behaviors. A modern day example would be the child or adolescent who lies to his or her parents in an effort to hide disordered eating.

Can gluttony be guarded against? Bowers (2015) shared ten ways to guard against gluttony:

1. Remember self-control through Christ is freeing; gluttony is a form of bondage breaking one's fellowship with God.
2. Remember the goal is self-control as a gift of the Spirit, not through one's own willpower.
3. Remember Jesus Christ atoned for the sin of gluttony, as with all sin, on The Cross. He offers everyone the gifts of Salvation and self-control.
4. Glut on Jesus, the Bread of Life. Remember, John 6:32-35:

[32] Then Jesus said to them, "Most assuredly, I say to you, Moses did not give you the bread from heaven, but My Father gives you the true bread from heaven. [33] For the bread of God is He who comes down from heaven and gives life to the world."

[34] Then they said to Him, "Lord, give us this bread always."

[35] And Jesus said to them, "I am the bread of life. He who comes to Me shall never hunger, and he who believes in Me shall never thirst.

"In the words of Jonathan Edwards, 'there is no such thing as excess in our taking of . . . spiritual food. There is no such virtue as temperance in spiritual feasting.'" (Bowers, p. 81-82)

5.   View taking communion (eating the bread; drinking the cup) as teaching self-control. First, during communion we are reminded of our need for God. Second, because we partake of the Lord's Supper with other Christians, we relinquish greedy overeating. "Finally, the regulated portions for each individual remind us of the beauty of self-control." (Bowers, p. 82)

6.   Periodically, take time to fast.

7.   Also know how to enjoy an occasional feast. In the Scriptures, Paul said, "I know how to be abased, and I know how to abound. Everywhere and in all things I have learned both to be full and to be hungry, both to abound and to suffer need." (Philippians 4:12)

8.   Say grace, a prayer of thanksgiving, before eating.

9.   Commit Scripture to memory. "[A] powerful defense against the deceitfulness of gluttony is having our mental refrigerators well-stocked with Scripture. It was by this means that Jesus withstood the temptation to satisfy his hunger unlawfully (Matt. 4:1–4; Luke 4:1–4)." (Bowers, p. 83)

10. Shun idleness. Keep physically active. Remember, Ecclesiastes 3:12-13: "[12] I know that nothing *is* better for them than to rejoice, and to do good in their lives, [13] and also that every man should eat and drink and enjoy the good of all his labor—it *is* the gift of God."

Gluttony as a Stronghold

"[3] For though we walk in the flesh, we do not war according to the flesh. [4] For the weapons of our warfare are not carnal but mighty in God for pulling down strongholds, [5] casting down arguments and every high thing that exalts itself against the knowledge of God, bringing every thought into captivity to the obedience of Christ," (2 Corinthians 10:3-5)

What is a Stronghold?

"Spiritually speaking, Paul defines strongholds as an 'argument or high thing that exalts itself against the knowledge of God'. A stronghold is a point of operation from where Satan can keep the unbeliever captive or the believer incapacitated." (The Spiritual War, n.d., What are Strongholds? section, ¶ 10)

"Strongholds" doesn't necessarily refer to something as extreme as "demon possession," but can merely be a "strong" influence or grip, persistent oppression, obsessions, hindrances or harassment. I do not believe that a child of God, in whom Christ's Spirit dwells, can simultaneously be demon possessed... but without a doubt many Christians are frequent victims of Satan's strongholds. (Robbins, 1990-2017, ¶ 3)

The unbeliever is bound by sin. Satan's desire for unbelievers is that they remain blinded from the light of the Gospel of Jesus Christ. Satan uses strongholds to keep the unbeliever lost. Once a person gets saved by repentance and surrendering to God's will, Satan still does not give up easily. The goal of Satan is to keep the light of Christ from shining through the Christian. "He does this through strongholds, if Satan can establish areas of operation in our life; he then will have the ability to attack at will. He can then keep us from being on the offensive, against his kingdom." (The Spiritual War, n.d., Overcoming Strongholds section, ¶ 3)

Demonic strongholds can exist in individuals, families, and even in churches. "Anyone who has fought an addiction, struggled with pride, or had to 'flee youthful lusts' knows that sin, a lack of faith, and a worldly outlook on life are indeed "strongholds." (Got Questions Ministries, 2002-2017c, ¶ 6). One can easily see how gluttony is a stronghold with individuals. In families, consider those parents who model gluttony to their children. Then the children, modeling their parents, become gluttons.

Can gluttony really be a stronghold in a church? Orgeron believes so. She knows there are churches where the majority of the congregation is overweight or obese. Yet the church members joke about the matter, as they pile their plates high with rich, unhealthy foods at Sunday covered dish dinners.

> Hebrews 13:9
>
> ". . . It is good that the heart be established by grace, not with foods which have not profited those who have been occupied with them."

Humans were made for fellowship with God. We need Him. Whether stuffing or starving for self-control, food cannot fill the void of not experiencing God's best. Only the Holy Spirit can fill our hungry souls. Unbelievers, Christians, Families, Churches, a better way exists. "You just have to get your heart to hear that it is safer to turn to God and that His presence is a better way to soothe yourself. He is waiting for you to let Him draw near." (Hall, 1999, Our Eating is Evidence section, ¶ 4) By letting the Holy Spirit control your appetite, you will not go wrong.

Overcoming the Stronghold of Gluttony

Satan as the ultimate enemy. In Matthew 16: 21-23 when Peter questioned Jesus' plan to go back to Jerusalem where He knew the Jewish leaders planned to kill Him,

> *Jesus did not rebuke Peter, but turned to Peter and rebuked Satan. "Get behind me Satan" (Matt. 16:23). Peter wasn't demon possessed, and probably didn't intend to be an offense. However, the Devil inspired Peter's statement, and Jesus went after the real source.*
>
> *Paul said that our battle is not with "flesh and blood" but with spiritual adversaries (Eph. 6:12). How important it is that we understand what the real root of the problem is -- "who" our real enemy is. It is Satan, not flesh and blood, not our brethren, not our family, not our children, not husbands and wives, not employers, nor our government! The Devil is the enemy!* (Robbins, 1990-2017, Getting to the Root of the Problem section, ¶s 3-4).

Putting on the armor of God. Paul told the Ephesians, "[10] Finally, my brethren, be strong in the Lord and in the power of His might. [11] Put on the whole armor of God, that you may be able to stand against the wiles of the devil." (Ephesians 6:10-11)

> *Paul uses the description of a Roman soldier, to illustrate to the Church at Ephesus, the need to put on the armor of God. Paul who was a Roman citizen (Acts 22:28) by birth, would have been familiar with the Roman legions, their weapons, and authority. He uses this to illustrate a spiritual parallel for the saints (Born-again believers). We are literally the army of the Lord, occupying the physical world. Paul uses the picture of a Roman soldier to cast the vision, of who we are in Christ. We are in every sense, a soldier for the kingdom of God.* (The Spiritual War, n.d., Background to the Armor of God, Part I section, ¶ 6)

What makes up the "full armor of God"? Ephesians 6:14-18 describes God's armor:

> [14] *Stand therefore, having girded your waist with truth, having put on the breastplate of righteousness,* [15] *and having shod your feet with the preparation of the gospel of peace;* [16] *above all, taking the shield of faith with which you will be able to quench all the fiery darts of the wicked one.* [17] *And take the helmet of salvation, and the sword of the Spirit, which is the word of God;* [18] *praying always with all prayer and supplication in the Spirit, being watchful to this end with all perseverance and supplication for all the saints—*

"The full armor of God—truth, righteousness, the gospel, faith, salvation, the Word of God, and prayer—are the tools God has given us, through which we can be spiritually victorious, overcoming Satan's attacks and temptations." (Got Questions Ministries, 2002-2017d, ¶ 9)

The spiritual disciplines. Orgeron recommends individuals with disordered eating practice the spiritual disciplines. What are spiritual disciplines? They are practices taken from Scripture to help Christians mature in Christ. How many are there? The number varies, depending on the author. Orgeron will discuss those disciplines she values in living out her Christian life. Among them are prayer, fasting, and daily Bible reading. Orgeron utilized prayer as a recovery tool in her path to recovery. She offers research (James & Wells, 2003; Matthews, 1998) supporting the inclusion of prayer. James and Wells reported that prayer might help reduce self-centeredness, improve mental control, and minimize symptoms of anxiety such as worry or rumination.

What about fasting? Allender (1990) reported, "Fasting is the choice to put aside legitimate satisfaction, for a time, to concentrate on a more pressing spiritual pursuit." (p. 194) This discipline, according to Allender, is more than abstaining from pleasure and an exercise in self-control, but fasting expresses a single-minded intention to pursue experiential knowledge of God. Orgeron does NOT recommend fasting for persons diagnosed with anorexia or for anyone who is underweight. She suggests consulting with a doctor before fasting.

Like prayer and fasting, Orgeron also used Scripture reading in her recovery process. Reading the Scriptures directs the mind and heart to issues of greatest concern to God. The Word of God searches our motives,

For the word of God is living and powerful, and sharper than any two-edged sword, piercing even to the division of soul and spirit, and of joints and marrow, and is a discerner of the thoughts and intents of the heart. (Hebrews 4:12)

Besides reading the Scriptures, Orgeron has benefitted from memorizing and meditating on Scripture. Through memorizing Scriptures an individual adds verses to his or her memory bank that the Holy Spirit can bring to recall in times of need later. Prayer with meditation on the Scriptures gives the Holy Spirit the opportunity to reveal personal application for specific verses to individual Christians. Other spiritual disciplines that Orgeron recommends include:

"Orgeron does **NOT** recommend fasting for persons diagnosed with anorexia or for anyone who is underweight. She suggests consulting with a doctor before fasting."

- Church Attendance (Hebrews 10:25)—"not forsaking the assembling of ourselves together, as *is* the manner of some, but exhorting *one another,* and so much the more as you see the Day approaching."
- Corporate Bible Study (Acts 17:11)-" These were more fair-minded than those in Thessalonica, in that they received the word with all readiness, and searched the Scriptures daily *to find out* whether these things were so."
- Corporate Prayer—Acts 1:14 and Acts 4:29-31 exemplify instances of corporate prayer in the Scriptures:

Acts 1:14

These all continued with one accord in prayer and supplication, [a] *with the women and Mary the mother of Jesus, and with His brothers.*

Acts 4:29-31

[29] *Now, Lord, look on their threats, and grant to Your servants that with all boldness they may speak Your word,* [30] *by stretching out Your hand to heal, and that signs and wonders may be done through the name of Your holy Servant Jesus."*

[31] *And when they had prayed, the place where they were assembled together was shaken; and they were all filled with the Holy Spirit, and they spoke the word of God with boldness.*

- Family Devotions and Bible Study with Children Involved (Deuteronomy 11:19)—" You shall teach them to your children, speaking of them when you sit in your house, when you walk by the way, when you lie down, and when you rise up." Clinton, Hindson, and Ohlschlager (2001) reported,

God commands parents to teach their children about Him and His love for them. Parental soul care involves a commitment to teach children in the ways of God. Parents should be able to sense teachable moments with their children. Then they can instruct them in God's ways. Home is the incubator where small hearts and hands are trained to serve God. (Soul Note, Teach Them Well section, p. 237)

- Observing the Sabbath (Exodus 20:8-11)

8 "Remember the Sabbath day, to keep it holy. 9 Six days you shall labor and do all your work, 10 but the seventh day is the Sabbath of the LORD your God. In it you shall do no work: you, nor your son, nor your daughter, nor your male servant, nor your female servant, nor your cattle, nor your stranger who is within your gates. 11 For in six days the LORD made the heavens and the earth, the sea, and all that is in them, and rested the seventh day. Therefore the LORD blessed the Sabbath day and hallowed it.

- Praise and Worship--Psalm 146:1-2 exemplifies individual praise and worship: "1Praise the LORD! Praise the LORD, O my soul! 2 While I live I will praise the LORD; I will sing praises to my God while I have my being." Psalm 149:1-4 exemplifies corporate worship:

1Praise the LORD!
Sing to the LORD a new song,
And His praise in the assembly of saints.
2 Let Israel rejoice in their Maker;
Let the children of Zion be joyful in their King.
3 Let them praise His name with the dance;
Let them sing praises to Him with the timbrel and harp.
4 For the LORD takes pleasure in His people;
He will beautify the humble with salvation.

- Service to others—When Jesus washed the disciples feet, he exemplified how Christians are to serve others. (John 13:1-17)
- Submission to God's will (1 John 2:17)—"And the world is passing away, and the lust of it; but he who does the will of God abides forever.

Nehemiah: A Biblical Example to Follow

Recovery from disordered eating requires a grieving process similar to that depicted by Nehemiah. In **Nehemiah 1:4**, Nehemiah began his journey with weeping, mourning, fasting, and prayer, all key elements in the recovery process. **Nehemiah 1:6** reveals how Nehemiah continued his journey with repentance for his sins and those of his people. Repentance involves breaking through denial, which many individuals with disordered eating prefer to live in rather than choosing the road to health and wellness.

The damage from poor choices made while in bondage need to be surveyed before anyone can move on from being enslaved to disordered eating. This is similar to Nehemiah as he went from gate to gate viewing the devastation of the temple walls. This scene is depicted in **Nehemiah 2:13-15**. On the road to healing, expect *opposition* just as Nehemiah (v.2: 10, 19; vv. 4:1-3; vv. 6:1-14) faced opposition on his journey. Nehemiah **responded to opposition** with four things. First, Nehemiah turned to **prayer** for deliverance when faced with opposition. Secondly, Nehemiah **called for help and unity** among the Jews (vv. 2:16-18). Thirdly, Nehemiah and the Jews building the wall **kept watch for their enemies** and were always ready for battle (vv. 4:16-18). Fourthly, Nehemiah and the others helping him **persisted in working to complete the** task (vv. 6:15-19).

With Nehemiah as the scriptural basis for needing to ponder or recount the effects of disordered eating, how does one apply Nehemiah's journey to the recovery process? Complete recovery of "removing the debris" left by abusing food requires a connection with and release of the emotions. Recall how Nehemiah wept over the devastation. *The recounting process* for Orgeron involved three things, which allowed emotional connection and release. First, *journaling* helped her discover her feelings and unlock repressed memories of abuse that were a catalyst for her developing disordered eating. Journaling also helped her keep track of her progress through recovery.

Secondly, **emotional connection and release** were found for Orgeron through *psychotherapy* with several different professional counselors. Different counselors and therapists have different styles. Orgeron recommends anyone considering counseling find a qualified therapist he or she is comfortable with preferably one who incorporates Christian ideology and techniques.

Thirdly, **emotional connection and release** can be found through the help of a *support group*. Recall how Nehemiah recruited and organized other Jews to help him complete the building of the wall. Orgeron's primary support group became her church family. Other support groups include the numerous 12-step groups, such as Codependent's Anonymous, Overeater's Anonymous, etc. In more recent years Orgeron participated in a local Celebrate Recovery group. This is a Christian based recovery network that Orgeron highly recommends to anyone who has any hurt, habit, or hang-up that he or she wants to overcome.

Before one can rebuild a life damaged by disordered eating, the losses and damages to the life need to be surveyed. Recall how Nehemiah surveyed the damage before rebuilding. Disordered eating and past abuse can result in losses in five different areas of life. First, losses from abuse can come in the form of missed opportunities. Orgeron thinks of how the chance for having a "normal" life was stolen from her. Secondly, negative effects of abuse may be cognitive in nature. For example, sometimes Orgeron experienced problems concentrating. Thirdly, negative effects of abuse and disordered eating may include physical illnesses. Orgeron had problems with TMJ, gastro esophageal reflux, nervous bladder, and other similar health issues. Fourthly, abuse damages our emotions. For example, Orgeron often felt that she could never be good enough so she strived for perfectionism, which is harmful because it's impossible to attain on earth. Fifthly, relationship problems also occur as a result of disordered eating and abuse. The lack of trust created during past abuse was a key factor for Orgeron as to why she could never maintain a healthy relationship in dating until she met her husband.

The "surveying" process for Orgeron included a lot of education. She continually educated herself on her particular issues. Her education came from reading books and articles, viewing documentaries, and tapping available community resources (for example, support groups and specialized counselors). The quick "forgive and forget" mode encouraged by others did not lead Orgeron to ultimate peace. The injury and its consequences had to be acknowledged. In offering forgiveness to her perpetrators and herself for damage caused from her disordered eating, she did not condone the actions of the offender. Through forgiveness she acknowledged the complete work of Christ's blood on the cross.

Even with the help of a therapist, a support group, etc., Orgeron experienced relapses. A person in recovery can expect to face opposition on the journey to wellness. For example, opposition can come in the form of family or friends embarrassed by the disordered eating and/or past abuse. When Orgeron first entered psychotherapy, other people begged her to not look back. However, she knew she had to in order to find peace and the answers she sought. She has no regrets of her decision to pursue the truth and the road to recovery. You won't either.

Another example of facing opposition in recovery is how Satan will throw stumbling blocks on the road to recovery (I Peter 5: 8). Just as Nehemiah faced attacks of criticism and ridicule (e.g.: vv. 4:1-3) and even an attempted assassination plot (v. 6:10), Orgeron too faced Satan's attempts to destroy the work God wanted and still wants to do in her. When this happens Orgeron protects herself from Satan's attacks. How? There are three ways she guarded against Satan. First, she put on the whole armor of God (Ephesians 6:11). Her spiritual weapons of defense based on Ephesians 6 include truth, righteousness, the gospel of peace, faith, salvation, and the word of God. Secondly, Orgeron resisted and continues to resist the devil (James 4:7). Thirdly, Orgeron does her best to not compromise her convictions when faced with temptation. Note how in Nehemiah 6, Nehemiah held fast and refused to give in to the enemy's tricks.

> *"A person in recovery can expect to face opposition on the journey to wellness."*

Before closing this section, Orgeron wants to stress that when a person has been victimized or experienced loss similar to Nehemiah, he or she must recount the experience and survey the effects before offering forgiveness and moving on with one's life. She would add two important points to remember. First, although circumstances may seem to get worse before they get better in recovery, it is only through Christ that one can grow to become known as a survivor rather than a victim of disordered eating and/or past abuse. She bases this on John 15:5. Secondly, although relapses occur, it's important to move on and not get stuck along the way. She found motivation to move on from her past in Philippians 3:12-16:

> John 15:5
>
> "I am the vine, you are the branches. He who abides in Me, and I in him, bears much fruit; for without Me you can do nothing."

[12] Not that I have already attained, or am already perfected; but I press on, that I may lay hold of that for which Christ Jesus has also laid hold of me. [13] Brethren, I do not count myself to have apprehended; but one thing I do, forgetting those things which are behind and reaching forward to those things which are ahead, [14] I press toward the goal for the prize of the upward call of God in Christ Jesus. [15] Therefore let us, as many as are mature, have this mind; and if in anything you think otherwise,

God will reveal even this to you. [16] Nevertheless, to the degree that we have already attained, let us walk by the same rule, let us be of the same mind.

Just as Nehemiah and the Jews reached their common goal of rebuilding the wall, Orgeron believes anyone with the help of God and others can rise above disordered eating.

***

Chapter 8: A Spiritual Approach to Healing

Key Terms/Concepts

ABC's of Salvation
Armor of God
Backsliders
Fasting
Gluttony
Prayer

Rededication
Repentance
Revival
Spiritual disciplines
Stronghold

Questions for Reflection:

1. Why are food addictions and other disordered eating patterns the hardest to break, in comparison to alcohol, drugs, and other types of addiction?
2. How does one make God their partner in overcoming disordered eating?
3. What are the steps in developing a personal relationship with Christ?
4. What is repentance?
5. What Scripture is often referred to as the prescription for revival?
6. How does revival begin?
7. According to Bowers, what are the dangers to gluttony?
8. According to Bowers, how can one guard against gluttony?
9. What is a stronghold?
10. What is Satan's goal in the life of a Christian?
11. Can gluttony be a stronghold in a church?
12. Who is the ultimate enemy in overcoming the stronghold of gluttony?
13. What are the spiritual disciplines?
14. Should individuals with eating disorders fast?
15. How is recovery from disordered eating similar to the grieving process? What biblical example did the author give?
16. What are ways Satan will try to oppose a person in recovery? (See page 80.)

***

A Biblical Path from Discovery to Recovery

1. Face the problem.
Identify the symptoms.
I Corinthians 11:28.

2. Recount the incident. Verbalize the details.

Nehemiah 2

3. Experience past and present emotions.

4. Place the responsibility on the offender. Joshua 7.

5. Trace problem behaviors to their origin. Replace them with healthy behaviors.

6. Observe others. Educate yourself.

7. Confront the aggressor. Matthew 18:15.

8. Forgive. Colossians 3:13.

9. Rebuild self-esteem and relationships. Nehemiah 4:17.

10. Reach out to others. II Corinthians 1:3-4.

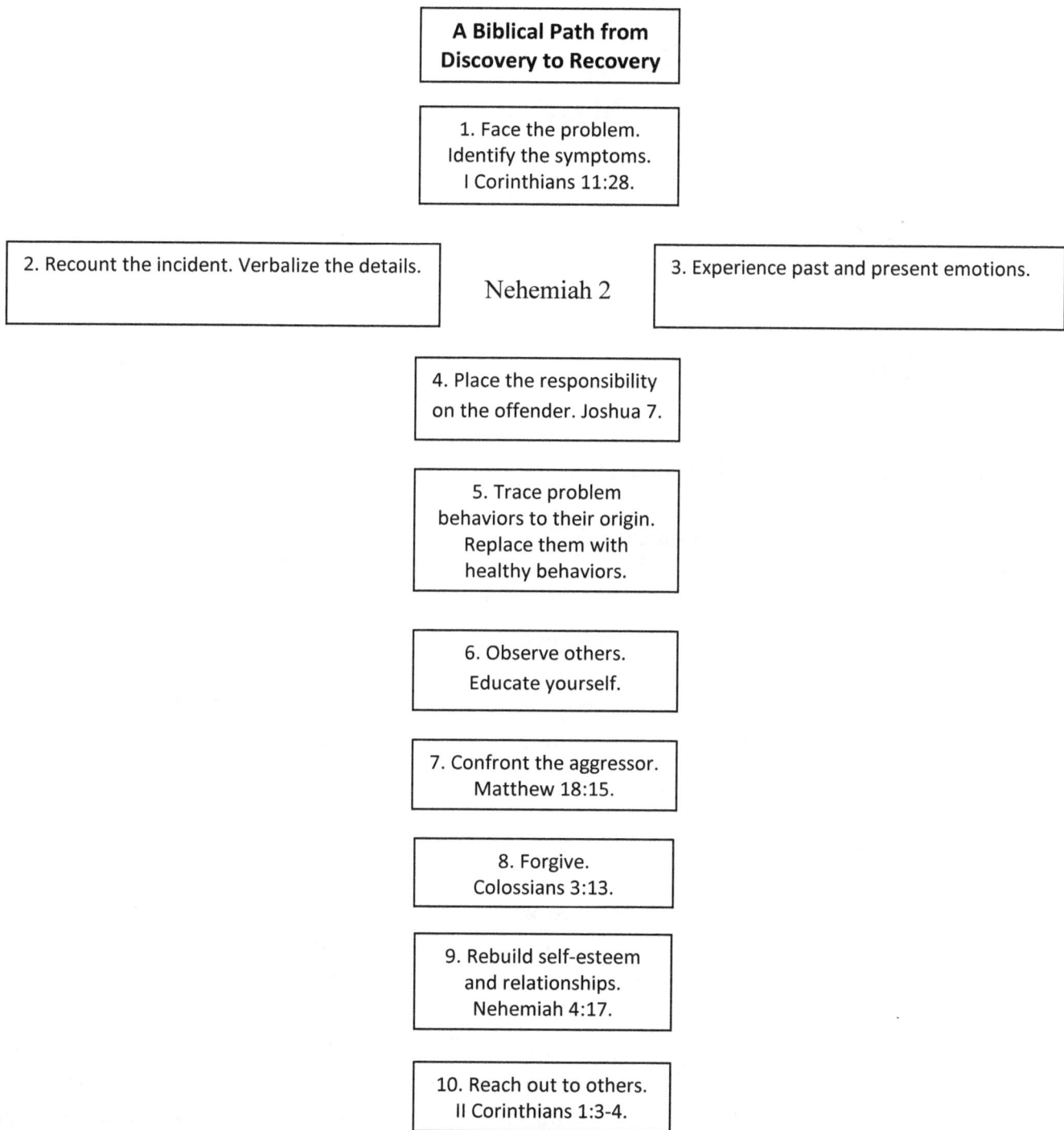

Figure 7: THE CROSS (Owens, 2001, Figure 2): A Biblical path to healing, based on Don and Jan Frank's 10 step "Critical Path Method for Emotional Recovery" from *When Victims Marry: Building a Stronger Marriage by Breaking Destructive Cycles (Here's Life, 1990)*, pp. 106-116.

Chapter 9: Christian Mindfulness:
A Path to Healing

2 Corinthians 10:3-5 King James Version (KJV)

³ For though we walk in the flesh, we do not war after the flesh: ⁴ (For the weapons of our warfare are not carnal, but mighty through God to the pulling down of strong holds;) ⁵ Casting down imaginations, and every high thing that exalteth itself against the knowledge of God, and bringing into captivity every thought to the obedience of Christ;

Colossians 3:5 New King James Version (NKJV)

⁵ Therefore put to death your members which are on the earth: fornication, uncleanness, passion, evil desire, and covetousness, which is idolatry.

Philippians 4:6-8 New King James Version (NKJV)

Be anxious for nothing, but in everything by prayer and supplication, with thanksgiving, let your requests be made known to God; ⁷ and the peace of God, which surpasses all understanding, will guard your hearts and minds through Christ Jesus.

Meditate on These Things

⁸ Finally, brethren, whatever things are true, whatever things are noble, whatever things are just, whatever things are pure, whatever things are lovely, whatever things are of good report, if there is any virtue and if there is anything praiseworthy—meditate on these things.

Though the term "mindfulness" does not appear in *The Holy Bible*, based on the above verses, the practice of mindfulness takes root in the Scriptures. Pete Walker, who "has been working as a counselor, lecturer, writer and group leader for thirty-five years, and as a trainer, supervisor and consultant of other therapists for 20 years" (Pete Walker, M.A., MFT, 2017, ¶ 1) offers one secular definition of mindfulness. "Psychologically speaking, *mindfulness* is taking undistracted time to become fully aware to your thoughts and feelings so that you can have more choice in how you respond to them." (Walker, 2014, p. 28) According to The Greater Good Science Center at the University of California, Berkeley (2017), mindfulness can be defined as "maintaining a moment-by-moment awareness of our thoughts, feelings, bodily sensations, and surrounding environment." (p. 1) Christian mindfulness adds a biblical perspective to secular views of mindfulness. According to Christian Simplicity (2017), "Mindfulness is paying attention. It is noticing what you are doing, feeling, and thinking at the time you are actually doing, feeling and thinking it. Because God is part of our everyday lives, paying attention to God and focusing on God's kingdom is a fundamental practice of Christian mindfulness. (What Christian mindfulness is section, ¶ 1) Godminders (2017) reported "Mindfulness and faith in Jesus are fully compatible. In fact, Jesus is likely the most mindful person to ever live." (¶ 1)

The verses 2 Corinthians 10:3-5 and Colossians 3:5 shared previously support thought stopping, a cognitive intervention recommended by therapists. According to *Wikipedia, the free encyclopedia* (2017d), the goal of *thought stopping* is to interrupt and remove recurrent though patterns that are problematic. The process described in Philippians 4:8 quoted previously could be one way we use *thought substitution* or how we reparent ourselves. In *reparenting* herself during her recovery, Orgeron meditated on and memorized applicable Scriptures to replace the internal negative messages she had received as a child.

Cooper (2012) discussed the value of mindfulness to those persons fighting EDs Negative eating disorder obsessions are common in individuals with EDs. "And the problem is, there is never just *one* thought; one leads to another to another. Soon they are tripping over each other, trying to take center stage, leaving the individual distracted and overwhelmed by negative emotions." (Cooper, ¶ 2) For example, one might think, *I'm fat. No one likes me…If I lose weight, people will like me…People won't like you, you're ugly…*and on in a downward spiral that may result in depression or anxiety.

> *This is why mindfulness has value. Instead of heading down that road of negativity, a person needs to STOP and consciously redirect their own thoughts, by looking, hearing, touching whatever it takes to **break the cycle**.*
>
> *Accessing one or all of the senses is always available. But mindfulness can also be practiced intentionally through meditation or prayer. Being still, allowing the mind to clear, focusing on positive issues or topics, and simply not permitting negative thoughts or emotion to encroach on this quiet time.* (Cooper, 2012, ¶s 2-3)

Ekern and Karges (2017) reported benefits to mindfulness practices in recovering from BED. These benefits include mindful eating, lowering anxiety and stress levels, and helping a person with self-acceptance." While eating disorders effectively numb emotions, practicing mindfulness can help a person reflect on what they are feeling or experiencing prior to a binge." (Ekern & Karges, Mindful Eating section, ¶ 1) This may lead the individual to ask questions such as, "Is this head hunger I'm feeling? Or am I really physiologically hungry? If not, what am I feeling now?" Depending on the answers to these questions, mindfulness may lead to resisting a binge and learning what the person's real need is at the moment rather than food.

For those persons who stress eat, Orgeron believes Christian mindfulness through the Word offers answers to eliminating stress eating. One of Orgeron's favorite verses that she used in her recovery from DE was 1 Peter 5:7 "casting all your care upon Him, for He cares for you." Additionally, in Orgeron's experience a common passage recommended by pastors and Christian therapists addressing stress and worry is Matthew 6:25-34 (NKJV):

25 "Therefore I say to you, do not worry about your life, what you will eat or what you will drink; nor about your body, what you will put on. Is not life more than food and the body more than clothing? 26 Look at the birds of the air, for they neither sow nor reap nor gather into barns; yet your heavenly Father feeds them. Are you not of more value than they? 27 Which of you by worrying can add one cubit to his stature?

28 "So why do you worry about clothing? Consider the lilies of the field, how they grow: they neither toil nor spin; 29 and yet I say to you that even Solomon in all his glory was not arrayed like one of these. 30 Now if God so clothes the grass of the field, which today is, and tomorrow is thrown into the oven, will He not much more clothe you, O you of little faith?

31 "Therefore do not worry, saying, 'What shall we eat?' or 'What shall we drink?' or 'What shall we wear?' 32 For after all these things the Gentiles seek. For your heavenly Father knows that you need all these things. 33 But seek first the kingdom of God and His righteousness, and all these things shall be added to you. 34 Therefore do not worry about tomorrow, for tomorrow will worry about its own things. Sufficient for the day is its own trouble.

Regarding the issues of low self-acceptance, low self-esteem and comparing ourselves with others that are often resolved through mindfulness, the Bible speaks about these issues also. Consider the following the verses:

Psalm 139:13-14

13 For You formed my inward parts;
You covered me in my mother's womb.
14 I will praise You, for I am fearfully and wonderfully made;[b]
Marvelous are Your works,
And that my soul knows very well.

In common English in layman's terms, Psalm 139:13-14 tells us that God does not make junk. God loves us just as we are; though he does chastise and purge us to draw us closer to Him; thus, we mature in Christ. Christ died for all.

2 Corinthians 10:12

12 For we dare not class ourselves or compare ourselves with those who commend themselves. But they, measuring themselves by themselves, and comparing themselves among themselves, are not wise.

To interpret the above verse, Orgeron believes Matthew Henry (1997) states it well in his discussion of 2 Corinthians 10:12-18:

There is not a more fruitful source of error, than to judge of persons and opinions by our own prejudices. How common is it for persons to judge of their own religious character, by the opinions and maxims of the world around them! But how different is the rule of God's word! (p. 1129)

Are there benefits to practicing Christian mindfulness? Yes, according to Kozlowski (2013). Kozlowski discussed three areas where mindfulness can benefit the Christian. First, mindfulness endorses the biblical commands to love and accept oneself and to accept others' differences.

Mindfulness allows everyone to bask in his or her own faith, belief and wishes — it opens the door to acceptance. It sees beyond the boundaries of religion, race, sex, age. It allows us to see our humanity and the bigger picture things that connects us beyond our titles, beyond our outward appearance, beyond our philosophies and dogmas.

It is a true coming together, a boundless exercise in caring and in the openness of the heart. It allows us to maintain our disagreements; however, in mindfulness we agree to disagree and to somehow find the balance and peace in that. (¶s 16-17)

The second benefit of mindfulness to Christians that Kozlowski (2013) discussed is how practicing mindfulness can help Christians to grow in their faith. For example, during worship services being mindful can help one experience God to the fullest. "As a practitioner of mindfulness, you minimize thinking about what you have to do after the service, who is sitting behind you, what you are wearing; you are more focused on your faith and the importance of it." (¶ 20)

Thirdly, Kozlowski (2013) reported mindfulness allows Christians to experience their bodies as "God's temple" more fully. "This allows Christians more clarity and power to help nurture the container of the soul. It also provides more strength to literally help *you* embody *your* faith." (¶ 22)

Orgeron recalls how she has had a problem with staying mindful all her life. Now she can laugh about how she got in trouble in the first grade for "daydreaming" and always looking out the window. Easily distracted she couldn't pay attention in class until her parents and first grade teacher mutually agreed on a new policy for her. She should always sit away from the window in the very front of the classroom in front of the teacher. Orgeron is grateful to her parents and early elementary teachers for enforcing the policy that was a catalyst to her developing a love of learning and allowing her to succeed academically. Even after her parents and teachers no longer enforced the policy, out of habit she always chose to sit in the front of the classroom. Still easily distracted, Orgeron still likes to sit in the front whenever she takes a class, attends a conference, or goes to church.

Orgeron reports other problems she has experienced and continues to experience due to a lack of mindfulness. One major problem that bothers Orgeron is her inability to remember names. She has always had that problem pointing out that in a graduating class of less than 90 students, when she graduated she could not tell you the names of every other student in her high school graduating class. Now she commonly has to ask new people she meets to repeat their name a few times before she can remember their name. She has found it helpful to write down someone's name when she meets a new person. Another problem Orgeron has at times is difficulty just relaxing and enjoying the moment. Instead, she's reflecting on the past or having big dreams for what she would like to do in the future.

Looking back, Orgeron realizes that her problems with attention, DE and other issues all stem from Complex PTSD, which developed as a result of emotional neglect and abuse that she experienced in her past. Fortunately, with Orgeron accepting Christ at a young age, He took the consequences of having cPTSD and used them for good (Romans 8:28). Without the OCD component of cPTSD, Orgeron doubts that she would have done as well academically or gone to college.

Orgeron also believes there is another benefit to her having grown up living with cPTSD. She believes that had she not been a "dreamer", she would not have taken as many risks and accomplished her childhood dream of being a professional writer. This too is biblical. Proverbs 29:18 (KJV) "Where there is no vision, the people perish: but he that keepeth the law, happy is he." Orgeron reports she is living out the happiest moments of her life with her husband and best friend Milton.

Orgeron concludes this chapter with the words of Walker (2014):

I cannot overstate the importance of becoming aware of your inner self-commentary. With enough practice, mindfulness eventually awakens your fighting spirit to resist the abusive refrains from your childhood, and to replace them with thoughts that are self-supportive. Mindfulness... Mindfulness tends to develop and expand in a progressive manner to all levels of our experience, cognitive, emotional, physical, and relational. Mindfulness is essential for guiding us at every level of recovering. (p. 29)

***

Chapter 9: Christian Mindfulness: A Path to Healing

Key Terms/Concepts

Mindfulness   Thought stopping
Reparenting   Thought substitution

Questions for Reflection:

1. What is mindfulness?
2. What is the purpose of thought stopping?
3. What are ways persons with DE can reparent themselves?
4. What Scriptures support the use of mindfulness?
5. According to Ekern and Karges, what are possible benefits in mindfulness practices in recovering from BED?
6. According to Kozlowski, what are three benefits to practicing Christian mindfulness?

Section 5:
Prevention
Of
Disordered Eating

Chapter 10: Prevention of Disordered Eating

Types of Prevention

Primary prevention. The best solution to the growing number of mental illnesses in society, including eating disorders, is prevention, according to World Health Organization (WHO) (2004) Department of Mental Health and Substance Abuse. Primary prevention prevents the occurrence of an eating disorder before it begins. Primary prevention promotes and sustains healthy development and demands the involvement of parents, teachers, clergy, and coaches.

Secondary prevention. Secondary prevention keeps individuals in the early stages of eating disorders from progressing to the point where the disorder is a part of one's "lifestyle" and where it is more likely to be associated with more significant problems like depression. This involves knowing the "warning signs" of eating disorders, knowing how to effectively reach out to distressed individuals, and knowing where to refer for appropriate treatment.

Secondary prevention also involves recognizing the individuals at greatest risk for eating disorders. Piran, Levine, and Steiner-Adair (1999) report the groups at greatest risk for developing eating disorders are athletes, dancers, and diabetics. The WHO (2004) reported that individuals in modeling and cooking also have higher rates of ED than the general public.

Tertiary prevention. Doctors and other specialists must be able to diagnose and refer individuals with full-blown eating disorders to appropriate treatment facilities. The major treatment facilities for eating disorders in the United States with one in Canada are listed as Appendix D.

> "The best solution to the growing number of mental illnesses in society, including eating disorders, is prevention."

Basic Principles of Prevention

Every family, group, and community is unique in what might trigger the development of an eating disorder in an individual. However, Minirth and Meier (1991) offer basic "dos" and "don'ts" for individuals to minimize the risk of developing an eating disorder. These principles apply especially to the obese person wanting to lose weight. They include:

Do. Using commonsense in the choices one makes regarding food goes a long way in preventing eating disorders. Minirth and Meier also recommend:

- Gaining insight about problems related to food and eating. Seek counseling, if necessary.
- Using behavioral incentives other than food. Never use food as a reward. Find other ways to reward yourself.
- Including healthy, regular physical activity in one's lifestyle. Find an exercise you enjoy. Exercise should be fun, and not just to lose or maintain weight.
- Maintaining a balanced diet. Eat more fiber and less fat.
- Having a support group of friends and family

- Using discipline in moderation. Avoid extremes.

Don't. Never base self-worth on looks. Society offers a lot of quick fixes for losing weight. Most of these quick fixes fail and need to be avoided, including crash programs, prolonged fasts, fad diets, diet drugs, and surgeries, such as stomach by pass.

Self-demand feeding. To prevent disordered eating, Hirschmann and Zaphiropoulos (1993) recommend self-demand feeding. They point out that physical hunger is the only reason anyone should eat, and define self-demand feeding as "responding to a child's physiological hunger with food and allowing the child to be self-directed." (p. 15)

Promoting resilience in children. With children our most prized possessions, they need protection and they need to know how to cope during times of stress, according to Hart (AACC, 2003). Research by Dent and Cameron (2003) and Siqueira and Diaz (2004) indicated that a lack of resiliency in children contributes to DE. What contributes to resiliency in children during times of stress? Alvord and Grados (2005) proposed six protective factors:

- Proactive orientation, which means the child has a realistic, positive self-esteem
- Self-regulation, which Sibcy (AACC, 2006) links to having a secure attachment. He explains self-regulation as a child having the ability to calm him or herself when stressful events occur.
- Proactive parenting, where the child has at least one supportive and loving parent or parent figure
- Connections and attachments that are positive and competent with peers, relatives, and other adults
- Involvement and accomplishment at school, IQ, and having special talents
- Community, which includes resources such as early prevention and intervention programs, recreational facilities available, sufficient health services, and church support.

Wolin and Wolin (1993), as cited by Siqueira and Diaz (2004), also identified characteristics in children that contribute to resiliency. These include having self-understanding/empathy, being able to disengage during stressful times, having meaningful relationships, having initiative, using creativity for self-expression, being able to see any humor in a stressful situation, and having a sense of goodness when surrounded by evil.

Promoting biblical attitudes. Orgeron recommends that adolescents be exposed to biblical principles regarding food and the body to minimize disordered eating. Miller and Miller (2006) outlined these principles in the chapter "Eating Struggles" of *Quick Scripture Reference for Counseling Youth*. Among these principles are recognizing one's body as God's temple, recognizing overeating as sin, and praying before eating. For adolescents with disordered eating and past abuse issues, the biblical principle of forgiveness also needs to be taught (Worthington, Mazzeo, & Kliewer, 2002).

Modeling and teaching a lifestyle promoting "wellness". Rayle and Myers (2004) recommend counseling adolescents to adopt a "wellness" lifestyle. Powers and Dodd (2003) define "wellness" as "a state of healthy living. This state is achieved by the practice of a healthy lifestyle, which includes regular physical activity, proper nutrition, eliminating unhealthy behaviors, and maintaining good emotional and spiritual health." (p. 373)

The Role of the Educator

Teachers can play a major role in the prevention of eating disorders, according to research (Grave, 2003; Levine & Smolak, 2012; NEDIC, 2014a; Piran et al., 1999; The Renfrew Center Foundation, 2017a). Transmitting cultural attitudes and shaping healthy student beliefs about the body and the self are key responsibilities of teachers. What can educators do to make a difference in the prevention of eating disorders? The Renfrew Center Foundation (2017a) offers preventive measures for educators who desire to prevent eating disorders in students and the community. These preventive measures include the following pointers.

Teach students about eating disorders. Health class curriculum needs to include information about shape diversity, eating disorders, body image concerns, and why diets don't work. Information about prevention and when to get help also should be included in the curriculum.

Plan activities during Eating Disorders Awareness Week (EDAW) and International No Diet Day (INDD). The NEDIC (2014b) advocated schools recognize EDAW that groups in Canada and internationally concerned about the high prevalence of eating disorders organized, scheduled in February every year. The purpose of EDAW is "to educate the public on the relationship between dieting, body dissatisfaction and eating disorders. The goal is to increase awareness of the factors causing individuals, particularly women, to develop anorexia, bulimia, and weight preoccupation." (Eating Disorders Awareness Week, EDAW, section, ¶ 1).

INDD (NEDIC, 2014b) is now recognized annually on May 6. Established goals for INDD are to:

- *Declare a moratorium on diet/weight obsession.*
- *Increase public awareness of the dangers and futility of dieting.*
- *Celebrate the beauty and diversity or our natural sizes and shapes.*
- *Affirm everybody's right to health, fitness and emotional well-being.*
- *Educate the public with the facts about weight-loss dieting, health and body-size.*
- *Increase public awareness of damage done to physical, emotional and financial health by society's obsession with thinness.*
- *Honor the victims of eating disorders and weight-loss interventions.*
- *Help change the prejudice with which fat people are perceived and treated.*
- *NEDIC is available to provide ideas, strategies, and consultation to individuals and groups wishing to develop an EDAW event or awareness campaign, or find out about listing of EDAW and INDD events in your area.* (NEDIC, 2014b, International No Diet Day, INDD, section, ¶ 3)

During EDAW and on INDD schools and other educational institutions can offer conferences and workshops dispelling myths about eating disorders and promoting healthy lifestyles. For a more extensive list on ideas to implement during these times, visit http://nedic.ca/give-get-help/prevention-health-promotion#edawindd.

Understand the role of the media. Teachers need to make students aware of the unhealthy advertising ploys by the media that idealize thinness. To counteract unhealthy messages from the media, Orgeron (2008) suggested educational institutions promote programs that develop character and "inner" qualities, such as honesty, kindness, and creativity.

Start peer support groups. Students can be trained to recognize eating disorders in others. These same students can lead support groups for peers whom they suspect face body image or food issues.

Prohibit school events promoting unhealthy diets and focusing on appearance. Orgeron offers the example of school beauty pageants as one such event. Research by Wonderlich, Ackard, and Henderson (2005)

may suggest that participating in beauty pageants as a child may lead to associated risk factors of eating disorders, but that other factors such as internalization of the thin ideal and parental pressure, may mediate the association between beauty pageant participation as a child and adult psychopathology. (p. 299)

While on the subject of appearance, Orgeron recommends all schools implement and enforce standard modest dress codes for all students. She believes having all students dress in the same general attire will minimize prejudice, bullying, and other negative occurrences that result from allowing students to have free reign of trying to keep up with the Joneses. By eliminating competition for being the best dressed student, etc. in class would likely decrease the number of students who develop disordered eating.

Set an example. Teachers should evaluate their own relationship with food. Students need role models who respect their bodies and others. To encourage healthy boundaries in student-teacher relationships, teachers also should be required to dress in modest, professional attire.

Confronting students with suspected ED. As cited by Owens (2002) and NEDA (2016g), Michael Levine, Ph.D. and Linda Smolak, Ph.D. offered pointers for faculty meeting with and referring students who may have eating disorders. Among the suggested guidelines are:

- Confront privately initially.
- Allow adequate time to avoid rushing and using the wrong words.
- Point out to the student specific observations that arouse concern.
- Communicate compassion and concern throughout the confrontation.
- Do not diagnose or become the student's therapist.
- Avoid arguing.
- Focus on the student's health and functioning effectively, not on weight, shape, or morality.
- Be knowledgeable about community resources where qualified help is available.

The Role of School Counselors

School counselors offer front line assistance in battling the problem of disordered eating in adolescents, according to Ray (2004). He recommends that school counselors be aware of risk factors specific to adolescents; know about eating disorder resources in the community; educate teachers, parents, and the community about disordered eating; and, offer on site school support for those students in outpatient treatment for eating disorders.

The Role of Parents/Primary Caregivers

Research (Dobson, 2010: Focus on the Family's Youth Culture department, 2000, 2002; Levine & Maine, 2002; Natenshon, n.d.) advocates parental involvement in preventing disordered eating in children. Natenshon pointed out that it is the parents who are primarily responsible for shaping body image and eating habits in children. Based on information taken from Focus on the Family's Youth Culture department (2000, 2002) and Levine & Maine and based on her personal experience, Orgeron compiled guidelines for parents to use in preventing eating disorders in children. These guidelines are:

•   Always love children unconditionally without showing preference for a specific child. NEVER display favoritism or prejudice towards any child. Try to treat each child equally, considering each child's age, developmental, and maturity level.

•   Never try to force a child to eat. Dobson and Dobson (1987) suggested,

> Instead of begging, pleading, bribing and threatening a child, I recommend that good foods be placed before him cheerfully. If he chooses not to eat, then smile and send him on his way. He'll be back. When he returns, take the same food out of the refrigerator, heat it, and set it before him again. Sooner or later, he will get hungry enough to eat. Do not permit snacking or substituting sweets for nutritious foods. But also do not fear the physical effects of hunger. A child will not starve in the presence of good things to eat. There is a gnawing feeling inside that changes one's attitude from "Yuck!" to "Yum!" usually within a few hours. (Food Section, ¶ 2)

> **1 Timothy 2:9 (KJV): "In like manner also, that women adorn themselves in modest apparel, with shamefacedness and sobriety; not with broided hair, or gold, or pearls, or costly array;"**

•   NEVER use food as punishment or as a reward. This is one sure way of setting a child up for disordered eating. For example, threatening a child to withhold his or her dinner if he or she doesn't obey. Another example would be promising a child a special treat, such as ice cream, pizza, etc., if they are well-behaved at church or wherever. In other words, do not try to manipulate a child's behavior with food.

•   Be a positive role model by eating healthy, exercising moderately, and maintaining a positive attitude.

•   Always dress modestly and dress your children likewise. NEVER dress yourself or your child, especially a girl, in clothing that draws attention to the body or appearance. This advice is biblical: **1 Timothy 2:9 (KJV)** "In like manner also, that women adorn themselves in modest apparel, with shamefacedness and sobriety; not with broided hair, or gold, or pearls, or costly array;" Furthermore, Dobson reported,

> *Child development experts warn that parents could be baiting pedophiles by dressing their daughters as raunchy women. The American Psychological Association (APA) warns that sexualizing children leads to three of the most common mental health problems among girls and women: eating disorders, low self-esteem, and depression.* (¶ 11)

- Teach children about disordered eating and to respect everyone, regardless of their weight or body shape.
- Build the self-esteem of children through educational, sporting, and social events.
- Limit media exposure. Screen telephone calls, emails, and Internet access. Keep computers for children in a central location of the home where they can be monitored easily.

Chapter 10: Prevention of Disordered Eating

Key Terms/Concepts

Eating Disorders Awareness Week
International No Diet Day
Modeling
Primary prevention
Resilience

Secondary prevention
Self-demand feeding
Tertiary prevention
Wellness

Questions for Reflection:

1. What is the best solution to the growing problem of disordered eating in society?
2. Identify and describe the three types of prevention.
3. According to Minirth and Meier, what are the basic "dos" and "don'ts" for individuals to minimize the risk of developing an eating disorder?
4. What factors characterize resiliency?
5. What biblical principles regarding food and the body contribute to resiliency?
6. What is wellness?
7. How can educators help prevent eating disorders?
8. How do the media contribute to the development of DE?
9. How should students with a suspected ED be confronted?
10. What is the role of school counselors in preventing disordered eating?
11. What are the guidelines recommended by Orgeron for parents to use in preventing disorders in children?
12. Why should food never be used as punishment or reward?

***

Chapter 11: Wellness as a Lifestyle for Preventing DE

To receive her Education Specialist Degree in Adult and Higher Education from Morehead State University, Orgeron completed the applied project *Exploration Linking Self-reported Disordered Eating and Wellness in Undergraduate Health Students*. (Owens, 2009) She explored self-reported disordered eating in students of higher education with emphasis given to determining whether a link exists between self-reported disordered eating and wellness attitudes and behaviors in MSU undergraduate health students using EAT-26 and 5F-Wel-A.

The EAT-26 (See Appendix C, as mentioned in Chapter 9: Treatment of Eating Disorders, The Road to Recovery, Assessment section.), an abbreviated version of the Eating Attitudes Test (EAT-40) (Garner & Garfinkel, 1997), contains 26 questions that measure attitudes and behavior patterns associated with anorexia nervosa. Research (Garner & Garfinkel; Garner, Olmsted, Bohr, & Garfinkel, 1982; Orbitello et al., 2006) identifies three subscales to the EAT-26: bulimia, dieting, and the tendency to self-control.

Orgeron has already given a thorough description of disordered eating previously in this book; but, what's wellness? Research reflects a number of definitions for wellness. For example, Powers and Dodd (2003) defined wellness "as a state of optimal health achieved by living a healthy lifestyle" (p. 10). According to Hettler (1980), "wellness is a positive approach to living—an approach that emphasizes the whole person" (p. 78). Hettler (1980, 1984) divided wellness into six dimensions, including intellectual, emotional, physical, social, occupational, and spiritual. Hettler (1980) reported that Halbert Dunn initially defined high-level wellness "in 1959 as 'an integrated method of functioning which is oriented toward maximizing the potential of which the individual is capable, within the environment where he is functioning'" (p. 77). Following Myers and Sweeney (2005), developers of the wellness instrument used for her study, Owens considered

> *wellness as a way of life oriented toward optimal health and well-being in which body, mind, and spirit are integrated by the individual to live more fully within the human and natural community. Ideally, it is the optimum state of health and well-being that each individual is capable of achieving.* (Myers, Sweeney, & Witmer, 2000, p. 252)

Reviewing the multiple definitions of wellness found in literature, Orgeron concludes that one's level of wellness would typically remain stable. However, one's level of wellness may vary with circumstances such as lifestyle choices (e.g., a decision to start drinking or smoking) or catastrophic events (e.g., a car accident or natural disaster affecting one's health or well-being unexpectedly).

The 5F-Wel-A, according to Myers and Sweeney (2005a, 2005b), is a 73-item instrument measuring "the single higher order wellness factor (Total Wellness), the five second-order factors (Creative, Coping, Social, Essential, and Physical Selves), and the original 17 discrete scales" (p. 41) assessed in the original version of the Wellness Evaluation of Lifestyle. Due to copyright regulations, Orgeron was unable to include a copy of 5F-Wel-A as an appendix in her applied project paper or in this book.

In her research Owens (2009) found no significant correlation between wellness and eating disorders. Regarding the limited population chosen for her study, Orgeron thinks that adding another group of individuals from a clinical setting diagnosed with eating disorders would have produced a more reliable result where the norms of the wellness scores of the students could be compared to the norms of the wellness scores of the clinically diagnosed subjects. Orgeron recommends such a study be conducted in the future.

Benefits to Applied Project and Wellness Promotion

With no foreseeable risks accompanying participation in Owens' (2009) research, students were not expected to encounter any risks before, during, or after completing the surveys. Potential participant benefits of the study included the opportunity to assess one's own wellness behaviors and eating attitudes and behaviors; thus, identifying areas where change is needed. Furthermore, "comprehensive wellness promotion on the university campus has the potential to increase students' retention in academic programs (thus increasing faculty retention). These programs also improve student chances for success once they have been graduated," (Hettler, 1980, p. 79) particularly since employers now realize the cost effectiveness of hiring healthy employees, which gives students who display healthy lifestyles a competitive advantage given equal academic qualifications.

Other long term benefits to promoting wellness in university students exist, according to Hettler (1980, 1984). He cited evidence that many contributing factors to premature death or disability, such as heart disease and cirrhosis of the liver, in mid-life stem from unhealthy behavior practices established in adolescence and the young adult years. Hettler pointed out how universities can help students develop healthy lifestyles beneficial not only in preventing premature deaths but in decreasing sick leave and minimizing illness-care costs, both sure signs of job effectiveness. Hettler (1980) concluded:

> *Wellness promotion is a responsibility of the university. If the citizens of tomorrow have more skills in dealing with the forces of society and develop positive health practices during the college years, they will be more productive citizens and decrease the amount of illness care required in future years.* (p. 91)

Keeling (2000) supports Hettler's (1980) conclusion that universities need to advocate for students to improve their health. Keeling compared the factors that make up health to "the components of some nonmonetary individual retirement account (IRA)" (p. 3). Keeling reported, "deposits made early on ('good' health behaviors, for example, and the more the better) eventually pay off with substantial returns, and there are significant penalties for premature withdrawals (risk behaviors, illnesses, and injuries)." (p. 3) Keeling emphasized disease prevention and reducing risks of harm in students remain important goals for colleges to advocate in students.

Etiological Factors of Disordered Eating Suggest Wellness Promotions and Interventions

Orgeron believes that since the causes of disordered eating are multifaceted, stemming from anywhere across the spectrum of individual, family, sociocultural, biological, and spiritual factors and since wellness covers all of these areas, promoting wellness would be a logical way to help prevent disordered eating. Additionally, she thinks that people might be more receptive to and less intimidated by offering a wellness program rather than an eating disorders program. She compares this to how people are more receptive to seeking life coaching than counseling. Life coaching does not have the negative stigma attached that counseling connotes. Likewise, wellness does not have the negative stigma that having an eating disorder connotes.

Full of Ourselves: A wellness program to advance girl power, health, and leadership (Teachers College Press, 2006). Based on research (NEDC, 2012a; Reel, 2013; Steiner-Adair & Sjostrom, 2006), Orgeron recommends that wellness education to prevent disordered eating begin much earlier than college age. With girls in elementary school now being diagnosed with eating disorders, the sooner preventative tools are used the better. One such tool is the Full of Ourselves (FOO) wellness program to prevent disordered eating. "FOO is a primary prevention program that targets the general population rather than eating disordered females." (Reel, p. 219) According to Steiner-Adair and Sjostrom, "FOO has been successfully implemented by schools, after-school programs, town libraries, summer camps, churches, and synagogues. All that's needed is a supportive community and one or two committed women to facilitate weekly program sessions." (p. xi) NEDC reported,

> *The book is organized around eight core 50-60 minute units: Full of Ourselves, Claiming Our Strengths, Body Politics, Standing Our Ground, Countering the Media Culture, Nourishing Our Bodies, Feeding Our Many Appetites, and the Power of Healthy Relationships. The book contains activities and handouts, and guides for adult and girl leaders. (¶ 1)*

> *Eating Disorders Recovery Center of Western New York promotes wellness.* (Eating Disorders Recovery Center of Western New York, n.d.a)

> *Our focus is on bringing families, schools, healthcare professionals, and youth to promote wellness and balance between preventing obesity and unhealthy weight control practices. . . . Only by working together can we make the changes required at home, at school, and in the community to find this middle ground and promote wellness. (¶s 1-2)*

Regarding school based programming, the Eating Disorders Recovery Center of Western New York (n.d.b) reported,

> School-based programming can significantly contribute to prevention of eating, body image and weight-related problems by observing the **4 C's of prevention** (Smolak & Levine, 2006. p. 369):
>
> 1. *Raising **consciousness** through education including gaining knowledge and building awareness*
> 2. ***Competency** building through developing skills, e.g., critical analysis of media advertising and the ability to resist wrong messages*
> 3. *Meaningful **connections** or relationships with peers, friends, families, adults, and community organizations and institutions, e.g., schools*
> 4. ***Change** in community messages, norms, and practices, e.g., acceptance of different body types and sizes. (Eating Disorders Recovery Center of Western New York, ¶ 1)*

A study by Russell-Mayhew, Arthur, and Ewashen (2007) supports the approach of Eating Disorders Recovery Center of Western New York (n.d.b). In this study the researchers looked at how effective a wellness-based prevention school program was on the body images, and eating attitudes and behaviors of students. "Results indicate that a one-time wellness-based eating disorder prevention program with students, which have in the past shown to be minimally effective, may be more effective in changing attitudes and behaviors when teachers and parents are involved." (Abstract, ¶ 1)

Considering the above research that advocates wellness as a preventive measure for disordered eating, Orgeron recommends parents, schools, day care centers, and other community youth centers implement wellness education into their programs. Not only should wellness education programs be utilized to prevent disordered eating, but children need role models who depict a wellness lifestyle. This should include parents, teachers, coaches, pastors, and other adults with any influence on children.

***

Chapter 11: Wellness as a Lifestyle for Preventing DE

Key Terms/Concepts

4 C's of prevention   Full of Ourselves
EAT-26   Wellness as a Lifestyle
5F-Wel-A

Questions for Reflection:

1. What two instruments did Orgeron use in her study linking disordered eating attitudes and behaviors with wellness lifestyles?
2. According to Hettler, what are long term benefits to promoting wellness in university students?
3. What is unique about the Full of Ourselves wellness program? (hint: target audience)
4. Discuss the 4 C's of prevention and why you think they are important.

***

Special Topics

- **Athletes and Disordered Eating**

- **Adolescents, Disordered Eating, & Obesity**

- **Disordered Eating and Pregnancy**

- **Disordered Eating in Higher Education**

- **Disordered Eating in Males**

- **Disordered Eating in the Church**

- **Linking Disordered Eating with Sexual Abuse**

Chapter 12: Athletes and Disordered Eating

Introduction

Athletes are at a greater risk of developing DE than non-athletes, according to research (Bulimia.com, 2017; Currie, 2010; EDReferral.com, n.d.a; Ferguson, n.d.; Koman & Hanson-Mayer, 2015; Sundgot-Borgen & Torstveit, 2004). "It is estimated that eating disorders affect a whopping 62 percent of athletes involved in organized sports." (Ferguson, Increased number of athletes plagued by eating disorders section, ¶ 3) Currie gave three main reasons why this is the case. These reasons are:

1. The nature of endurance sports (e.g.: long-distance running) where "leanness is related to performance for obvious physiological reasons. Runners who are several kilogrammes over their optimum performance weight will perform less well." (p. 64)

2. The nature of weight category sports (e.g.: boxing) where "athletes will not be allowed to compete if their weight is above the upper limit for that category.... This can create considerable pressure to achieve the necessary weight loss and often in a very short period of time." (p. 64)

3. The nature of aesthetic sports (e.g.: gymnastics) where "an aesthetic evaluation is attached to a particular body composition which is then promoted and encouraged in competitors." (p. 64)

Key studies cited by Currie have unfailingly reported a greater incidence of DE in the three aforementioned types of sports (Byrne & McLean, 2002; Johnson, Powers, & Dick, 1999; Sundgot-Borgen, 1993; Sundgot-Borgen & Torstveit).

Athletes, their families, and coaches, must recognize the problem, its seriousness, and be pro-active against DE. Otherwise; EDs can bring athletes to a point where they are unable to perform. The medical problems for athletes with EDs are "Electrolyte imbalances; Cardiac arrhythmia and increased risk of cardiac arrest; Osteoporosis; Severe dehydration and fatigue; Muscle weakness and loss; [and] Kidney failure." (Ferguson, n.d., Medical Issues section) Furthermore, EDs also can be deadly conditions when not addressed appropriately. "Even if the more serious morbidity can be avoided, an athlete with an eating disorder can expect to be more prone to injury, and to have a shorter sports career that is troubled by inconsistent performances." (Currie, 2010, p. 64)

Risk and Safety Influences for Athletes

NEDA (2016a) reported influences specific to athletes that can put members of this population at either a greater or less risk of developing DE. What are these influences?

> *Risk factors.*
> - Any sport that emphasizes looks, weight regulations, or muscularity. Examples include gymnastics, swimming/diving, bodybuilding, and boxing/wrestling.
> - Participating in individual sports (e.g.: a gymnast, runner, or figure skater) rather than team sports (football or basketball player)
> - Participating in sports that demand stamina (e.g.: a swimmer or runner)
> - Overrated belief that weighing less will result in a better performance

- Participating in a sport from a young age or being a top athlete
- Low self-worth; "family dysfunction (including parents who live through the success of their child in sport); families with eating disorders; chronic dieting; history of physical or sexual abuse; peer, family and cultural pressures to be thin, and other traumatic life experiences." (NEDA, Risk Factors for Athletes section, Bullet 6)
- Having coaches who are more concerned about winning rather than about the player's well-being.

Ferguson (n.d.) reported additional risk factors. These factors are: having a perfectionistic personality, competitive nature, and a fear of losing; "Critical eye of judges and subjective nature of some judging in competitions (i.e. judging on technical and artistic merit, etc.)[; and,] Media messages about health and body shape size (i.e.-thin means healthy; thinness means success, etc.)." (At Risk Facts for Athletes section)

Risk factors thought to be more specific to female athletes are "social influences emphasizing thinness, performance anxiety and negative self-appraisal of athletic achievement." (NEDA, 2016a, Risk Factors for Athletes section, ¶ 2) A final factor is finding one's self-worth through sports participation only.

Safety factors

- *Positive, person-oriented coaching style rather than negative, performance-oriented coaching style.*
- *Social influence and support from teammates with healthy attitudes towards size and shape.*
- *Coaches who emphasize factors that contribute to personal success such as motivation and enthusiasm rather than body weight or shape.*
- *Coaches and parents who educate, talk about and support the changing female body.* (NEDA, 2016a, Protective Factors for Athletes section)

Assessing for DE in Athletes

Sports medicine workers play a significant role in assessing and diagnosing DE. "Physicians, athletic trainers, sport psychologists, sport dietitians and physical therapists interact with athletes and active persons, and may have an opportunity to identify eating disordered behaviours." (Joy, Kussman, & Nattiv, 2016, Diagnosis and Evaluation of Athletes with Eating Disorders section, ¶ 1) What tools are available to assist them in this process?

Preparticipation physical evaluation (PPE, 4th Ed.). The PPE was developed by the collaboration of the following professional American medical associations, including

- American Academy of Family Physicians
- American Academy of Pediatrics
- American College of Sports Medicine
- American Medical Society for Sports Medicine
- American Orthopedic Society for Sports Medicine
- American Osteopathic Academy of Sports Medicine. (Bernhardt & Roberts, 2010; PPE Coalition for Youth Sports Health & Safety, 2010)

The main purpose in giving a PPE is "to promote health and safety of the athlete in training and competition. The PPE has traditionally been considered a screening tool for injuries, illness, or factors that might place the athlete or others at risk for preventable illness or injury." (Bernhardt & Roberts, 2010, p. 1) According to Bernhardt and Roberts, as cited by Joy et al. (2016),

> *The PPE includes several questions aimed at identification of disordered eating behaviours:*
> 1. *Do you worry about your weight?*
> 2. *Are you trying to, or has anyone recommended that you gain or lose weight?*
> 3. *Are you on a special diet or do you avoid certain types of food?*
> 4. *Have you ever had an eating disorder?*
> 5. *Have you ever taken any supplements to help you gain or lose weight or improve your performance?*
>
> *Additional questions on the PPE questionnaire screen for downstream consequences of eating disorders including menstrual dysfunction (in female athletes), and stress fractures, mood disturbance and substance use (in female and male athletes).* (Joy et al., Screening for Eating Disorders in Athletes section, ¶s 1-2)

Despite a lack of research to support the effectiveness of the PPE, "the examinations are widely performed, with every state requiring some level of PPE for scholastic athletes." (Bernhardt & Roberts, p. 1) For more information on the PPE, please visit the following Web page: https://www.aap.org/en-us/about-the-aap/Committees-Councils-Sections/Council-on-sports-medicine-and-fitness/Pages/PPE.aspx

Periodic health evaluation (PHE). The PHE is valuable for many reasons, according to the International Olympic Committee (2009).

> *It includes a comprehensive assessment of the athlete's current health status and risk of future injury or disease and, typically, is the entry point for medical care of the athlete. The PHE also serves as a tool for continuous health monitoring in athletes. Recent advances in this field relate to: (i) data on sudden cardiac death and other noncardiac medical problems, and the detection of risk factors and groups; (ii) a consensus conference on concussion; (iii) data on eating disorders and (iv) data on risk factors for musculoskeletal injuries.* (p. 538)

Treatment of DE in Athletes

Due to the complexity of eating disorders in athletes, the treatment team for an athlete with an ED must include at least "a physician, a sports dietitian, a mental health professional and the athletic trainer." (Joy et al., 2016, Treatment of Disordered Eating and Eating Disorders in Athletes section, ¶ 1) The treatment team members may also include specialists such as psychiatrists, gastroenterologists, etc.. "Communication among team members is critically important. The individual affected by the eating disorder must feel like he or she is receiving a cohesive and consistent message from the treatment team." (Joy et al., Treatment of Disordered Eating and Eating Disorders in Athletes section, ¶ 1)

A disadvantage to treating athletes with DE is that these clients value being slim as a foundation for athletic achievement. Furthermore, the distinction between functioning as a committed athlete and exercising compulsively is unclear since optimum effort is required of these high-energy players. Nevertheless, breaking out of denial to acknowledge that there is a problem is the first step to treating DE in athletes. (Bulimia.com, 2017)

Types of Treatment

Cognitive behavioral therapy (CBT). One key to treating athletes with an ED is CBT. During CBT clients examine their attitudes, behaviors, and thought patterns affecting their health; understand root causes of their disorder; and, work to change maladaptive beliefs and behaviors to improve health and well-being.

Group therapy. Group therapy gives an athlete with an ED another avenue to further explore their relationships with food, exercise, etc., "where other patients suffering from the same illnesses provide support and understanding. Group therapy also helps alleviate feelings of shame, stigma or isolation." (Bulimia.com, 2017, Treating Anorexia and Bulimia in Athletes section, ¶ 2)

Family counseling. Another key to successful treatment of an ED in an athlete is family counseling or therapy. This is crucial to make sure any negative environmental factors are discovered and eliminated.

Nutritional counseling. A nutritionist also is an important member of the treatment team for an athlete with an ED. The nutritionist can help the client recognize nutritional foods needed by his or her body. The nutritionist also will teach the client "how to plan meals, how to avoid excessive dieting and how to develop healthy eating habits." (Bulimia.com, 2017, Treating Anorexia and Bulimia in Athletes section, ¶ 3)

Medication. Medication is not routinely given to athletes diagnosed with an ED alone. However, if the ED is accompanied by depression, anxiety, or suicidal ideation, then medication combined with therapy is usually the best treatment option.

Dual diagnosis treatment. When athletes with EDs also are diagnosed with "substance abuse (an extremely common co-occurring condition), athletes must undergo **dual diagnosis treatment** that addresses both problems in order to avoid relapse. A medical team must devise an integrated treatment plan, and patients must go through a preliminary phase of detoxification." (Bulimia.com, 2017, Treating Anorexia and Bulimia in Athletes section, ¶ 3)

Authorization and Returning to Play Concerns

A significant issue of concern for the treatment team is deciding if and when an athlete should resume play after being diagnosed with an ED. "Of note, athletes diagnosed with anorexia nervosa who have a BMI <16 kg/m^2 or athletes with moderate-to-severe bulimia nervosa (purging >4 times/week) should be categorically restricted from training and competition." (De Souza, Nattiv, & Joy et al., 2014, as cited by Joy et al., 2016, Clearance and Return to Play Considerations, ¶ 1) Before returning to play, "athletes who fall into moderate and high- risk categories should have a written contract completed and signed by the athlete and each member of the multidisciplinary team." (De Souza et al., 2014, as cited by Joy et al., Clearance and Return to Play Considerations, ¶ 1) Due to copyright concerns, a sample copy of a return to play contract will not be included in this book. However, a sample contract is available as Table 2 at the following link: http://www.medscape.com/viewarticle/857680_9

DE in Female Athletes

Disordered eating commonly occurs among female athletes. In fact, according to Sundgot-Borgen and Torstveit (2004), the incidence of EDs is "higher in female athletes than in male athletes." (p. 25) However, EDs are "sorely under recognized by coaches, teachers, parents, therapists and physicians." (Eating Disorder Hope, 2014, Impact of Eating Disorders on Athletes section, ¶ 1). Denial is a common problem with female athletes and their authority figures. Why?

> *The fire of denial can be fed by coaches who rely on the exceptional talent and extreme drive for success that many athletes possess to win games, titles, awards, etc. When a female athlete is still winning or competing and ill, it may be easier to deny an active problem with food or eating.* (Eating Disorder Hope, Characteristics of Eating Disorders in Athletes section, ¶ 2)

Eating Disorder Hope also identified two common personality characteristics or traits for both female athletes and women diagnosed with EDs. These traits are perfectionism and competitiveness.

The Female Athlete Triad

"Sport and exercise are part of a balanced, healthy lifestyle. But for some girls and women, especially in competitive sport, not balancing the needs of their bodies and their sports can have major consequences, called the female athlete triad." (Healthy Body Image, 2017, Learn More About the Female Athlete Triad section, ¶ 1). The female athlete triad frequently occurs in female sports participants with DE, particularly those women who restrict food intake. Why the concern? "The annual mortality rate associated with anorexia nervosa is more than 12 times higher than the death rate of all causes of death for females 15 to 24 years old in the general population." (Renfrew Center Foundation for Eating Disorders, n.d., ¶ 10)

Definition. The female athlete triad refers to three separate but inter-related disorders that include low energy from DE or over-exercising; amenorrhea or other menstrual dysfunctions; and, osteoporosis [De Souza,et al., 2014; Nattiv, et al., 2007; Winstead & Willard, 2006, as cited by Joy, et al., 2016, Consequences of Eating Disorders section]. "Although any one of these problems can occur in isolation, inadequate nutrition for a woman's level of physical activity often begins a cycle in which all three occur in sequence - hence the term '**Female Athlete Triad**'". (International Olympic Committee, 2017, p. 2) "Low energy availability (whether inadvertent, intentional or psychopathological), can result from low energy intake relative to high energy expenditure during training and is the underlying factor contributing to negative effects on reproductive and skeletal health. [De Souza, et al.; Nattiv, et al]." (Joy et al., 2016, Consequences of Eating Disorders; Health Consequences section, ¶ 3)

Triad Consensus Panel Screening Questions. This screening test is a type of PHE that the Consensus Panel recommends female athletes complete annually. The Triad-specific self-report questionnaire is included as Table 3.

Table 3: Triad Consensus Panel Screening Questions
(Retrieved July 29, 2017 from De Souza, et al., 2014, p. 3, Box 1)

Box 1 Triad Consensus Panel Screening Questions*
▸ Have you ever had a menstrual period?
▸ How old were you when you had your first menstrual period?
▸ When was your most recent menstrual period?
▸ How many periods have you had in the past 12 months?
▸ Are you presently taking any female hormones (oestrogen, progesterone, birth control pills)?
▸ Do you worry about your weight?
▸ Are you trying to or has anyone recommended that you gain or lose weight?
▸ Are you on a special diet or do you avoid certain types of foods or food groups?
▸ Have you ever had an eating disorder?
▸ Have you ever had a stress fracture?
▸ Have you ever been told you have low bone density (osteopenia or osteoporosis)?
*The Triad Consensus Panel recommends asking these screening questions at the time of the sport pre-participation evaluation.

While PHEs are usually given at the collegiate sports level, the Consensus Panel recommends those of younger ages also be given the assessment.

A major point that the Panel emphasised is that existence of any one Triad component should prompt more thorough investigation for the others. Screening and early intervention in adolescent females for components of the Triad are especially important when one considers that 90% of peak bone mass is attained by 18 years of age, [Matkovic, Jelic, Wardlaw, et al. (1994), as cited by De Souza, et al.] thereby providing a window of opportunity for optimizing bone health. (De Souza, et al., 2014, p. 3)

Preventing DE in Women Athletes

For women who want to prevent the development of DE, Eating Disorder Hope (2014) recommended the following:

Tips for women on how to avoid eating disorder behaviors while training:
- *exercise and train with a partner or in groups with other women (avoid isolation and secrecy around exercise and food);*
- *replenish fluids and follow a well-balanced food plan (including enough protein, iron, calcium, and fat intake);*
- *get guidance and help from a sports nutritionist;*
- *contact your physician if you begin to experience menstrual irregularity or lose menses;*
- *take 1-2 days off per week;*

- *avoid looking at "calories burned" displays on cardio equipment;*
- *seek professional help if you start to experience unmanageability in your eating, exercise, or weight and/or body concerns;*
- *avoid using diuretics, laxatives, stimulants, steroids for performance or training enhancement;*
- *Women with histories of eating disorder: continue to receive maintenance care from a professional; continue to attend support groups for people in recovery from eating disorders.* (Tips for women on how to avoid eating disorder behaviors while training section, ¶ 7)

Preventing DE in Athletes

Prevention of eating disorders is the key to success and that starts at home. Adopting and committing to a healthy lifestyle is first and foremost. This means eating a regular well-balanced diet, exercising and embracing a 'fitness is fun' attitude rather than emphasizing body size, shape or weight. (Ferguson, n.d., What motivates you when it comes to fitness? section, ¶ 5)

Preventive Strategies

The National Collegiate Athletic Association (NCAA), as cited by Joy et al. (2016) developed 10 tactics for their coaches and other leadership officials to implement with the goal of preventing EDs in their athletes. These strategies are:

1. *Be aware of the symptoms of disordered eating.*
2. *Consult a registered dietitian who specialises in sport, particularly a Board Certified Specialist in Sports Dietetics (CSSD) to prescribe appropriate nutrition for optimal sport performance.*
3. *De-emphasise weight: Be aware of how you are communicating to athletes about weight and performance. Focus on ways for athletes to enhance their performance that do not involve weight.*
4. *Keep an open dialogue with athletes about the importance of nutrition and staying injury-free for optimal athletic performance.*
5. *Recognise that the body composition and training required for optimal health and performance are not identical for all athletes.*
6. *Screen student-athletes before the start of the season for risk factors of disordered eating using a validated screening instrument.*
7. *Ensure that all stakeholders (coaches, strength and conditioning coaches, athletic trainers, student-athletes, student-athlete affairs administrators and athletics department staff) are educated about the factors that put athletes at risk for disordered eating.*
8. *Understand your institution's referral protocol for student-athletes who are in need of assistance with nutrition or disordered eating issues.*
9. *Encourage help-seeking for all mental health concerns, including disordered eating.*

10. *Develop a plan with other stakeholders (such as university counselling services or a sports registered dietitian) for how to identify and treat student-athletes with eating disorders.* (Joy et al., Prevention section, ¶ 2)

The Role of Coaches and Trainers

The Renfrew Center Foundation for Eating Disorders (2017b) gave the following preventive measures for coaches and trainers to use with their athletes to decrease the incidence of eating disorders in this population. These measures are:

1. Coaches and trainers should know and be able to identify the warning signs of eating disorders. They also should recognize and appreciate their role in helping to prevent the development of an ED.

2. Coaches and trainers should share with athletes correct information about body makeup, healthy eating, and sports performance to counter false information and to minimize unhealthy and counterproductive practices. They should know about local ED specialists who can help teach the athletes.

3. Stress the negative impact of being under weight, particularly for women athletes with amenorrhea or other menstrual problems. Refer such individual athletes to eating disorder specialists for a medical evaluation.

4. If an athlete diets chronically and/or displays atypical eating, refer the athlete to an eating disorder specialist. The sooner treatment is received the better the chances are that the treatment will be successful.

5. Do NOT weigh athletes. This takes the focus off the weight. Focus on intellectual and affective abilities to give the athlete more control to increase performance.

6. Never assume losing weight will improve performance. "Studies show this does not necessarily apply to all athletes. Additionally, some individuals may respond to weight loss attempts with eating disorder symptoms. Improved performance should not be at the expense of the athlete's health." (¶ 6)

7. "Understand why weight is such a sensitive and personal issue for many women. Since weight is emotionally charged for many, eliminate derogatory comments or behaviors, no matter how slight, about weight." (¶ 7) Again, if a concern exists related to an athlete's weight, refer that athlete to a professional trained to work with eating disorders in athletes.

8. Do not spontaneously limit athletic participation when an athlete is diagnosed with an ED, except justified by a medical illness. "Consider the athlete's health, physical and emotional safety and self-image when making decisions regarding an athlete's level of participation in his/her sport." (¶ 8)

9. Sport leaders need to evaluate their personal attitudes and values about body image, dieting, and weight. They need to realize how their outlooks and standards may unintentionally impact their athletes. They need to promote and reflect a healthy self-perception and self-regard to their players.

A final word to coaches who have players with symptoms of EDs:

"When approaching an athlete you suspect may have an eating disorder do so privately. Provide evidence of your concerns with specific behaviors you have noticed. Reassure the athlete that you want to assist in any way you can. Alleviate any concerns the athlete may have about losing their position on the team, etc. Do not back down when you have concerns; tell the athlete you feel the matter needs to be addressed with someone who understands eating disorders. Do not be afraid to make this a requirement - it can save a life! Adapted from Eating Disorder Awareness and Prevention, EDAP (1998), www.edap.org, Athletes and Eating Disorders." (Ferguson, n.d., For Coaches section, ¶ 11)

Lastly, Joy et al. (2016) recommends sports medicine doctors use the PPE as a way to teach the parents or guardians of young athletes about DE and its possible health consequences. "Emphasising the role of nutrition in optimising performance and health is an important strategy to avoid unhealthy dietary manipulation." (Joy et al., Prevention section, ¶ 3)

Final Remarks

Of all the research articles Orgeron found about DE in athletes, she found only one article that she believes even came close to the ultimate answer to resolving DE issues in athletes, including treatment and prevention. What element is missing from all the articles cited thus far that Orgeron believes will help curtail, prevent, and assist in the treatment of DE? Of course! With Orgeron's biblical emphasis in *Food as an Idol* (ABC's Ministries, 2017) that component would be spiritual in nature.

"Physical fitness expressed through exercise [including sports] can be, if done with the right intention, a form of spiritual discipline that reflects the relational love of humanity to God as well as an expression of a healthy love of the embodied self." (Greenwood & Delgado, 2013, Abstract) Greenwood and Delgado reported that striving for one's optimum wellness, "including weight and cardiovascular training and nutrition, is an affirmation of three foundational theological principles of human embodiment: as created in the 'imago Dei', as unified body/spirit, and as part of God's creation calling for proper stewardship." (Abstract).

The Scriptures, what should be the ultimate authority in one's life, speak of physical fitness being beneficial: 1 Timothy 4:8—"[8] For bodily exercise profits a little, but godliness is profitable for all things, having promise of the life that now is and of that which is to come." The key with exercise and competing in sports is moderation or self-control, a fruit of the Spirit (See Galatians 5:22-23.). One's relationship with God must come first. When anyone focuses on his or her physical body to the degree that his or her spiritual life is neglected, that individual has "missed the mark" (sinned).

The apostle Paul also mentions physical training in illustrating spiritual truth in 1 Corinthians 9:24-27. He equates the Christian life to a race we run to "get the prize." But the prize we seek is an eternal crown that will not tarnish or fade. In 2 Timothy 2:5, Paul says, "Similarly, if anyone competes as an athlete, he does not receive the victor's crown unless he competes according to the rules." Paul uses an athletic analogy again in 2 Timothy 4:7: "I have fought the good fight, I have finished the race, I have kept the faith." While the focus of these Scriptures is not physical exercise, the fact that Paul uses athletic terminology to teach us spiritual truths indicates that Paul viewed physical exercise, and even competition, in a positive light. We are both physical and spiritual beings. While the spiritual aspect of our being is, biblically speaking, more important, we are to neglect neither the spiritual or physical aspects of our health. (Got Questions Ministries, 2002-2017b, ¶ 2).

What one should avoid regarding exercise and competition is doing these things for vain glory. The Bible speaks against vanity through the following Scriptures:

1 Samuel 16:7

[7] *But the LORD said to Samuel, "Do not look at his appearance or at his physical stature, because I have refused him. For the LORD does not see as man sees,[a] for man looks at the outward appearance, but the LORD looks at the heart."*

Proverbs 31:30

[30] *Charm is deceitful and beauty is passing,*
But a woman who fears the LORD, she shall be praised.

1 Peter 3:3-4

[3] *Do not let your adornment be merely outward—arranging the hair, wearing gold, or putting on fine apparel—* [4] *rather let it be the hidden person of the heart, with the incorruptible beauty of a gentle and quiet spirit, which is very precious in the sight of God.*

In conclusion, Orgeron believes a person's main goal or motive behind exercising and competing determines whether the behaviors are pleasing to God. Exercise and competition are not to develop the appearance of people's physiques to be noticed and admired by others. Instead, the ultimate purpose of exercising and competing should be to develop people's physical well-being so that they will have added physical energy for God to use them for His ultimate purposes of glorifying Him and building His kingdom.

***

Colossians 3:23

[23] *And whatever you do, do it heartily, as to the Lord and not to men,*

Chapter 12: Athletes and Disordered Eating

Key Terms/Concepts

Female athlete triad   Preparticipation physical evaluation (PPE)
Periodic health evaluation (PHE)   Triad Consensus Panel Screening Questions

Questions for Reflection:

1. Why are athletes at a greater risk of developing DE than non-athletes, according to Currie?
2. According to NEDA, what are influences specific to athletes that put members of this population at a greater risk of developing DE?
3. What are safety factors that decrease the risk of athletes developing DE?
4. Why is assessing athletes for ED important?
5. What specialists should be a part of the treatment team for an athlete with an eating disorder?
6. What types of treatment are used with athletes diagnosed with eating disorders?
7. What concerns must be addressed before an athlete can return to play?
8. Why do women with EDs sometimes fall through the cracks in regards to diagnosis?
9. What disorders make up the female athlete triad?
10. What are some tips for women athletes to avoid DE behaviors during training?
11. What ten tactics, according to Joy et al. (2016), did the NCAA create for coaches and other leadership officials to implement with the goal of preventing EDs in their athletes?
12. What other preventive measures for coaches and others to use with athletes were given by Renfrew Center Foundation for Eating Disorders?
13. What does Orgeron believe is the ultimate answer to resolving DE issues in athletes, including treatment and prevention?
14. What Scriptures speak of physical fitness as being beneficial?
15. What would be a biblical perspective to those who exercise and participate in sport activities?

***

Chapter 13: Adolescents, Disordered Eating, & Obesity

Adolescents "are the most at-risk group of people in developing an eating disorder," according to Eating Disorders Victoria (2016, ¶ 1). Adolescents are at high risk of developing disordered eating due to the common stressors they face (Garcia-Grau, Fuste, Miro, Saldana, & Bados, 2002; McVey, 2003). The stressors adolescents face include adapting to physical maturation and pressures from family, peers, school, and the community. As part of her graduate studies Owens (2008) conducted a literature review of disordered eating in adolescence, including classifications, etiology, treatment, and prevention. The first part of this chapter is built upon Owens' work in 2008. Orgeron discusses the issue of obesity in adolescents in the later part of the chapter. Although, obesity is not considered an eating disorder, due to the epidemic proportions of obesity among adolescents around the world and the high risk of medical problems, even to the point of death, Orgeron would feel amiss not covering the topic.

Before getting too deep into the topic of disordered eating in adolescents, let's look at how parents can determine whether their children are at a healthy weight. The NIH (2017a) reports

a healthy weight is usually when your child's BMI is at the 5th percentile up to the 85th percentile, based on growth charts for children who are the same age and sex. To figure out your child's BMI, use the Center for Disease Control and Prevention (CDC) BMI Percentile Calculator for Child and Teen. (Screening and Prevention section, ¶ 2)

The *BMI Percentile Calculator for Child and Teen* is available online at https://nccd.cdc.gov/dnpabmi/calculator.aspx. For children, underweight is considered less that the fifth percentile; healthy weight is considered the fifth percentile to below the 85th percentile; overweight is from the 85th percentile to below the 95th percentile; and, obese is considered above the 95th percentile.

Why the Concern in Adolescents?

Ray (2004) reported the initial onset of eating disorders typically occurs in adolescence. "The problem often starts with weight gain at adolescence, which can make kids feel self-conscious and out of control, which then leads to exercise, dieting, or a combination of the two" (Rabinor, 2002, p. 113). However, more recent research shows younger children too are at risk of developing disordered eating. Consider the following statistics reported by NEDA (2016d) about children and adolescents:

- *42% of 1st-3rd grade girls want to be thinner (Collins, 1991).*
- *In elementary school fewer than 25% of girls diet regularly. Yet those who do know what dieting involves and can talk about calorie restriction and food choices for weight loss fairly effectively (Smolak, 2011; Wertheim et al., 2009).*
- *81% of 10 year olds are afraid of being fat (Mellin et al., 1997).*
- *46% of 9-11 year-olds are "sometimes" or "very often" on diets, and 82% of their families are "sometimes" or "very often" on diets (Gustafson-Larson & Terry, 1992).*

- *Over one-half of teenage girls and nearly one-third of teenage boys use unhealthy weight control behaviors such as skipping meals, fasting, and smoking cigarettes, vomiting, and taking laxatives (Neumark-Sztainer, 2005).*

- *35-57% of adolescent girls engage in crash dieting, fasting, self-induced vomiting, diet pills, or laxatives. Overweight girls are more likely than normal weight girls to engage in such extreme dieting (Boutelle, Neumark-Sztainer, Story, & Resnick, 2002; Neumark-Sztainer & Hannan, 2001; Wertheim et al., 2009).*

- *Even among clearly non-overweight girls, over 1/3 report dieting* (Wertheim et al., 2009). (¶ 1)

That's not all the concern. Here's more:

- Teenage girls comprise the largest cohort of patients with eating disorders. (Kanel, 2007)

- One study reported by Dotinga (2006) revealed obese adolescents 12 to 17 years old consumed a daily average of 687 to 1,017 calories more than needed for growth and daily requirements. Obesity, according to Powers and Dodd (2003) "increases the risk of developing at least 26 diseases." (p. 194)

- Kubetin (2001) reported one study revealed nearly one-third of girls participating in the first nationwide eating disorders survey of high school students had a significant number of eating disorder symptoms.

- While 95% of adolescents use computers more than other age groups (Madden, Lenhart, Duggan, Cortesi, & Gasser, 2013), an increasing number of pro-eating disorder websites exist.

- Eating problems in adolescence are linked to medical and mental health concerns, according to Dinsmore and Stormshak (2003). These concerns include depression and suicidality (Dinsmore & Stormshak; Kanel), heart disease and other cardiovascular problems (Kelley & Kelley, 2015; Panagiotopoulos, 2000; Powers & Dodd), osteoporosis (Bone Density . . . , 2005), diabetes (Excess Androgen . . . , 2006; Powers & Dodd); self-mutilation (Kanel; Levenkron, 1998), and electrolyte imbalances associated with dehydration, malnutrition, or seizures (Kanel).

With the information above reflecting the seriousness of disordered eating in adolescents, Orgeron believes she would be amiss to not discuss this topic further. For diagnostic criteria of the different classifications of eating disorders presented in this chapter, Orgeron encourages readers to review chapter 5, Classifications of Eating Disorders.

Types of Disordered Eating Found in Adolescents

According to The Healthy Teen Project (2015), "The most common eating disorders among adolescents are anorexia, bulimia and binge-eating disorder." (Types of Eating Disorders section, ¶ 1) Other reported types of disordered eating found among adolescents are Pica, Night-Eating Syndrome, Nocturnal Sleep-Related Eating Disorder, and Prader-Willi Syndrome.

Anorexia Nervosa

Attitudes and behaviors toward food in adolescents with anorexia are similar to those found in adults with anorexia. The APA (2013) does point out the importance of finding the BMI appropriate for age and for the child's anticipated growth when diagnosing. The Healthy Teen Project (2015) and Walden

Center for Education and Research (2015b) reported adolescents commonly take serious steps to keep from eating, often in an effort to control what, how much, when and where they will eat. They often speak of being "too fat" while in reality they are too thin. According to the Walden Center for Education and Research, individuals with anorexia are often perfectionistic and high achieving in school. Yet, they have low self-esteem. The Healthy Teen Project reported adolescents with anorexia not only limit food intake, but they also cut off relationships, social events, and positive experiences.

Bulimia Nervosa

Adolescents with BN who have a normal weight often slip through the eyes of parents unnoticed, according to The Healthy Teen Project (2015). The Walden Center for Education and Research (2015b) reported, "Teenagers with bulimia can frequently hide the signs of throwing up by running water while spending long periods in the bathroom." (Bulimia Among Teenagers section, ¶ 4) Since purging associated with BN creates such a serious health threat, Orgeron encourages parents of teenagers to know the signs indicating that their child may have BN. These signs include missing food, finding an excessive amount of food packaging containers, smelling vomit frequently, overusing fluid pills, taking an excessive amount of trips to the kitchen while others are asleep or not around, and over exercising. Parents also need to be aware that "many teenagers who have bulimia also have binge-eating disorder." (Walden Center for Education and Research, Binge-Eating Disorders Among Teenagers section, ¶ 1)

Binge Eating Disorder

While most teens with BN have normal weights, teenagers with BED are usually overweight, some even obese. These teens feel a loss of control over eating, often eating secretly and when not hungry. "Most of the physical signs and symptoms associated with binge eating disorder are long-term including weight gain (often leading to obesity), high blood pressure, diabetes, irregular menstrual cycle, skin disorders and heart disease." (The Healthy Teen Project, 2015, Binge Eating Disorders section, ¶ 4)

Etiology of Disordered Eating in Adolescents

Just as with any other age group, the causes of DE in adolescents are multifaceted, including developmental, sociocultural, individual, family, etc. Orgeron recommends reviewing chapter 7, Etiology of Disordered Eating as a reminder of common factors that contribute to the development of DE. Only those causal factors specific to adolescents or not discussed thoroughly in chapter 7 will be discussed thoroughly in this section.

Developmental Factors.

Nash (1999) reports three transitions put adolescents at greater risk for the development of disordered eating. These transitions include changes associated with physical maturation, the beginning of dating, and the increase of academic requirements occurring around the same period of time.

Sociocultural Factors

Messages from the media. As mentioned in chapter 7, Mintle (2016) and NEDA (2016f) recognize the power of the media, advertising and celebrity spotlights in the development of eating disorders. Jaffe (1998), Kanel (2007), and Vandereycken (2006) concur with the influence of the media in developing DE in adolescents.

Pro-eating disorder websites. As opposed to pro-recovery websites that emphasis recovery from disordered eating, "Pro-eating disorder Web sites are communities of individuals who engage in disordered eating and use the Internet to discuss their activities." (Wilson, Peebles, Hardy, & Litt, 2006, Abstract: Objective section) Pro-eating disorder websites online by far outnumber the number of available pro-recovery websites. (WebMD, 2005)

The pro-ana online communities promote attitudes and behaviors exhibited by individuals with AN; the pro-mia online communities similarly to BN. Sometimes these terms are used interchangeably. (Wikipedia, 2017e) Research (Futures, 2016; Mariani, 2016; NEDIC, 2014c; WebMD, 2005; Wikipedia, 2017e; Wilson et al., 2006) points out the dangers of pro-eating disorder sites, and how adolescents, especially young girls, are at high risk of being captivated by unhealthy information found at these sites.

> *You won't find facts and statistics about the health complications of anorexia on pro-ana websites. Instead, you'll find a lot of support for distorted views about eating disorders and unattainable physical ideals. For girls on the brink of developing an eating disorder, these sites can be dangerous traps.* (Futures, 2016, The Allure of Pro-Ana Communities section, ¶ 3)

Pro-eating disorder communities target young unhappy girls with low self-esteems encouraging them to practice behaviors harmful to the body. At such communities, members may:

> ➢ *Endorse anorexia and/or bulimia as desirable (84% and 64% respectively in a 2010 survey).*
> ➢ *Share crash dieting techniques and recipes (67% of sites in a 2006 survey, rising to 83% in a 2010 survey).*
> ➢ *Coach each other on using socially acceptable pretexts for refusing food, such as veganism (which is notably more prevalent in the eating-disordered in general).*
> ➢ *Compete with each other at losing weight, or fast together in displays of solidarity.*
> ➢ *Commiserate with one another after breaking fast or binging.*
> ➢ *Advise on how to best induce vomiting, and on using laxatives and emetics.*
> ➢ *Give tips on hiding weight loss from parents and doctors.*
> ➢ *Share information on reducing the side-effects of anorexia.*
> ➢ *Post their weight, body measurements, details of their dietary regimen or pictures of themselves to solicit acceptance and affirmation.*
> ➢ *Suggest ways to ignore or suppress hunger pangs.* (Wikipedia, 2017e, Online Presence section, ¶ 2)

According to NEDIC (2014c), the developers of such sites have disordered eating. Developing the sites gives them a false sense of security believing their attitudes and behaviors are okay, and erroneously allowing them to believe disordered eating is a choice and that others support them in their choice.

What do the victims of these communities have in common? According to Futures (2016), easy access and too much alone time on computers; pre-existing symptoms of disordered eating; feelings of not fitting in; and, they lack social support/friends in reality off-line.

What about the parents of girls involved in pro-eating disorder websites? Survey results in the study by Wilson et al. (2006) reflected, "Parents frequently (52.8%) were aware of pro-eating disorder sites, but an equal number did not know whether their child visited these sites, and only 27.6% had discussed them with their child. Most (62.5%) parents, however, did not know about pro-recovery sites." (Abstract: Results section)

Peer influence. Bullying and teasing from other children set adolescents up for disordered eating (Garner & Garfinkel, 1997; Nash, 1999; Paxton, 1999; Rabinor, 2002; The Healthy Teen Project, 2015). According to the Healthy Teen Project,

> *Many teenagers report that the onset of their eating disorder involved comments or teasing by peers, usually about appearance. Whether done in the context of an innocent family nickname or in a malicious bullying event, these instances of feeling shame, or being shamed, based on size or physical appearance are powerful contributors to a teenager developing an eating disorder. The tendency for females, specifically, to 'bond' around 'fat talk' and negative body discussions have also been associated with the development of an eating disorder.* (Bullying/"Fat Talk" section, ¶ 1)

Paxton (1999) reported that the eating attitudes and behaviors of an adolescent's immediate circle of friends are also important. They may increase or diminish the risk of DE. An adolescent perceiving a friend's focus on dieting and weight control is positively correlated to an increased risk for DE, according to Paxton.

Action toys/dolls depicting ideal image. With actions toys, such as G.I. Joe and Star Wars, boys receive messages that an ideal male body has "a hugely muscular figure that we believe no man could attain without massive doses of steroids." (Pope, Phillips, & Olivardia, 2000, p. 44) These same messages are received into adolescence through exposure to professional wrestling and unrealistic male body images in magazines such as *Playgirl*, according to Pope et al. (2000).

Individual Factors

Personal history of dieting. From a cohort study of adolescent health in Victoria, Australia, Patton (1999) concluded, "dieting is the most important predictor of new eating disorders." (p. 1) Results from this study suggested that females who dieted more strictly were 18 times more likely to develop an eating disorder than non-dieters. Moderate female dieters were five times more likely to develop an eating disorder than the non-dieters were.

Food as a drug. Similar to alcohol with an alcoholic, food also may be an addictive agent in the life of an adolescent (Luftman & Marciano, 1994; Minirth et al., 1990; Nash, 1999). Nash points out that the addiction model of eating disorders "assumes that some individuals are biologically vulnerable to certain foods (e.g., sugar) that cause chemical dependence." (p. 85).

Poor body image. Research (Body image concerns . . . , 2006; Brown, Cash, & Lewis, 1989; Insel & Roth, 2004; Luftman & Marciano, 1995; Nash, 1999; Natenshon, n.d.a, n.d.b; O'Dea, 2002;

Paxton, 1999; Piran et al., 1999; Pope et al., 2000; Russell-Mayhew, 2005; van den Berg, Wertheim, Thompson, & Paxton, 2002; Vandereycken, 2006; Wade & Lowes, 2002) links disordered eating and poor body image. Results of studies by Brown et al. (1989), Paxton, van den Berg et al. (2002), Vandereycken, and Wade & Lowes support the link between DE and poor body image in adolescent females.

Regarding adolescent males, the results of one study by Pope et al. (2000) of boys aged 11 to 17 years old revealed that discrepancies between one's ideal body image and one's actual body image put boys at risk of developing eating disorders. These at-risk boys often turned to steroids and other dangerous, illegal drugs.

Prior emotional, sexual, or physical abuse. Mary Anne Cohen, Director of The New York Center for Eating Disorders and author of *French Toast for Breakfast: Declaring Peace with Emotional Eating* (Gurze Books, 1995) reported the following:

> *In my eating disorder practice, 40 to 60 percent of the men and women who come to therapy for an eating problem have been sexually or physically abused. "It was my father's best friend." "It was my father." "It was my brother." "It was my mother's boyfriend." "It was my mother." "And so I starved myself." "And so I binged and purged." "And so I got fat." "And so I started using laxatives."*
>
> *What is the connection between sexual abuse and developing an eating disorder? The answer is guilt, shame, anesthesia, self-punishment, soothing, comfort, protection and rage.* (Cohen, 2016, ¶s 1-2)

Other research (Costin, 1996; Garner & Garfinkel, 1997; Gati, Tenyi, Tury, & Wildmann, 2002; Kinder, 1997; Larkin, Rice, & Russell, 1999; Neumark-Sztainer, Story, Hannan, Beuhring, & Resnick, 2000; Sanci, Coffey, Olsson, Reid, Carlin, & Patton, 2008; Schwartz & Cohn, 1996) supports a link between DE and prior emotional, sexual, or physical abuse in adolescents. Orgeron also discussed the link between sexual abuse and DE in her book *We Survived Sexual Abuse! You Can Too!* (ABC's Ministries, 2016).

Why don't children and adolescents tell on their abusers? Cohen (2016) offered several reasons, including not understanding the abuse is wrong; denial that the abuse is wrong; fear of not being believed; threatened by abuser; and, bribery from abuser to keep quiet.

Poor coping skills. Garcia-Grau et al. (2002) conducted a study of 216 middle class adolescent high school girls linking DE and coping style. "The results suggest that subjects who avoid the problem and cope nonadaptively with the emotions that the problems generate show a higher predisposition to developing an eating disorder." (p. 119)

Impulsivity and control issues. A study by Gowers and Shore at the University of Liverpool, England, as cited in Where do . . . (2001), revealed multiple pathways to DE. In addition to sociocultural and family factors, "an alternative pathway may be impulsivity and fear of loss of control." (Where do . . ., Concerns arise late in childhood section, ¶ 1) Insel and Roth (2004) and Minirth et al. (1990) also linked DE to control issues citing perfectionism and unrealistic demands for self-control as behaviors leading to an ED.

Prescription medication side effects. According to Schwarz (2016) some medications may cause adolescents to gain weight. Among those medicines are:

- *Cortisol and other glucocorticoids*
- *Megace*
- *Sulfonylureas*
- *Tricyclic antidepressants (TCAs)*
- *Monoamine oxidase inhibitors (MAOIs), such as phenelzine*
- *Oral contraceptives*
- *Insulin (in excessive doses)*
- *Thiazolidinediones*
- *Risperidone*
- *Clozapine* (Etiology and Pathophysiology section, ¶ 3)

Family Factors

Dysfunctional parenting. Because of the strong impact of parents on children and adolescents, Orgeron believes the following information also reported in Chapter 7, Etiology of Disordered Eating is well worth repeating. Research (DeGoede & Drews, 1998; Minirth et al., 1990) indicates family environment plays a key role in the occurrence of eating disorders. Children learn false beliefs and emotional feelings about food from their parents and extended families. Parental commands such as "Clean up your plate", and "you eat too much" cause children to mistrust their natural appetites (DeGoede & Drews). Dysfunctional eating attitudes and behaviors also are learned when parents model chronic dieting, excessive exercising to lose weight, and eating too much without getting any exercise. Minirth et al. consider the environment around the dinner table important in determining whether an individual develops an eating disorder. According to Minirth et al., unhealthy emotional feelings learned from families of origin may stem from:

➢ Experiencing family meals as a battleground. Is the atmosphere at the dinner table a shooting gallery? Do family members overeat? These are crucial questions to consider when assessing the etiology of an eating disorder.

➢ "You must eat" syndrome. One case described by Minirth et al. involved a female adult who recalled her mother forcing her to sit at the table for hours when she failed to eat everything on her plate. When the woman as a young child wanted to rebel, she also received the powerful, hypnotic message: "You must eat."

➢ Using food as a comforter, as a reward or as part of celebration rituals. Most true food addicts, similar to the alcoholic, eat for comfort when they feel bad and overeat at celebrations. Every individual with an eating disorder has trigger foods and situations that may result in an uncontrollable "rush". Minirth et al. report sugar and chocolate as the most popular trigger foods. Trigger situations may include family gatherings, parties, award banquets, grocery shopping, the smell of food, and for some individuals just driving past a fast food restaurant.

➢ Overeating to please others. Dr. Meier shared his own experience here of how he grew up eating to please his mother:

I grew up in a German home. My mother was a wonderful cook, and still is, at age eighty, a wonderful cook. And, like good old-world eaters, we put butter on everything. Sometimes I used to food my butter rather than butter my food. (p. 32)

He added that his eating to please his mother became a type of codependency.

Biological Factors

Genetic/biological factors. While Orgeron believes most disordered eating is learned and a choice made by an individual, one cannot rule out genetic/biological factors, such as Prader-Willi Syndrome discussed previously, as a cause of obesity in children and adolescents. Orgeron encourages parents of obese children/adolescents to have medical doctors screen their children for such causes.

Hormonal factors. According to Scjwarz (2016), hormonal problems linked to childhood obesity are:

- *Growth hormone deficiency*
- *Growth hormone resistance*
- *Hypothyroidism*
- *Leptin deficiency or resistance to leptin action*
- *Glucocorticoid excess (Cushing syndrome)*
- *Precocious puberty*
- *Polycystic ovary syndrome (PCOS)*
- *Prolactin-secreting tumors* (Etiology and Pathophysiology section, ¶ 1)

Does Your Adolescent Have Disordered Eating?

Parents need to wake up and educate themselves on the dangers of DE in children and adolescents. What are the indicators that a child or adolescent has DE? Center for Discovery (2017) identified these indicators. They include:
- Eating small amounts of food or not eating at all
- Missing meals
- Eating alone; won't eat around anyone else
- Storing food privately
- Hiding figure by wearing loose-fitting clothes
- Obsessing/talking about weight and body/self image
- Finding reasons to diet
- Over exercising
- Withdrawing socially
- Being irritable or depressed
- Frequent trips to the bathroom after meals
- Modifications in sleep habits
- Cheeks that are swollen (caused from vomiting)
- Abnormal menstrual cycles

➢ Injuries to fingers from forced vomiting
➢ Cavities in teeth
➢ Extreme weight fluctuations
➢ Constantly feeling cold
➢ Weak muscles
➢ Hair loss
➢ Development of lanugo (thin white hair) on body.

Based on the above indicators, what should parents do when they suspect their child has an ED? Gerson (2017) offered the following tips:

- *-Set a private time & place to speak*
- *-Use "I" Statements*
- *-Feeling anxious? Rehearse what you want to say*
- *-Avoid 'simplistic solutions' e.g. Just stop, Just eat." This isn't' helpful and can leave your loved one feeling misunderstood.*
- *-Encourage them to seek professional help as getting timely and effective treatment will drastically increase their chances for recovery.*
- *-Stick to the facts (e.g. "I have seen you run to the bathroom at mealtimes, it makes me worried that you may be making yourself throw up."). (¶ 2)*

Often parents hesitate to speak with their child about such behaviors afraid that the child will react negatively. Parents ought not to cower from discussing such important issues with their children. Children need to be confronted lovingly and with concern. Additionally, listening to the child's responses rather than lecturing will be received more positively by the child. During the discussion, have as much information available about DE and ask whether your child will cooperate in getting treatment.

Treatment of DE in Adolescents

Jaffe (1998) reported eating disorders in adolescents are difficult to treat so the sooner they are diagnosed, the better the chances for recovery. What might make treating DE in adolescents more difficult? "A significant proportion of overweight or obese adolescents in the United States and the United Kingdom think they are just about the right weight and are not concerned about their weight status, two new studies suggest." (Harrison, 2015, ¶ 1) The studies referred to by Harrison are by Lu, Tarasenko, Asgari-Majd, Cottrell-Daniels, Yan, and Zhang (2015) and Jackson, Johnson, Croker, and Wardle (2015). Additionally, Jackson et al. (2015) reported "A number of studies have examined rates of under- and overestimation of body size in adolescent samples, with results indicating that up to 25% of normal-weight girls and around 5% of normal-weight boys perceive themselves to be too heavy. [Brener, Eaton, Lowry, & McManus, 2004; Hayward, Millar, Petersen, Swinburn, Lewis, 2014; Martin, Frisco, & May, 2009; Talamayan, Springer, Kelder Gorospe &, Joye, 2006; Viner, Haines, Taylor, Head, Booy, & Stansfeld, 2006; Yang, Turk, Allison, James, & Cjasems, 2014]" (p. 1488) Whether these inaccurate self-perceptions are a result of denial, ignorance, or whatever, adolescents in such cases may not want to cooperate with parents' efforts to help their child overcome DE. Before these adolescents can be treated effectively, they must realize they have a problem, and also have the motivation to change. Motivation is determined by what level of change an adolescent is at. The stages of change are precontemplation, contemplation, preparation, action, and maintenance (Victorian Centre of Excellence in Eating Disorders, n.d.). If anorexia is suspected or diagnosed, research by Pauli, Aebi, Metzke, and Steinhausen, (2017) and Rieger, Touyz, and Beumont, (2002) supports using the Anorexia Nervosa Stages of Change Questionnaire, which Orgeron found online as a PDF. However, due to copyright concerns, she will not be including the questionnaire in this book.

"Treatment of eating disorders usually involves a combination of psychotherapy and medical management." (Insel & Roth, 2004, p. 419) For adolescents with life-threatening complications due to DE, Jaffe (1998) reported hospitalization is the first step to treatment. Eating Disorder Hope (2005-2017) stressed the importance of using a comprehensive team approach to treating adolescents with disordered eating. This treatment team should consist of "a medical doctor, a psychologist or therapist, a psychiatrist, a dietitian and a physical therapist." (Comprehensive Eating Disorders Treatment for Teens a Must section, ¶ 1) Families too play a key role in treating adolescents with DE. Subject to the seriousness of the DE, Insel and Roth noted treatment might continue for not many months to years. Relapses of the DE are common in adolescents, according to Jaffe, with indicators suggesting a poorer prognosis depression, suicide attempts, and alcohol abuse.

Prevention of DE in Adolescents

"Prevention is the most important thing," Wang said. Children "start having a small energy gap, then it becomes bigger over time. [We] need to start early and establish healthy habits. It requires more than just one strategy -- everyone has to participate, including the government, community, schools, families, and the food and beverage industries." (Wang, Gortmaker, Sobol, & Kuntz, 2006, as cited by Dotinga, 2006, ¶ 12)

Obesity in Adolescents

"Childhood obesity is a global phenomenon affecting all socio-economic groups, irrespective of age, sex or ethnicity." (Raj & Kumar, 2010, Abstract) Why the concern?

➢ Today in the United States about 20% of school aged children are obese.

➢ Worldwide, according to research conclusions of a study about the occurrence of overweight and obesity in adolescents by Bibiloni, Pons, and Tur (2013), the prevalence of obesity in adolescents is high; though the obesity rate for boys was found to be higher, it could not be determined which sex had the higher obesity rate among adolescents.

➢ "Without intervention, extremely obese children may continue to suffer from obesity as adults. Overweight adolescents have a 70% chance of becoming overweight or obese adults and an 80% chance if a parent is overweight or obese." (American Society for Metabolic and Bariatric Surgery, 2011, Prevalence of Obesity in Adolescents section, ¶ 2)

➢ Many of the preventable illnesses that develop as an adult take their roots during the adolescent years from unhealthy behaviors such as unhealthy eating, inadequate exercise, smoking, and lack of sleep.

➢ "Obese adolescents are more than twice as likely than non-obese adolescents to die prematurely, before age 55, of illness or self-inflicted injury." (Franks, 2010, as cited by American Society for Metabolic and Bariatric Surgery, 2011, Risks Associated With Obesity in Adolescents, ¶ 1)

Etiopathogenesis of Adolescent Obesity

The *"Aetiopathogenesis* [British form of etiopathogenesis (n.d.), which means 'the cause and development of a disease or abnormal condition'] of childhood obesity is multi-factorial and includes genetic, neuroendocrine, metabolic, psychological, environmental and socio-cultural factors." (Raj & Kumar, 2010, Abstract). Let's look closer at each of these factors:

   Genetics and adolescent obesity. Stanford Children's Health (2017) and Raj and Kuman (2010) reported that obesity can be inherited from parents to child through single or polygenic gene abnormalities. Genetic conditions found in adolescents predisposing them to obesity are Bardet-Biedl syndrome, Cohen syndrome, and Prader-Willi syndrome, all discussed previously.

   Does having a genetic predisposition towards obesity mean that an adolescent is destined to being obese? Research (Hausenblas, Cook, & Chittester, 2008; Kelley & Kelley, 2015; Ruiz, Labayen, Ortega, Legry, Moreno, Dallongeville, et al., 2010) reported not if that adolescent exercises regularly meeting the daily requirements established by the U.S. Department of Health and Human Services. "They suggested that children and adolescents should participate in physical activity for 60 min/d or longer, and most of the activity should be of moderate to vigorous intensity." (Ruiz, et al., 2010, p. 328)

   Energy metabolism and adolescent obesity. Everyone's metabolism, or how fast one's body burns energy or stored fat, is different. An individual may also raise or lower his or her metabolism. Metabolism is regulated by intricate neuroendocrine connections. When adolescents fast or lose weight metabolism slows down with their bodies going into a "starvation" mode. What can adolescents do to raise their metabolism? WebMD.com (2015) offers 10 suggestions:

1. Do strength training exercises to develop muscle. "Every pound of muscle uses about 6 calories a day just to sustain itself, while each pound of fat burns only 2 calories daily." (Slide 2).
2. Increase aerobic exercise.
3. Drink plenty of water.
4. Although energy drinks are okay for adults, American Academy of Pediatrics recommends adolescents avoid them due to the risk of anxiety, high blood pressure, and sleep problems.
5. Eat smaller amounts more often.
6. Eat foods with green or red chili pepper or flakes, which can speed up your metabolism rate.
7. Add more protein to one's diet. (More calories are burned digesting protein-rich foods than with digesting fat or carbohydrates.)
8. While WebMD recommends drinking coffee, Orgeron does not advocate drinking coffee. Caffeine, a stimulant, in coffee can interact with a number of prescriptions medications. Furthermore, Got Questions Ministries (2002-2017a) reports,

Similar to gluttony, caffeine addiction is something that Christians are often hypocritical about. Christians are quick to condemn addiction to alcohol and tobacco, but tend to ignore other more "socially acceptable" addictions such as over-eating and caffeine. Alcohol clearly can have more dangerous effects on behavior and can be harmful to health when abused. Tobacco is harmful to health in even small quantities. In comparison, caffeine might not seem so bad, but "it's not as bad as…" is not something Christians should live by. Rather, Christians should live by "Is it right? Is it honoring to God?" (¶ 2)

9. Drink Green Tea. For the same reasons Orgeron does not advocate drinking coffee, she does not advocate drinking Green Tea.
10. Avoid fasting and diets less than 1,200 calories daily for females, 1,800 calories daily for males.

Environmental factors putting adolescents at risk for obesity. Environmental factors of adolescents are often out of their control. For example, as Orgeron has always heard, "You can't choose the family that you were born into." What makes an adolescent more at risk of developing obesity? Here are factors commonly reflected in research:

➢ Poor parental models in regards to eating and exercise habits; parents who are obese
➢ Lack of encouragement
➢ Lower socio-economic levels
➢ Not enough sleep
➢ Frequently eating at fast-food restaurants
➢ Eating extra-large portions
➢ Too many high calorie foods available
➢ Too many sweetened drinks, such as sodas and fruit drinks, available
➢ Lack of healthy snacks, such as fruit and nuts, available
➢ Watching too much television
➢ Too much time on the computer

Additionally, McCall (2016) reported that adolescents with developmental disabilities, such as autism also are at greater risk of being and staying obese. According to Zeller et al. (2015), children who experience any form of abuse, with emotional abuse the worst, also are at a greater risk of becoming obese.

How should parents approach adolescents with obesity to encourage them to get help to overcome their problem? "[C]onsideration should be given to word choice when talking to youth about body weight." (Puhl, 2017, Talking About Weight: Youth Language Preferences section, ¶ 5) Puhl reported that recently a group of researchers surveyed 50 adolescents with obesity about what expressions they preferred their families use in talking to them about their body weight. Words that the adolescents found offensive are "extremely obese," "fat," "obese," "chubby," and "weight problem." Puhl recommended that parents NEVER use these expressions to talk to an adolescent with obesity. Terms adolescent girls preferred include "weight," "Curvy," "higher body weight," and "BMI". Adolescent boys preferred the terms "weight," "overweight," "heavy/big," and "higher body weight". Puhl also pointed out that the study has strong implication as to how healthcare providers should talk to adolescents and their families about problems related to weight.

Early puberty (in girls). "Puberty refers to breast budding and pubic hair; it does not begin, as is popularly thought, with the first period." (Frellick, 2015, ¶ 5) Frellick reported that excessive body fat creates estrogen which the ovaries release during puberty. With more body fat, breast development begins earlier.

Girls who hit puberty early are "at higher risk of being depressed, developing an eating disorder, abusing drugs, and engaging in sexual behavior earlier," Dr. Greenspan told attendees at TEDMED 2015 in Palm Springs, California. And as adults, those girls have a higher risk for breast cancer and heart disease, she added. (Frellick, ¶s 2-3)

Treating Obesity in Adolescents

Permanent lifestyle changes as treatment. For adolescents who are obese, parents must intervene in their child's life to encourage and make the home environmentally friendly to promote weight reduction. This means not bringing sweet, high-fat, and high-caloric food into the home. In some cases if the child is a compulsive eater, this may mean locking the pantry and having healthy foods only available to the adolescent at meals and snack time. Though eating out seems to be the norm in a lot of households in today's society, this should not be the case where a child is dealing with obesity.

In addition to monitoring the diet of an adolescent who is obese, parents and other caretakers also must limit sedentary activities, such as watching television and working on the computer. Raj and Kumar (2010) reported,

Screen time should be restricted to less than two hours per day as the opposite is associated with increased adiposity and higher weight status. . . . Excessive TV viewing is associated with higher intakes of energy, fat, sweet and salty snacks and carbonated beverages in addition to reducing consumption of fruits and vegetables. This makes TV time restriction an excellent opportunity to complement dietary management. (Restriction of Sedentary Behavior section, ¶ 1)

Not only should screen time for adolescents be limited, but parents need to monitor all technology used by an adolescent. (Jantz, 2016) Jantz reported many parents fail to do this because they use the television or Internet as a babysitter, they try to be the adolescent's friend, and they want to appease guilt from being busy with too many other personal commitments (e.g.: work). Among the ways that Jantz reported parents and caretakers of children can monitor a child's use of technology include helping and teaching children to make appropriate choices based on designated ratings for any form of media; encouraging children to use non-electronic media, such as reading books or playing board games; limiting media for educational purposes only; and, creating screen-free areas in the home, including all bedrooms.

In addition to assisting adolescents with obesity to manage their diet and limit sedentary activities, parents also need to motivate adolescents to start moving more. This can be done by asking them to help with chores, walk the family pet, and/or taking a walk with them.

Prescription medications as treatment. Prescription medications are available to treat obesity but not without side effects. Thus, "Pharmacotherapy should be reserved as a second line of management and should be considered only when insulin resistance, impaired glucose tolerance, hepatic steatosis, dyslipidaemia or severe menstrual dysfunction persist in spite of lifestyle interventions." (Raj & Kumar, 2010, Pharmacological Treatment section, ¶ 1)

Surgical therapy. "Gastric bypass surgery can help obese adolescents lose weight, and many maintain the weight loss over the longer term, but there may be ongoing nutritional deficiencies and the need for further surgery." (Davenport, 2017, ¶ 1) Due to her personal experience of knowing someone who had surgery to lose weight Orgeron has a bias against performing surgery for weight loss. For purposes of this discussion, this individual will be given the fictitious name Jill. Orgeron asked Jill once, "Do you regret having the surgery?"

Jill replied in a definitive tone, "Yes, I do. In hind sight, I wish I had pushed back from the table more and exercised to lose weight, whatever I had to do. I wouldn't recommend this to anyone." Unfortunately, Jill died an early death due to problems associated with her weight loss and health issues.

Due to her personal bias against surgical therapy, Orgeron recommends this treatment method only be used as a last resort in extremely obese adolescents who have undergone extensive medical evaluations by multiple physicians, who have had extensive counseling, after much prayer, and where the adolescent is willing to work with parents and doctors to monitor their health lifelong. For more information on using surgical interventions in adolescents to lose weight, see the following resources:

➢ Davenport, 2016
➢ Inge, Jenkins et al., 2017
➢ Inge, Miyano et al, 2009
➢ Michalsky et al., 2015
➢ O'Brien et al., 2010
➢ Olbers et al., 2017
➢ Saber, 2016
➢ Taylor & Taylor, 2015, Surgical Management section

Preventing Obesity in Adolescents

"The ideal preventive strategy for obesity is to prevent children with a normal, desirable BMI from becoming overweight or obese. Preventive strategies should start as early as newborn period." (Raj, & Kuman, 2010, Prevention of Obesity section, ¶ 1) Families, physicians, schools, and the community must all work together to overcome the obesity epidemic in children and adolescents.

The family: first line of defense. Orgeron believes that preventing obesity in children and adolescents *must* start with the parents or primary caregivers and their having a home environment that promotes a permanent healthy lifestyle. Stanford Children's Health (2017) gave recommendations on how parents and caregivers can help prevent obesity in children. These recommendations are:

➢ NEVER focus on the child's weight; slowly implement changes into the home that promotes a healthier environment and lifestyle.

➢ Set a positive example. Children often model parents' behaviors.

➢ Inspire your children to exercise at least an hour daily as much as possible. If an extremely obese child is resistant to or cannot exercise, at least get them moving more initially. Try the "Sit-Less" intervention (Jenkins, 2016). This is where one "breaks up sedentary behavior with standing and light-intensity walking." (¶ 1) Because the "Sit-Less" intervention strategies are easier to do than formal exercise, the chances for long-term compliance are better.

> **"Preventing obesity in children and adolescents *must* start with the parents or primary caregivers and their having a home environment that promotes a permanent healthy lifestyle."**

➢ Limit "screen" time (television and computer combined) to no more than two hours each day. Homework may require occasional exceptions. Research by Busko (2016b) and by Kenney and Gortmaker (2017) support limiting screen time in children and adolescents.

➢ Never reward or punish a child with food.

➢ Keep healthy snacks available; don't buy soft drinks or high sugar and high fat foods.

➢ Keep plenty of fruits and vegetables available each day.

➢ Don't buy drinks with added sugar, including sodas, fruit juices, and sports drinks. Offer water to children to drink as an alternative.

Orgeron believes one of the most important keys in the home to preventing obesity is having daily family meals together. Advantages to the parents of having regular family meals are reported by Golden, Schneider, and Wood (2016).

Postulates for why family meals are protective include the following: families will consume healthier foods than teenagers would choose on their own; parents can model healthy food choices; family meals provide a time for teenagers and parents to interact; and parents can monitor their child's eating and address issues earlier when they are aware of their child's eating behavior. (Evidence-Based Management Strategies Associated with Both Obesity and EDs in Teenagers section, ¶ 3)

"What can health care providers do?" (Neumark-Sztainer, 2009) While pediatricians typically assess for and treat obesity and other health-related problems in children, Vine, Hargreaves, Briefel, and Orfield (2013) reported the role needs to be expanded to include primary care providers and community clinics. "The primary care practice may be an ideal site in which to identify overweight and obese children, educate parents and children about the health risks of obesity, and establish and implement therapeutic interventions." (Jortberg et al., 2016, Introduction section, ¶ 4) Vine et al. (2013) pointed out "with the right interventions and activities, PCPs can effectively play an expanded role in preventing and treating obesity among children and adolescents. Obstetricians and gynecologists also play an important role in prenatal care, monitoring maternal weight gain, and encouraging and supporting breastfeeding." (Motivation for the Study section, ¶ 2) What can these clinicians do? According to Vine et al., their roles can include:

• Assessing and monitoring weight and BMI

• Promoting healthy lifestyles

• Treating the patient (e.g. counseling within the office setting for patients diagnosed as overweight or obese)

• Developing their own knowledge and skills regarding obesity

• Improving their care models

• Referring patients with obesity to specialized obesity treatment centers

• Giving out literature promoting obesity prevention

• Participating in community initiatives to promote obesity prevention

• Advocating for policy changes and legislation that will help in the prevention of obesity.

Neumark-Sztainer (2009) discussed five suggestions grounded in research for clinicians to do to help prevent obesity in adolescents. These include promoting healthy eating and regular exercise;

promoting a healthy body image; encouraging families to have pleasant and more family meals together; and, encouraging families to emphasize weight less and have an environment at home that promotes healthy eating and regular physical activity.

Some physicians may think I *became a doctor to treat people, not prevent diseases.* That's not the attitude of sports medicine doctor Bert R. Mandelbaum, MD, DHL (Hon). Mandelbaum (2015) reported,

> *I believe that we all have a higher calling. Our most important job is to motivate our patients to take control of their fitness—and to get their family members to join them. And in the long run, what's best for our patients is best for us as well.* (A Sports Doctor's Most Important Job section, ¶ 2)

School interventions. Schools and school faculty and staff also are important components of the battle to overcome the obesity epidemic in adolescents. However, the battle must begin long before high school; but *must* start in pre-school and primary education, even in pre-school day care centers. Orgeron believes there are four main interventions for such institutions and their employees. These include providing access to healthier food and limiting unhealthy snacks; making more physical activity available to students; mentoring programs; and providing at least one full time staff nurse at every school to assist in monitoring students' weight and health status.

To help prevent obesity in children, Orgeron believes school cafeterias should be required to serve only healthy well balanced meals, omitting sugary and high-fat items from the daily menu. Orgeron also believes vending machines with sodas, candy, chips, and other unhealthy foods should be prohibited from being on school property. If vending machines are available at a school, they should only contain healthy snack items, and should only be accessible before and after school, not during lunchtime or while classes are in session. Not only is providing a healthy diet at school important to help prevent obesity, but according to a study by Rosettie, Micha, Penalvo, Cudhea, and Mozaffarian (2017) as cited by Busko (2017b), if all schools, elementary through senior high school, would provide fresh fruits and vegetables and restrict the accessibility of sugar-sweetened drinks to students the number of deaths from heart disease, diabetes, and stroke would be lower years later in the population at large.

Regarding physical activity in schools, Orgeron remembers years ago during her childhood when recess and physical education were mandated in schools. In today's world, not all schools offer recess or physical education classes due to an increased emphasis on academics to meet testing standards or due to budget cutbacks in schools. Sometimes, some teachers even withhold recess as a type of punishment for classroom misbehavior. Orgeron asks, with increasing overweight and obesity in children and adolescents, has the sacrifice been worth the cost of students' declining health?

> *Taking away physical activity because it is a privilege or something that is just fun or is not necessary sends the wrong message. Exercise along with nutrition is important to health. We want to make sure that kids take that seriously and develop good habits.* (Caplan, 2017, ¶ 4)

Orgeron agrees with Caplan (2017). Other research that supports the value of including exercise as a part of school curriculum include Mei et al. (2016), Phillips (2016), and Roth et al. (2015).

What types of mentoring programs are available in schools to prevent obesity? "Healthy Buddies" (Stock et al., 2007) is an elementary school intervention to prevent obesity and ED where older students (4th thru 7th graders) mentor the younger children on the importance of eating healthy and exercise. From the results of a pilot study conducted at two elementary schools in Canada, Stock et al. concluded that the

> *student-led curriculum improved knowledge not only in older schoolchildren but also in their younger buddies. It also decreased weight velocity in the older students. Student-led teaching may be an efficient, easy-to-implement way of promoting a healthy lifestyle from kindergarten to 7th grade.* (Conclusions section, ¶ 1)

Why does Orgeron advocate for school nurses at every school? "A new policy statement by the American Academy of Pediatrics (AAP) [American Academy of Pediatrics, 2016] calls for a minimum of one full-time registered nurse in every school and a school physician in every district." (Frellick, 2016) With the increasing prevalence of obesity and other health issues in today's children, Orgeron believes this policy is appropriate, as poor health often affects one's ability to concentrate; thus, affecting academic performance.

Frellick (2016) recommends different roles school nurses can have in today's academic setting. They include "surveillance, emergency preparedness, health education, chronic disease management, and behavioral health assessment. They also liaise between schools and the public health arena, facilitating immunization, obesity prevention, smoking cessation, and substance abuse and asthma education." (Role Has Expanded section, ¶s 1-2)

Before closing the section on school interventions for obesity in adolescents, Orgeron wants to point out that school environments also need to be safe. In a study by Dr. Carolyn Côté-Lussier and colleagues at the University of Montreal and its affiliated Research Centre at CHU Sainte Justine children's hospital, as cited by Tucker (2015), living in poverty and not feeling safe at school put children at a greater risk for obesity. Orgeron suggests all school entrance doors be locked while classes are in session and halls be monitored by school security or other school personnel on a regular basis.

Community interventions. First, and foremost, Orgeron believes community interventions to prevent obesity in adolescents should complement the interventions implemented at home and at school. Communities need to be advocates for families and schools to create environments conducive to a healthy lifestyle, including diet, exercise, etc. Two communities in the United States are doing just that, according to Cohen (2017) and Busko (2017a). The nations of United Kingdom and Mexico also are taking steps to reduce obesity and become healthier, according to Tucker (2016) and Busko (2016a), respectively.

Communities need to be advocates for families and schools to create environments conducive to a healthy lifestyle, including diet, exercise, etc.

"San Francisco makes the healthy choice the easy choice," Cohen (2017, article title) reported. In 2015, the University of California, San Francisco Medical Center stopped selling "all sugar-sweetened beverages from every store, cafeteria, food truck and restaurant on its sprawling campuses." (¶ 2) Furthermore, San Francisco, the city, is poised to eliminate sugary drinks from all its hospitals; according to Cohen, researchers believe the sugary drinks feed the national diabetes and obesity epidemics. These efforts stem from the movement by the San Francisco Health Improvement

Partnership, which has already lowered sugar-sweetened drink consumption, restricted the sale of alcohol by retailers, and made dental care available to formerly underserved children. The campaign to decrease the sale and availability of sugary drinks was modelled after an earlier campaign to control tobacco, where the largest impact resulted from increasing taxes on tobacco sales, and from environmental sanctions on smoking.

> *Nutrition epidemiologist Barry Popkin, a professor at the University of North Carolina at Chapel Hill, applauded the effort of the San Francisco partnership.*
> *"This is the kind of change we need at the national, state and local level if we're going to remove some of the major health disparities," he said in a phone interview.*

Howard County, Maryland also is on the bandwagon to decrease obesity and improve the health of residents in their community, Busko (2017a) reported. After a community campaign from 2013 to 2015 to decrease the drinking of sugary drinks, soda sales in supermarkets dropped by 20% with sales remaining the same in "control" supermarkets outside the county. The "Howard County Unsweetened campaign" components included the following:

> • *The educational component included television ads, outdoor billboards, direct mail, and Twitter, Facebook, and YouTube posts, and a Better Beverage Finder online tool that lists hundreds of brands of unsweetened beverages.*
> • *Forty providers (in 13 practices) participated in an American Academy of Pediatrics collaborative to improve practice behaviors related to childhood obesity.*
> • *Professional marketers set up booths at community events such as sporting events and distributed healthy drinks.*
> • *The Better Choices Coalition of 50 community organizations collaborated in diverse efforts such as improving vending-machine choices and educating their members.*
> • *A contest was held for youths to produce the best documentary about sugary drinks.*
> • *Campaign members were successful in getting laws passed that removed student-accessible vending machines in middle schools; required that food sold in schools meet national nutrition standards; and required that childcare facilities serve beverages such as water, plain or low-fat milk, or small sizes of 100% fruit juice.* (Busko, 2017a, Complex Campaign to Get People to Switch to "Better Beverages" section, ¶ 3)

Dr. Lawrence J. Appel (Johns Hopkins Medical Institutions, Baltimore, Maryland) said as part of his presentation during the *EPI\LIFESTYLE 2017 Scientific Sessions*, "'The point at which the obesity epidemic takes off, particularly in girls,' is in adolescence, and, on average, adolescents in the US obtain 200 to 300 calories a day from sugar-sweetened beverages." Busko (2017a, ¶ 5) reported. Appel, as cited by Busko, also said, "Given the scale of the obesity epidemic . . . I think this [public-health] effort—I'm not saying ours is perfect; it's more expensive than a taxation approach—is the way to go." (¶ 5)

The development of legislation in the United Kingdom requiring manufacturers to gradually and imperceptibly lower the sugar amounts in sugary drinks by 40% over five years could significantly lower the number of people who are overweight, obese, and who have type 2 diabetes, according to a modeling study by Ma, He, Yin, Hashem, and MacGregor (2016), Tucker (2016) reported.

Dr. MacGregor told Medscape Medical News *that the current study was aimed at quantifying the benefits of such a policy, which is modeled after a salt-reduction program instituted in the UK in 2003–2004, also led by him, and which is credited with a 42% decrease in stroke mortality within 8 years, among other health benefits.* (Modeling Sugar Cuts on Salt Reduction—UK Leading the Way section, ¶ 2)

Based on findings from the current study, researchers estimated half a million less cases of overweight and one million less obesity cases in the UK. Based on the results of the salt-reduction policy, and because human taste buds adapt to smaller, incremental changes, Tucker (2016) believes the intervention is feasible. " . . . Once you get used to it, you prefer foods with less salt and sugar," Dr. MacGregor said. (Tucker, But How Feasible Is It? section, ¶ 2)

Ma et al. (2016) concluded, "The proposed strategy should be implemented immediately, and could be used in combination with other approaches, such as taxation policies, to produce a more powerful effect." (Interpretation section) Dr. MacGregor said, "We want to set it up in the UK, and then once we've demonstrated that it's possible to get the food industry to work with it, spread it out to the rest of the world." (Tucker, Modeling Sugar Cuts on Salt Reduction—UK Leading the Way section, ¶ 5)

With one third of Mexican children between the ages of 2 and 18 overweight or obese, and with one third of Mexican adults obese, Mexico enacted a 10% sales tax on sugary drinks in an effort to fight adiposity and other related health issues. (Busko, 2016a) In an observational study Colchero, Popkin, Rivera, and Ng (2016) looked at how the tax on sugary beverages affected purchases of drinks in Mexican stores. They found "purchases of taxed beverages decreased by an average of 6% (-12 mL/capita/day), and decreased at an increasing rate up to a 12% decline by December 2014. All three socioeconomic groups reduced purchases of taxed beverages, but reductions were higher among the households of low socioeconomic status." (Study answer and limitations section)

Sassi (2016) indicated the greatest impact of taxes on sugary drinks as part of a public health campaign is giving the message to consumers and those in the food industry that the government is concerned about the harmful effects of unhealthy lifestyles and is not afraid to address them. "This is the strongest incentive for consumers to reconsider choices often made automatically, based on habits or environmental influences, and for players in the food supply chain to reorient their production towards healthier options," he said. (¶ 4) Sassi also pointed out,

Other, complementary, policies are also needed. A broad menu includes regulatory measures (for example, nutrition labelling, regulation of health claims, and advertising), health education based on a sound behavioural understanding of consumers' food choices, incentives for research and development in food production, voluntary initiatives with agreed targets and independent monitoring, changes in the environment of food choice, and counselling by general practitioners of people at higher risk. (¶ 5)

Summary/Conclusions

To write this article, Orgeron conducted a literature review of DE and obesity in adolescence, including classifications, etiology, treatment, and prevention. After reviewing the literature, Orgeron thinks that the most important factors to minimizing DE and obesity in adolescents include educating parents, school personnel, and adolescents about disordered eating; adopting biblical attitudes toward food and the body; building resiliency in children, and modeling a lifestyle promoting wellness. In concluding, Orgeron agrees with Cornell (2000) that recovery from disordered eating for adolescents "begins with a conscious choice" (¶ 8) and requires "finding a better way to deal with the pressures from others, or the abuse suffered, or the lies of the culture." (¶ 9)

***

Chapter 13: Adolescents, Disordered Eating, & Obesity

Key Terms/Concepts

Anorexia Nervosa Stages of Change
    Questionnaire
BMI Percentile Calculator for Child and Teen
Etiopathogenesis

Healthy Teen Project
Metabolism
Puberty

Questions for Reflection:

1. Why are adolescents an at-risk group for developing disordered eating?
2. How can parents determine whether their child is at a healthy weight?
3. Why is there a greater concern for eating disorders in adolescent girls over adolescent boys?
4. What types of DE attitudes and behaviors are found in adolescents?
5. Why do parents often miss the signs of bulimia in their adolescents?
6. Discuss the etiology of disordered eating in adolescents.
7. What four sociocultural factors greatly influence adolescents in the development of disordered eating?
8. How do pro-eating disorder communities on line influence young girls towards the development of eating disorders?
9. How does an adolescent's immediate circle of friends impact the risk of disordered eating in adolescents?
10. What individual factors put adolescents at greater risk in developing an eating disorder?
11. What links developing an ED with past abuse?
12. Why don't children and adolescents tell on their abusers?
13. According to Center for Discovery (2017), what are indicators parents and other primary caregivers need to be aware of to recognize a possible ED in their child or adolescent?
14. How should a parent confront a child or adolescent with a suspected ED?
15. Why is getting treatment for an adolescent with an ED as soon as possible important?
16. Why is there a concern for obesity in adolescents?
17. Does having a genetic predisposition towards obesity mean that an adolescent is destined to being obese?
18. What can adolescents do to raise their metabolism?

19. What makes an adolescent more at risk of developing obesity?

20. How should parents approach adolescents with obesity to encourage them to get help to overcome their problem?

21. What can parents do to promote weight reduction in an overweight or obese child or adolescent?

22. How can parents monitor the use of technology by a child or adolescent?

23. What are ways to treat obesity in adolescents?

24. How soon should parents start using ED preventive strategies in children?

25. Where does Orgeron believe the first line of defense against obesity in children and adolescents should begin?

26. According to Stanford Children's Health, what can parents and caregivers do to help prevent obesity in children?

27. What are advantages of parents having regular family meals?

28. How can primary care givers help prevent and treat obesity among children and adolescents?

29. How can schools intervene to overcome the obesity epidemic in adolescents?

30. What types of mentoring programs are available in schools to prevent obesity?

31. Why does Orgeron advocate for school nurses at every school?

32. How can communities be advocates for families and schools to create environments conducive to a healthy lifestyle?

33. What are San Francisco and Howard County, Maryland doing to decrease obesity and improve the health of their residents?

34. What did the nation of Mexico do to decrease the obesity epidemic in their nation? Do you think the United States should do likewise?

***

Chapter 14: Disordered Eating and Pregnancy

Anticipating the arrival of a child is one of the most important times in the life of a woman, and should be one of the most special times. During this time and even before getting pregnant a woman who wants a healthy pregnancy, a healthy delivery, and a healthy child later needs to practice self-care, in particular maintaining a healthy weight throughout the pregnancy.

For women planning to have a child, doctors and other clinicians recommend that these women have a healthy weight prior to pregnancy and maintain a healthy weight throughout the duration of the pregnancy and even postpartum. Unfortunately, as cited by Davenport (2016a), "Dr. Hillier said that the 'bottom line' is that there are few opportunities to intervene with women before they become pregnant. 'They come as they are, if you will, when they are pregnant — whether that's normal weight, overweight, or obese.'" (¶ 5)

What do the statistics say? Rapaport (2015) reported that about 50% of first time pregnant women in the United States are overweight when they become pregnant. That is the same proportion of pregnant women who put on an excessive amount of weight while pregnant. These statistics, according to Rapaport, came from a study by "Dr. Joachim Dudenhausen, an obstetrics researcher at Charite University Medicine in Berlin," (¶ 3) and his colleagues who compared information on over 2 million American women with statistics from about 1,650 German peers

Dudenhausen, Grunebaum, and Kirschner (2015) reported that before getting pregnant only about half (47%) of the American women had a normal weight, 4% were underweight, and 48% exceeded recommended weight standards. Of the German women, 72% had a normal weight with 4% underweight and only 24% weighed too much. "Weight gains for German and American pregnancies were calculated for each BMI group for those staying below, within, and above the recommended gestational weight recommendations by ACOG/IOM." (p. 591) Overall, in the U.S. only 32% of the women complied with recommended weight gain standards; 48% gained more than recommended; with 20% of the expectant mothers not gaining enough weight. Those statistics compared to 34%, 27%, and 39% in German women, respectively. Dudenhausen et al. (2015) reported results from the study

> *confirm that the obesity epidemic reaches outside the United States. It is important to counsel women in the Unites States and Germany well before and during pregnancy about proper nutrition with the goal to prevent perinatal risks associated with failures of optimal prepregnancy weight and gestational weight gains.* (p. 592)

Throughout the remainder of this chapter Orgeron will discuss important information for pregnant mothers to know during and postpartum to a pregnancy. She also will include special sections on EDs and pregnancy, and on obesity and pregnancy.

During the Pregnancy

Orgeron believes having a healthy pregnancy for both mother and baby involves making healthy lifestyle choices daily. Healthy lifestyle choices include decisions to eat healthy foods in moderation, to get enough rest and exercise, to maintain healthy relationships, and to minimize stress in one's life. To do otherwise can result in negative consequences for both mother and baby. (Brown, 2015; ACOG, 2013a, 2015; Hillier, Pedula, Vesco, Oshiro, & Ogasawara, 2016; Rapaport, 2015)

Healthy Lifestyle Choices

Healthy weight gain guidelines. OB/GYN's and other clinicians who treat "pregnant women should determine a woman's body mass index at the initial prenatal visit and counsel her regarding the benefits of appropriate weight gain, nutrition and exercise, and, especially, the need to limit excessive weight gain to achieve best pregnancy outcomes." (ACOG, 2013a, Abstract) How much weight should a woman gain during pregnancy? The answer to that question depends on her initial weight at the beginning of her pregnancy.

> *Women who are underweight at the start of pregnancy should gain 28 to 40 pounds, while women who are normal weight are advised to gain 25 to 35 pounds, according to the U.S. Institute of Medicine. For overweight women, a 15- to 25-pound gain is recommended and obese women should gain just 11 to 20 pounds.* (Rapaport, 2015, ¶ 6)

"Body-positive pregnancy". Davidson and Lewin (2017) recommend pregnant mothers strive for a "body-positive pregnancy".

> *Working towards a body positive pregnancy means seeking out affirming support, honoring your body history, nourishing yourself and your baby, protecting yourself from other people's body politics and critical voices, and recognizing your critical body thoughts as something you can work to reframe.* (¶ 2)

Davidson and Lewin (2017) offered seven tips to achieving a body positive pregnancy. These tips are:

1. Get acquainted with your past body weight and figure. Challenging old false beliefs and negative thinking are powerful means to be body positive, along with using affirmative self talk.
2. Have a support group.
3. Develop a supportive birth team, including your OB/GYN or midwife and the baby's father. Other team members might include close friends or family.
4. Make taking care of yourself a priority. Be intuitive listening to body cues as to when you need to eat, rest, etc.
5. Stay off the scale, [except at the doctor's office]. Use other means, such as how you feel and how the baby is developing, to determine whether you are having a healthy pregnancy.
6. Understand that gaining weight and other physiological changes in a pregnant woman's body are normal and necessary to have a healthy pregnancy. Remember, "Weight gain includes the

growth of the baby, increased blood volume, your placenta, breast tissue growth, and amniotic fluid." (Understand the Changes section, ¶ 1)

7. Pregnant women are not immune to the media's unrealistic images of beauty. Keep the negative and intimidating messages and images from the media in perspective. Expose yourself to healthier more realistic positive images.

Physical activity (PA). Being active in any stage of life is healthy, maintaining and improving cardiorespiratory health; reducing the chances of obesity and other linked comorbidities; and, resulting in greater longevity. Staying active while pregnant has slight risks and has proved to help most women; although, a few changes to exercise habits may be required due to normal body changes and fetal needs. "Regular physical activity during pregnancy improves or maintains physical fitness, helps with weight management, reduces the risk of gestational diabetes in obese women, and enhances psychologic well-being." (ACOG, 2015, p. 1) However, as with anyone else, pregnant women should consult with a physician before beginning any exercise program.

Pregnant mothers with normal pregnancies should engage in both aerobic and strength-training exercises prior to getting pregnant, for the duration of the pregnancy, and postpartum. With the approval of a physician, the exercise goal for the healthy pregnant mother is to have an exercise program that leads to an eventual goal of moderate-force exercise for a minimum of 20–30 minutes daily on most, if not all days. When medically necessary, the exercise program should be modified. (ACOG, 2015)

What physical activities are safe for pregnant women? According to ACOG (2015), the following activities are safe for pregnant mothers to start or continue during pregnancy: "walking; swimming; stationary cycling; low-impact aerobics; Yoga, modified; Pilates, modified; running or jogging; racquet sports; and, strength training." (p. 3, Box 3)

Which exercises should pregnant women refrain from doing? ACOG (2015) reports the following physical activities should be avoided during pregnancy: "contact sports (e.g., ice hockey, boxing, soccer, and basketball); activities with a high risk of falling (e.g., downhill snow skiing, water skiing, surfing, off-road cycling, gymnastics, and horseback riding); scuba diving; sky diving; and, 'Hot yoga' or 'hot Pilates'." (p. 3, Box 3)

Should a pregnant woman ever stop exercising? Warning signs for a pregnant woman to stop exercising are

- *Vaginal bleeding*
- *Regular painful contractions*
- *Amniotic fluid leakage*
- *Dyspnea before exertion*
- *Dizziness*
- *Headache*
- *Chest pain*
- *Muscle weakness affecting balance*
- *Calf pain or swelling.* (ACOG, 2015, p. 4, Box 4)

Unhealthy Lifestyle Risks

Are there risks to not complying with the weight gain recommendations established by the IOM? If so, what are the risks? One risk that Orgeron found researchers focused on is an increased risk of obesity in the child. (Davenport, 2016a; Hillier et al., 2016) Hillier et al. conducted a study "to determine, among children with *normal* birth weight, if maternal hyperglycemia and weight gain independently increase childhood obesity risk in a very large diverse population." (p. 1) The researchers "found that gestational diabetes increased the risk of obesity in the first 10 years of life of the child by almost 30%, while excessive gestational weight gain increased the risk by over 15%." (Davenport, ¶ 2)

The Postpartum Period

The new mother's self-care habits postpartum are important to her and her child's health. This is especially true regarding the mother's ability to reach and maintain a healthy weight. "Weight loss after pregnancy takes time, but it's possible." (Mayo Clinic Staff, 2015b, ¶ 1) New mothers should focus on eating healthy foods and getting physical activity back into their daily schedule. In the best interest of herself, and especially her baby, a new mother needs to avoid weight gain postpartum. Why? Just as gaining an excessive amount of weight during pregnancy increases the child's risk of being obese, weight gain during the postpartum period also increases the risk of obesity in the child. (Doyle, 2015) "Dr. Lenie van Rossem of University Medical Center Utrecht in The Netherlands" (Doyle, ¶ 2) gave three possible reasons for the connection between weight gained during and after pregnancy and the child's risk of obesity: "genes, lifestyle, and 'intra-uterine programming'," (Doyle, ¶ 10)

> *It is still not clear whether post-delivery weight gain has an independent effect on child's weight or if weight gain during pregnancy drives most of the child's risk, and also happens to coincide with post-pregnancy weight gain, according to Dr. Jihong Liu of the Arnold School of Public Health at the University of South Carolina in Columbia.*
>
> *"Weight management is very important for women before, during and after pregnancy," Liu, who wasn't involved in the study, told Reuters Health by email. "It has the potential to break the vicious cycle of weight-related health issues in women and their offspring." (Doyle, ¶s 13-14)*

Healthy Eating After Pregnancy

While pregnant, women typically adjust their diets to support the fetus' need for nourishment. After the delivery, it's time to readjust their diet again. The Mayo Clinic Staff (2015b) offers the following tips to new mothers to establish a healthy diet:

- ***Focus on fruits, vegetables, monounsaturated fats, and whole grains.*** *Foods high in fiber — such as fruits, vegetables, nuts and whole grains — provide you with many important nutrients while helping you feel full longer.*

- ***Eat smaller portions.*** *Eating smaller portions is linked with weight loss and weight maintenance over time. Don't skip meals or limit the amount of fruits and vegetables in your diet, though — you'll miss vital nutrients.*
- ***Avoid temptation.*** *Surround yourself with healthy foods. If junk food poses too much temptation, keep it out of the house.*
- ***Don't try quick fixes.*** *There's no magic bullet for losing weight.* (Consider your eating habits section, ¶ 1)

Physical Activity after Giving Birth

What about exercise in the postpartum period? After a woman has given birth is a fitting time for the woman's medical providers to encourage her to continue her healthy lifestyle to develop a permanent lifestyle of wellness. Getting back to exercise routines developed during the pregnancy and adding new exercises is a key in supporting a permanent lifestyle of wellness. After pregnancy a woman may start exercising again "as soon as medically safe, depending on the mode of delivery, vaginal or cesarean, and the presence or absence of medical or surgical complications. Some women are capable of resuming physical activities within days of delivery." (ACOG, 2015, p. 5)

Can mothers who breastfeed exercise?

Regular aerobic exercise in lactating women has been shown to improve maternal cardiovascular fitness without affecting milk production, composition, or infant growth. [Cary & Quinn, 2001] Nursing women should consider feeding their infants before exercising in order to avoid exercise discomfort of engorged breast. Nursing women also should ensure adequate hydration before commencing physical activity. (ACOG, 2015, pp. 6-7)

Breastfeeding Benefits

Breastfeeding offers three benefits, according to LaFleur, (2017). These benefits include nourishing the baby, protecting the baby from illness, and helping the mother lose extra pounds put on while pregnant.

What happens when a mother breastfeeds that promotes weight loss? When a woman breastfeeds she uses stored fat cells and calories from the food she eats to produce milk that feeds her baby. Doctors recommend the mother who breastfeeds eat an extra 300-500 calories daily to fuel her energy needs and the production of milk for the baby. Even eating these extra calories, according to LaFleur, breastfeeding mothers can drop pounds.

Initial weight lost immediately after birth averages about 15 pounds. After that, most mothers for the next six months lose 1 to 2 pounds each month and at slower rates thereafter. Typically losing all the weight gained during pregnancy takes on average 6 to 9 months. (LaFleur)

Myths to Overcome Postpartum

You need to regain the figure you had prior to being pregnant. (Rollin, 2017) Soon after giving birth new mothers are bombarded with the message that they need to start working on getting their prepregnancy figures back. Having a variety of feelings regarding body changes a new mother has experienced during her pregnancy is normal. Rollin suggested, "What if instead of seeing stretch marks and post-baby body-differences as 'flaws,' you took some time to be thankful for the amazing thing that your body just enabled you to do?" (Myth # 1: Our bodies are meant to stay the same over time section, ¶ 8)

Women's worth is determined by appearance. (Rollin, 2017) This myth applies to all women. Pregnant women are not immune to the false messages portrayed by the media. Rollin reported,

> *When women spend their time fixating on their appearance and body, they are devoting precious time-which they could be using to impact real change in the world.*
> *When you fixate on how your body looks it takes away valuable time that you could be using to pursue your passions, strengthen your relationships, or reflect on other things. No one writes in someone's obituary: "she was so thin" or "she was the perfect weight." What would you like to be remembered for? Work to shift focus to the things and people in your life that truly matter.* (Myth # 2: Women's worth is found in their appearance, weight, and body section, ¶s 2-3)

ED's and Pregnancy

Eating disorders can complicate pregnancy, and vice versa. An eating disorder can be a pre-existing condition of pregnancy or develop during the pregnancy. (Farrar, 2014b) According to Farrar,

> *"Pregorexia" is a term that was coined by the media to describe eating disorders that persist through or emerge during pregnancy. Calorie restriction, binge eating, purging through exercise or vomiting, using laxatives excessively and eating only particular types of food are all symptoms which may be experienced.* (¶ 2)

In many women with an ED, getting pregnant makes the ED worse. Farrar (2014b) reported that the stress associated with being pregnant can trigger a relapse or the onset of a new ED in pregnant women. Pregnancy can make the already difficult diagnosing of an ED even more difficult. "Sufferers themselves may be less likely to understand that something is wrong. Families and loved ones may notice a change in behavior or an additional element of stress, but may dismiss their concerns and attribute the behaviors to the hormonal aspects of the pregnancy." (Farrar, Pregnancy and Eating Disorder Complications section, ¶ 2)

What are the risks of having an ED and being pregnant simultaneously? Baker (2017) reported,

> *Some studies have shown that women with AN have an increased risk of low weight babies, preterm birth, and a C-section. Women with BED are at increased risk for maternal hypertension, large-for-gestational-age babies, and a longer duration of labor. Thus, is it important that women with a current eating disorder or a history of an eating disorder find a practitioner they are comfortable sharing this information with so that proper services and monitoring can take place. After birth, women with a history of an eating disorder are at increased risk for postpartum depression and anxiety, with up to 35% of women with an eating disorder history experiencing postpartum depression.* (¶ 7)

Orgeron recommends that if a pregnant woman suspects she has an ED, that woman needs to seek treatment as soon as possible to avoid harm to herself and/or the baby due to inadequate nutritional support. Orgeron also believes it is important to realize that another complication of eating disorders, especially with AN, is not being able to get pregnant in the first place due to gynecological problems brought on by an ED. Baker (2017) reported,

Some studies suggest that women who have received inpatient treatment for AN, and thus may be more medically compromised, have a lower prevalence of pregnancy compared with women without a history of AN most studies show no severe long-term effects. An important caveat is that, while those with a history of AN may not struggle with infertility, some women who currently have AN may. If a woman is experiencing amenorrhea, then she may not be ovulating. And if a woman is not ovulating, she would not be able to become pregnant. However, it is possible to ovulate in the absence of menstruation. In contrast, women with a history of both AN and BN are more likely to have conceived using fertility treatment and to take longer than 6-months to conceive. Women with BED are at increased risk for miscarriage, which may be an indirect result of the fact many individuals with BED are obese. (¶ 6)

Obesity and Pregnancy

"Obesity is the most common health care problem in women of reproductive age. Obesity in women is such a common problem that the implications relative to pregnancy often are unrecognized, overlooked, or ignored because of the lack of specific evidence-based treatment options." (Catalano & Koutrouvelis, 2015, Abstract) Being obese makes getting pregnant more difficult, if at all possible and increases the likelihood of having a miscarriage, according to Grunebaum, as cited by Rapaport (2015). Being obese during pregnancy also increases the chances of gestational diabetes mellitus (GDM) developing. (Catalano, 2007; Simmons et al., 2015) Catalano also reported, "In women with pregestational glucose intolerance, hypertension, central obesity, and lipid disorders, the physiologic changes in pregnancy increase the risk of problems previously not routinely encountered during pregnancy. These include chronic cardiac dysfunction, proteinuria, sleep apnea, and nonalcoholic fatty liver disease." (Abstract) Other risks of being obese while pregnant, as reported by ACOG (2013b), include

hypertension, preeclampsia, cesarean delivery, and postpartum weight retention [Baeten, Bukusi, & Lambe, 2001; Cedergren, 2001; Sebire et al.,2001; Weiss et al., 2004; Vesco et al., 2009]. Similarly, fetuses of pregnant women who are overweight or obese are at increased risk of prematurity, stillbirth, congenital anomalies, macrosomia with possible birth injury, and childhood obesity [Stothard, Tennant, Bell, & Rankin, 2009; Oken, Taveras, Kleinman, Rich-Edwards, & Gillman, 2007]. Additional concerns include potential intrapartum, operative, and postoperative complications and difficulties related to anesthesia management. Obese women are also less likely to initiate and sustain breastfeeding [Li, Jewell, & Grummer-Strawn, 2003]. (Pregnancy Complications section, ¶ 1)

What about the baby? Are there risks to the child when a pregnant woman is overweight or obese? "When counseling obese women about potential pregnancy complications, it is important to inform them of the associated fetal risks, including prematurity, stillbirth, congenital abnormalities (e.g., neural tube defects), macrosomia, and childhood and adolescent obesity." (ACOG, 2013b, Fetal Complications section, ¶ 1) Additionally, a greater risk for babies to have cerebral palsy also has been linked to overweight and obese mothers during early pregnancy according to the results of a "Population-based retrospective cohort study of women with singleton children born in Sweden from 1997 through 2011. Using national registries, children were followed for a cerebral palsy diagnosis through 2012." (Villamor et al., 2017, Abstract, Design, Setting, and Participants section) .Approximately 45% of the links among the mothers' BMIs and the proportions of children born full-term with cerebral palsy resulted from the child's not getting enough oxygen, according to Villamor et al.. "Although the effect of maternal obesity on cerebral palsy risk may seem small compared with other risk factors, the authors highlight its relevance by emphasizing the rising obesity rates." (Parry, 2017)

In an initial multicenter randomized experiment Simmons et al. (2015) compared the effect of implementing "healthy eating [HE], physical activity [PA], and both HE and PA [HE+PA]) on GDM risk" (Objective section, ¶ 1) in obese pregnant women from nine European nations. Simmons et al. found "an HE intervention among obese European women led to lower GWG, fasting glucose, and 2-h insulin concentrations by 35–37 weeks gestation than a PA intervention or a combination of the two." (p. 7) Hackethal (2015) reported that senior author of the study "Mireille van Poppel, PhD, of the VU University Medical Center in Amsterdam, the Netherlands" (¶ 2) said,

> *"More is not always better. Combining counseling on healthy eating and physical activity seems less or equally effective compared with healthy eating alone....."*
> Combining healthy eating plus physical activity might "dilute the message" or require too much change that could ultimately undermine motivation, the authors point out. (Combining Advice May Dilute the Message section, ¶s 2-3)

Study results suggest clinicians need to encourage pregnant women who are overweight and obese to implement healthy eating as a permanent part of their lifestyle.

Final Reflections

What greater miracle than to be blessed to bring a new life into the world? This new life is completely dependent on the mother's care while in the womb. Any self-respecting mother should want what's best for her child. Doing what's best involves more than just self-care for nine months. Doing what's best starts long before conception. It starts by developing a lifestyle of healthy habits at a young age. It continues throughout one's pregnancy, and even long after the child is born.

Being realistic, Orgeron knows not all pregnancies are positive experiences for women nor are all the babies wanted. In such cases, Orgeron wants to encourage these mothers experiencing unexpected, unwanted pregnancies to not abort but to seek help through counseling professionals, local homes for unwed mothers, and through local adoption agencies, if they are not in a position to give their child a good home. Psalm 127:3 tells us, "Behold, children *are* a heritage from the LORD, The fruit of the womb *is* a reward."

God alone gives life, and only He has the right to take that life. To end a child's life through abortion or any other means is murder. Too many couples are infertile wanting children. Giving one of these families the child would make a better option than having murder on one's conscience. Orgeron knows from her personal experience. Her paternal grandparents were one of those childless couples. Orgeron will probably never know who her biological paternal grandparents were or any of their families but she wants to thank them for doing the right thing. Her dad had a good life, and touched many lives on his journey to Heaven where he now resides.

Orgeron closes by encouraging birth mothers to please give any unplanned, unwanted children the opportunity to live the life God intends for them. It's the right thing to do.

.

***

Deuteronomy 5:17:
"You shall not murder."

Chapter 14: Disordered Eating and Pregnancy

Key Terms/Concepts

Body positive pregnancy   Pregorexia

Questions for Reflection:

1. What do statistics say about disordered eating among pregnant women or those women planning a pregnancy?
2. How much weight should a woman gain during pregnancy?
3. What is a body positive pregnancy? What are seven tips for pregnant women to achieve a body positive pregnancy?
4. With the approval of a physician, what should be the exercise goal for the healthy pregnant mother?
5. What physical activities are safe for pregnant women?
6. Which exercises should pregnant women refrain from doing?
7. What are the warning signs for a pregnant woman to stop exercising?
8. Are there risks to not complying with the established weight gain recommendations? If so, what are the risks?
9. Why should a new mother avoid weight gain postpartum?
10. What are three possible reasons for the connection between weight gained during and after pregnancy and the child's risk of obesity?
11. After delivery, what should mothers do to readjust their diet again, according to Mayo Clinic Staff?
12. Can mothers who breastfeed exercise?
13. What are the benefits of breastfeeding?
14. What two myths do women need to overcome postpartum
15. What are the risks of having an ED and being pregnant simultaneously?
16. What are possible consequences of being obese before and during pregnancy?
17. What about the baby? Are there risks to the child when a pregnant woman is overweight or obese?
18. Why should unexpected, unwanted pregnancies NEVER be aborted?

***

Chapter 15: Disordered Eating in Higher Education (Adapted from Owens, 2003a)

"Eating disorders affect people of all ages, but are especially prominent among college students." (Walden Center for Education and Research, 2015a, ¶ 1) Multi-Service Eating Disorders Association (MEDA), as cited by the Walden Center, reported:

> *The following statistics on college student eating disorders:*
> - *15% of women 17 to 24 have eating disorders.*
> - *20% of college students said they have or previously had an eating disorder.*
> - *91% of female college students have attempted to control their weight through dieting.* (¶ 1)

One of the biggest challenges of campus counseling centers is to identify and help students with disordered eating. According to Chelsea Kronengold, M.A., Program Coordinator at NEDA, as cited by Best Colleges (2017),

> *Eating disorders are a growing epidemic on college campuses. A longitudinal study over a 13 year period found that the rate of eating disorders among college students has risen from 7.9% to 25% for males and 23.4% to 32.6% for females (White, 2011) College is a period of development in which disordered eating is likely to arise, resurface, or worsen for many young men and women. The increased social pressure to make friends, have romantic relationships, achieve academically, and fear of the "freshman 15" are all potential risk factors for disordered eating and other maladaptive coping mechanisms for college students.* (The Rise of Eating Disorders on Campus section, ¶ 3)

Let's look further at why disordered eating is prevalent among students in higher education:

Preexisting Conditions

With disordered eating more prominent among younger populations, more students are coming into college already having experienced disordered eating. According to a national research project about college students, as cited by Eisenberg, Nicklett, Roeder, and Kirz (2011), 20% of students who responded reported they had suspicions they had experienced disordered eating in their past. Best Colleges (2017) reported "4/10 students have personally experienced an eating disorder or know someone who has." (Eating Disorders in College Section, ¶ 1)

Environmental Triggers

"Freshman 15" (Worthington, 2001). The "Freshman 15" described by Worthington is a common occurrence in college students. This is where students used to structured, healthy eating habits succumb to the temptation of having too much freedom to decide what and when to eat. Until these students learn how to make healthy choices about eating habits, weight gain may result. However, based on the results of a research study by Zahorsky and Smith (2011), NEDA (2013) suggests that the "Freshman 15" is over exaggerated on how much weight students in their first year of college gain. Zahorsky and Smith reported,

> *Freshmen gain between 2.5 to 3.5 pounds, on average, over the course of their first year of college. Compared to same-age noncollege attendees, the typical freshman gains only an additional half-pound. Instead of a spike in weight during the freshman year, college-educated individuals exhibit moderate but steady weight gain during and after college.* (Results Section, ¶ 1)

Sociocultural influences. Garner, as cited by Moriarty and Moriarty (1993), identified five sociocultural influences linked to eating disorders. These include pressure to be thin, glorification of youth, changing roles of women, the popular media, and athletic elitism and cosmetic fitness.

In college, appearance ranks high in determining a student's self-value, according to Baker (2003). College students who become strangers in a homogenous student body without the support of families often develop distorted views of society in terms of age, race, class, and body size. Even though pressures to conform are high, college students may gain weight to relieve social expectations and competition; to avoid issues such as sexual intimacy, orientation, experimentation, or intimidation; or to escape conflicting gender or ethnic role expectations. With Caucasian males still primarily dominating academia, females on campuses are at greatest risk of developing eating problems.

Stress. With stress an individualized phenomenon, according to Hudd (2000), what stresses any one student is unique. Hudd identifies different factors that can cause stress in college students, including general transition to college life, absence of family and high school friends, and the need to develop new systems of social support. Baker (2003) points out that finances can be an area of stress when college students have to deal with academics and odd jobs to afford the costs of college and living expenses. Retreating into unhealthy eating habits can be a way for college students to try to control or escape the various stressors of life.

Athletic programs. Moriarty and Moriarty (1993) report that a recent survey given by the NCAA sports-science division shows that eating disorders are now a significant problem among college athletes. Physical activity alone does not trigger eating disorders; but when physical and health educators and coaches emphasize elitism, winning and body image; they may serve to predispose students to eating disorders.

Prior Research

University students serve as the population for much prior research related to eating attitudes and behaviors. The areas studied in prior research are broad, and those included in this literature review include:

Competitive Attitude and Achievement Orientation Related to Disordered Eating

Burckle (1999) gave 198 Caucasian females from introductory psychology classes at a largely middle-class university in Maine packets of inventories that would enable her to determine the relationship between hypercompetitiveness (unhealthy) and disordered eating, personal development competitiveness (healthy) and eating disorders, and achievement orientation and disordered eating. Results of the student responses lead Burckle to conclude:

- Hypercompetitiveness, associated with various pathologies and which requires success at any cost, is related positively to DE.
- A healthy generalized competitive attitude is not linked to DE.
- A generalized need to achieve is not related to DE; but, when attractiveness was the primary domain of competition for the subjects, the motivation to achieve was related significantly to bulimic and anorexic symptoms.

Sexual Abuse and Eating Disorders

Whether sexual abuse and eating disorders are linked is debatable based on conflicting results of prior research studies. Prior research reviewed related to this topic includes:

Kinzl et al. (1994). A stratified sample of 350 females attending the University of Innsbruck, a large public institution, were asked to complete three questionnaires to assess how dysfunctional family dynamics and childhood sexual abuse relate to adult sexual dysfunctions, eating disorders, and personality development. The researchers concluded from their results that childhood sexual abuse is neither necessary nor sufficient for the later development of an eating disorder; however, results reveal that an adverse family background may be a key etiological factor.

Connors and Morse (1993). Connors and Morse reviewed research literature that investigated a possible relationship between sexual abuse and eating disorders and that used university students and clinical populations as subjects of investigation. They attributed the discrepant results found by earlier researchers to methodological issues such as diagnostic criteria, study design, and assessment techniques and to the comorbidity of eating pathology with personality disorders. Connors and Morse concluded that in general prior sexual abuse might be regarded as a risk factor in a biopsychosocial etiological model of eating disorders.

Thunberg. From the results of his study, Thunberg concluded that women who report having been sexually abused as a child seem to face a greater risk of developing an eating disorder than those who report no prior abuse. He attributed low self-esteem as one possible marker contributing to this link.

Beckman and Burns (1990). The purpose of this study was to explore the relationship between self-report of previous sexual abuse and self-report of current eating behaviors consistent with bulimia.

Results of this study offer limited support for a link between sexual abuse and bulimia. Beckman and Burns proposed that perception of control might be a key variable that mediates the possible link between sexual abuse and bulimia.

Cultural Differences in Eating Disorders

Nielsen (2000) conducted a study that compared eating disorders in 56 black female undergraduates and 353 white female undergraduates in a small, southern, coeducational, predominantly white, private university. Almost 25% of the white students reported previously or currently having an eating disorder while only 9% of the black women gave an account to an earlier or current eating disorder. A study by Heesacker (2000) comparing disordered eating in American college women with Israeli college women revealed higher levels of disordered eating among American college women. The findings were consistent with the idea that sociocultural factors may cause disordered eating.

Exercise Habits and Eating Disorders

Matheson and Crawford-Wright (2000) examined risk factors displayed by undergraduate obligatory exercisers and whether any differences in the profiles of undergraduate obligatory and non-obligatory exercisers were exhibited. Obligatory exercise, considered unhealthy, refers to exercise that causes excessive physical pain, interferes with significant relationships or work, results in a lack of time for other leisure activities, becomes an obsession, or results in other psychological problems. Among the risk factors found by Matheson and Crawford-Wright in a student obligatory exercise population that might lead to disordered eating are a feeling of social isolation, high anxiety, and body dissatisfaction.

Eating Behaviors and Grade Point Average

Trockel, Barnes, and Egget (2000) analyzed a random sample of 200 students living in on-campus residence halls at a large private university to determine the effect of several health behaviors on grade point averages. Results revealed that students who eat breakfast on average have higher grade point averages than students who go without breakfast.

Prevention Programs

Hotelling (1999) reported that before 1989 little literature could be found about disordered eating prevention in higher education. In that year Whitaker and Davis (1989) edited the book *The Bulimic College Student: Evaluation, Treatment, and Prevention*. Prevention programs by Clark, Levine, and Kinney (1989), Hotelling (1989), and Sesan (1989) were included in this book.

Martz and Bazzini (1999) conducted two studies at a rural Southeastern university to evaluate the impact of one-shot interventions aimed at preventing eating disorders. Both studies indicated only minimum benefits to the implementation of the programs.   Another prevention program at Stanford, according to Marble (1997), as cited by Owens (2003a), proved of little value. This prevention program consisted of attending a 90-minute discussion lead by two students. One student was a recovered anorexic patient and the second student was in recovery from bulimia.

Phelps, Dempsey, Sapia, and Nelson (1999) applied a six session prevention program initially designed for high school students to college-aged females by comparing two sororities, one of which its members completed the program and a second group used as a control group. The prevention model was altered to be age-appropriate which resulted in four sessions designed to reduce the internalization of sociocultural pressures, to increase physical self-esteem and build personal competence, to reduce body dissatisfaction and explore healthy methods of weight management and to give participants an example of a personal success story of an individual recovered from an eating disorder. Experimental-control posttest comparisons revealed that the program significantly lowered current utilization and future intentional use of fasting, excessive exercise, purging, diet aids, water pills, or laxatives as weight management tools. Likewise, pre- to posttest comparisons with the experimental group confirmed the efficacy of the program in significantly increasing physical self-esteem; notably increasing personal efficacy; and, significantly decreasing body dissatisfaction.

EDReferral.com (n.d.b) lists the current major eating disorder centers affiliated with a college or university. For colleges or universities not listed, Orgeron recommends checking with the specific institution's health or wellness center to see what is available on campus for students.

The Role of Student Personnel

All physical and health education teachers, coaches, administrators, and guidance counselors play key roles in the prevention of eating disorders among college students. These professionals are in a position to offer healthy alternatives to the sociocultural influences that often lead to eating disorders. Moriarty and Moriarty (1993) encouraged teachers and coaches to familiarize themselves with the following five "Ps":

Predisposition. Teachers, coaches, counselors and other persons working with college students need to know who is predisposed to developing eating disorders. Caucasian women, athletes, and dancers are among those most commonly reported to be at high risk for having issues related to eating and body image.

Precipitation. What precipitates disordered eating in students? Knowing the answer to this question and being sensitive to changes in the lives of students and athletes can help teachers; coaches and other professionals identify students and athletes at-risk for disordered eating.

Perpetuation. In terms of perpetuation, individuals working with college students need to recognize the addictive nature of unhealthy eating patterns. Reasoning with students wrapped up in unhealthy attitudes and behaviors towards eating is difficult. "Tough love" often must be used to facilitate students with disordered eating in getting help.

Professional help. What type of professional help is available to students? All personnel at the higher educational level should know what resources are available on campus to help students with eating or body image issues. If campus facilities are inadequate, students should be referred to reputable doctors and therapists who treat eating disorders off campus.

Prevention. A common theme found in this literature review related to the prevention of eating disorders is that prevention is the best form of treatment. When teachers, coaches, and other administrators fulfill the role of detection and referral of students with disordered eating, more serious consequences of eating disorders that can lead to death may be prevented. At this point feel free to review the preventive measures offered by The Renfrew Center (2002) cited earlier in Chapter 9: Prevention of Disordered Eating, The Role of the Educator section.

Haberman and Luffey (1998) gave suggestions to help prevent obesity and combat disordered eating on college and university campuses. Among these suggestions are:

- College health services can take proactive roles in promoting healthy exercise by referring students to fitness resources on campus. If exercise facilities are unavailable on a campus, health services can advocate for such a facility.

- College health clinicians should routinely provide consultations for weight loss, eating disorders, cholesterol control and healthy nutrition topics. They also can offer large group sessions on topics such as sports nutrition, women's nutrition, and men's health that are applicable to large numbers of students.

- College food services in collaboration with college health services should ensure that quick and healthy meals and snacks are easily accessible and easily recognizable.

- Off-campus dining facilities and food markets can be advertised in campus newsletters and Web sites.

In summary, in this article Orgeron highlights literature reviewed concerned with disordered eating in students of higher education. Initially the etiology of this problem was considered. Then prior studies that related to disordered eating and that used college or university students as subjects were outlined. Lastly, Orgeron discusses the role of student personnel in higher education in the prevention of disordered eating in student bodies.

Based on her research, Owens (2003a) recommended that all student personnel in higher education take an active role individually and collectively in trying to reduce the amount of disordered eating on campuses. In addition to offering classes, brochures, seminars and individual guidance directly related to disordered eating, educating students on other indirectly related topics might help to reduce disordered eating on campuses. Among these topics would be anger and stress management, overcoming adversity, sexual abuse, and how to help a friend or loved one with disordered eating. When personnel at the highest levels of higher education realize the scope of disordered eating and actively decide to make a difference, through the trickle-down effect that results in a comprehensive defense against disordered eating, more serious health conditions and perhaps even a premature death in a student might be avoided.

***

Chapter 15: Disordered Eating in Higher Education

Key Terms/Concepts

Five "Ps" of prevention for student personnel   Hypercompetitiveness
Freshman 15   Obligatory exercise

Questions for Reflection:

1. What are potential risk factors for DE and other unhealthy coping behaviors in college students?
2. What things in the environment of college students can trigger an eating disorder?
3. What do studies show about cultural differences and DE?
4. In a study by Matheson and Crawford-Wright, what were the risk factors found in a student obligatory exercise population that might lead to disordered eating?
5. Do eating behaviors affect grade point averages?
6. What roles can student personnel play in the prevention of eating disorders among college students?
7. What are suggestions given to help prevent obesity and combat disordered eating on college and university campuses?

***

Chapter 16: Disordered Eating in Males

With eating disorders traditionally known as a "woman's illness", "males suffering from eating disorders and body image issues have an immense stigma to overcome…." (Strother, Lemberg, Stanford, & Turberville, 2014, p. 13) Child and Adolescent Psychologist Mae Sokol, M.D. (Menninger Psychiatric Hospital, Topeka, Kansas), as cited by Brooks, (2001), said,

> *"The public thinks of it as a 'girl disease,' and these guys don't want to have to come out and say, 'I have a girl disease.' Plus, to have to come to a [treatment facility] where most of the patients are women -- they don't feel good about that at all."* (Brooks, ¶ 14)

"…The availability of treatment and difficulty admitting to a problem means men are much less likely than women to get help. The Center • A Place of HOPE offers eating disorder programs designed specifically for men." (The Center – A Place of Hope, 2017, ¶ 1)

Why the Concern in Males?

With research on disordered eating in men mostly neglected throughout history, Anderson (2014) reports seven reasons this ought not to be:

- Eating disorders are dangerous and can lead to death.
- Eating disorders in men are commonly overlooked, minimized, or ignored completely for somewhat inexplicable reasons.
- Eating disorders in men "raise intellectually intriguing scientific, sociocultural, and historical questions." (p. 4)
- Eating disorders in men present physicians and therapists with challenges in diagnosis and treatment.
- Eating disorders in men exemplify tendencies in public and medical prejudice over time.
- Eating disorders in men seem to be increasing significantly in onset and incidence.
- Eating disorders in men "raise issues of spirituality and what constitutes a peaceable relationship to the factual and imagined body in which we live and move." (p. 4)

The National Association for Males with Eating Disorders (NAMED) (2017) is dedicated to guidance in the male disordered eating arena. They offer support to boys and men touched by disordered eating. NAMED provides access to combined knowledge from experts in the field. They also encourage the improvement of effective medical intervention and investigation of males with disordered eating.

NAMED (2017) reported 10 facts that should raise more concern for the problem of disordered eating in males. These are:

1. *25-40% of people with eating disorders are males (Hudson, [Hiripi, Pope, & Kessler] 2007).*
2. *As many men as women want to change their weight (Andersen, [Cohn, & Holbrook], 2000).*

3. *Men engage in eating-disordered behaviors nearly as often as women (Mond, [Mitchison, & Hay,] 2014).*

4. *Eating disorders assessment tests underscore males (Darcy [& Lin], 2014 [sic]).*

5. *Additionally, prevalence of eating disorders in males is greater than estimated because men are often too stigmatized to seek treatment for "women's problems." (Cohn, 2013)*

6. *Despite popular beliefs, eating disorders have never been "women's diseases," and professionals in the field are realizing this fact more and more (Cohn [& Lemberg], 2014).*

7. *The earliest case descriptions of anorexia nervosa by Richard Morton in 1690 included cases of a man and a woman (Andersen, 2014).*

8. *Media objectification and sexualization of males is just as rampant as for females (Cohn, 2013).*

9. *A high percentage of comorbid conditions exist for males in treatment, such as excessive exercise, poor body image, and issues with sexuality (Weltzin [et al.], 2014)*

10. *Attention to gender dynamics is critical in the process of treatment.* (Bunnell [& Maine], 2014). (MALES & ED link, 10 Facts about males and eating disorders section)

How EDs Differ in Males and Females

Raevuori, Keski-Rahkonen, and Hoek (2014) reported that research has "…consistently shown that symptoms and risk factors for eating disorders vary by sex…." (Conclusion section, ¶ 1) A number of issues exist where the manifestation of disordered eating differs between males and females. "Included among these are: weight history, sexual abuse and other trauma, gender orientation, depression and shame, exercise and body image, comorbid chemical dependency, and media pressures." (Strother et al., 2014, p. 14) Raevuori et al., (2014) also reported distinctions between disordered eating in males and females. Differences they reported are "risk factors, clinical presentation, comorbidity, and consequences." (Risk Factors, Clinical Presentation, and Comorbidity section, ¶ 1) In terms of evaluating EDs in males and females, Welles (2017) reported, "Common 'red flags' used for assessing the degree of medical compromise in women—amenorrhea, low body mass index (BMI)—do not exist in male patients with eating disorders, potentially causing delayed referrals to appropriate levels of care." (¶ 2)

Weight History

The first distinction noted by Strother et al. (2014) where males and females differ in the presentation of eating disorders is with weight histories. Males commonly have experienced mild to moderate obesity sometime prior to developing an ED and are especially vulnerable if they were obese as children. This differs from women where they only felt overweight with no history of abnormal weight. Research reported by Raevuori et al. (2014) supports the work by Strother et al..

The motives of using compensatory behaviors to maintain or lose weight also differ with the sexes, according to Strother et al. (2014). Males typically use compensatory behaviors, for example exercise, to ward off medical conditions experienced by their fathers; while, women's motives are grounded in the desire to be thin. Additionally, Raevuori et al. (2014) and Strother et al. report more males than females want to lose or gain weight for athletic reasons, such as to be able to play their best at a particular sport. In the cases of males where weight gain is desired for athletic reasons, the goal would be to gain weight in the form of muscle rather than losing fat. (Cohn & Murray, 2014; NEDC, n.d.) NEDC reported, "Over-exercising and the extreme pursuit of muscle growth are frequently seen as healthy behaviours for males and can even be actively encouraged. The truth is that these activities can indicate a significant disorder and lead to severe physical health problems." (What are the warning signs of eating disorders in males? section, ¶ 3)

Sexual Abuse and Other Trauma

PTSD and disordered eating often co-exist, "particularly as individuals suffering from an eating disorder usually report a history of trauma." (Ekern, 2017a, Connection and Relationship between Trauma and Eating Disorders section, ¶ 1) Farrar (2014) reported, "Trauma comes in the form of neglect, abuse, accidents, and of course attacks such as sexual assault or rape." (¶ 1) Orgeron would add natural disasters to Farrar's list. "It is suggested that engagement in eating disorder behaviors may be a method of coping with the discomforting emotions and experiences correlated with PTSD." (Ekern, Connection and Relationship between Trauma and Eating Disorders section, ¶ 1)

As Farrar (2014) reported, Orgeron understands that "correlations do not necessarily indicate causes." (¶ 2) However, in her situation she believes that her past abuse was a strong catalyst for the development of her past ED. Farrar reported, "If abuse and trauma actually caused eating disorders, then every person suffering from Post Traumatic Stress Disorder would go on to develop an eating disorder. This is simply not the case…" (¶ 2) Orgeron proposes that in such cases where an ED doesn't develop following abuse or other type of trauma there may have been a third mediating factor that thwarted the development of an ED—for example, a strong emphasis on healthy eating with it exemplified by the family in the home.

In 2004 Orgeron explored the questions of whether sexual trauma influences eating behavior, and if so, how and why does sexual abuse affect eating attitudes and behaviors. Her literature review linked the etiology, treatment, and prevention of sexual abuse and disordered eating. "After reviewing the literature and considering her own experience, Orgeron concluded that sexual abuse does predispose a victim to develop disordered eating attitudes and behaviors later. However, the researcher surmises stress is the primary mediating factor between sexual abuse and disordered eating." (Orgeron, 2004, p. 69)

One study at Michigan State University found that although women experience sexual harassment more than men, "men who experience high levels of sexual harassment are much more likely than women to induce vomiting and take laxatives and diuretics in an attempt to control their weight." (Buchanan, 2013, ¶ 1) What is sexual harassment? Nordqvist (2013) reported,

> *There are different forms of sexual harassment, it is generally considered to be bullying of a sexual nature. It typically includes giving inappropriate rewards or privileges in exchange for some form of sexual favor. Sexual harassment is a major cause of anxiety and depression as well as a leading cause of dysfunctional eating and concerns about body image. (¶s 8-9)*

Nicole Buchanan, central author in the investigation, reported to her surprise that the results are the first to show "men are significantly more likely to engage in purging 'compensatory' behaviors at high levels of sexual harassment." (Buchanan, ¶ 3)

Brewerton (2016) reported,

> *Individuals with an eating disorder complicated by trauma and PTSD require treatment for both conditions using a trauma-informed, integrated approach (Brewerton, 2004; Brewerton, 2007; SAMHSA, 2014). If the trauma is not addressed during the treatment of an eating disorder, then it is likely that successful recovery will be thwarted.* (Treatment section, ¶ 1)

Gender Orientation

Having a homosexual gender orientation places males at a greater risk for disordered eating. (Brooks, 2001; EdReferral.com, n.d.a; Hall, 2017; Raevuori et al. 2014; Strother et al., 2014) While the increased incidence of EDs among men is now being recognized, what is less well known "is that eating disorder rates are increased amongst the sexual minority community compared to their 'straight' counterparts." (Hall, ¶ 2) According to NEDA (2016c), "Gay men are thought to only represent 5% of the total male population but among men who have eating disorders, 42% identify as gay." (Research on LGBT Populations and Eating Disorders section, Bullet 6) "Some men, who experience confusion around sexual orientation, find comfort in weight loss as a product of restricted eating. In anorexia, severe weight loss creates changes in the body's physiology, including lower testosterone levels, resulting for some, in asexuality." (Strother et al., p. 16) For males who report being a transgender, Hall reported that "an eating disorder can develop in conjunction with body dysmorphia, as a way of changing the way their body looks, because they have so many negative associations with it in its existing form." (An Attempt to Change The Body section, ¶ 1)

Why the higher risk? NEDA (2016c) reported possible influences interact in men who identify as anything outside of heterosexuality that put them at higher risk for developing ED. These influences are:

- *Coming out: Fear of rejection/experience of rejections by friends, family and co-workers*
- *Internalized negative messages/beliefs about oneself due to sexual orientation, non-normative gender expressions, or transgender identity*
- *Experiences of violence (gay bashing), contributing to development of Post-Traumatic Stress Disorder, which research shows sharply increases vulnerability to an eating disorder*
- *Discrimination*
- *Being bullied*
- *Discordance between one's biological sex and gender identity* (¶ 3)

Challenges in receiving treatment. In addition to having unique etiological factors, homosexual men have problems finding help with recovery. One barrier is the lack of professionals trained in this issue. Legislation and professional associations protect clinicians from being forced to treat such cases that are out of their areas of expertise. To exemplify, Orgeron includes an updated excerpt from *We Survived Sexual Abuse! You Can Too!* (ABC's Ministries, 2016):

The state of Tennessee recently passed a bill protecting the religious rights of therapists and counselors. According to Locker and Meyer (2016, April 27), Tennessee Governor Bill Haslam

> *signed into law a controversial bill that says no licensed counselor or therapist must serve a client whose "goals, outcomes or behaviors" conflict with the counselor's "sincerely held principles" — a measure the American Counseling Association had denounced as a "hate bill" against gay and transgender people.*
>
> *Senate Bill 1556 also shields from civil lawsuits, criminal prosecution and sanctions by the state licensing board counselors who refuse to provide services — provided they coordinate a referral of the client to another counselor who would serve them.*
>
> *The bill's provisions, which go into effect immediately, also will not apply in cases where the person seeking or undergoing counseling is "in imminent danger of harming themselves or others." (¶ 1)*

Orgeron believes Haslam did the right thing, and that this law should become national legislation. Why? One of the first responsibilities of a counselor is to do no harm. Throughout her counseling coursework in primarily secular counseling courses students were taught a key principle to remember in counseling is to refer out whenever a client's issues are outside our area of expertise or whenever we feel that we are not a good "fit" for the prospective client. This is very similar to how medical doctors work. MD's like Counselors have areas of expertise. Would you want a heart surgeon treating a high risk pregnancy or a brain surgeon treating a pre-mature baby? No, of course not! That's why counselors should refer out when the client's issues are outside his or her area of expertise or comfort zone.

As an AACC member, Orgeron is committed to following the standards of this organization. As a Christian, ultimately she is accountable to following the words of Scripture, which she believes the AACC Code of Ethics also endorses ultimately, The AACC Y-2014 Code of Ethics, regarding LGBT behaviors, stipulates under "1-120: Refusal to Participate in the Harmful Actions of Clients":

1-120-f: Application to Homosexual, Bisexual and Transgendered Behavior

Christian counselors do not condone or advocate for the pursuit of or active involvement in homosexual, bisexual or transgendered behaviors and lifestyles. Counselors may agree to and support the desire to work through issues of homosexual and transgendered identity and attractions, but will not describe or reduce human identity and nature to sexual orientation or reference, and will encourage sexual celibacy or biblically-prescribed sexual behavior while such issues are being addressed. Counselors acknowledge the client's fundamental right to self-determination and further understand that deeply held religious values and beliefs may conflict with same-sex attraction and/or behavior, resulting in anxiety, depression, stress, and inner turmoil.

Given the truth in the above statement, as long as a counselor refers out to a reputable secular counselor where the person would be a better "fit" for the issue at hand, no harm is done. The referral should be interpreted as if a Medical Specialist were referring to another Medical Specialist. (pp. 51-53)

A second barrier to homosexual, asexual, and transgendered men getting help may be the absence of an accepting family or friend support group. There are incidents where males have been excommunicated from their families of origin or circle of friends after "coming out" that they do not identify with the "normal" and only biblically moral male sexual orientation, heterosexuality.

Regardless of a male's sexual orientation, recovery from disordered eating is not easy. However, Orgeron believes that men identifying as homosexual, asexual, or transgendered can find the same cleansing, forgiveness, and healing of DE through the blood of Jesus Christ that she herself experienced.

Depression and Shame

Men with disordered eating frequently feel depressed and shameful (Brooks, 2001; EdReferral.com, n.d.a; Strother et al., 2014; Weltzin et al., 2014; Winter & Lemberg, 2014). "Hidden depression drives several of the problems we think of as typically male: physical illness, alcohol and drug abuse, domestic violence, failures in intimacy, self-sabotage in careers" (Real, 1997, p. 22), "and now eating disorders are added to this list." (Strother et al., p. 16)

"We tend not to recognize depression in men because the disorder itself is seen as unmanly. Depression carries, to many, a double stain—the stigma of mental illness and also the stigma of 'feminine' emotionality." (Real, 1997, p. 22) Furthermore, similar to disordered eating, due to customary gender socialization, "men tend to manifest depression differently than women." (Real, p. 23) To exemplify this difference, Orgeron suggests a man feeling depressed might turn to alcohol or drugs to repress his feelings while a woman feeling depressed might isolate from others to cry out what she is feeling.

Exercise and Body Image

Exercise and body image concerns commonly present with both men and women displaying disordered eating attitudes and behaviors, according to research. (EdReferral.com, n.d.a; Klass, 2015; Mitchison & Mond, 2015; Morgan, 2002; NEDC, 2017; Pope, Phillips, & Olivardia, 2000; Strother et al., 2014; Weltzin, 2014) However, the motives behind and the consequences from these concerns differ with the sexes. How so? First, women talk about the issues; men don't. "No man is in the locker room talking about our abs," said Keon Addison, owner of Unleashed Potential, a boot camp in Montgomery. "We're talking about the lawn we're about to go mow. Cars. We actually want to show our strength and communicate in a different way. The locker room talk is not what (women) talk about." (Klass, ¶ 6) Although, men do not discuss their exercise and body image concerns like women do does not mean they do not think about them. According to Klass,

Nearly half of men surveyed in a TODAY Health/AOL Body Image survey last year said they think about their personal appearance several times each day. Of those surveyed:
• 63 percent of guys said they always feel like they could lose weight.
• 53 percent don't like having their picture taken.
• 41 percent said they worry that people judge their appearance.
• 44 percent feel uncomfortable wearing swim trunks. (What the numbers show section, ¶ 1)

Addison, as cited by Klass (2015), also pointed out, men look in mirrors. Addison said, "We are some vain people. We are our worst critic. One of the things we do when we look in the mirror, is we flex. And while we're getting our arms strong and our chest strong, there's a belly." (Klass, ¶ 6) Addison attributed the "belly" to some men's drinking and/or not eating healthy. Speaking of adult men having a "belly", Mitchison and Mond (2015) reported BED has the highest incidence of all the EDs in grown men.

"Exercise concerns are common in males with eating disorders as over 50 percent of males presenting for eating disorder treatment at Rogers Memorial Hospital report problematic exercise behaviors," (Weltzin, 2014, ¶ 2) according to "Theodore E. Weltzin, MD, FAED, FAPA, Medical Director of Eating Disorders Services at Rogers Memorial Hospital and Assistant Clinical Professor of Psychiatry at the Medical College of Wisconsin, Milwaukee." (¶ 1) Weltzin reported males with EDs who have exercise concerns typically exercise for one of two reasons. First, men can use exercise similar to how alcoholics use alcohol as an addictive agent to elevate one's mood. Strother et al. (2014) reported this behavior "is sometimes referred to as Anorexia Athleticism." (p. 16) The second group of men with EDs abusing exercise is the "'compulsive' exercisers. These individuals have highly ritualized exercise behaviors that create anxiety when disrupted and often have co-occurring obsessive-compulsive symptoms not related to exercise." (¶ 5)

NEDC (2017) reported, "For males, body dissatisfaction is more commonly manifested as the pursuit of a muscular, lean physique rather than a lower body weight." (Body Dissatisfaction section, ¶ 1) When this pursuit of muscularity becomes an obsessive preoccupation, Pope et al. (2000) call it "muscle dysmorphia".

No longer is ED and body image problems considered just a part of the woman's world. Morgan (2002) reported,

> *A growing number of researchers say that men are suffering as well – and are reluctant to seek help. Some student health directors say they see an increasing number of college men who have eating disorders or unhealthy obsessions with their appearance – although few if any colleges have set up programs tailored to men. And some researchers cite studies that show that binge eating has become as prevalent for college men as binge drinking – with about 40 percent of them doing it. One group of researchers has a name for severe body-image problems in men: "the Adonis complex." (It's a Man's World, Too section, ¶ 1)*

What is the Adonis Complex? Pope et al. (2000), authors of the book *The Adonis Complex: How to Identify, Treat, and Prevent Body Obsession in Men and Boys* (Simon & Schuster, 2002) noted "'Adonis Complex' isn't an official medical term." (p. 6) They use the expression "Adonis Complex" to denote a group of "usually secret, but surprisingly common, body image concerns of boys and men. These concerns range from minor annoyances to devastating and sometimes even life-threatening obsessions—from manageable dissatisfaction to full-blown psychiatric body image disorders." (pp. 6-7) When these concerns are extreme, body dysmorphic disorder (BDD) may be diagnosed. "The general category of BDD refers to all types of serious unfounded body image concerns. Muscle dysmorphia is simply the form of BDD in which muscularity, as opposed to some other aspect of the body, becomes the focus." (Pope et al., p. 154) According to Pope et al., the Adonis complex makes up all the different forms of body obsessions present in today's world in men. Among them are: chest needs to be bigger; stomach needs to be flatter; body needs more muscle (muscle dysmorphia); hair is too thin; breasts are too fat; and penis isn't big enough. Based on her understanding of the Adonis Complex, Orgeron believes one of the worst forms of the disorder would be gender dysphoria. The DSM-5 (APA, 2013) identifies the criteria for a diagnosis of gender dysphoria in grown men and adolescents as a striking difference between one's biological gender and experienced gender for a minimum period of six months, as expressed by a minimum of two of the following criteria:

1. *A marked incongruence between one's experienced/expressed gender and primary and/or secondary sex characteristics (or in young adolescents, the anticipated secondary sex characteristic).*

2. *A strong desire to be rid of one's primary and/or secondary sex characteristics because of a marked incongruence with one's experienced/expressed gender (or in young adolescents, a desire to prevent the development of the anticipated secondary sex characteristics).*

3. *A strong desire for the primary and/or secondary sex characteristics of the other gender.*

4. *A strong desire to be of the other gender (or some alternative gender different from one's assigned gender).*

5. *A strong desire to be treated as the other gender (or some alternative gender different from one's assigned gender).*

6. *A strong conviction that one has the typical feelings and reactions of the other gender (or some alternative gender different from one's assigned gender).* (p. 452)

Additionally, "The condition is associated with clinically significant distress or impairment in social, occupational, or other important areas of functioning." (p. 453) In the context of the APA's criteria reported above,

> *"experienced/expressed gender" refers to the gender that the person subjectively identifies as or wishes to be publicly recognized as—what is often referred to as "gender identity"—while "assigned gender" refers in almost all cases to his or her unambiguous biological sex. (In rare cases, a person's biological sex is difficult to determine; such "intersex" individuals are born with biological features of both sexes. Most transgender individuals are not biologically intersex. [Rothkopf, & John, 2014])"* (Hruz, Mayer, & McHugh, 2017, pp. 3-4)

With the previously mentioned unhealthy preoccupations, males are "dieting" more; abusing exercise, diet aids and other drugs to "muscle up"; and wasting money on products and surgeries that often turn out to be worthless. For anyone who knows someone identifying with any of the previously mentioned body dissatisfactions, Orgeron's advice is to get professional help.

Comorbid Chemical Dependency

Dennis and Helfman (2016) and Strother et al. (2014) reported around 57% of men with BED also wrestle with substance abuse. That's compared with 28% of women. (Strother et al.) Costin (2007) reported around 24 % of individuals who are diagnosed with bulimia abuse or depend on alcohol.

"Although alcohol use in anorexia is not as common, this combination results in the highest death rate." (Costin, p. 33)

Stimulants used to lose weight among those with EDs are on the rise. (Costin, 2007; Strother et al., 2014)

> *Drugs such as cocaine and methamphetamine are increasingly used to curtail appetite and lose weight rather than to get high. Drug treatment programs often miss this fact. Celebrities who have obvious eating disorders are unfortunately ending up in drug rehab for this reason and because it is more acceptable to have a drug problem than an eating disorder.* (Costin, p. 33)

"Eating disorders and substance abuse are independently correlated with higher than expected rates of death both from medical complications as well as suicide." (Dennis & Helfman, 2016, ¶ 1) Thus, Orgeron cannot stress enough the importance of getting help for anyone suffering from an ED and substance abuse problem. The first step to treating an individual with an ED and substance abuse problem is to make sure the person has been detoxed with all the substance out of their system. Only after detoxing can an individual be treated effectively. Treatment works best when both the ED and the substance abuse issue are treated simultaneously.

Media Pressures

Messages from the media can negatively affect both males and females. "'Male body image industries'—purveyors of food supplements, diet aids, fitness programs, hair-growth remedies, and countless other products—now prey increasingly on men's worries, just as analogous industries have preyed for decades on the appearance-related insecurities of women." (Pope et al., 2000, p. 5) However, according to NEDC (n.d.), four negative cultural or media messages are exclusive to males. These are:

- *Males should only have one body type – the ideal physical body shape for men is now more prescribed with lean, muscular body types in fashion to the exclusion of other male body types*
- *You are what you look like - males are more at risk if they conflate having a 'perfect body' with success in other areas such as dating, getting a good job, and social desirability*
- *Males need to be in control – males can be expected to 'take charge' and be 'in control'. When coping with particular issues beyond their control, males can sometimes displace these anxieties onto their bodies, manifesting in control over the body through excessive exercise and dieting*
- *Eating disorders and other mental illnesses are not masculine – males can be expected to conceal personality traits and vulnerabilities that have traditionally been associated with females. A desire not to appear weak or vulnerable has led to a stigma around mental illness that has delayed treatment and support for many males with eating disorders. This stigma has been further exacerbated by the popular misconception that eating disorders are a 'female's disease'.* (What are the risks for males? section, ¶ 1)

Cultivation theory (Morgan, Shanahan, & Signorielli, 2008) suggests that regular exposure to the media cultivates an inaccurate perception of reality in individuals as over time they accept these inaccurate images as reality. "Accordingly, the surge in media portrayals of the muscular male ideal may lead men to believe that it is possible, even necessary, to achieve a v-shaped, muscular body oneself." (Schooler & Ward, 2006, p. 28)

Warning Signs of ED in Males

NEDC (2017) reported warning signs that more commonly occur in males than females. These are:

- *Preoccupation with body building, weight lifting or muscle toning*
- *Weight lifting when injured*
- *Lowered testosterone*
- *Anxiety/stress over missing workouts*
- *Muscular weakness*
- *Decreased interest in sex, or fears around sex*
- *Possible conflict over gender identity or sexual orientation*
- *Using anabolic steroids* (What are the warning signs of eating disorders? section, ¶ 2).

Disordered Eating in Boys

"A survey shows that L.A. male high school students are about as likely as females to use diet aids or laxatives or vomiting to lose weight. The numbers challenge old assumptions." (Alpert, 2013, Subtitle) Professionals report boys now face the same influences as girls, as unrealistic images of muscle men thrive in pop culture. The constant talk of social websites such as Facebook and Twitter also fuels the fire, Alpert reported.

> *Los Angeles isn't the only city where boys have been increasingly likely to purge or turn to diet substances, with higher-than-average rates also seen in Chicago, Houston, Charlotte, N.C., and elsewhere. Government estimates show that the number of males hospitalized for eating disorders rose 53% between 1999 and 2009. Some experts say they are unsure whether more boys and men are in fact suffering such disorders or whether more are now willing to seek help.* (Alpert, ¶ 12)

"'Eating disorders don't discriminate,' says Julia Taylor, a school counselor at Apex High School, in Apex, North Carolina, and author of *Perfectly You*, a children's book on body image." (Rubenstein, 2010, ¶ 3) Taylor, as cited by Rubenstein, reported having worked with innumerable boys with poor body image and harmful eating and exercise habits. Yet, Taylor said, "[n]one has had a diagnosed eating disorder—and that's part of the problem." (Rubenstein, ¶ 3) In their experience, Pope et al. (2000) noted "A recurrent theme … is that their parents often had no idea of what was happening in their sons' minds." (p. 193)

How Boys Differ From Girls

As with older males and females, EDs affect boys and girls differently. Below are differences Orgeron found through her literature review:

- Young males are able to hide their illness longer from parents than young females. (Brooks, 2016; Pope et al., 2000)
- Young males also have higher rates of "comorbid depression, substance use, and a history of suicidal ideation." (Brooks, Sex Differences section, ¶ 4)
- Despite having more psychiatric issues, young males are less likely to receive treatment. (Brooks) According to Brooks, "Samuel Ridout, MD, PhD, Department of Psychiatry and Human Behavior, Butler Hospital, Providence, Rhode Island" (Brooks, ¶ 2) said, for young males to have more psychiatric issues is significant "'because males complete suicide at much higher rates, at about 3 to 1.' Therefore, consequences of missed opportunities for intervention may be higher in young male adolescents, Dr. Ridout said." (¶ 7)
- "Boys are more likely to focus on building huge muscle mass, exercising to extremes, and even taking unhealthy supplements or steroids -- though not all boys with eating disorders do." (Rubenstein, 2010, ¶ 8) Research reported by Pope et al. (2000) supports Rubenstein's statement.

Risk Factors of DE in Boys

What makes a boy more susceptible to developing DE? Below are the main factors Orgeron found in her literature review:

- Identifying as gay or bisexual. "In one study, gay and bisexual boys reported being significantly more likely to have fasted, vomited or taken laxatives or diet pills to control their weight in the last 30 days." (NEDA, 2016c, Research on LGBT Populations and Eating Disorders, Point 3)
- Being homeless or having a dangerous home environment. NEDA reported:

  * Up to 42% of homeless youth are LGBT-identified
  * 33% of youth who are homeless or in the care of social services experienced violent assault when they came out. (Potential factors that may interact with LGBT person's pre-disposition for developing an eating disorder may include, but are not limited to: section, Bullet 7)

- Athletic participation
- Dieting
- Perfectionism
- Having an unhealthy relationship with fathers (May, Kim, McHale, & Crouter, C., 2006).
- "Overvaluation of body weight and/or shape" (Mitchison & Mond, 2015, p. 4)

The Role of the Media

"Mass media exposure is a key factor in the development of body image disturbance and disordered eating among youth and adolescents." (Levine & Harrison, 2008, p. 490) Over the years male action figures have gone from looking like "normal" healthy men to looking like men with muscles that could only be acquired through the use of steroids. "Boys are exposed to these figures while they are still very young—long before they are old enough to form an independent opinion about what a realistic man's body should look like." (Pope et al., p. 44) As they age, boys are exposed to wrestlers and other professional athletes who sometimes developed their muscles through the inappropriate use of steroids. Add to that the exposure to all the air brushed images in health and fitness magazines—not to mention comic books, movies, and television that depict men with unhealthy, unrealistic builds for males. Is it any wonder why young boys and adolescents are presenting with an increasing number of body image and DE problems?

The Adonis Complex in Boys

The Adonis Complex exemplified in boys. Pope et al. (2000) reported the Adonis Complex has a number of forms in boys. Among these forms are body shape dissatisfaction, not being tall enough, having acne, not having enough muscle, having too much fat, and not having enough pubic hair, hair on their legs, or on other areas of their body. If "a strong dislike of one's sexual anatomy" (APA, 2013, p. 452) exists, these boys may be developing gender dysphoria. Among other criteria for a diagnosis of gender dysphoria in boys includes wearing girls' clothes, preferring to take on girl roles in play, playing with dolls and other activities stereotypically played with by girls, and rejecting masculine toys and other activities typically played with by boys.

Warning signs. What should parents and others who work with boys look for if they suspect a boy has the Adonis Complex? Pope et al. (2000) listed twelve "clues" highlighting the key behaviors to watch for. These clues or warning signs are:

1. Working out unduly
2. Preoccupation with looking like male images depicted in the media
3. Using too many "dietary supplements, such as creatinine or protein powders, hoping to build up his body and become more muscular." (p. 194)
4. Using drugs bought in health food stores (e.g.: ephedrine) to develop muscle
5. Symptoms of steroid use (e.g.: mood swings during rapid muscle growth)
6. Unhealthy weight fluctuations
7. Using unsafe weight loss methods (e.g.: fasting, using laxatives or fluid pills)
8. Spending an excessive amount of time looking in a mirror or other reflective surface
9. Spending an excessive amount of time primping or spending an excessive amount of money on products to improve appearance (e.g.: skin and hair products)
10. Wearing bulky clothes to camouflage his appearance
11. Constantly asking others how he looks
12. Hesitating to leave the house for any reason (not wanting to be seen by others at school, etc.)

For boys with gender dysphoria, "natal boys may shave their legs at the first signs of hair growth. They may sometimes bind their genitals to make erections less visible." (APA, p. 454)

While there is much that is not known with certainty about gender dysphoria, there is clear evidence that patients who identify as the opposite sex often suffer a great deal. They have higher rates of anxiety, depression, and even suicide than the general population. Something must be done to help these patients, but as scientists struggle to better understand what gender dysphoria is and what causes it, it would not seem prudent to embrace hormonal treatments and sex reassignment as the foremost therapeutic tools for treating this condition. (Hruz, Mayer, & McHugh, 2017, p. 27)

Ryan T. Anderson (2017), author of the upcoming book *When Harry Became Sally: Responding to the Transgender Moment* (Encounter Books, 2018) reports, "80 to 95% of children with gender dysphoria will come to identify with and embrace their bodily sex." (¶ 11) Furthermore, Anderson noted 41% of those claiming to be transgender attempt suicide in comparison to 4.6 % of the over-all population. Additionally, those who have undergone sex-change operations "are 19 times more likely than average to die by suicide." (¶ 13)

In terms of treatment, "As I explain in 'When Harry Became Sally,' the most helpful therapies focus not on achieving the impossible—changing bodies to conform to thoughts and feelings—but on helping people accept and even embrace the truth about their bodies and reality." (Anderson, 2017, Puberty Blocking May Have Long-Term Health Consequences section, ¶ 10) Agreeing with Anderson's approach to treatment for gender dysphoria (with application also to other forms of the Adonis Complex), Orgeron encourages parents or other caregivers who know boys who manifest any of the aforementioned "clues" or warning signs to not ignore the behaviors but take them seriously and get professional counsel, preferably biblically based.

The Role of the Parents

What should parents and other caretakers do when they suspect a boy has DE or the Adonis Complex? Pope et al. (2000) offered 10 suggestions that can be integrated into the daily schedule if a parent or caretaker suspects a boy has the Adonis Complex. Orgeron adapts their list to include DE as follows:

1. Self-educate on the issues at hand.
2. Look for the signs of DE or the Adonis Complex. Don't ignore the signs.
3. Listen to what the boy has to say.
4. Discuss the boy's body image or weight concerns with him.
5. Don't blame. Educate him on how what he might be doing can harm him.
6. Avoid criticism and teasing. Criticizing and teasing one about appearance only makes the situation worse.
7. Reassure the boy about his appearance. If that doesn't help, suggest professional help for the boy.
8. "Encourage your son not to buy into society's unrealistic, media images." (Pope et al., p. 199)
9. Encourage the boy to find other ways to build a healthy self-esteem. "Athletic achievement, scholastic skills, mastering a hobby, making friends, and having an appealing personality are all

things that should help a boy develop good self-esteem. Show him that you consider these things to be more important than the look of his body." (Pope et al., p. 199)

10. If following the above steps is unsuccessful and a boy continues to endanger himself, seek professional help.

Orgeron offers one last suggestion for parents and caregivers. In fact, she considers this suggestion the most important compared to any above. What would that be? Teach boys about and exemplify the love of God to them.

We spend incredible amounts of time and energy preparing our children to be successful and accomplished. We send them to the best schools, help them with their homework, worry with them over emotional issues, but far too often we neglect the very foundation of their lives—their spiritual selves. (Glennon, 2000, p. 207)

Orgeron recommends parents and other caregivers begin teaching boys to pray at a young age. Involving them in family devotionals also is important. Another important key is finding a strong biblically-based, child-friendly church to attend with them. Don't just send or drop children off at church. Go with them. Orgeron believes this leaves a more lasting impression and will motivate them to stay in church as they grow older. As Orgeron has heard and read many times, "The family that prays together stays together."

"An informed parent, sensitive to these issues, and following the recommendations above, can do a lot to ease these burdens in a son as he faces the challenges of growing up." (Pope et al., 2000, p. 200) In closing this section, Orgeron reminds parents and caretakers of the following Scriptures:

Ephesians 6:4

"[4] And you, fathers, do not provoke your children to wrath, but bring them up in the training and admonition of the Lord."

Proverbs 22:6

"**Train up a child** in the way he should go, And when he is old he will not depart from it."

Prevention of Disordered Eating in Males

"Our proactive goal should be to help growing boys and young men to internalize a healthy self-esteem and deep respect for their body." (Andersen, 2014, p. 9) One way Orgeron believes this can be accomplished is by fathers being more pro-active in the prevention of DE and body image problems in their sons' lives. Since unhealthy relationships with fathers put boys at risk of developing DE and body image issues, it stands to reason that fathers getting involved and having healthier relationships with their sons would help prevent these problems from developing. According to the results of a study by Wong et al. (2017), as cited by Frellick (2017), *when dads helped more often with tasks such as dressing, teeth brushing, and bathing, their children were 33% less likely to become obese from ages 2 to 4 (odds ratio [OR], 0.67; P < .05). And a one-level increase in how frequently fathers took their children out for walks or play was linked with a 30% decrease in obesity (OR, 0.70). (Frellick, ¶s 4-5)*

Orgeron believes the principles of prevention for DE presented in Section 6 of this book apply to both males and females, and don't need to be repeated here. What is on Orgeron's heart to share here? Because of the strong links of past sexual abuse and the high risks of suicides linked with DE and body image problems, what Orgeron shares in this section are preventive factors for sexual abuse and for suicide. Of course, these factors are applicable to both sexes.

Preventing Sexual Abuse

The role of parents. The American Academy of Pediatrics (AAP) (2011) recommends the following:

Tips that can minimize your child's risk of molestation:

- *In early childhood, parents can teach their children the name of the genitals, just as they teach their child names of other body parts. This teaches that the genitals, while private, are not so private that you can't talk about them.*
- *Parents can teach young children about the privacy of body parts, and that no one has the right to touch their bodies if they don't want that to happen. Children should also learn to respect the right to privacy of other people.*
- *Teach children early and often that there are no secrets between children and their parents, and that they should feel comfortable talking with their parent about anything -- good or bad, fun or sad, easy or difficult.*
- *Be aware of adults who offer children special gifts or toys, or adults who want to take your child on a "special outing" or to special events.*
- *Enroll your child in daycare and other programs that have a parent "open door" policy. Monitor and participate in activities whenever possible.*
- *As children age, create an environment at home in which sexual topics can be discussed comfortably. Use news items and publicized reports of child sexual abuse to start discussions of safety, and reiterate that children should always tell a parent about anyone who is taking advantage of them sexually.*
- *If your child discloses any history of sexual abuse, listen carefully, and take his or her disclosure seriously. Too often, children are not believed, particularly if they implicate a family member as the perpetrator. Contact your pediatrician, the local child protection service agency, or the police. If you don't intervene, the abuse might continue, and the child may come to believe that home is not safe and that you are not available to help.*
- *Support your child and let him or her know that he or she is not responsible for the abuse.*
- *Bring your child to a physician for a medical examination, to ensure that the child's physical health has not been affected by the abuse.*

- *Most children and their families will also need professional counseling to help them through this ordeal, and your pediatrician can refer you to community resources for psychological help.*
- *If you have concerns that your child may be a victim of sexual abuse, you should talk with your pediatrician. Your physician can discuss your concerns, examine your child, and make necessary referrals and reports.* (¶ 3)

Based on her personal experience of sexual abuse, her educational background and with all the horrid stories being reported on the news in today's world regarding sexual abuse, Orgeron adds her own recommendations to the AAP list. Her recommendations, as initially compiled in *We Survived Sexual Abuse! You Can Too!* (ABC's Ministries, 2016) include separate bedrooms for boys and girls; no alone time outside without adult supervision; modesty in front of children; and, individual baths for boys and girls, not together, regardless of age.

The role of educators. Teachers and other school officials can play a major role in the prevention of childhood sexual abuse. Transmitting appropriate cultural attitudes and shaping healthy student beliefs about sex and the body are key responsibilities of teachers. What can educators do to make a difference in the prevention of sexual abuse? Orgeron offered these suggestions in *We Survived Sexual Abuse! You Can Too!* (ABC's Ministries, 2016):

- Teach students about sexual abuse. Whether through health class or another school-based sexual abuse prevention program, Orgeron believes that students need to be educated about the signs to look for in potential perpetrators, about how to keep themselves pure for marriage (abstinence), about the harm done by sexual abuse, and about what to do if they or someone they know is being sexually abused.
- The Safe Dates Program. One example of a school-based prevention program is the Safe Dates Program (Foshee et al., 2004). Foshee et al. (2004) reported about Safe Dates, an intervention to prevent and reduce dating violence amid adolescents, which is offered to 8th graders teaching them knowledge and skills helpful throughout high school. Explicit to impeding sexual dating violence, educators teach students how to analyze verbal and nonverbal signs that a peer is unprepared to have sex, encourage students to be honest with others about sexual boundaries, and discuss dating tips with students about how to minimize the risk of experiencing sexual dating violence and how to respect others. Foshee et al. (2004) concluded from their study that Safe Dates offers hope to preventing dating violence. For more information about Safe Dates please see the following link: https://www.hazelden.org/web/public/safedates.page
- Understand the role of the media. Teachers need to make students aware of the unhealthy advertising ploys by the media that idealize sex and violence. To counteract unhealthy messages from the media, educational institutions can promote programs that develop character, establish appropriate boundaries, and that teach respect of self and others.

"Transmitting appropriate cultural attitudes and shaping healthy student beliefs about sex and the body are key responsibilities of teachers."

- Set an example. News stories of

teachers, coaches, and other school officials molesting and having consensual sex with children are common in today's world. That should NEVER happen! Students need role models who respect their bodies and maintain appropriate boundaries.

- Report students who are suspected child abuse victims. The law requires that anyone who knows of a child being sexually, or otherwise, being abused, that person needs to file a report to the local police or the Department of Children's Services. School officials also should be knowledgeable about other qualified community resources such as counselors, social workers, and doctors who are trained to work with sexual abuse victims and perpetrators. (pp. 49-51)

The role of government and legislatures. Based on information reported in this book and in *We Survived Sexual Abuse! You Can Too!* (ABC's Ministries, 2016), Orgeron recommends more legal sanctions against sexual harassment be developed and enforced. She also believes law-makers should mandate schools to offer character development courses to all students from kindergarten through 12th grade.

The most important legislation that Orgeron believes the U.S. Congress needs to do is "adopt a national 'bathroom bill' to protect women [men too] and children." (Orgeron, 2016, p. 53) Though the current pleas for needing such legislation are focused toward protecting women and girls, who is to say that a biological female will not cross-dress to enter a men's restroom to molest a young boy? Young boys need protecting as well as young girls and women. To explain her position for the need for a nationwide "bathroom bill, she includes the following updated excerpt from *We Survived Sexual Abuse! You Can Too!* (ABC's Ministries, 2016).

To understand my position, first, consider why people, particularly males, cross-dress. Two main reasons exist why men cross-dress: one, the man has gender identity disorder, where he believes he is a woman. Two, he is a transvestite. This is a man who knows he is a man; but, he cross dresses for sexual gratification

One exception to the above two reasons why a person might cross-dress is when that individual is diagnosed with Klinefelter syndrome or another biological anomaly. Normal chromosomal makeup for a male is XY; while, for the female the normal chromosomal makeup is XX.

Klinefelter syndrome is a genetic condition that results when a boy is born with an extra copy of the X chromosome. Klinefelter syndrome is a common genetic condition affecting males.

Klinefelter syndrome adversely affects testicular growth, and this can result in smaller than normal testicles. This can lead to lower production of the sex hormone testosterone. Klinefelter syndrome may also cause reduced muscle mass, reduced body and facial hair, and enlarged breast tissue. The effects of Klinefelter syndrome vary, and not everyone with it develops these signs and symptoms.

Klinefelter syndrome often isn't diagnosed until adulthood. Most men with Klinefelter syndrome produce little or no sperm. But assisted reproductive procedures may make it possible for some men with Klinefelter syndrome to father children. (Mayo Clinic Staff, 2016c, ¶ 1-3)

Stochholm et al. (2012) studied criminal activity among the XXY population, and another chromosomal abnormality population, XYY Syndrome. According to Stochholm et al., XXY and XYY syndromes are the two most common male chromosomal abnormalities where live births can result. The Stochholm study shows both XXY and XYY populations have higher crime rates than normal populations. Why might this be true? For reflection: Did these populations choose to be born with these syndromes? No, these anomalies would go back to original sin. Here's another question: if a male is diagnosed too late to prevent the development of female breasts, which would be the easiest to hide in public, large breasts or a penis? Of course, a penis! Orgeron thinks for this reason that an untreated individual with XXY Syndrome might dress as a woman and use the women's restroom. Sometimes Orgeron thinks we can be too quick to judge cross-dressers, etc. without knowing the cause/motive behind the behavior.

With gender identity disorder mentioned previously, a disturbance of gender identification exists where the affected individual has an overpowering desire to alter their sexual anatomy or insists that he or she is of the opposite sex. These individuals have a persistent disturbance about their assigned sex and about how to live out the norms for the assigned sex's gender role. Gender identity disorder may become apparent early in childhood or not surface until later. These individuals sometimes try to live as the opposite sex. Some go as far as to seek medical treatment to bring his or her biological anatomy into conformance with his or her desires. When those with gender identity disorder have sought sex change operations, then these individuals become known as transsexuals.

Orgeron believes the motive behind why an individual might choose to use any particular restroom needs to be given consideration. However, the problem is that there is no way at first glance one can determine whether an individual is cross dressing because he/she is a transvestite, a transsexual, or whether the person really thinks he or she is of the opposite sex than indicated by one's chromosomal makeup. Orgeron thinks the transvestites who cross dress for sexual gratification are the ones to be most concerned about. Additionally, Orgeron believes that regardless of the reason why people cross dress, they don't need our judgement or criticism. They need our prayers. They also need psychiatric treatment.

> "the problem is that there is no way at first glance one can determine whether an individual is cross dressing because he/she is a transvestite, a transsexual, or whether the person really thinks he or she is of the opposite sex than indicated by one's chromosomal makeup."

For example, when Klinefelter's syndrome is diagnosed early enough as a baby, doctors can give the person testosterone and other hormones to promote normal development as a male and to prevent the development of breasts and other female characteristics during puberty.

The issues surrounding a "bathroom bill" are complex with no easy answers. Given the complexity, Orgeron supports legislation requiring individuals using public restrooms of the sex listed on one's birth certificate. This keeps the safety of children a number one priority. Otherwise, the door is wide open for pedophiles and other sex offenders to dress in women's [or men's] attire just to be able to enter a woman's [or man's] restroom seeking potential victims. One such case has already occurred in a Target store in Texas [and more since then]. For the rare cases of Klinefelter's and other genetic or other biological anomalies, Orgeron suggests that a separate Family bathroom be available for such individuals to use. (pp. 53-56)

While on the topic of bathrooms, Orgeron believes there is another matter the U.S. Congress needs to deal with to prevent body image issues and even DE. After reading the numerous accounts of grown men who reported how intimidated and uncomfortable they felt as boys having to take showers after gym class in open showers, and knowing how uncomfortable she herself was in junior and senior high school physical education courses where open showers were only available, Orgeron believes open showers, especially in schools, need to be banned. Requiring closed stalls for shower rooms in all athletic facilities would minimize students' ability to be able to compare, tease, and/or bully those who may be over or under developed for their age. Not to mention, the matter of modesty also should be a factor in developing such legislation.

Suicide Prevention in Clients/Patients with EDs

"Eating disorders are oftentimes accompanied with thoughts of suicide or suicide attempts. In fact, suicide is the most common cause of death among individuals with eating disorders." (Berman, n.d., ¶ 1) Castlewood Treatment Center (2016) reported,

> *Individuals with anorexia are about 31 times more likely to make a fatal suicide attempt when compared to members of the general population. For individuals with bulimia, meanwhile, the rate is 7.5 times higher than in the general population. These numbers show that eating disorders are life threatening, and frequently lead to individuals committing suicide.* (Eating Disorder Mortality Rates section, ¶ 1)

One important reason why Orgeron chose to include factors for preventing suicide in this chapter is because of the "gender paradox of suicidal behavior." (Wikipedia, 2017b, ¶ 2) What is this paradox? "**Gender differences in suicide** rates have been shown to be significant; there are highly asymmetric rates of *attempted* and completed *suicides* between males and females." (Wikipedia, ¶ 1) While females attempt suicide more; males are more successful at completing the act. What causes this gap? While males attempt suicide less, they typically use more lethal means, such as hanging or shooting themselves. Female suicide attempts typically are through less fatal means such as overdosing on drugs or slashing one's wrist. With treatment for DE typically delayed in males where they reach the stage of having suicidal ideation and may be at greater risk of dying with them choosing more lethal means to attempt to kill themselves, Orgeron believes much more attention needs to be given to the prevention and treatment of ED in males.

What can be done to help lower the incidence of suicide among individuals with DE? First, Eating Disorder Hope (2013) reported, "It is crucial to be aware of warning signs of suicide as much can be done to prevent tragic outcomes for these people." (¶ 1) What are the warning signs? Berman (n.d.) listed the following "red flags" that someone may be contemplating suicide:

- *Talking about wanting to die or to kill oneself.*
- *Looking for a way to kill oneself, such as searching online or buying a gun.*
- *Talking about feeling hopeless or having no reason to live.*
- *Talking about feeling trapped or in unbearable pain.*
- *Talking about being a burden to others.*

- *Increasing the use of alcohol or drugs.*
- *Acting anxious or agitated; behaving recklessly.*
- *Sleeping too little or too much.*
- *Withdrawn or feeling isolated.*
- *Showing rage or talking about seeking revenge.*
- *Displaying extreme mood swings.*
- *Preoccupation with death.*
- *Suddenly happier, calmer.*
- *Loss of interest in things one cares about.*
- *Visiting or calling people to say goodbye.*
- *Making arrangements; setting one's affairs in order.*
- *Giving things away, such as prized possessions.* (Warning Signs section, ¶ 1)

Besides knowing the warning signs, how else can these at risk individuals be helped?

The most important element is support from friends and family members. Never abandon a loved one who is struggling with an eating disorder. Never give up, and never allow them to become isolated. Offer your compassion and your understanding. Be available to talk with them. Let them know that you love them, are concerned about them, want them to get better, and believe in their ability for recovery. Also, encourage them to seek treatment, and let them know you will be with them every step of the way. (Castlewood Treatment Center, 2016, Suicide Prevention section, ¶ 1)

Orgeron also stresses the importance of taking every suicide threat or attempt seriously. In some cases, the person may not really want to end their life; but, their actions may be a cry out for attention and help. However, as Orgeron believes and has heard many times, "It's better to err on the side of safety, than sorry." "If someone is in a psychiatric emergency they should go to their nearest emergency room, call 911, and/or call the National Suicide Prevention Lifeline 1-800-273-TALK (8255)." (Berman, n.d., Warning Signs section, ¶ 2)

Concluding Remarks on DE in Males

Though DE signs and symptoms differ in the sexes, EDs are no less complicated or serious for men and boys than for women and girls. As Mitchison and Mond (2015) reported,

The impairment in quality of life, lost productivity, and psychosocial wellbeing associated with eating disorders and related disturbances appears to be comparable in males and females. It is thus vital that barriers to help-seeking, such as stigma, ignorance more generally, and female-centric services, are addressed. (p. 7)

In concluding, Orgeron reminds parents of the importance of leaving a legacy of love and faith in the Lord Jesus Christ. In closing she shares the following words of encouragement from the Scriptures.

Psalm 103:2-4

2 Bless the LORD, O my soul,
And forget not all His benefits:
3 Who forgives all your iniquities,
Who heals all your diseases,
4 Who redeems your life from destruction,
Who crowns you with lovingkindness and tender mercies,

***

Chapter 16: Disordered Eating in Males

Key Terms/Concepts

Adonis Complex

"Bathroom bill"

Body dysmorphic disorder (BDD)

Cultivation theory

Gender dysphoria

Gender identity disorder

Gender paradox of suicide behavior

Muscle dysmorphia

Transsexual

Transvestite

XXY and XYY syndromes

Questions for Reflection:

1. Why are eating disorders a concern in men?
2. How does NAMED support boys and men with disordered eating?
3. How do EDs manifest differently in males and females?
4. What does Orgeron believe is the mediating factor between sexual abuse and disordered eating?
5. What are possible influences that might cause men who identify as anything outside of heterosexuality to be at a higher risk for developing EDs?
6. What are the challenges for homosexual men getting treatment?
7. If a client's gender identity is outside of a clinician's area of expertise, why should that clinician refer the client out to another clinician?
8. How do exercise and body image issues differ in males and females?
9. Traditionally, EDs have been known as a "woman's illness". How and why has this changed?
10. What is the Adonis Complex?
11. According to the DSM-5, what are the criteria for diagnosing gender dysphoria?
12. What is the first step in treating an individual with an ED and a substance abuse problem?
13. According to NEDC, what four negative cultural or media messages are exclusive to males?
14. What are warning signs that more commonly occur in males than females?
15. Why is DE now a concern in boys?
16. How do EDs affect boys differently than girls?
17. What makes a boy more susceptible to developing DE?
18. How is the Adonis Complex manifested in boys?

19. What should parents and other caretakers do when they suspect a boy has DE or the Adonis Complex?

20. What does Orgeron believe is the most important suggestion for parents to prevent DE in boys?

21. Why should fathers get more involved with their sons?

22. According to the Academy of Pediatrics, what can parents do to minimize the risk of sexual abuse in a child?

23. What other recommendations does Orgeron give to supplement the AAP suggestions for parents in minimizing the risk of sexual abuse in children?

24. What role can teachers and other school officials play in the prevention of childhood sexual abuse?

25. What can legislators and other government officials do to minimize the risk of sexual abuse in children?

26. Why do people cross dress?

27. Why are the issues surrounding a "bathroom bill" so complex?

28. Do you think "open showers", especially in schools, should be banned? Why? Or why not?

29. According to the Castlewood Treatment Center, what is the most common cause of death among individuals with EDs?

30. Explain the gender paradox of suicidal behavior.

31. What are the "red flags" or warning signs that someone may be contemplating suicide?

32. According to Castlewood Treatment Center (2016), what is the most important element of support those struggling with EDs need?

***

Chapter 17: Disordered Eating in the Church

Introduction

One might expect Christians in churches to be among the healthiest groups of people in the world. This is not the case according to research (Moritz, 2013; Premier Life, 2014). Moritz reported, "Recent studies show that Christians are not portraying a good testimony of honoring God with their bodies." (p. 1) One study by the Pawtucket Heart Health Program, as cited by Moritz, found church attenders are more apt than non-attenders "to be 20 percent overweight and have higher cholesterol and blood pressure numbers." (p. 2) Another study conducted by Matthew J. Feinstein (Northwestern University Medical Center), as reported by Moritz, found 50 percent of young persons who attend church at least once weekly are more apt to be obese as they reach middle age than those persons who attend church less. According to Premier Life, a part of Premier Christian Media Trust, a charity registered in England and Wales,

> *Research carried out at events and conferences found that 90% of church members knew someone who was suffering with an eating disorder. 70% of them knew someone in their own church. The majority said that their church was not able to offer sufferers, or their families, any help or support in their battle toward recovery.* (¶ 1)

Not only are Christians in general not setting good examples to others, but pastors too are not doing well in this area, according to Moritz (2013). He reported,

> *A national survey of more than 2,500 religious leaders conducted in 2002 by the Pulpit & Pew research project on pastoral leadership based at Duke Divinity School found that 76 percent of clergy were either overweight or obese, compared with 61 percent of the general population.* (pp. 4-5)

Arterburn and Mintle (2004) reported how gluttony is rarely addressed in churches today. "In fact, some of the best Christian speakers have never resolved their own food issues, so they do not address them with followers. . . . They scream an unspoken message that food is the one acceptable addiction in the church." (pp. 2-3)

In 1 Timothy 3:2 pastors are instructed to be blameless, without reproach. "However, they seem to think that obesity is exempt from the list of sins. Pastors and Christians have become apathetic in this area, and the worst offenders in this health crisis." (Moritz, p. 16) What's wrong with this picture? How could this have happened?

New Life Ministries (2017) reported, "[I]f we can apply God's light to the dark places of our soul, we will remove the need to eat in excess as a defective means to find comfort and relief." (¶ 2) Orgeron believes this cannot happen unless we are willing to dig out the roots to disordered eating in the church.

This chapter will include sections on "The Roots to Disordered Eating in the Church", "The Solution to Disordered Eating in the Church," and "Health and Wellness Programs in the Church." Additionally, Orgeron thinks with the strong links between sexual abuse and DE she would be amiss to not include a section on how the church can help prevent sexual abuse. This part of the chapter will be excerpted from *We Survived Sexual Abuse! You Can Too!* (ABC's Ministries, 2016).

The Roots to Disordered Eating in the Church

Although Satan is the ultimate enemy as discussed earlier in chapter 11, we cannot blame him for all the problems with gluttony in the church. God gave mankind freewill (Joshua 24:15) to decide whether to give in to the wiles of the Devil or to submit to the Holy Spirit's leading. God also promised that for every temptation, He would provide a way of escape. (1 Corinthians 10:13) Each individual has to make the choice as to which path he or she will choose. Similarly, church bodies must decide whether they want to be healthy or complacent towards taking care of the body. Remember, "An obese Church is not in health physically or spiritually, and it is obvious that it is not well either." (Moritz, p. 25)

Based on her research and her personal experience Orgeron believes there are influences both within the church and outside the church that have contributed to the church's poorer state of health than the general public and that continue to allow the church to be a breeding ground for disordered eating. Orgeron will discuss those influences below.

Internal Roots

Unhealthy foods served at church. (Association of Black Cardiologists, Inc. (ABC), 2013; Moritz, 2013; Ryder, 2011) Christians, we need to be honest. "Potlucks, ice cream socials, pancake breakfasts, spaghetti dinners and donuts are not good for the body, brain or soul." (Ryder, ¶ 19) Neither are all the pizza parties some churches have to attract today's youth. Based on John 6:44, Orgeron believes the Holy Spirit should be what draws people to come to church, not their taste buds.

Based on 1 Corinthians 10:31, "Christians should take care not to use their liberty to the hurt of others, or to their own reproach. In eating and drinking, and in all we do, we should aim at the glory of God, at pleasing and honouring him." (Henry, 1997, pp. 1107-1108) Orgeron believes the purpose of whatever one puts in one's mouth should line up with His intended purpose for eating—for nourishment. Not to say that one should not enjoy his or her meals. However, "Church fellowships meals need to be looked at with the question in mind, "Will this meal glorify God?" Why do we ask God to bless food that is not nourishing to us?" (Moritz, 2013, p. 30) Again, food's purpose is to provide nourishment to our bodies—not for celebration or to bribe children and teenagers to attend church.

Misunderstandings of Scripture and false teachings regarding one's body. Research (Briggs, 2016; Christians for Biblical Equality, CBE, International 2017; Goulet, Henrie, & Szymanski, 2017; Jacobson, Hall, Anderson, & Willingham, 2016; Moritz, 2013) supports what Orgeron knows first-hand through stories told to her—unbiblical attitudes about the body among Christians are linked to disordered eating. What types of unbiblical attitudes exist? Orgeron found two main ones in her research. First, some Christians do not see a problem with neglecting the body. Moritz (2013) reported, "Many Christians consider their physical bodies mere "shells," like one of an alien, and most Christian circles place their emphasis on spiritual development and not physical development." (p. 81) Another view is radical dualism, which sees the body as separate from the spirit, and evil. (Jacobson et al., 2016) These believers "see the body as largely a source of pollution and temptation." (Briggs, ¶ 6)

Failure to educate about sexuality and God's purpose for sex. (CBE International, 2017) "[T]he history of the Church demonstrates a decidedly negative view of the body and sexuality." (CBE International, ¶ 1) Orgeron knows this to be truth from her educational and life experiences. First, there are those Christians who believe sex is only for procreation, and not to be enjoyed. Then, other Christians see sex and sexuality as "dirty" and not to be discussed. Both of these attitudes go against Scriptural teachings that our bodies are the temple of God and that sex is for procreation and enjoyment between one man and his wife.

Toxic faith. (Arterburn & Felton, 1991, 2001) What is toxic faith? Arterburn and Felton defined toxic faith as "a destructive and dangerous involvement in a religion that allows the religion, not a relationship with God, to control a person's life . . . It is abusive and manipulative and can become addictive." (p. 19) Before one can rid oneself of toxic faith, a person must first recognize the false beliefs. One example of toxic faith is self-obsession, or self-centeredness often a characteristic of those persons with disordered eating. Self-centered individuals are not concerned with helping others but are consumed with meeting their own needs.

Laziness also is one type of self-defeating behavior that can manifest through toxic faith. Orgeron gives an example of Christian individuals who know they need to lose weight. Rather than taking action by starting to move more and eat less, these individuals pray for a miracle, or rationalize that if God wanted them thin, He would have made them that way.

External Roots

Peer pressure from friends. Steve Reynolds wrote in his book, *Get off the Couch: 6 Motivators to Health* (Regal, 2012)

> If a person's overweight friends think fat is beautiful, that person may begin to think the same thing in order not to be left out. On the other hand, if thin is in with a person's friends, they may adopt that attitude. From there, it is a short step to choosing food and exercise habits that will enable them to soon look like the rest of the crowd, whether that means eating more food to look like their plus-sized friends or less food to look like their thin ones. (Reynolds, 2012, pp. 209-210, as cited by Moritz, 2013, p. 132)

The food and fashion industries. (Arterburn, & Mintle, 2004, 2011; Moritz, 2013) Food is advertised everywhere—TV commercials, billboards, magazines. How can anyone resist all the temptations? Not to mention the easy access to high fat super-sized meals advertised at a bargain. Additionally, Arterburn and Mintle report that some experts believe carbonated soft drinks are the number one source contributing to society's obesity problem. "When it comes to eating, American culture is toxic." (Arterburn & Mintle, p. 2)

The fashion industry also plays a role in the disordered eating problem. "Society today lives in a Photoshop world, and people compare themselves to images that do not really exist and reject their God-given body. People live lives of comparing and perfecting. . . . This constant pressure is on everyone to look a certain way." (Moritz, 2013, p. 101) "Thanks to media, any chance for a healthy body image is gone before puberty hits. Food becomes our enemy and our lover, truly a relationship as complicated as any other." (Arterburn & Mintle, p. 2) Orgeron would like to point out that she believes an exception exists to the statement by Arterburn and Mintle, "Thanks to media, any chance for a healthy body image is gone before puberty hits." Orgeron believes there are exceptions to this statement such as when God intervenes and has his hand on the life of a child.

The Solution to Disordered Eating in the Church

"The local Church should not only be a place that promotes spiritual health, but one that promotes and advocates for physical health and wellness." (Moritz, 2013, p. 21) Additionally, most Americans (70.6%) call themselves Christian (Pew Research Center, 2017), "which means that churches may be in a key position to improve the health of the nation. Not only are churches potential points of contact with the public, they also tend to hold regular events that involve food and relationships." (Centers for Disease Control and Prevention (CDC), 2013, ¶ 1) According to Church Health Programs . . . (2013), "In a survey of more than 1,200 members of 11 African-American churches in North Carolina, an overwhelming majority of congregants said they believe that *the church has a responsibility to promote healthy living* within the community they serve." (¶ 2) What can churches do to help reverse the epidemic of disordered eating?

First and foremost, churches need pastors and other leaders who exemplify and promote healthy lifestyles. (Cox, 2011; Moritz, 2013) Moritz reported,

> *In creating a health and wellness ministry, the program must begin with the pastor. . . . [T]he senior pastor is the most effective example in the church because it is his job to lead the flock. . . . When the pastor steps up and leads, so does his church. Therefore, the senior pastor should care about being a person of overall health.* (pp. 71-72)

One way a pastor can begin to address disordered eating issues in congregations is through a sermon-based campaign with gluttony a key focus.

Change the types of food people consume at church. (Allicock et al., 2013; Church health programs . . . , 2013) In an effort to curb the epidemic of heart disease in the African-American community in New York, cardiologist Ola Akinboboye and the ABC (2013) recommend churches change the unhealthy foods they serve to healthier food items, which in turn would influence how congregants eat at home. To push the message, Akinboboye and the ABC created a documentary entitled "Before You Eat the Church Food Watch This Video" (ABC), which links heart disease to lifestyle choices. Orgeron watched this documentary, and recommends all pastors and other church leadership watch the program. The program "offers a model for faith communities across the country that public health advocates say is needed to see church-based health programs truly succeed." (Church health programs . . . , ¶ 8)

Believe and teach truths about the body that line up with Scripture. Orgeron believes that the Scriptures are the ultimate source of truth. Thus, she agrees with Focus on the Family's (2000) report that

If we're going to start believing the truth about appearance and weight, we've got to go to the ultimate Source. What does our loving heavenly Father have to say about our bodies and real beauty? Check out these Scriptures:

- *Genesis 1:27 – You were made in the image of God.*
- *Psalm 8 – In the whole wonderful universe, He gives you a place of honor.*
- *Proverbs 31:30 – Outward appearances don't matter as much as what's inside.*
- *Zephaniah 3:17 – The God of the universe takes delight in YOU!*
- *Romans 5:8 – God loves you enough to send His Son to die for you.*
- *1 Peter 3:3 – How you look is not what really makes you beautiful.*

*Look especially at Psalm 139. The author of that poem knew that the human body is among God's most miraculous creations. He thanked God for carefully forming our bodies even before birth – for creating us each unique and incredibly special. If God created our bodies, then they are **good**!* (Nothing but the Truth section, ¶s 1-2)

"Renew the mind" where unbiblical attitudes and behaviors exist about the body and sexuality. Orgeron gleans this from Romans 12:2, "And do not be conformed to this world, but be transformed by the renewing of your mind, that you may prove what *is* that good and acceptable and perfect will of God." Just as individuals can be brought up with unbiblical attitudes and behaviors and need to renew the mind, churches too can have biblically unsound doctrine and practices that need to be reevaluated and replaced with biblically sound attitudes and behaviors.

Offer biblically based courses and mentoring programs about the body and sexuality. What about smaller churches and those with limited financing who might think, *we can't do that. We're too small or don't have the funding.* Cox (2011) reported that these barriers can be overcome by groups of churches in a community banding together to offer programs. Long-term partnerships with hospitals or other community agencies also can be effective. What types of biblically based courses are available about the body and sexuality? For adults, Orgeron recommends church groups use the following curriculum:

- American Association of Christian Counselors (2001). *Healthy Sexuality.* Forest, VA: Author.
- American Association of Christian Counselors (2007). *Fresh Starts Recovery Series: Forgiveness: Getting beyond your pain & past.* Forest, VA: Author.
- Sledge, T. (1992). *Making peace with your past: Help for adult children of dysfunctional families.* Nashville: LifeWay Press.

For parents who want biblically based training on how to teach their children about healthy sexuality, a church might utilize *Teaching Your Children Healthy Sexuality DVD Curriculum Kit* (Bethany House, 2009), by Jim Burns. For youth group leaders looking for a way to teach biblically sound principles about sexuality to male teens, Orgeron recommends *Every Young Man's Battle* Book and Workbook (Waterbrook, 2009). These books are available for purchase in bulk at lower rates through http://www.fredstoeker.com/book/everyyoungmansbattle.shtml. For the females in youth groups, don't forget the book and workbook, *Every Young Woman's Battle: Guarding Your Mind,*

Heart, and Body in a Sex-Saturated World (The Every Man Series) (Waterbrook, 2004). These books can be purchased through Amazon.com or christianbook.com.

Train children to think critically about what's popular and what the media portrays as attractive. CBE International (2017) reported, "Equipping girls who are genetically predisposed to eating disorders with faith-based critical thinking skills may decrease their need to adopt maladaptive coping tools such as rigidity and perfectionism." (The Church and Prevention of Disembodiment section, ¶ 3) This in turn would decrease the numbers of disordered eating.

> *Older women cannot leave it to the next generations to find their way through the tumultuous waters of sexual maturation alone. Kristen Ritzau, a research coordinator at Azusa Pacific University who mentors young women in various ministry capacities, says, "We need to talk about these things in the open, in a normalized way. We need to stop making sex shameful. And we need mentoring. Younger people need older people who've been through stuff, to share it with us".* (CBE International, 2017, The Church and Prevention of Disembodiment section, ¶ 5)

Now that what churches need to do to help stop the disordered eating epidemic around the world has been discussed, Orgeron feels she would be amiss not to include the six mistakes people make in starting health and wellness campaigns. (Moritz, 2013) These are:

- People neglect the truth that the Bible is the ultimate authority and contains all the answers for any problem, including disordered eating. Instead, they look to the world for their answers about how to manage one's weight.

- People minimize the problem thinking it's just a "plate problem" when the problem

> *starts long before one puts anything into their mouth. A persons mind can be their worst enemy with "stinking thinking". So they must trust God that He can and will change believers in a positive light if they are willing to surrender their thoughts to Christ and eat so that their brain can retain a good memory.* (p. 78)

- Rather than living in victory over problems through the faith of Jesus Christ, too many people operate out of fear and other emotions.

- Most people do not understand and honor their bodies as "God's temple".

- Many people fail to understand and practice the biblical concept of moderation. They also are impatient wanting deliverance now without seeing the importance of taking small daily steps to recovery.

- Most people fail to trust God with their bodies. "Believers have to fully rely on God for all things including weight loss. God challenges every human being to follow him. . . . God guarantees to change one's waistline and life, one pound at a time if we trust Him." (p. 83)

Health and Wellness Programs in the Church

Health and wellness programs in churches should be unique and have a deeper purpose than programs in the secular world. How so? According to the Ministry Tools Resource Center (2010), three biblical principles and practices need to be implemented into all church-based health and wellness programs. These are:

1. Churches need to teach the principle of our bodies as "God's temple", based on 1 Corinthians 6:19-20.

2. Based on Mark 12:30, "a church can minister to the whole person, integrating physical, spiritual, emotional, mental, and social health and wellness." (¶ 5)

3. Based on John 10:10, a church can assist individuals in living out the abundant life not only spiritually but also physically as much as possible on earth by teaching them how to prevent medical problems that affect one's entire being.

Benefits

Orgeron believes one of the most important benefits and reasons for having health and wellness programs in churches is being able to use the program as an outreach tool. Moritz (2013) reported,

> The local Church exists to get the Gospel to lost people in many ways and through many opportunities. The ability to meet felt needs and using the Gospel to get people well and healed is a God-ward effort. This will result in life change that people will physically and visually be able to communicate to other people. A person's story of losing weight in a Church is a launching pad for evangelism. (p. 84)

Are there other benefits to having health and wellness programs in churches? According to Moritz (2013), "When a church has a health and wellness ministry that promotes lifestyle change, if pain is decreased or eased, pleasure increases. If people decrease their pain of sin of gluttony, they automatically increase their pleasure in God." (p. 104)

Programs Available

Bod4God. (Bloom, 2009; Bod4God, 2017; Dahl, 2012; Donvan, & Thompson, 2012) "Bod4God is a diet and fitness program that delivers sustainable weight loss. It was developed by Pastor Steve Reynolds of Capital Baptist Church in Annandale, Virginia (part of the greater D.C. area)." (Bloom, ¶ 1) After his own weight struggles and losing over 100 pounds, Reynolds wrote the book *Bod4God* (Regal, 2009) which explains "the simple lifestyle changes, both inside and out, that have led to his incredible weight loss. He shows how you can change your life forever by committing your body to God's glory." (Bod4God, Bod4God Tab, About Bod4God section, ¶ 3) According to Reynolds, there are four basic keys to the program that are illustrated by the acronym "D-I-E-T". The four keys are:

- o *Dedication: Honoring God with Your Body*
- o *Inspiration: Motivating Yourself for Change*
- o *Eat and Exercise: Managing Your Habits*
- o *Team: Building Your Circle of Support* (Bod4God, Bod4God Tab, About Bod4God section, ¶ 2)

Reynolds believes that without these keys one cannot reach a healthy sustainable weight.

Body and Soul. (Allicock et al., 2013; Campbell, Resnicow, Carr, Wang, & Williams, 2007; CDC, 2013; Resnicow et al., 2004) "Blacks appear to have less healthful diets than whites [Kimmo's, J., Gillespie, C., Seymour, J., Serdula, M., & Blanck, H, M., 2009; McCabe-Sellers, Bowman, Stuff, Champagne, Simpson, & Bogle, 2007]. Data for 2009 indicate only 22.4% of blacks reported eating recommended amounts of fruits and vegetables." (Allicock et al., Introduction section, ¶ 1) Thus, the need for the Body and Soul program, designed to be utilized in African-American churches.

The Body and Soul program consists of four parts:

1. Pastoral support
2. Educational events (e.g. healthy food fairs; bulletin inserts about healthy eating)
3. Changes in church environment (e.g., establishing policies requiring healthy foods to be served at church events)
4. "peer counseling (provide one-on-one support from trained volunteer church members by using motivational interview principles [Allicock, Campbell, Valle, Carr, Resnicow, & Gizlice, 2012] with training provided via a DVD and detailed implementation manuals)." (Allicock et al., Body and Soul program section, ¶ 2)

Allicock et al. (2013) reported the Body and Soul program has been effective in getting African-Americans to eat more fruits and vegetables. Additionally, some churches have added an exercise component to the program. Allicock also pointed out that though the program was designed for African-American churches, the program could be adapted to work with any racial or ethnic congregation.

Celebrate Recovery. (Celebrate Recovery, 2015). "Celebrate Recovery is a biblical and balanced program that helps us overcome our hurts, hang-ups, and habits. It is based on the actual words of Jesus rather than psychological theory." (What is Celebrate Recovery? section, ¶ 1) These groups utilize the Christian 12 Steps, and eight principles based on the Beatitudes.

Orgeron has participated in two different Celebrate Recovery groups, one at a Baptist church and the other at a Seventh Day Adventist Church in her area. The programs consisted of a meal, a praise and worship service, and small group discussions. On a side note, the meals at the Seventh Day Adventist Church were much healthier than at the Baptist Church. As vegetarians, Seventh Day Adventists know how to eat healthy and well. Additionally, from Orgeron's observations they appear to have fewer members who are overweight or obese. Orgeron is not Seventh Day Adventist but commends them for their focus on healthy eating.

The Daniel Plan. (Daniel Plan, 2013) *"The Daniel Plan Church Campaign Kit* is a great way to encourage everyone in your church toward a healthy lifestyle, explore biblical principles for health, and unite your congregation around the single purpose of honoring what God has given us." (The Daniel Plan Store, 2017, Church Campaign Link, ¶ 1) What is The Daniel Plan? After Pastor Rick Warren realized how he had neglected taking care of his body for 30 years and the negative example this was having on his congregation at Saddleback Church in Southern California, he took action. He recruited three doctors to help him create what he called The Daniel Plan. The plan is named after Daniel in the Scriptures, who along with his three brothers refused to eat food and drink wine from King Nebuchadnezzar's table. Instead, they ate vegetables and drank water. (Daniel 1)

In chapter one, "How It All Began", of the book *The Daniel Plan* (Zondervan, 2013) Pastor Rick Warren wrote,

The Daniel Plan is far more than a diet. It is a lifestyle program based on biblical principles and five essential components: Food, Fitness, Focus, Faith, and Friends. These last two components—faith and friends—are what I call the secret sauce that makes The Daniel Plan so effective. When you have God and a group helping you, you now have far more than willpower helping you make positive changes, and you are far more likely to stay consistent. (Warren, Amen, & Hyman, 2013, p. 16)

Individualized church model. (Todd, 2017)   With changing demographics in the surrounding community, under the ministry of Senior Minister Rev. Daniel U'Ren, Western Oaks Christian Church in Oklahoma City, based on the second greatest command from God to love one's neighbor (Mark 12:31; Matthew 22:39), "made the choice to learn the stories, needs, and struggles of the people in the community. In order to achieve this goal, Western Oaks Christian Church is now offering new ministry initiatives that seek to further embed the congregation among its neighbors." (Todd, ¶ 3) One of those initiatives is a commitment to promoting healthy lifestyles. Tools used to do this include having a yearly health fair offering amenities such as free immunizations and free screening for blood pressure problems. The church also has a completely smoke-free campus. Walking also is highly encouraged by the church leadership.

"When asked how these initiatives are helping the congregation of Western Oaks to become more aware of its sense of ministry and purpose, Rev. U'ren's reply was simple: 'We want this to be a church that would be missed by the community'." (Todd, ¶s 7-8)

By sharing the example of Western Oaks Christian Church's commitment to "love thy neighbor" through their health and wellness ministry, Orgeron hopes and prays other churches will do likewise. If all churches worked together to promote holistic health, Orgeron believes this would have a large impact on stamping out the epidemic of disordered eating.

Life Recovery/Lose It for Life. (Arterburn, & Mintle, 2004, 2011; Trinity Health Weight Loss, 2011). In the "Getting Started" section of *Lose It for Life* (Thomas Nelson, 2011) Stephen Arterburn, M.Ed. wrote

Lose It for Life is the culmination of a lifelong journey of first having a weight problem, then finding a way to be free of it for life, and sharing the method of that victory with others. I also bring with me thirty years of experience of working with fellow strugglers of all types of addiction and dependence. (Arterburn, & Mintle, 2011, p. XIV)

Arterburn is *New Life Ministries* Founder and Chairperson; host of *New Life Live!,* a Christian radio show; *New Life TV* (web-based) host; and founder of *Women of Faith* conferences, which Orgeron has attended in the past. "He also serves as a teaching pastor in Indianapolis, Indiana." (New Life Ministries, 2017b, Meet the Hosts section, ¶ 1)

Orgeron recalls thinking as she read the first edition of *Lose It for Life* (2004), *this guy gets it. He knows what he's talking about.* She found more encouragement in recovery from her disordered eating from reading *Lose It for Life* than any other books she has read on the subject, with *Love Hunger* (Thomas Nelson, 1990) a close second favorite book. At some point Orgeron would be interested in starting a *Lose It for Life* or *Life Recovery* group in her area.

What makes Lose It for Life work? According to Arterburn and Mintle (2004, 2011), the seven keys to making this program work are surrender, acceptance, confession, responsibility, transformation, and preservation. Surrender refers to humbling oneself before God, based on 1 Peter 5:6. Acceptance refers to one breaking out of denial and accepting that he or she needs help. Confession, based on James 5:16, requires one to talk about their problem with both God and others. Responsibility requires one to not blame others but to take responsibility for his or her actions, particularly one's mistakes. Forgiveness (Matthew 6:14) demands that an individual forgive him or herself, along with anyone else who has offended him or her. Transformation means being able to transform one's experience to be able to help others, based on 2 Corinthians 1:3-4. Preservation requires one to persevere through life's struggles without relapsing to regain weight lost.

The *Lose It for Life* resources also may be used in conjunction with other weight loss programs. For example, Trinity Health Weight Loss uses the *Lose It for Life Workbook* to cover the spiritual aspect of their program. (Trinity Health Weight Loss, 2011) These groups too can meet in churches. "In most groups participants spend about half the time in study/discussion and half the time sharing, praying and enjoying a healthy meal." (Trinity Health Weight Loss, Where are the Meetings Held? section, ¶ 2)

The Church's Role in Sexual Abuse Prevention
[Excerpted and Updated from We Survived Sexual Abuse! You Can Too! (ABC's Ministries, 2016), pp. 56-62]

Why do churches need to be concerned and be pro-active towards the epidemic of sexual misconduct? Orgeron explains why. First, churches need to develop church policies that protect themselves, the children and adolescents in the church, and those who are caretakers over children and adolescents. Let's not forget singles need protection too!

Why do churches need to protect themselves? One local church in Orgeron's community now faces a $10 million lawsuit from a sexual abuse victim whose perpetrator was a member of that church. The victim claims the church tried to cover up the sexual abuse. Not likely, as the perpetrator is in prison now serving time for the offense. Orgeron thinks larger mega churches are at greatest risk of facing such circumstances. When child victims grow up to become money hungry adults out to get compensation for pain and suffering, and perhaps even hurt the reputation of the church, these larger mega churches need to be sure church officials always report allegations made regarding any church member or attender as either being a victim or perpetrator. When strict policies are adopted and enforced, chances too are less likely that false allegations can be made against church staff and volunteers.

Why do children and adolescents, and their overseers need protection? Orgeron believes many perpetrators seek out church children and adolescents due to the ignorance among church members about the seriousness of sexual abuse. Church parents and other members often have the "it will NEVER happen to my child", or it won't happen here" mentality that leaves church children more vulnerable to perpetrators because of their ignorance about matters relating to sexual abuse. The truth is sexual abuse can and does happen in Christian homes and churches.

> "Church parents and other members often have the 'it will NEVER happen to my child', or 'it won't happen here' mentality that leaves church children more vulnerable to perpetrators because of their ignorance about matters relating to sexual abuse."

Overseers of children and adolescents in churches need protecting too. One allegation of sexual abuse made against a pastor, a deacon, or whoever in the church can have his or her reputation and ministry ruined for life, regardless of whether the accusation is true.

Why do church singles need education about and protection from sexual abuse? Orgeron herself was a targeted victim of a male who was visiting her home church's singles department years ago to hit on the single women there. None of the women in the singles group realized what the male was all about until two or three of them shared about how each of them were unknowingly simultaneously supposedly seriously dating the same person. Perpetrators who hit on single church members know that by being with Christians, the likelihood of them picking up AIDS or another sexually transmitted disease is probably less.

Promote and teach biblical attitudes towards sex and about sexual abuse. The Bible is clear that sex is a gift from God inherent in our created male or female nature, and that this gift is not to be abused. Genesis has God saying that it is not good for man to be alone, and He created a fitting and complementary partner for Adam in Eve. God then commands them, "Be fruitful and multiply; fill the earth and subdue it" (Genesis 1:28), to have sexual relations which will produce many children. So God's intention for sex is for a man and woman to have intimacy that results in children as a reflection of their one-flesh union. Sex in God's plan is not dirty, shameful or ugly, but is intended to bring joy to a married couple, to seal their bond, and to glorify God by bringing people created in His image and spirit into His world.

The Fall (See Genesis, Chapter 3.) brought a lack of transparency between husband and wife in clothing what had been naked innocence, and in Eve now being subject to her husband even while striving with him. This is revealed in Genesis 3:16: "To the woman He said: 'I will greatly multiply your sorrow and your conception; In pain you shall bring forth children; Your desire *shall be* for your husband, And he shall rule over you.'"

> "Sex in God's plan is not dirty, shameful or ugly, but is intended to bring joy to a married couple, to seal their bond, and to glorify God by bringing people created in His image and spirit into His world."

Polygamy is depicted in the Bible, but only in the Old Testament, and all those families were marred by strife which was a direct result of polygamy. Polygamy is never held up as an example to be imitated.

A Biblical ethic of sex is further developed in the Gospels and the New Testament, discarding the ritual purity requirements of the Mosaic Law while retaining its moral code. Jesus affirmed marriage as one man to one woman for life, while challenging the misuse of the Law by some of the Pharisees to justify easy divorce. (Matthew 19:3-9; Mark 10:2-12) Paul added abandonment to adultery as justification for divorce. But even in the case of a believer married to an unbeliever, divorce was a last resort allowed only in the case of abandonment. (1 Corinthians 7:10-16) The New Testament sexual ethic is developed in this framework of lifelong, male-female monogamous marriage, both for its own merits in producing harmonious relations within families and society and for the living picture provided of the intimate bond between Christ the bridegroom and His bride, the church. (Ephesians 5:22-33)

In summary of what Jesus taught about sex and marriage, He defined marriage as between one man and one woman for life. He also limited sexual activity to marriage. Any sex outside of the marital relationship is sin, and that includes any kind of sexual abuse. The aforementioned biblical principles regarding sex and marriage need to be preached from pulpits, taught by youth directors and Sunday school teachers, and, especially at home, taught by Christian parents in order to minimize and perhaps prevent today's youth from straying from God's ideal for sex and marriage.

In addition to the basic biblical principles explained above, church staff, lay leaders, and parents need to teach children and youth at an age appropriate level the dangers of sex outside of marriage. This discussion should also include what signs to look for in a person who may have targeted them or another child as a potential sex abuse victim.

Develop church safety systems to prevent sexually inappropriate behavior. MinistrySafe is one organization that assists churches and other ministries in developing a safety plan to help keep the church or ministry environment free from inappropriate sexual conduct.

> *Programs that serve children and youth play a vital role in the lives of our children and in our community. Ministry programs help to develop each child's intellectual, social, spiritual or physical capacity. As they serve, ministry leaders cannot forget their responsibility to safeguard each child, as well as those who serve them.*
>
> *MinistrySafe was created by legal professionals who are sexual abuse experts. After decades of litigating sexual abuse cases, Gregory Love and Kimberlee Norris founded MinistrySafe to help ministries meet legal standards of care and reduce the risk of sexual abuse by creating preventative measures tailored to fit the needs of churches, camps and ministry programs.*
>
> *MinistrySafe offers a comprehensive program utilizing a 5-Part Safety System that creates overlapping layers of protection to ensure no situation is overlooked. MinistrySafe offers customized systems of protection to fit each program type.* (MinistrySafe, 2016, The Safety System section, ¶ 1-3)

Orgeron's former home church's denomination, Church of the Nazarene has joined forces with MinistrySafe to combat the problem of child and adolescent sexual abuse by requiring all Nazarene Churches to adopt the Nazarene Safe program. While a Nazarene church member, Orgeron received a certificate for the completion of Ministry Safe Child Sexual Abuse Awareness Training.

Nazarene Safe. The Board of General Superintendents of the Church of the Nazarene embraces a zero tolerance policy regarding sexual abuse:

> *The Church of the Nazarene has adopted a zero tolerance policy for sexual misconduct and inappropriate behavior with minors. All workers, leaders, and pastoral staff are to be above reproach in their conduct and to act in the best interest of others. This requires not only that they themselves refrain from engaging in any abusive or suspicious behavior involving minors; they will also be required to report without delay to the proper authorities anyone seen engaging in*

such behavior. (Church of the Nazarene Board of General Superintendents, 2017, Zero Tolerance of Sexual Misconduct with Minors section, ¶ 1)

The developers of Nazarene Safe created a seven part course that anyone working with children in the Nazarene Church must complete. The video tutorial

answers the questions: what is a safety system and how is one created? The video tutorial is designed to help Nazarene Churches better understand the five key components of a system designed to keep children safe from sexual abuse. Viewers will learn the WHY, WHAT and the HOW of an effective Safety System:

- *WHY a safety system is necessary*
- *WHAT a safety system includes*
- *HOW to implement a safety system* (Nazarene Safe, 2017, Safety System section, ¶ 1)

The seven sessions to the Nazarene Safe program include the safety system introduction; information correcting misconceptions about sexual abuse; and MinistrySafe's 5-Part Safety System (Entire System Overview, Session 3), which requires sexual abuse awareness training, appropriate criminal background checks (Session 4); skillful screening (Session 5); tailored policies and procedures (Session 6); and, monitoring and oversight (Session 7). The Nazarene Safe course may be taken on-line for a fee, or in a classroom setting with a qualified instructor. For more information, see the MinistrySafe or Nazarene Safe Web site.

---

1 Cor. 6:9-10 (NKJV)

"**9 Do you not know that the unrighteous will not inherit the kingdom of God? Do not be deceived. Neither fornicators, nor idolaters, nor adulterers, nor homosexuals,[a] nor sodomites, 10 nor thieves, nor covetous, nor drunkards, nor revilers, nor extortioners will inherit the kingdom of God.**"

Final Reflections

Christians, remember the Church did not get in its current unhealthy state overnight. It will take time, perhaps years, to reverse the effects of years of unhealthy attitudes, beliefs, and behaviors that have contributed to the sin problems of gluttony and sexual abuse in the Church. If God has called someone as an individual, or as part of a church body, to work for, and to advocate for renewing the health of Christians and others in these areas, Orgeron encourages him or her to not give up the fight. The church needs revival. The lost world needs spiritual awakening. Before spiritual awakening can occur, Orgeron believes the church must get its house in order through revival by way of repentance. Remember, we may lose a battle here and there, but know the war was won at the Cross by Jesus Christ. Orgeron closes this chapter with three Scriptures that have offered her encouragement to continue following her call to full time vocational ministry:

1 Thessalonians 5:24 (KJV)

24 Faithful is he that calleth you, who also will do it.

Galatians 6:9 (KJV)

9 And let us not be weary in well doing: for in due season we shall reap, if we faint not.

Isaiah 40:31 (KJV)

31 But they that wait upon the LORD shall renew their strength; they shall mount up with wings as eagles; they shall run, and not be weary; and they shall walk, and not faint.

***

Chapter 17: Disordered Eating in the Church

Key Terms/Concepts

Bod4God   MinistrySafe
Body and Soul   Nazarene Safe
Celebrate Recovery   The Daniel Plan
Life Recovery/Lose It for Life   Toxic faith

Questions for Reflection:

1. What do statistics show about disordered eating in the church?
2. Discuss the internal roots to disordered eating in the church.
3. What types of unbiblical attitudes regarding food and the body exist in the church?
4. What is toxic faith?
5. What external influences affect disordered eating in the church?
6. Why is it important for churches to promote healthy lifestyles?
7. What can churches do to help reverse the epidemic of disordered eating?
8. What are six mistakes people make in starting health and wellness campaigns at a church?
9. How should health and wellness programs in churches differ from those programs in secular settings?
10. What are benefits to having health and wellness programs in churches?
11. What are six possible programs churches can utilize to promote health and wellness in the church?
12. Why do churches need to be concerned and be pro-active towards the epidemic of sexual misconduct?
13. Why do children and adolescents, and their overseers need protection from sexual predators in churches?
14. What mentality in church parents and others leave church children more vulnerable to perpetrators?
15. What was and continues to be God's design for sex?
16. How did Jesus define marriage?

***

Chapter 18: Linking Disordered Eating with Sexual Abuse

Introduction

As an overcomer of an eating disorder and as a survivor of sexual abuse, Orgeron developed an interest in how disordered eating and sexual abuse relate. Thus, in writing this article her intent is to share what she has learned through her studies, research, and personal observations.

Does sexual trauma influence eating behavior? If so, how and why does this occur? Orgeron explored these key questions in her research of literature that linked sexual abuse and disordered eating, including etiology, treatment, and prevention. In this article she will cover etiology and treatment, as the topic of the prevention of sexual abuse, particularly the role of the church was discussed in the previous chapter.

In reviewing the literature, "common themes" were sought out. For example, a common theme is that sexual abuse predisposes a victim to developing disordered eating. Rader Programs (2004), the first to ascertain a significant link between sexual abuse and disordered eating, reported that over 80 percent of their clients recall some form of abuse.

Throughout her literature reviews over the years Orgeron has considered sexual abuse as defined by Allender (1990). He reported that in addition to sexual contact, sexual abuse can be verbal, visual, or psychological. Any violation of a child's physical/sexual boundaries is considered abuse. This includes actions ranging from very severe contact (genital intercourse and oral or anal sex—forcible or non-forcible)

> "a common theme is that sexual abuse predisposes a victim to developing disordered eating."

to least severe contact (sexual kissing and sexual touching of buttocks, thighs, legs, or clothed breasts or genitals); exposure to or use for pornography; and, even use of a child as a spouse surrogate.

As in writing *Food as an Idol*, Orgeron considered disordered eating throughout her literature review as being on a continuum. For a review of what disordered eating entails, please see the Introduction.

Etiology Linking Sexual Abuse and Disordered Eating

Researchers have explored associations between sexual abuse and disordered eating for years. Smolak and Murnen (2002) explored such research and conducted meta-analysis on their findings. Results reflected a positive correlation between sexual abuse and disordered eating. As mentioned in Chapter 4, to review, Schwartz and Gay (1996) used existing research linking sexual abuse and disordered eating, along with information from their clinical experience, to compile a table of the functions, or purposes that ED symptoms can serve. The "Adaptive Function of Eating Disorder Symptoms" (Schwartz and Gay, p. 95) is listed in Appendix B.

The Self-Medication Hypothesis

Gurze (2003) reported the self-medication hypothesis stipulates that eating binges may be an attempt to manage anxiety and depression, which stem from sexual abuse. According to this hypothesis, in an attempt to deal with the abuse the anticipated sequence of the disorders follows: abuse; anxiety or mood disorders, and then bulimia nervosa (BN) or substance abuse disorders. Research by Schoemaker, Smit, Bijl, and Vollebergh (2002) supports the self-medication hypothesis. Schoemaker et al. tested the hypothesis by comparing BN cases with four mutually exclusive diagnostic control groups: psychiatric controls, substance abuse controls, dual diagnosis controls, and healthy controls. Results indicated that a history of psychological or multiple abuses was a specific risk factor for dual diagnosis disorder and for BN.

Posttraumatic Stress Disorder (PTSD) Response

Root (1991), as cited by Schwartz and Gay (1996), reported that ED symptoms are a masked PTSD response for some clients. Root found that for some clients who gave up the ED symptoms before they dealt with the abuse, other trauma-related symptoms such as flashbacks, self-mutilation, or suicidal tendencies increased.

Unhealthy Body Image

"Body image disturbance is a primary feature of eating-disordered, sexually abused individuals" (Costin, 1996, p. 125). Studies by Tripp and Petrie (2001) and by Van den Berg, Wertheim, Thompson, and Paxton (2002) support this link. Tripp and Petrie studied 330 female undergraduates to compare relationships among sexual abuse, eating disorders, bodily shame, and body disparagement. The researchers found that body disparagement explicitly predicts eating disorder symptoms. Van den Bern et al. studied 410 Grade 10 girls comparing body mass index, body dissatisfaction, teasing history, global psychological performance, and dietary restraint techniques used, and bulimic behaviors. The researchers concluded from the results that body dissatisfaction influenced the occurrence of bulimic behaviors.

Sexual Barrier Weight

Weiner and Stephens (1996) surveyed 42 female ED patients, two-thirds reporting sexual trauma histories. Using graphic analysis, age versus weight, Weiner and Stephens found that body weight fluctuations followed sexually significant life events, especially for those study participants reporting experiences of rape and sexual relationships that ended. From the study results, Weiner and Stephens proposed "that sexually traumatized persons may resist a specific body weight due to fear of sexual attractiveness or impulses relating to specific sexual trauma that occurred at that weight" (p. 68).

Desire to Self-Injure

Schwartz and Cohn (1996) reported disordered eating as one form of self-injury in victims of sexual abuse. Because sexual abuse violates such extreme boundaries and disrupts attachment and bonding, Schwartz and Cohn pointed out that some clients display self-injury symptoms.

Control and Dysfunctional Issues

Dinsmore and Stormshak (2003) investigated the possible mediating significance of adolescent intrapersonal aptitude, gauged by self-control and coping, on the connection between ED symptoms and family functioning in early at-risk adolescents. Results revealed a correlation between weight concerns and both self-control deficiencies and negative coping skills. Furthermore, family factors, such as cohesion, significantly correlated with adolescent self-control deficiencies and negative coping skills.

Emotional Expression

Miller (2003) reported that sexual abuse victims struggling with weight issues use food and other related behaviors to cope with the emotional upheaval resulting from the abuse. According to Miller,

> *Eating can be used as a way to express emotions. Eating soothes the "soul". People eat when they are depressed, discouraged, lonely, scared, anxious, tired, and bored and for many other emotional reasons. Relieving the pain of negative emotions through eating can cause obesity and present a barrier to weight control once the client decides to lose weight* (p. 82).

One study by Murray and Waller (2002) indicated that significant levels of internalized shame exist in clients reporting sexual abuse and bulimic symptoms. According to Murray and Waller, the shame results from the sexual abuse with the bulimic attitudes and behaviors as coping methods to deal with the shame.

A Multifactorial Model

Rorty and Yager (1996) proposed that the development of eating disorders in victims of sexual abuse is a complex process composed of many facets, including child temperaments, vulnerability to comorbid conditions, affect regulation, and family and peer influences. Figure 7 depicts the complicated genesis developed by Rorty and Yager (p. 26).

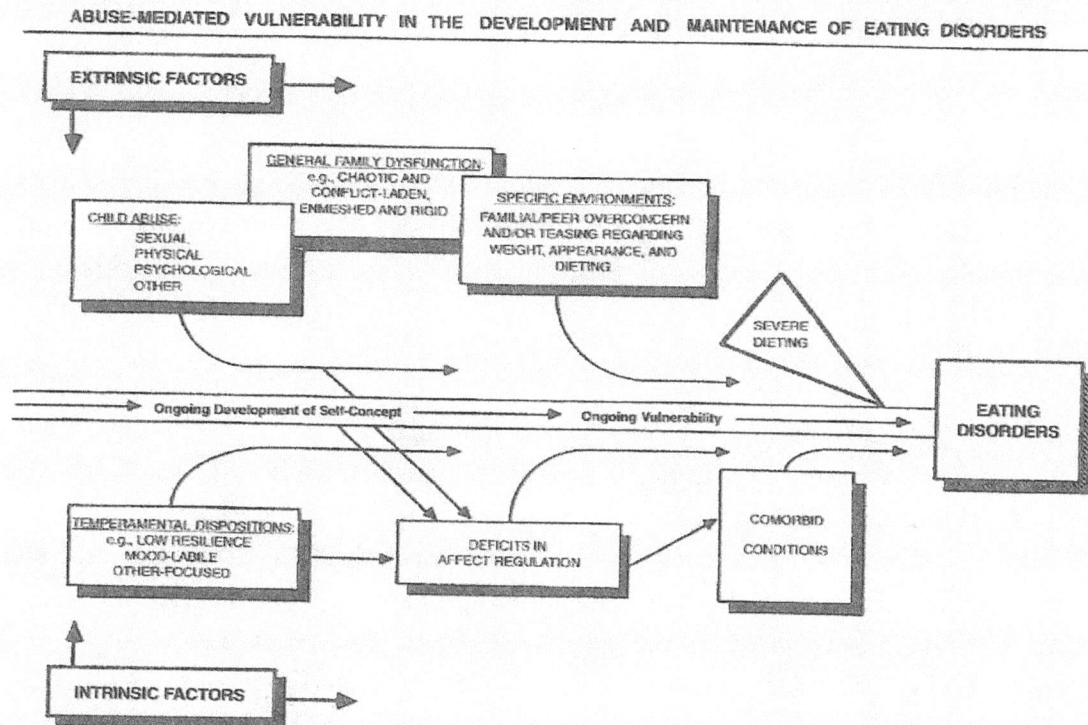

ABUSE-MEDIATED VULNERABILITY IN THE DEVELOPMENT AND MAINTENANCE OF EATING DISORDERS

Figure 7: A multifactorial model for the emergence of eating disorders in some women who have been abused in childhood. (Rorty & Yager, 1996, p. 26)

Other Related Studies

Orgeron found two studies linking sexual harassment, a form of sexual abuse, to ED behaviors. Harned and Fitzgerald (2002) surveyed 472 active-duty military women, 254 active-duty military men, and 1,853 women with a lawsuit against a national corporation for sexual harassment. The survey questions assessed unwanted sex-related experiences at work, job satisfaction, ED symptoms, psychological distress, and health status. Results indicated a link between sexual harassment and ED symptoms in women. No correlation existed between sexual harassment and ED symptoms among men in the study. A case study by Gati, Tenyi, Tury, and Wildmann (2002) supports the results of the Harned and Fitzgerald study. Gati et al. reported about an adolescent female diagnosed with anorexia nervosa. The diagnosis significantly correlated with being sexually harassed via the Internet.

Worth noting are key statements by Schwartz and Cohn (1996):

Certainly some eating-disordered clients were not sexually or physically abused or neglected, and many sexually abused clients do not have eating disorders. Eating disorders are determined by a multitude of factors, and there are many syndromes associated with eating disorders, some of which are directly and indirectly influenced by sexual trauma (pp. IX-X).

Other factors in addition to sexual abuse that could precipitate ED symptoms researched by Striegel-Moore, Dohm, Pike, Wilfley, and Fairburn (2002) are bullying and discrimination from peers.

Striegel-Moore et al. found that physical and sexual abuse, bullying from peers and discrimination are all risk factors for developing binge eating disorder.

Assessment

The assessment process to determine whether a person has an ED should include both a thorough physical examination and a complete family and individual history of eating behaviors and other related disorders. Additionally, patients may be given one or more available tests used in the screening process.

ED Assessment Tools

Eating Attitudes Test (EAT-26). EAT-26 (2017) reports that this test developed by Dr. David Garner is probably the most popular measure of symptoms and issues related to eating disorders. This test may be taken on-line at http://www.eat-26.com/.

  Other on-line testing. The website psychcentral.com (Grohol, 2018) offers free on-line screening tests for eating disorders. These tests include Binge Eating Disorder Quiz; Eating Disorder Screening Test; Do I Have an Eating Disorder? Quiz; and the EAT-26 mentioned previously.

  Cambridge Eating Disorder Center (CEDC) and Screening for Mental Health, Inc. (SMH) partnered to offer a free on-line screening tool for eating disorders. (CEDC, 2017). This screening tool is available at http://www.mybodyscreening.org/

Other Tools for Diagnosing

In addition to the ED self-report instruments, personality tests may be used with persons diagnosed with eating disorders to identify factors such as anxiety, depression, and impulsivity commonly associated with EDs. Psychcentral.com also offers a number of personality assessments available at https://psychcentral.com/quizzes/personality-tests/.

  To establish an official diagnosis, criteria from the Diagnostic and Statistical Manual of Mental Disorders, Fifth Edition (DSM-5) (American Psychiatric Association, 2013) must be met. The DSM-5 contains diagnostic descriptions for anorexia, BN, binge eating disorder, and other related eating disorders; PTSD, and other mental illnesses, such as substance use disorders often associated with disordered eating.

Treatment

Pharmacological Treatments

The use and effectiveness of treating individuals diagnosed with eating disorders using medication depends on the type of ED, such as AN, BN, or BED; and on whether co-existing diagnoses, such as depression, obsessive compulsive disorder, alcohol or substance abuse, anxiety disorders, PTSD and attention deficit disorder, exist. Regarding pharmacological treatment for anorexia, Mayo Clinic Staff (2016a) and WebMD Staff (2017a) reported that no medications have been approved by the FDA as treatment for anorexia, as no medication used has been very effective. David T. Tharp M.D., M.Div., Medical Director and founder of Stonebriar Psychiatric Services (n.d.b) and a former "staff psychiatrist at the Remuda Ranch Center for Anorexia and Bulimia in Arizona, a treatment program for women with eating disorders and dual diagnoses," (Stonebriar Psychiatric Services, n.d.a, ¶ 2) reported in treating AN:

> Some studies have found Periactin and other medications which stimulate appetite to be helpful. However, many of these young women already live with constant hunger, and the idea of a medicine that tries to "make them eat" is frequently terrifying for them. If depression is present, anti-depressants may be helpful if one understands that you cannot achieve full therapeutic benefit until there has been some weight restoration. Some of the newer "antipsychotic" medications have also been helpful in low doses, and it is felt that this is partly due to alleviating some of the body image anxiety and possibly some of the distortion, which at times almost seems to take on delusional proportions. (Tharp, 2006a, p. 2)

A study by Kaye et al. (2001) offers evidence that Prozac is effective in treating anorexia. Subjects of the study were 35 people with anorexia discharged from the hospital after regaining weight. Sixteen of the 35 patients received Prozac while the remaining 19 received a placebo. After a year of outpatient treatment, results showed that 10 of the 16 individuals treated with Prozac maintained a healthy body weight without relapsing, as compared to 3 of the 19 patients treated with placebo.

Bulimia pharmacological treatment. Mayo Clinic Staff (2016b) and WebMD Staff (2017b) report antidepressants in conjunction with psychotherapy are helpful in the treatment of BN. WebMD Staff report "Antidepressants, such as selective serotonin reuptake inhibitors (SSRIs) – including Prozac, Zoloft, Celexa and Lexapro – in combination with psychological therapies, are now a mainstay in bulimia therapy." (Medications for bulimia section, ¶ 1) However, Mayo Clinic Staff report Prozac is the only antidepressant approved by the FDA to treat bulimia.

BED Pharmacological Treatment. Tharp (2006b) reported:

> There are a number of antidepressants, as well as some anti-obesity agents and anticonvulsants which have shown to be of some benefit with BED. However, these have generally not yet been approved for the treatment of BED by the FDA. These would include Meridia (sibutramine) and Xenical (orlistat) as anti-obesity agents, along with Topamax as one of the anticonvulsants that has at times been helpful. Fluoxetine (Prozac) in its higher dose ranges of 60-80 mg per day has frequently been helpful in reducing the frequency of binges and often with accompanying weight loss. Other medications in the SSRI group, such as the Zoloft, Celexa, and Luvox have shown similar trends. (p. 2)

Nutrition Therapy

Nutrition education and intervention, by a registered dietitian, is a key element of treating eating disorders, according to Ozier, Henry, and American Dietetic Association (2011). Ozier et al. (2011) notes the responsibilities of the dietitian as assessing the nutritional status, knowledge base, motivation, and current eating and treatment plan; developing the nutrition section of the proposed treatment; implementing the treatment plan and supporting the patient in achieving his or her goals. The dietitian continuously relates with the patient throughout the course of treatment and assists the primary medical provider with monitoring lab results, vital signs, and any physical symptoms related to malnutrition.

Exercise Therapy

Although concerns exist for using exercise to treat ED, especially in those individuals who exercise compulsively, Hausenblas, Cook, and Chittester (2008) concluded that exercise may be beneficial as an intervention for ED. Hausenblas et al. (2008) reported

> *Theoretical justification suggests that by improving physical fitness through regular healthy exercise, patients with ED may experience improved self-esteem, body image, and mood, as well as a reduction in the uncomfortable sensations of bloating and distention during eating [Fossati, 2004]. Additionally, exercise promotes self-regulation. Therefore, exercise may reduce bodily tensions and negative mood and increase tolerance to everyday stress, which are all triggers for binging and purging [Alpers & Tuschen-Caiffier, 2001].* (p. 44)

Psychotherapy

Another vital member of the treatment team for a person with an ED is a psychologist. Treatment procedures that are recommended by any one therapist will reflect his or her treatment philosophy, according to Freeman, Miller and Mizes (2000). In treating eating disorders psychologists often need to fill the role of educator as well as help the client deal with the broader problems that led to the disorder. Most professionals, according to The Something Fishy Website on Eating Disorders (1998-2018), adopt an eclectic approach that combines cognitive, behavioral, and psychodynamic models with family therapy and psychoeducation.

Cognitive-behaviorists presume the primary vehicle for permanent recovery is cognitive; although, they assume lasting change occurs at many levels, including behavioral, cognitive, and emotional. The goal of cognitive-behavioral therapists is to have the patient change overrated concepts about the desirability of thinness and to overcome fears about weight gain (Williamson & Netemeyer, 2000).

Cognitive techniques. Ridding the patient of self-defeating attitudes and beliefs that precipitated the disorder is the goal of cognitive therapists treating eating disorders. Old beliefs and attitudes are replaced with realistic, healthy ones.

The integrative cognitive therapy (ICT) treatment method for eating disorders proposed by Wonderlich, Peterson, Mitchell, and Crow (2000) differs from other cognitive and interpersonal models by placing a greater clinical emphasis on cultural factors, self-oriented cognition, interpersonal schemas, interpersonal relationship styles, and affect regulation. In this multifaceted treatment method, multitudes of strategies for overcoming eating disorders exist but the authors focus on three, which they consider crucial to recovery. The first goal of the ICT therapist is to promote behavioral change in food consumption, meal planning, and poor nutritional habits. This goal is accomplished through teaching clients about the maladaptive nature of dieting, the cultural factors that encourage it, and providing healthy alternatives to eating behaviors which can be implemented into the client's lifestyle. The second mechanism of change advocated by ICT is to modify the actual self-perception and improve self-esteem. Finally, *helping the patient to adopt an interpersonal stance that allows her to be interpersonally attached to others, but very much aware of boundaries and limits, is considered optimal. Helping the patient to identify and express her thoughts and feelings in relationships is considered an essential element to the healthy functioning of an autonomous self.* (p. 279)

Behavioral therapy. Many hospital and day programs incorporate behavior therapy into their programs. This approach is tailored to the needs of each patient individually and involves the gradual increase in activities with weight gain or loss.

Psychodynamic models. Psychodynamic therapists focus on early experiences that may have contributed to the course of development in an ED. The goals of psychodynamic therapists include: understanding the different purposes that maintaining eating disordered symptoms serve for a client, improving the client's self-esteem, increasing the client's self-differentiation, improving the eating disorder symptomatology, and improving social functioning. Mechanisms of change that psychoanalysts use include corrective emotional experiences, making the unconscious conscious, gaining insight, and internalization (Fallon & Bunce, 2000).

Self psychology therapy is a psychoanalytic theory reported by Sands (2000) to treat eating disorders. Self psychology theory emphasizes the inner world of the patient. Sands separated "out four mechanisms of change offered either explicitly or implicitly by self-psychology over the years which, in their most simplified form, can be called forms of (1) internalization, (2) resumption of development, (3) desomatization, and (4) integration." (p. 203) Kohut (1971, 1977, 1984), as cited by Sands, describes the way clients change as "transmuting internalization process." (Sands, p. 203) For this process to be successful an empathic relationship must exist between the client and therapist, as the client internalizes behaviors, such as self-calming, learned from the therapist. The second method of change "resumption of development" "suggests that empathic understanding serves as a facilitating medium reinstating self-developmental processes." (Sands, p. 204)

As cited by dictionary.com, psychiatrists define somatization as "the conversion of anxiety into physical symptoms." (Somatization, n.d.) Using desomatization as a way to help clients change, the client learns to express emotions verbally rather than stuffing them to manifest in the form of physical symptoms.

As cited by dictionary.com, psychologists define integration as "the organization of the constituent elements of the personality into a coordinated, harmonious whole." (Integration, n.d.) According to Sands (2000), "it is the empathic responsiveness of the therapist which allows disowned domains of the self to become recognized, understood, and slowly integrated into the patient's central self-structure." (p. 205)

Psychoeducation. Treasure, Schmidt, and Troop (2000) view anorexia not just as a dieting disorder but also as a form of stress response to severe life events or problems. Initial treatment sessions focus on answering the questions "where is the patient at; where is she coming from and how can we help her move in the direction of sustained change?" (p. 284). Therapy goals include teaching the patient that the "cons" of maintaining anorexia outweighs the "pros". Self-esteem is monitored during the entire treatment process. The techniques of motivational interviewing are utilized, which requires the therapist to express empathy, develop discrepancy, avoid arguments, and roll with resistance and support self-efficacy.

Family Therapy

Bryant-Waugh (2000) described family therapy as an approach to treating eating disorders that integrates developmental psychology, Bowenian systems theory, and feminist ideology. Exploring the patient's developmental history and analyzing past patterns of response to life changes and stress manifest the influence of developmental psychology in this approach.

Bowenian therapists view therapy as an opportunity for people to learn more about themselves and their relationships, so that they can assume responsibility for their own problems. This is a process of active inquiry that helps family members get past blaming and fault-finding in order to face and explore their own roles in family problems. Understanding, not action is the key to solving dysfunctional behavior. Treatment involves placing the problem in a multigenerational framework through a timeline and a genogram, lowering anxiety in the patient, increasing differentiation, and using process questions and relationship experiments. (Nichols & Schwartz, 2001, as cited by Owens, 2002)

For treating eating disorders, DeGiacomo and Antonietta (2000) proposed the Elementary Pragmatic Model that evolved out of general systems theory and has a strong focus on family participation and intervention. This approach also embraces intensive, multidisciplinary Day Hospital treatment that includes psycho-education on eating disorders, group therapy, nutrition therapy, creativity groups, and physical rehabilitation.

Group therapy

"Group therapy is just as effective as individual therapy – for treating a wide range of symptoms – and … group participation offers a unique therapeutic advantage." (Rosenfeld, 2017, ¶ 3) The advantage is group members can identify with each other, they can learn from each other, and support one another. As members interact, group therapists also can offer insight to members on how to improve one's boundaries or communication skills. Furthermore, "Group therapy offers a cost-effective alternative to individual therapy, and group treatment allows access to a larger population of individuals, who might not otherwise receive care." (Rosenfeld, ¶ 5)

Equine therapy.

Eating Disorder Hope (2012) defines equine therapy as

> a form of psychotherapy in which horses are utilized as tools for a man or woman to develop greater self-understanding and assist in emotional growth. Equine Therapy is a form of animal assisted therapy, an aspect of mental health that acknowledges the bond between animals and humans in addition to the opportunity for emotional healing that can occur when a relationship is initiated between two species, such as human and horse. (What is Equine Therapy? Section, ¶ 1)

According to Eating Disorder Hope (2012), "many *eating disorder therapists and professionals* recognize the benefits of equine therapy as a method of improving lives and refer patients to riding programs." (What is Equine Therapy? Section, ¶ 2)

"Founded in 1999, the Equine Assisted Growth and Learning Association (EAGALA) is the leading international nonprofit association for professionals incorporating horses to address mental health and personal development needs." (Welcome section, ¶ 1) The website of EAGALA (2009-2010) sites the goals and opportunities offered by the organization. Among these objectives and opportunities are training and certifying therapists in the field of Equine Assisted Psychotherapy (EAP); annual conferences; and providing educational, training, and support resources. In addition, EAGALA offers a map and search options to find where their programs are located.

EAP patients learn about themselves when they participate in activities with horses and then discuss feelings and behavior patterns learned. Canopy Cove (2016) and Remuda Ranch (2014b, 2016) are located in settings that allow them to utilize Equine Therapy as a part of the recovery process for patients. Horse care, grooming procedures, saddlery, and basic equitation (horseback riding) may be a part of eating disorder treatment for patients at Remuda Ranch. Research from Remuda Ranch indicates a number of benefits to EAP. These benefits include:

- Enhanced self-esteem
- Overcoming fears
- Impulse modulation
- Renewed self-efficacy
- Feelings of belonging
- Reaching out
- Improved body image awareness
- Self-acceptance
- Assertiveness
- Development of trust
- Outward direction of focus
- Improved communication skills
- Improved emotional awareness
- Improved emotional regulation
- Improved self-control
- Healing relationships
- Freedom from inhibitions
- Spiritual growth.

Expressive Creative Therapy

As a part of their multi-disciplinary treatment program, the staff of Remuda Ranch (2017b) offers expressive arts therapy as a component of treating eating disorders. Through expressive arts therapy patients explore their identities and problems using their personal creativity. Self-worth, self-concept, and a sense of individual purpose may be discovered using therapeutic music, dance/movement (DMT), art, and creative writing. Relationship systems also are examined through the expressive therapies. (Owens, 2002)

Remuda Ranch (2017b) lists the benefits to expressive arts therapy:

- *Patients share their perceptions and viewpoints that might otherwise be difficult to express through more traditional therapies.*
- *Promoting a sense of freedom allows patients to unearth and dissect their inner feelings during the healing process.*
- *Using images to express their feelings may be easier than conveying these feelings in words.* (Healing Through Art section, ¶ 1)

Music/DMT. According to Wennerstrand (2002), as cited by Owens (2002), research shows that many individuals with eating disorders have alexithymia, "defined as difficulty in putting feelings and fantasies into words (Zerbe, 1995)." (Wennerstrand, ¶ 2) Through DMT patients express that which cannot be expressed with words. Dance/movement therapy practiced by trained dance/movement therapists certified by The American Dance Therapy Association is a body-based therapy that combines interpersonal, object-relations theory, movement analysis, and dance technique.

Art/writing. Many researchers and practitioners recommend that persons recovering from eating disorders keep daily food journals and a journal to uncover and express both stuffed and current feelings. Orgeron has found journaling helps to release pent-up emotions, to discover one's trigger foods and situations, and to facilitate in positive self-talk. DeGoede and Drews (1998) recommend 15 to 20 minutes of journaling daily.

> *When you use your daily journal, allow yourself to write without worrying about grammar, sentence structure, or spelling: it doesn't even have to make sense. This is an exercise in beginning to get to know the "inside" you from the "outside" you.* (p. 17)

Restoring Powerlessness, Betrayal, & Ambivalence from Sexual Abuse

Persons who were sexually abused will find no quick answers, no easy cures, and will struggle with some issues related to the abuse all their life, according to Allender (1990, 1995, 2008). He described the effects of sexual abuse and what is necessary to heal from these effects. Allender identified powerlessness, betrayal, and ambivalence resulting from the sexual abuse as the effects that must be overcome on the journey to healing. The three things Allender pointed out that are keys to overcoming these effects are honesty, willingness to change, and a desire to help others. By honesty, Allender means not living in denial, accepting the damage done, and grieving over the losses. Furthermore, persons who were abused need to look at how they have harmed themselves and others by living out the effects of the abuse. Repentance is crucial to this process. The willingness to change may result in the abused confronting the abuser; although, Allender pointed out that confrontation is not a must for healing to occur. In some instances, confrontation is not possible. Furthermore, Allender reported that a major key to moving ahead on the journey to healing is allowing the abuse to open the heart to want to do good for others.

Wholistic Approaches to Disordered Eating

There are two wholistic approaches to healing that Orgeron endorses. One of those wholistic approaches to healing that she recommends to others is that of Dr. Phil McGraw, which he discussed in the book *The Ultimate Weight Solution: The 7 keys to Weight Loss Freedom* (Free Press, 2003). Please see

Chapter 1 of *Food as an Idol* to review the highlights of Dr. McGraw's 7 keys to successful weight loss and weight maintenance.

The other wholistic approach to healing that Orgeron recommends to others is that of Dr. Gregory Jantz. To review this model, see Chapter 7 entitled "A Wholistic Model in Treating Disordered Eating".

Improving Body Image

"The creation of a positive body image is not only a worthwhile pursuit, especially for persons who've experienced an eating disorder, it is also an objective that's really possible to achieve" (Cash, 2003, p. 13). Cash reported about an 8-step cognitive behavioral approach that he developed and published as *The Body Image Workbook* (New Harbinger Publications, 1997). This approach to developing positive body image includes techniques such as taking personal inventories, journaling, using positive self-talk and avoiding individuals who lead to feelings of self-consciousness and negative body image.

Closing Remarks

After reviewing the literature linking sexual abuse and disordered eating, Orgeron is more convinced that sexual abuse sets individuals up to develop disordered eating. This conclusion parallels her personal experience where she attributes many of her food and body image issues with having been sexually abused at an early age. However, her conclusion may not be applicable to men as most of the study participants were females. The one reported study that used males found no link between sexual abuse and disordered eating. Further study using male victims of sexual abuse would be needed to determine if a link between sexual abuse and disordered eating exists in males.

Orgeron can identify with many of the theories presented linking sexual abuse and disordered eating. For example, she used to eat to self-medicate and to express emotions. Several psychiatrists and psychologists have diagnosed PTSD in her. She also identifies with body image problems having been teased all through school for being "short" and "fat". Above all, she recognizes a lot of truth in the Sexual Barrier weight hypothesis because she knows that she used to sabotage weight loss efforts by overeating when she got to a certain point because she feared being raped again.

Of all the alternatives for treatment to maintain a healthy weight, Orgeron recommends those with sexual abuse and disordered eating issues try one of the wholistic approaches. However, she does want to stress the importance of not traveling the journey to healing alone. Seek professional help.

***

Chapter 18: Linking Disordered Eating with Sexual Abuse

Key Terms/Concepts

Ambivalence

Betrayal

Body image

Desomatization

Integration

Integrative cognitive therapy (ICT)

Internalization

Multifactorial model

Powerlessness

Resumption of development

Self-medication hypothesis

Sexual barrier weight

Somatization

Questions for Reflection:

1. Does sexual trauma influence eating behavior? If so, how and why does this occur?
2. What etiological theories exist regarding the link between disordered eating and sexual abuse?
3. Discuss the self-medication hypothesis?
4. What is meant by the phrase sexual barrier weight?
5. What is the premise of the multifactorial model in the development of eating disorders?
6. What did studies exploring a link between sexual harassment and ED behaviors reveal?
7. What are treatment options when a person diagnosed with an ED reports past sexual abuse?
8. What is the goal of cognitive therapists treating eating disorders?
9. What are the goals of psychodynamic therapists in treating a client with an eating disorder?
10. According to Sands (2000), what are four tools used in self psychology to treat eating disorders?
11. What are advantages to group therapy over individual psychotherapy?
12. According to Allender, what are three keys to overcoming the powerlessness, betrayal, and ambivalence experienced by victims of sexual abuse?

***

Afterword

Thank you to those who have made the journey to read *Food as an Idol: Finding Freedom from Disordered Eating.* I realize I have stepped on a lot of toes writing this book. However, just as a friend of mine, Rev. James Kahler, pastor of Bible Holiness Church, Madison, TN, pointed out a few days ago, "it's easy for us as Christians to point fingers at those who abuse alcohol and drugs, but when it comes to food, we don't want to deal with it. More people have probably hurt their bodies with food than with alcohol or drugs. That ought not to be."

In the concluding remarks, I want to stress that though *Food as an Idol* may be quite extensive in the knowledge offered about disordered eating, also referred to as gluttony, this book is not intended to be used as a substitute for professional treatment from a psychiatrist, therapist, or eating disorder treatment center. Furthermore, including the resources listed in the appendix of this book is not intended as an endorsement or a recommendation for the source. Persons reading *Food as an Idol* who need help or just want to learn more should check out each resource and decide what resources would best help them individually. For those who have read *Food as an Idol* and who see themselves within the pages of this book realizing they too may have issues related to disordered eating, I urge those individuals to seek professional help to walk alongside them on the road to freedom and healing; but, above all, I encourage you to seek God's forgiveness and His deliverance from disordered eating. He delivered me! He can deliver you too!

Parents, may I have your attention please? If you see your child through the pages of this book, please take your child to have a professional assessment. Eating disorders are progressive in nature and can lead to serious consequences, including death. The sooner you can get help for your child the better. Additionally, I encourage you to have family meals together. However, keep the atmosphere around meals and snack time pleasant. Stress and negative talk around the dinner table can upset your and your child's digestive processes. Dinner time is not the time for you and your spouse to be discussing family problems or other disturbing news that would upset children. Keep serious, negative conversations behind closed doors.

To teachers, coaches, church youth leaders, etc., I want to encourage you to be alert to the symptoms of DE that children you work with may be displaying. If you notice DE symptoms I encourage you to speak with the child and the parents or other caregivers. If they give you no satisfaction and the symptoms continue in the child, please do not hesitate to report the situation to your superiors and if necessary, your local children's services, especially if the child looks thin and malnourished.

In conclusion, Piper (2015) pointed out that when gluttony is present in an individual's life:

The way back may involve many external controls and disciplines outside. But in the end, the only way out will be when God himself through Jesus Christ becomes our satisfying soul food and contentment in him becomes the governor and the regulator of all our appetites and desires. (¶ 17)

I believe that the "external controls" and "disciplines" referred to by Piper may come in a variety of forms, including medication, individual psychotherapy, group therapy, inpatient treatment, spiritual disciplines, and the various other forms of treatment mentioned in this book. These treatment options are tools that God can use to bring healing and freedom from disordered eating. I encourage those with disordered eating and those who know someone who exhibits symptoms of disordered eating to take advantage of "God's tools", the resources provided in this book and elsewhere to get help. After all, as The Renfrew Center Foundation (n.d.) reported,

> *Eating disorders are not just fads, phases, lifestyle choices, or trivial eccentricities. They are extremely serious diseases that have the highest mortality rate of any psychiatric disorder.*
>
> *Patients with eating disorders deserve and require professional evaluation, diagnosis, and treatment. If someone close to you had cancer, you would do everything in your power to get them the finest professional care available. Eating disorders require that same level of treatment.* (p. 9)

Pamela K. Orgeron, Author & Editor

ABBREVIATIONS USED IN THIS BOOK:

AACC	American Association of Christian Counselors
AAP	American Academy of Pediatrics
ABC	Association of Black Cardiologists
ACOG	American College of Obstetricians and Gynecologists
ADD	attention deficit disorder
AN	anorexia nervosa
APA	American Psychiatric Association
ARFID	avoidant/restrictive food intake disorder
BBS	Bardet Biedi syndrome
BDD	body dysmorphic disorder
BED	binge eating disorder
BFLS	Börjeson-Forssman-Lehmann syndrome
BFP	body fat percentage
BMI	body mass index
BN	bulimia nervosa
CBE	Christians for Biblical Equality
CBT	cognitive behavioral therapy
CDC	Centers for Disease Control and Prevention
cPTSD	Complex PTSD
DE	disordered eating
DMT	dance movement therapy
DSM–5	Diagnostic and Statistical Manuel of Mental Disorders, Fifth Edition (APA, 2013)
EAGALA	Equine Assisted Growth and Learning Association
EAP	equine assisted psychotherapy

EAT	Eating Attitudes Test
ED	eating disorder
EDAW	Eating Disorders Awareness Week
ED-NOS	eating disorder, not otherwise specified
FOO	Full of Ourselves
FXS	Fragile X syndrome
GDM	gestational diabetes mellitus
HE	healthy eating
ICT	integrative cognitive therapy
INDD	International No Diet Day
IOM	Institute of Medicine
NAMED	National Association for Males with Eating Disorders
NCAA	National Collegiate Athletic Association
NCHS	National Center of Health Statistics
n.d.	no date
NEDA	National Eating Disorders Association
NEDC	National Eating Disorders Collaboration
NEDIC	National Eating Disorder Information Centre
NIH	National Institutes of Health
NEDC	National Eating Disorders Collaboration
NORD	National Organization for Rare Disorders
OCD	obsessive-compulsive disorder
PA	physical activity
PCP	primary care provider
PHE	periodic health evaluation
PPE	preparticipation physical evaluation

PTSD   posttraumatic stress disorder

PWS   Prader-Willi syndrome

WHO   World Health Organization

***

About our medical director, board certified in psychiatry, Dr. Tharp . . . . (n.d.). Retrieved March 28, 2017 from http://www.stonebriarps.com/DrTharp.html

Allender, D. (1990,1995, 2008). *The Wounded Heart: Hope for adult victims of childhood sexual abuse.* Colorado Springs, CO: Navpress.

Allicock, M., Campbell, M. K., Valle, C. G., Carr, C., Resnicow, K., & Gizlice, Z. (2012). Evaluating the dissemination of Body and Soul, an evidence-based fruit and vegetable intake intervention: challenges for dissemination and implementation research. *Journal of Nutrition, Education and Behavior, 44*(6), 530–538. Abstract. Retrieved May 31, 2017 from https://www.ncbi.nlm.nih.gov/pubmed/22406012

Allicock M, Johnson L, Leone L, Carr C, Walsh J, Ni A, et al. (2013). Promoting fruit and vegetable consumption among members of Black churches, Michigan and North Carolina, 2008–2010. *Preventing Chronic Disease.* Retrieved May 30, 2017 from https://www.cdc.gov/pcd/issues/2013/12_0161.htm

Alpers, G., & Tuschen-Caiffier, B. (2001). Negative feelings and the desire to eat in bulimia nervosa. *Eating Behaviors, 2*(4), 339-352.

Alpert, E. (2013, June 13). Eating disorders plague teenage boys, too. *Los Angeles Times.* Retrieved June 22, 2017 from http://articles.latimes.com/2013/jun/13/local/la-me-boys-eating-disorders-20130614

Alvord, M. K., & Grados, J. J. (2005). Enhancing resilience in children: A proactive approach. *Professional Psychology: Research and Practice, 36*(3), 238-245.

American Academy of Pediatrics. (2011, November). Parent Tips for Preventing and Identifying Child Sexual Abuse. Retrieved June 26, 2017 from https://www.aap.org/en-us/about-the-aap/aap-press-room/news-features-and-safety-tips/pages/Parent-Tips-for-Preventing-and-Identifying-Child-Sexual-Abuse.aspx

American Academy of Pediatrics. (2016, May). *Role of the school nurse in providing school health services.* Retrieved May 16, 2017 from http://pediatrics.aappublications.org/content/early/2016/05/19/peds.2016-0852

American Association of Christian Counselors. (2003). *Heal our land: Trauma response and grief counseling resource library.* Forest, VA: Author.

American Association of Christian Counselors. (2006). *Caring for kids God's way biblical counseling certificate program.* Forest, VA: Author.

American Association of Christian Counselors. (2016) AACC Christian counseling best practice series eating disorders 2.0 workbook. Forest, VA: Light University.

American College of Obstetricians and Gynecologists. (2013a). ACOG committee opinion no. 548: Weight gain during pregnancy. PDF file retrieved July 11, 2017 from https://www.acog.org/Resources-And-Publications/Committee-Opinions/Committee-on-Obstetric-Practice/Weight-Gain-During-Pregnancy

American College of Obstetricians and Gynecologists. (2013b). ACOG committee opinion no. 549: Obesity in pregnancy. *Obstetrics and Gynecology, 121*(1), 213-217. Retrieved June 12, 2017 from http://journals.lww.com/greenjournal/Fulltext/2013/01000/Committee_Opinion_No__549___Obesity_in_Pregnancy.48.aspx

American College of Obstetricians and Gynecologists. (2015). Physical activity and exercise during pregnancy and the postpartum period. *Committee Opinion No. 650.* PDF Format retrieved June 11, 2017 from http://www.acog.org/Resources-And-Publications/Committee-Opinions/Committee-on-Obstetric-Practice/Physical-Activity-and-Exercise-During-Pregnancy-and-the-Postpartum-Period

American Psychiatric Association. (2013). *Diagnostic and statistical manual of mental disorders* (5th ed.). Washington, DC: Author.

American Society for Metabolic and Bariatric Surgery. (2011, May). *Adolescent obesity.* Retrieved May 9, 2017 from https://asmbs.org/resources/adolescent-obesity

Anderson, A. (2014). A brief history of eating disorders in males. In L. Cohn & R. Lemberg (Eds.), *Current findings on males with eating disorders* (pp. 4-10). New York, NY: Taylor & Francis.

Andersen, A., Cohn, L. and Holbrook, T. (2000) *Making Weight: Men's Conflicts with Food, Weight, Shape & Appearance.* Carlsbad, CA: Gürze Books.

Anderson, N. T., Zuehlke, T. E., & Zuehlke J. S. (2000). *Christ-Centered Therapy.* Grand Rapids, MI: Zondervan.

Anderson, R. T. (2017, June 20). Gender-confused kids need therapy, not puberty-blocking drugs: New study. *The Daily Signal.* Retrieved June 24, 2017 from https://www.lifesitenews.com/opinion/gender-confused-kids-need-therapy-not-puberty-blocking-drugs-new-study

Arterburn, S. & Felton, J. (1991, 2001). *Toxic faith: Experiencing healing from painful spiritual abuse.* Colorado Springs, CO: Waterbrook.

Arterburn, S. & Mintle, L. (2004, 2011). *Lose it for life: The total solution—spiritual, emotional, physical—for permanent weight loss.* Nashville: Integrity.

Association of Black Cardiologists, Inc. (Producer). (2013). Before you eat the church food watch this video [Documentary]. Retrieved May 30, 2017 from https://www.youtube.com/watch?v=L21mK9pRcOI

Baeten, J. M., Bukusi, E. A., & Lambe, M. (2001) Pregnancy complications and outcomes among overweight and obese nulliparous women. *American Journal of Public Health, 91,* 436–440.

Bailey, E. (2013, March 25). *Hyperarousal.* Retrieved June 30, 2017 from https://www.healthcentral.com/article/hyperarousal

Baker, C. (2003). *Fed up: College students & eating problems.* New York: Gurze.

Baker, J. (2017, May 11). *Eating disorders can do real damage to women's gynecological health—at any age.* Retrieved June 12, 2017 from https://uncexchanges.org/2017/05/11/eating-disorders-can-do-real-damage-to-womens-gynecological-health-at-any-age/

Bardet Biedi Syndrome Family Association. (n.d.). *What is* Bardet Biedi Syndrome? Retrieved April 24, 2017 from https://www.bardetbiedl.org/what-is-bbs/

Beckman, K. A., & Burns, G. L. (1990). Relation of sexual abuse and bulimia in college women. *International Journal of Eating Disorders, 9,* 487-492.

Belak, L. B. (2016, March 21). *Avoidant-restrictive food intake disorder.* Retrieved May 18, 2017 from http://emedicine.medscape.com/article/2500040-overview#a4

Berman, R. (n.d.). *Eating disorders and suicide.* Retrieved June 27, 2017 from https://www.eatingdisorderhope.com/treatment-for-eating-disorders/eating-disorders-and-suicide

Bernhardt, D. T., & Roberts, W. O. (Eds.), (2010) *PPE: preparticipation physical evaluation (*4th ed.). Elk Grove Village, IL: American Academy of Pediatrics.

Best Colleges. (2017). *Eating Disorders*. Retrieved April 10, 2017 from
http://www.bestcolleges.com/resources/eating-disorders/

Bibiloni, M. D. M., Pons, A., & Tur, J. A. (2013). Prevalence of overweight and obesity in adolescents: A systematic review. *International Scholarly Research Notices, 2013,* Article ID 392747. Retrieved May 9, 2017 from https://www.hindawi.com/journals/isrn/2013/392747/

Blair, H. (2013, February 22). Discovering the biological basis of anorexia. Retrieved March 21, 2017 from
http://www.nami.org/About-NAMI/NAMI-News/Discovering-the-Biological-Basis-of-Anorexia

Bloom, B. (2009, February/March). Bod4God is dieter's answer to prayer. *Faith & Fitness*. Retrieved May 31, 2017 from http://faithandfitness.net/node/2771

Bod4God. (2017). *Home Page*. Retrieved May 30, 2017 from http://www.bod4god.org/

Body image concerns among male adolescents with AN. (2006, March/April). *Eating Disorders Review, 17,* 6.

body mass index. (n.d.). *Dictionary.com unabridged*. Retrieved April 14, 2017 from Dictionary.com website http://www.dictionary.com/browse/body-mass-index

Bone density in teens with anorexia nervosa. (2005, September/October). *Eating Disorders Review, 16*(5). Retrieved May 5, 2017 from http://eatingdisordersreview.com/bone-density-in-teens-with-anorexia-nervosa/

Boutelle, K., Neumark-Sztainer, D., Story, M., & Resnick, M. (2002). Weight control behaviors among obese, overweight, and nonoverweight adolescents. *Journal of Pediatric Psychology, 27, 531-540.*

Bowden, D. J., Kilburn-Toppin, F. & Scoffings, D. J. (2013: July/August). Radiology of eating disorders: A pictorial review. *RadioGraphics: The Journal of Continuing Medical Education in Radiology, 33,* 1171-1193. Retrieved March 23, 2017 from http://pubs.rsna.org/doi/full/10.1148/rg.334125160

Bowers, J. (2015). Gluttony. In M. Segal (Ed.), *Killjoys: The seven deadly sins* (pp. 73-84). Minneapolis, MN: Desiring God.

Bramen, L. (2011, July 6). *Gourmand syndrome*. Retrieved April 21, 2017 from
http://www.smithsonianmag.com/arts-culture/gourmand-syndrome-26067295/

Brener, N. D., Eaton, D.K., Lowry, R., & McManus, T. (2004). The association between weight perception and BMI among high school students. *Obesity Research, 2004*(12), 1866–1874.

Brewerton, T. D. (2004). Eating disorders, victimization, and comorbidity: Principles of treatment. In T. D. Brewerton (Ed.), *Clinical Handbook of Eating Disorders: An Integrated Approach* (pp. 509-545). New York: Marcel Decker.

Brewerton, T. D. (2007). Eating disorders, trauma, and comorbidity: focus on PTSD. *Eating Disorders*, 15(4), 285-304. doi:10.1080/10640260701454311

Brewerton, T. D. (2016). *Trauma, posttraumatic stress and eating disorders*. Retrieved June 20, 2017 from https://www.nationaleatingdisorders.org/trauma-posttraumatic-stress-disorder-and-eating-disorders

Briggs, D. (2016, October 26). This is my body: How Christian theology affects body image. *Christianity Today*. Retrieved June 6, 2017 from http://www.christianitytoday.com/news/2016/october/how-christian-theology-affects-body-image-body-shaming.html

Brooks, J. (2001, April 4). *Eating disorders not just a girl problem.* Retrieved June 16, 2017 from http://www.webmd.com/mental-health/eating-disorders/news/20010404/eating-disorders-not-just-girl-problem#1

Brooks, M. (2016, May 16). *Boys with eating disorders carry higher psychiatric load.* Retrieved June 16, 2017 from http://www.medscape.com/viewarticle/863318

Brown, T. (2015, December 28). *ACOG updates guidelines on prenatal obesity, exercise.* Retrieved May 16, 2017 from http://www.medscape.com/viewarticle/856536

Brown, T. A., Cash, T. F., & Lewis, R. J. (1989). Body-image disturbances in adolescent female binge-purgers. *Journal of Child Psychology and Psychiatry, 30,* 605-613.

Bryant, J., & Oliver, M. B. (Editors), (2008). *Media Effects: Advances in Theory and Research* (3rd ed.). New York, NY: Taylor & Francis.

Bryant-Waugh, R. (2000). Developmental-systemic-feminist therapy. In A. Freeman (Series Ed.), K. J. Miller, & J. S. Mizes (Vol. Eds.). Springer series on comparative treatments for psychological disorders. *Comparative Treatments for Eating Disorders (pp. 160-181).* New York: Springer.

Buchanan, N., Bluestein, B., Woods, K., Nappa, A., & Depatie, M. (2013, May 9). *The link between sexual harassment and 'purging' – in men.* Retrieved June 20, 2017 from http://msutoday.msu.edu/news/2013/the-link-between-sexual-harassment-and-purging-in-men/

Bulimia.com. (2017). *Finding the best anorexia, bulimia, and eating disorder treatment for athletes.* Retrieved April 4, 2017 from http://www.bulimia.com/topics/athletes/

Bunnell, D., & Maine, M. (2014) Understanding and treating males with eating disorders. In L. Cohn & R. Lemberg (Eds.), *Current findings on males with eating disorders* (pp. 168-182). New York, NY: Taylor & Francis.

Burckle, M. A. (1999, June). Forms of competitive attitude and achievement orientation in relation to disordered eating. *Sex Roles: A Journal of Research, 40*(11), 853-870.

Busko, M. (2016a, January 8). *Sales of sweet drinks in Mexico dip in first year of 'sugar' tax.* Retrieved May 16, 2017 from http://www.medscape.com/viewarticle/856927

Busko, M. (2016b, December 20). *Excessive screen time tied to poor health habits in teens.* Retrieved May 12, 2017 from http://www.medscape.com/viewarticle/873482

Busko, M. (2017a, March 14). *It worked! Sugary-drink sales fell after community campaign.* Retrieved May 16, 2017 from http://www.medscape.com/viewarticle/877195

Busko, M. (2017b, March 15). *Healthy foods in schools might avert deaths from diabetes, CVD.* Retrieved May 16, 2017 from http://www.medscape.com/viewarticle/877237

Byrne, S., & McLean, N. (2002). Elite athletes: Effects of the pressure to be thin. *Journal of Science and Medicine in Sport, 5*(2), 80-94.

Cambridge Eating Disorder Center. (2017). Online screening & helpful resources. Retrieved March 25, 2017 from http://www.eatingdisordercenter.org/eating-disorder-education/helpful-resources.html

Campbell, M.K., Resnicow, K., Carr, C., Wang, T., & Williams, A. (2007). Process evaluation of an effective church-based diet intervention: Body & Soul. *Health Education & Behavior: the official publication of the Society for Public Health Education, 34*(6), 864-880. Abstract. Retrieved May 30, 2017 from https://www.ncbi.nlm.nih.gov/pubmed/17200096

Canopy Cove. (2016). *Using equine therapy to treat anorexia, bulimia, and other eating disorders.* Retrieved March 27, 2017 from https://www.canopycove.com/equine-therapy/

Caplan, A. L. (2017, April 27). *School recess: A right or a privilege?* Retrieved May 12, 2017 from http://www.medscape.com/viewarticle/878673

Cappuccio, F. P., Taggart, F. M., Kandala, N. B., Currie, A., Peile, E., Stranges, S. et al. (2008). Meta-analysis of short sleep duration and obesity in children and adults. *Sleep, 31*(5), 619-626.

Carcieri, E. (2015). *Self-injury and eating disorders.* Retrieved March 22, 2017 from http://www.mirror-mirror.org/selfinj.htm

Cary, G. B., & Quinn, T. J. (2001). Exercise and lactation: are they compatible? *Canadian Journal of Applied Physiology, 26*(1), 55-75.

Casey, J. (2003). *Body fat measurement: Percentage vs. body mass.* Retrieved April 22, 2017 from http://www.webmd.com/diet/features/body-fat-measurement#1

Cash, T. F. (2003, Summer). Body image: Learning to like your looks and yourself. *Eating Disorders Today, 1,* 1, 12-13.

Castlewood Treatment Center. (2016, September 7). *A closer look at eating disorders and suicide.* Retrieved June 27, 2017 from http://www.castlewoodtc.com/2016/09/closer-look-eating-disorders-suicide/

Catalano, P. M. (2007, February). *Management of obesity in pregnancy.* Obstetrics & Gynecology, 109(2), 419-433.

Catalano, P. M., & Koutrouvelis, G. O. (2015, December). Practice bulletin no. 156 summary: Obesity in pregnancy. *Obstetrics & Gynecology, 126*(6), 1321-1322. Abstract. Retrieved July 7, 2017from https://www.researchgate.net/publication/289629386_Obesity_in_Pregnancy

Cedergren, M. I. (2001) Maternal morbid obesity and the risk of adverse pregnancy outcome. *Obstetrics & Gynecology, 103,* 219–224.

Celebrate Recovery. (2015). *Home page.* Available: http://www.celebraterecovery.com/

Center for Discovery. (2017, April 13). *Does my child have an eating disorder?* Retrieved May 6, 2017 from http://www.centerfordiscovery.com/blog/child-eating-disorder/

Centers for Disease Control and Prevention. (2013, April). *Body & Soul: Churches impact their members' food choices.* Retrieved May 30, 2017 from https://www.cdc.gov/prc/stories-prevention-research/stories/churches-impact-food-choices.htm

Centers for Disease Control and Prevention. (2015a, November 9). *Childhood overweight and obesity.* Retrieved March 22, 2017 from https://www.cdc.gov/obesity/childhood/

Centers for Disease Control and Prevention. (2015b, October 27). *Strategies to prevent obesity.* Retrieved April 23, 2017 from https://www.cdc.gov/obesity/strategies/index.html

Centers for Disease Control and Prevention. (2016a, August 15). *Adult obesity causes & consequences.* Retrieved April 24, 2017 from https://www.cdc.gov/obesity/adult/causes.html

Centers for Disease Control and Prevention. (2016b, September 1). *Adult obesity facts.* Retrieved April 24, 2017 from https://www.cdc.gov/obesity/data/adult.html

Centers for Disease Control and Prevention. (2017, Jan. 4). *Prevention Strategies & Guidelines*. Retrieved April 26, 2017 from https://www.cdc.gov/obesity/resources/strategies-guidelines.html

Chaput, J.-P., Després, J.-P., Bouchard, C., & Tremblay, A. (2007). Short sleep duration is associated with reduced leptin levels and increased adiposity: Results from the Quebec Family Study. *Obesity, 15*(1), 253-261.

Chaput, J.-P., Després, J.-P., Bouchard, C., & Tremblay, A. (2011). The association between short sleep duration and weight gain Is dependent on disinhibited eating behavior in adults. *Sleep, 34*(10), 1291–1297. http://doi.org/10.5665/SLEEP.1264

Christensen, C. K., & Hainline, B. E. (2016). Prader-Willi syndrome and obesity and PWS lookalikes. Retrieved April 24, 2017 from http://www.pwsausa.org/conditions-resembling-pws/

Christian Simplicity (2017). *Christian mindfulness*. Retrieved October 13, 2017 from http://christiansimplicity.com/christian-mindfulness/

Christians for Biblical Equality International. (2017). *The church, sexuality, and eating disorders*. Retrieved June 6, 2017 from https://www.cbeinternational.org/resources/article/other/church-sexuality-and-eating-disorders

Church health programs needed, but not at the pulpit, African-American Survey Shows. (2013, April 14). *The Huffington Post*. Retrieved May 29, 2017 from http://www.huffingtonpost.com/2013/04/14/church-health-programs-needed-african-american-survey-shows_n_3072164.html

Church of the Nazarene Board of General Superintendents. (2017). *Nazarene Safe. Zero Tolerance*. Retrieved June 27, 2017 from http://nazarenesafe.org/zero-tolerance/

Cipolia, G., & Berman, M. (2015). 7 Things to remember during a relapse in eating disorder recovery. *Walden Eating Disorders Treatment*. Retrieved May 22, 2017 from http://www.waldeneatingdisorders.com/7-things-to-remember-during-a-relapse-in-eating-disorder-recovery/

Clark, L. V., Levine, M. P., & Kinney, N. E. (1989). A multifaceted and integrated approach to the prevention, identification, and treatment of bulimia on college campuses. In L. C. Whitaker & W. N. Davis (Eds.). *The bulimic college student: Evaluation, treatment, and prevention* (pp. 257-298). New York: Haworth Press.

Clinton, T. (Executive Editor), Hindson, E. (General Editor), & Ohlschlager, G. (Consulting Editor) (2001). American Association of Christian Counselors. *The Bible for Hope: Caring for People God's Way*. Nashville, TN: Nelson.

Cohen, M. A. (2016). *Sexual abuse and eating disorders*. Retrieved May 7, 2017 from https://www.edreferral.com/blog/sexual-abuse-and-eating-disorders-by-mary-anne-cohen-csw-director-aaa-the-new-york-center-for-eating-disorders-206

Cohen, R. (2017). *San Francisco makes the healthy choice the easy choice*. Retrieved May 16, 2017 from http://www.medscape.com/viewarticle/878208

Cohn, L. (2013). *Male gender roles and other sociocultural factors in navigating access to treatment*. International Conference on Eating Disorders (plenary session), Montreal, Canada.

Cohn, L., & Lemberg, R. (Eds.) (2014). *Current findings on males with eating disorders*. New York, NY: Taylor & Francis.

Cohn, L., & Murray, S. B. (2014, October 1). *The facts about males and eating disorders*. Retrieved June 16, 2017 from https://www.edcatalogue.com/facts-males-eating-disorders/

Colchero, M. A., Popkin, B. M., Rivera, J. A., & Ng, S. W. (2016). Beverage purchases from stores in Mexico under the excise tax on sugar sweetened beverages: Observational study. *BMJ*. Retrieved May 17, 2017 from http://www.bmj.com/content/352/bmj.h6704

Collins, M. E. (1991). Body figure perceptions and preferences among pre-adolescent children. *International Journal of Eating Disorders,10*(2), 199-208.

Comer, R. J. (2001). *Abnormal psychology* (4th ed.). New York: Worth.

Conners, M. E., & Morse, W. (1993). Sexual abuse and eating disorders: a review. *International Journal of Eating Disorders, 13*, 1-11.

Cooper, D. (2012). *Eating disorders and mindfulness*. Retrieved October 11, 2017 from https://www.eatingdisorderhope.com/recovery/self-help-tools-skills-tips/mindfulness

Costin, C. (1996). Body image disturbance in eating disorders and sexual abuse. In M. F. Schwartz & L. Cohn (Eds.), *Sexual abuse and eating disorders* (pp. 109-127). Bristol, PA: Brunner/Mazel.

Costin, C. (2007). *The Eating Disorder Sourcebook* (3rd. ed.). New York, NY: McGraw-Hill.

Cox, L. (2011, October 24). Churches can help congregations get healthy, study finds. Live Science. Retrieved June 7, 2017 from http://www.livescience.com/16683-churches-congregations-healthy.html

Craigen, K. (2017). *8 Myths About Binge Eating Disorder*. Retrieved July 10, 2017 from http://www.waldeneatingdisorders.com/8-myths-about-binge-eating-disorder/

Crevar, D. (2013, February 22). *5 ways to fight obesity and being overweight*. Retrieved April 26, 2017 from https://www.bodybuilding.com/fun/5-steps-help-fight-obesity.htm

Currie, A. (2010). Sport and eating disorders – Understanding and managing the risks. *Asian Journal of Sports Medicine, 1*(2). 63-68.

Dahl, M. (2012, January 31). Bod4God: How faith can help fitness. *NBC News, TODAY*. Retrieved May 31, 2017 from http://www.today.com/health/bod4god-how-faith-can-help-fitness-1C9381845

Darcy, A., & Lin, I. H. (2012). Are we asking the right questions? A review of assessment of males with eating disorders. *Eating Disorders: The Journal of Treatment and Prevention, 20*(5), 416-426.

Davenport, L. (2016a, May 12). Obesity/diabetes in pregnancy affects even normal babies. Retrieved June 13, 2017 from http://www.medscape.com/viewarticle/863217

Davenport, L. (2016b, June 5) *Keep an eye on mental health after bariatric surgery in teens*. Retrieved May 12, 2017 from http://www.medscape.com/viewarticle/864319

Davenport, L. (2017, January 10). *Cautious optimism on gastric bypass surgery in teenagers*. Retrieved May 11, 2017 from http://www.medscape.com/viewarticle/874235

Davidson, M., & Lewin, S. (2017). *7 Steps for a body-positive pregnancy*. Retrieved May 16, 2017 from https://www.nationaleatingdisorders.org/blog/steps-for-body-positive-pregnancy

Dawson, L., Rhodes, P., & Touyz, S. (2014). "Doing the Impossible" The Process of Recovery from Chronic Anorexia Nervosa.*Qualitative Health Research, 24*(4), 494-505.

De Souza, M. J., Nattiv, A., Joy, E., *et al.* (2014). Female athlete triad coalition consensus statement on treatment and return to play of the female athlete triad: 1st International Conference held in San Francisco, California, May 2012 and 2nd International Conference held in Indianapolis, Indiana, May 2013. *British*

Journal of Sports Medicine, 48(4), 289. PDF Retrieved July 26, 2017 from http://bjsm.bmj.com/content/48/4/289.long

DeGiacomo, P., & Rugiu, A. S. (2000). The Elementary Pragmatic Model. In A. Freeman (Series Ed.), K. J. Miller, & J. S. Mizes (Vol. Eds.). Springer series on comparative treatments for psychological disorders: *Comparative treatments for eating disorders (pp. 236-257)*. New York: Springer.

DeGoede, D. L., & Drews, D. (1998). *Belief therapy: A guide to enhancing everyday life*. Lake Elsinore, CA: E. D. L.

Dennis, A. B., & Helfman, B. (2016). *Substance abuse and eating disorders what parents and families need to know*. Retrieved June 21, 2017 from https://www.nationaleatingdisorders.org/substance-abuse-and-eating-disorders

Dennis, K. (Speaker) (2016). *Medical implications and health risks of anorexia and bulimia.* (AACC Christian Counseling Best Practice Series Eating Disorders 2.0 102). Forest, VA: Light University.

Dent, R. J., & Cameron, R. J. (2003). Developing resilience in children who are in public care: The educational psychology perspective. *Educational Psychology in Practice, 19*(1), 3-19.

diet. (n.d.). *Dictionary.com unabridged.* Retrieved March 28, 2017 from Dictionary.com website http://www.dictionary.com/browse/diet

Dinsmore, B. D., & Stormshak, E. A., (2003). Family functioning and eating attitudes and behaviors in at-risk early adolescent girls: The mediating role of intra-personal competencies. *Current Psychology: Developmental, Learning, Personality, Social, 22*(2), 100-116.

dissociation. *Dictionary.com.* Retrieved June 30, 2017 from http://www.dictionary.com/browse/dissociation?s=t

Dobson, J. C. (2010). *Girls in peril.* Retrieved April 6, 2017 from http://www.dobsonlibrary.com/resource/article/d1f8cf04-8ed3-4f84-a066-e99cfc549dce

Dobson, J. C., & Dobson, S. (1987). *Power games.* Retrieved April 6, 2017 from http://www.dobsonlibrary.com/resource/article/94920047-92b3-406f-a795-5c72a8df1ffe

Donvan, J., & Thompson, V. (2012, April 30). Bod4God: Faith-based weight loss plan to honor God. *abc NEWS.* Retrieved May 31, 2017 from http://abcnews.go.com/US/bod4god-faith-based-weight-loss-plan-honor-god/story?id=16244990

Dotinga, R. (2006). *Average U.S. child consumes too many calories.* Retrieved May 4, 2017 from http://www.foodconsumer.org/777/8/Average_U_S_Child_Consumes_Too_Many_Calories.shtml

Doyle, K. (2015, October 20). *Mom's weight gain after giving birth may increase child's obesity risk.* Retrieved June 11, 2017 from http://www.medscape.com/viewarticle/852883

Dreher, C. (1999-2014). Maker's Diet: Seven keys to health. Retrieved June 2, 2017 from http://www.transformyourhealth.com/webnewsletters/may06/nl0506md7keys.htm

Dudenhausen, J. W., Grunebaum, A., & Kirschner, W. (2015). Prepregnancy body weight and gestational weight gain-recommendations and reality in the USA and in Germany. *American Journal of Obstetrics & Gynecology, 213*(4), 591-592. PDF version retrieved July 6, 2017 from http://www.ajog.org/article/S0002-9378(15)00599-2/fulltext

EAT-26. (2009-2017). *Eat-26 self-test.* Available: http://www.eat-26.com/

Eating Disorder Hope. (2005-2017). *Teen, adolescent and children's eating disorders.* Retrieved May 8, 2017 from https://www.eatingdisorderhope.com/treatment-for-eating-disorders/special-issues/teen-adolescent-children

Eating Disorder Hope. (2012). *Equine therapy.* Retrieved March 27, 2017 from https://www.eatingdisorderhope.com/treatment-for-eating-disorders/types-of-treatments/horse-equine-therapy

Eating Disorder Hope. (2013). *Suicide risk increased with eating disorders.* Retrieved June 27, 2017 from https://www.eatingdisorderhope.com/blog/suicide-eating-disorders

Eating Disorder Hope. (*2014*). *Athletes & eating disorders.* Retrieved April 4, 2017 from https://www.eatingdisorderhope.com/treatment-for-eating-disorders/special-issues/athletes

Eating Disorder Referral & Information Center. (2017a). *Athletes and eating disorders.* Retrieved April 4, 2017 from https://www.edreferral.com/athletes-ed

Eating Disorder Referral & Information Center. (2017b). *Consequences of eating disorders.* Retrieved March 22, 2017 from https://www.edreferral.com/consequences

Eatingdisordersonline.com. (2016). *Vision impairment.* Retrieved March 23, 2017 from http://www.eatingdisordersonline.com/medical/vision.php

Eating Disorders Recovery Center of Western New York. (n.d.a). *Prevention: Overview and statement of purpose.* Retrieved April 12, 2017 from http://www.nyeatingdisorders.org/prevention/

Eating Disorders Recovery Center of Western New York. (n.d.b). *School prevention programs.* Retrieved April 12, 2017 from http://www.nyeatingdisorders.org/prevention/schoolprevprog.php

Eating Disorders Victoria. (2016). *Eating disorders and adolescents.* Retrieved May 8, 2017 from https://www.eatingdisorders.org.au/eating-disorders/eating-disorders-children-teens-and-older-adults/eating-disorders-a-adolescents

EdReferral.com. (n.d.a). *Do men get eating disorders?* Retrieved June 15, 2017 from https://www.edreferral.com/males-ed

EDReferral.com. (n.d.b). *Help at college – What are the resources at my college for eating disorder treatment?* Retrieved April 10, 2017 from https://www.edreferral.com/college-counseling

Eikey, E. V., & Reddy, M. C. (2017). "It's definitely been a journey": A qualitative study on how women with eating disorders use weight loss apps. *Proceedings of the 2017 CHI Conference on Human Factors in Computing Systems* (pp. 642-654). Abstract. Retrieved July 20, 2017 from http://dl.acm.org/citation.cfm?id=3025591

Eisenberg, D., Nicklett, E. J., Roeder, K., & Kirz, N. E. (2011), Eating disorder symptoms among college students: Prevalence, prsistence, crrelates, and treatment-seeking. *Journal of American College Health, 59*(8), 700-707.

Ekern, J. (2017a). *PTSD/trauma and eating disorders.* Retrieved June 20, 2017 from https://www.eatingdisorderhope.com/treatment-for-eating-disorders/co-occurring-dual-diagnosis/trauma-ptsd

Ekern, J. (2017b). Spirituality and eating disorders. *Eating Disorder Hope.* Retrieved May 22, 2017 from https://www.eatingdisorderhope.com/recovery/faith-and-spirituality

Ekern, J., & Karges, C. (2017). *Binge eating disorder and mindfulness/DBT.* Retrieved October 11, 2017 from https://www.eatingdisorderhope.com/information/binge-eating-disorder/binge-eating-disorder-and-mindfulnessdbt

Emily Program. (2017a). *Fitness trackers and disordered eating.* Retrieved July 20, 2017 from https://www.emilyprogram.com/blog/fitness-trackers-and-disordered-eating

Emily Program (2017b). *ADHD and eating disorders.* Retrieved July 24, 2017 from https://www.emilyprogram.com/blog/adhd-and-eating-disorders

Equine Assisted Growth and Learning Association, Inc. (2009-2010). *Welcome.* Retrieved March 27, 2017 from http://home.eagala.org/

etiopathogenesis. (n.d.) *Merrian-Webster Medical Dictionary.* Retrieved May 9, 2017 from https://www.merriam-webster.com/medical/etiopathogenesis

Excess androgen in obese adolescent girls. (2006, September/October). *Eating Disorders Review, 17*(5). Retrieved May 5, 2017 from http://eatingdisordersreview.com/excess-androgen-in-obese-adolescent-girls/

Fabian, L. J., & Thompson, J. K. (1989). Body image and eating disturbance in young females. *International Journal of Eating Disorders, 8,* 63-74.

Fallon, A., & Bunce, S. (2000). The psychoanalytic perspective. In A. Freeman (Series Ed.), K. J. Miller, & J. S. Mizes (Vol. Eds.). Springer series on comparative treatments for psychological disorders. *Comparative Treatments for Eating Disorders (pp. 82-127).* New York: Springer.

Farrar, T. (2014a). *Abuse and eating disorders.* Retrieved June 20, 2017 from http://www.mirror-mirror.org/physex.htm

Farrar, T. (2014b). *Eating disorders and pregnancy.* Retrieved June 11, 2017 from http://www.mirror-mirror.org/pregnancy.htm

Ferguson, A. (n. d.). *Athletes and eating disorders.* Retrieved April 4, 2017 from https://www.edreferral.com/athletes-ed

Ferre, F., Cambra, J., Ovejero, M., & Basurte-Villamor, I. (2017). Influence of attention deficit hyperactivity disorder symptoms on quality of life and functionality in adults with eating disorders. *Actas espanoles de psiquiatria, 45*(3), 98-107. Abstract. Retrieved July 24, 2017 from https://www.ncbi.nlm.nih.gov/pubmed/28594055

Fetters, K. A. (2017). 14 Fad diets you shouldn't try. Retrieved April 17,2017 from http://www.health.com/health/gallery/0,,20833428,00.html

Flot, R. (2006). *Coping with college series: Eating disorders and disordered eating.* Retrieved February 20, 2008 from Illinois State Student Counseling Services Web site: http://counseling.illinoisstate.edu/search/

Focus on the Family. (1999). *Starving for acceptance: A parent's guide to eating disorders.* Colorado Springs: Author.

Focus on the Family. (2000). *The truth about eating disorders.* Retrieved May 30, 2017 from http://www.focusonthefamily.com/parenting/teens/truth-about-eating-disorders

Focus on the Family's Youth Culture Department. (2000, 2002). *Preventing Eating Disorders.* Retrieved April 6, 2017 from http://www.focusonthefamily.com/parenting/parenting-challenges/eating-disorders/preventing-eating-disorders

Folsom, V., Krahn, D., Nairn, K, Gold, L., Demitrack, M. A., & Silk, K. R. (1993). The impact of sexual and physical abuse on eating disordered and psychiatric symptoms: A comparison. *International Journal of Eating Disorders, 13*, 249-257.

food. (n.d.) *Miller-Keane Encyclopedia and Dictionary of Medicine, Nursing, and Allied Health, Seventh Edition.* (2003). Retrieved March 15, 2017 from http://medical-dictionary.thefreedictionary.com/food

Foshee, V. G., Bauman, K. E., Ennett, S. T., Linder, G. F., Benefield, T., & Suchindran, C. (2004). Assessing the long-term effects of the Safe Dates Program and a booster in preventing and reducing adolescent dating violence victimization and perpetration. *American Journal of Public Health, 94*(4), 619-624.

Fossati, M., Amati, F., Painot, D. Reiner, M. Haenni,C., and Golay, A. (2004). Cognitive-behavioral therapy with simultaneous nutritional and physical activity education in obese patients with binge eating disorder. *Eating and Weight Disorders, 9*(2), 134-138. doi:10.1007/BF03325057

Frank, D. & Frank, J. (1990). *When victims marry: Building a stronger marriage by breaking destructive cycles.* San Bernardino: Here's Life.

Franks, P. W. et al. (2010). Childhood obesity, other cardiovascular risk factors, and premature death. *New England Journal of Medicine* (NEJM). 362(6), 485-493.

Freeman, A., Miller, K. J., & Mizes, J. S. (2000). Springer series on comparative treatments for psychological disorders. *Comparative treatments for eating disorders.* New York: Springer.

Frellick, M. (2015, Nov. 23). *Obesity and stress may push girls' puberty earlier.* Retrieved May 12, 2017 from http://www.medscape.com/viewarticle/854868

Frellick, M. (2016, May 23). *AAP calls for a full-time nurse in every school.* Retrieved May 16, 2017 from http://www.medscape.com/viewarticle/863648

Frellick, M. (2017, June 27). *Dads' increasing role can help lower kids' obesity risk.* Retrieved June 27, 2017 from http://www.medscape.com/viewarticle/882129

Friedman, J. K. (2016). *Sleep: The one thing you're not doing that could improve your eating disorder recovery.* Binge Eating Disorder Association. Retrieved June 3, 2017 from http://bedaonline.com/sleep-one-thing-youre-not-improve-eating-disorder-recovery/

Futures. (2016). *Dangers of pro-ana communities.* Retrieved May 5, 2017 from https://www.futuresofpalmbeach.com/eating-disorder-treatment/anorexia-treatment/dangers-of-proana/

Gallagher, D., Heymsfield, S. B., Heo, M., Jebb, S. A., Murgatroyd, P. R., & Sakamoto, Y. (2000). Healthy percentage body fat ranges: an approach for developing guidelines based on body mass index[1-3]. *The American Journal of Clinical Nutrition, 72*, 694–701. Retrieved April 22, 2017 from http://ajcn.nutrition.org/content/72/3.toc

Garaulet, M., Gómez-Abellán, P. (2013). Chronobiology and obesity. *Nutricion Hospitalaria, 28(Supl. 5),* 114-120. Retrieved June 5, 2017 from https://www.ncbi.nlm.nih.gov/pubmed/24010751

Garcia-Grau, E., Fuste, A., Miro, A., Saldana, C., & Bados, A. (2002). Coping style and disturbed eating attitudes in adolescent girls. *International Journal of Eating Disorders, 32*(1), 116-120.

Garner, D. M., & Garfinkel, P. E. (1997). *Handbook of treatment for eating disorders* (2nd ed.). New York: Guilford.

Garner, D. M., Olmsted, M. P., Bohr, Y., & Garfinkel, P. E. (1982). The eating attitudes test: Psychometric features and clinical correlates. *Psychological Medicine, 12*, 871-878.

Gati, A., Tenyi, T., Tury, F., & Wildmann, M. (2002). Anorexia nervosa following sexual harassment on the Internet: A case report. *International Journal of Eating Disorders, 31,* 474-477.

Genetic and Rare Diseases Information Center. (2012, October 17). *Albright's hereditary osteodystrophy.* Retrieved April 24, 2017 from https://rarediseases.info.nih.gov/diseases/5770/albrights-hereditary-osteodystrophy

Gerson, M. (2017, May 16). From identification to treatment: 4 Steps to effectively intervening with your child's eating disorder. Retrieved June 2, 2017 from https://columbuspark.com/2017/05/16/identification-treatment-4-steps-effectively-intervening-childs-eating-disorder/

Giacomo, P. D., & Rugiu, A. S. (2000). The elementary pragmatic model. In A. Freeman (Series Ed.), K. J. Miller, & J. S. Mizes (Vol. Eds.). Springer Series on Comparative Treatments for Psychological Disorders. *Comparative Treatments for Eating Disorders (pp. 236-257).* New York: Springer.

Gledhill, N., & Jamnik, V. K., (1992). Development and validation of a fitness screening protocol for firefighter applicants. *Canadian Journal of Sport Sciences, 17*(3), 199-206.

Glennon, W. (2000). *200 Ways to raise a boy's emotional intelligence.* Berkeley. CA: Conari Press.

Godminders LLC (2017). *Mindfulness Jesus-style.* Retrieved October 13, 2017.

Goldberg, R. L. (2017, May). *How to break free from the "diet mentality".* Monthly Insights. Retrieved May 16, 2017 from http://www.askaboutfood.com/insights.html

Golden, N. H., Schneider, M., & Wood, C. (2016). Preventing obesity and eating disorders in adolescents. *Pediatrics, 138*(3). Retrieved May 12, 2017 from http://pediatrics.aappublications.org/content/pediatrics/early/2016/08/18/peds.2016-1649.full.pdf

Gonnissen, H. K., Hursel, R., Rutters, F., Martens, E.A., & Westerterp-Plantenga, M.S. (2013). Effects of sleep fragmentation on appetite and related hormone concentrations over 24 h in healthy men. *British Journal of Nutrition, 109,* 748-756.

Goode, E. (1999, May 20). Study finds TV alters Fiji girls' view of body [Electronic Version]. *The New York Times.* Retrieved March 21, 2017 from http://www.nytimes.com/1999/05/20/world/study-finds-tv-alters-fiji-girls-view-of-body.html

Got Questions Ministries. (2002-2017a). *Is caffeine addiction a sin?* Retrieved May 10, 2017 from https://www.gotquestions.org/caffeine-addiction.html

Got Questions Ministries. (2002-2017b). *Should a Christian exercise? Is exercise something Christians should be focused on?*

Got Questions Ministries. (2002-2017c). *Spiritual strongholds – what is the biblical view?* Retrieved May 23, 2017 from https://www.gotquestions.org/spiritual-strongholds.html

Got Questions Ministries. (2002-2017d). *What is the full armor of God?* Retrieved May 26, 2017 from https://www.gotquestions.org/full-armor-of-God.html

Goulet, C., Henrie, J., & Szymanski, L. (2017). An exploration of the associations among multiple aspects of religiousness, body image, eating pathology, and appearance investment. Journal of Religion and Health, 56(2), 493-506. Abstract. Retrieved June 6, 2017 from https://link.springer.com/article/10.1007%2Fs10943-016-0229-4

Grave, R. D. (2003). School-based prevention programs for eating disorders: Achievements and opportunities. *Disease Management & Health Outcomes, 11*(9), 579-593.

The Greater Good Science Center at the University of California, Berkeley (2017). What is mindfulness? *Greater Good Magazine.* Retrieved October 11, 2017 from https://greatergood.berkeley.edu/mindfulness/definition

Greenwood, T. C., & Delgado, T. (2013). A journey toward wholeness, a journey to God: Physical fitness as embodied spirituality. *Journal of Religion and Health, 52*(3), 941-954. Abstract. Retrieved June 6, 2017 from https://link.springer.com/article/10.1007%2Fs10943-011-9546-9

Grohol, J. M. (1995-2017). *Psychological tests & quizzes.* Available: https://psychcentral.com/quizzes/

Gunnars, K. (2012-2017), *Mediterranean diet 101: A meal plan and beginner's guide.* Retrieved April 19, 2017 from https://authoritynutrition.com/mediterranean-diet-meal-plan/

Gurze Books (2003, May/June). Bulimia nervosa and child abuse. *Eating Disorders Review, 14,* 7. Website available: http://eatingdisordersreview.com/category/eating-disorders/

Gustafson-Larson, A. M., & Terry, R. D. (1992). Weight-related behaviors and concerns of fourth-grade children. *Journal of American Dietetic Association,* 818-822.

Haberman, S. & Luffey, D. (1998). Weighing in college students' diet and exercise behaviors. *Journal of American College Health, 46,* 189-191.

Hackethal, V. (2015, July 6). *Healthy eating beats exercise to limit weight gain in pregnancy.* Retrieved May 16, 2017 from http://www.medscape.com/viewarticle/847472

Hall, A. (2017, February 23). Male eating disorders in the LGBT community. Retrieved June 18, 2017 from http://namedinc.org/?p=397

Hall, B. (1999). *You can correct and prevent eating disorders by training you heart to feed yourself with God!* Retrieved May 23, 2017 from http://tasteheavennow.net/understanding_yourself/eating_disorders.htm

Harned, M. S., & Fitzgerald, L. F. (2002). Understanding a link between sexual harassment and eating disorder symptoms: A mediational analysis. *Journal of Consulting and Clinical Psychology, 70*(5), 1170-1181.

Hartel, K. (n.d.). *9 Diets you should avoid.* Retrieved April 17, 2017 from http://www.fitday.com/fitness-articles/nutrition/the-9-most-unhealthy-diets.html

Hausenblas, H. A., Cook, B. J., & Chittester, N. I. (2008). Can exercise treat eating disorders?. *Exercise & Sport Sciences Reviews, 36,* 43-47.

Hayward, J., Millar, L., Petersen, S., Swinburn, B., Lewis, A. J. (2014). When ignorance is bliss: Weight perception, body mass index and quality of life in adolescents. *International Journal of Obesity, 38,* 1328–1334.

Healthy body image. (2017). Retrieved July 26, 2017 from https://www.olympic.org/hbi

Heesacker, M., Samson, A. W. & Shir, J. S. (2000). Assessment of disordered eating by Israeli and American college women. *College Student Journal, 43,* 572-584.

Henretty, J. (n.d.). What's eating our patients? The link relationship between trauma and eating disorders. *StressPoints, a quarterly eNewsletter.* International Society for Traumatic Stress

Studies. Retrieved July 24, 2017 from http://sherwood-istss.informz.net/admin31/content/template.asp?sid=54146&brandid=4463&uid=1044618441&mi=6440456&mfqid=33021250&ptid=&ps=54146

Henry, M. (1997). *Matthew Henry's concise commentary on the whole Bible.* Nashville, TN: Nelson.

Hettler, B. (1980). Wellness promotion on a university campus. *Family & Community Health, 3*(1), 77-95.

Hettler, B. (1984). Wellness: Encouraging a lifetime pursuit of excellence. *Health Values, 8*(4), 13-17.

Hillier, T. A., Pedula, K. L., Vesco, K. K., Oshiro, C. E. S., & Ogasawara, K. K. (2016). Impact of maternal glucose and gestational weight gain on child obesity over the first decade of life in normal birth weight infants. *Maternal and Child Health Journal, 20*(8), 1559-1568. Abstract. Retrieved June 13, 2017 from https://link.springer.com/article/10.1007/s10995-016-1955-7

Hirschmann, J. R., & Zaphiropoulos, L. (1993). *Preventing childhood eating problems: A practical, positive approach to raising children free of food & weight conflicts.* Carlsbad, CA: Gurze.

Homme, M. (2000). Eating Disorders. In N. T. Anderson, T. E. Zuehlke, & J. S. Zuehlke. *Christ-Centered Therapy* (pp.239-242). Grand Rapids, MI: Zondervan.

Hotelling, K. (1989). A model for addressing the problem of bulimia on college campuses. In L. C. Whitaker & W. N. Davis (Eds.). *The bulimic college student: Evaluation, treatment, and prevention* (pp. 241-255). New York: Haworth Press.

Hotelling, K. (1999). An integrated prevention/intervention program for the university setting. In N. Piran, M. P. Levine, & C. Steiner-Adair (Eds.), *Preventing eating disorders: A handbook of interventions and special challenges* (pp. 208-221). Ann Arbor: Taylor & Francis.

Hruz, P. W., Mayer, L. S., & McHugh, P. R. (2017, Spring). Growing pains: Problems with puberty suppression in treating gender dysphoria. *The New Atlantis, 52,* 3-36. PDF version retrieved June 24, 2017 from http://www.thenewatlantis.com/publications/growing-pains

Hudd, S. S. (2000, June). Stress at college: Effects on health habits, health status and self-esteem. *College Student Journal, 34*(2), 217.

Hudson, J., Hiripi, E., Pope, H., & Kessler, R. (2007). The prevalence and correlates of eating disorders in the national comorbidity survey replication. *Biological Psychiatry, 61,* 348–358.

Hursel, R., Gonnissen, H. K., Rutters, F., Martens, E. A., & Westerterp-Plantenga, M. S. (2013). Disadvantageous shift in energy balance is primarily expressed in high-quality sleepers after a decline in quality sleep because of disturbance. *American Journal of Clinical Nutrition, 98,* 367-373.

idol. (1995). In Youngblood, R. F. (General Ed.) & Bruce, F. F., & Harrison, R. K. (Consulting Eds.). *Nelson's new illustrated Bible dictionary* [computer file], electronic ed., Logos Library System. Nashville: Nelson.

Inge, T. H., Jenkins, T. M., Xanthakos, S. A., Dixon, J. B., Daniels, S. R., Zeller, M. H. et al. (2017, March). Long-term outcomes of bariatric surgery in adolescents with severe obesity (FABS-5+): a prospective follow-up analysis. *The Lancet Diabetes & Endocrinology, 5*(3), 165-173.

Inge, T. H., Miyano, G., Bean, J., Helmrath, M., Courcoulas, A., Harmon, C. M. et al. (2009). Reversal of type 2 diabetes mellitus and improvements in cardiovascular risk factors after surgical weight loss in adolescents. *Pediatrics, 123*(1), 214-222.

Insel, P. M., & Roth, W. T. (2004). *Core concepts in health* (9th ed.). New York: McGraw-Hill.

Institute of Medicine. 1998. *Assessing readiness in military women: The relationship of body, composition, nutrition, and health.* Washington, DC: National Academies Press. https://doi.org/10.17226/6104.

integration. (n.d.). *Dictionary.com Unabridged.* Retrieved March 28, 2017 from Dictionary.com websitehttp://www.dictionary.com/browse/integration

International Olympic Committee (2009). The International Olympic Committee (IOC) consensus statement on periodic health evaluation of elite athletes: March 2009. *Journal of Athletic Training, 44*(5), 538-557. Retrieved July 28, 2017 from https://www.ncbi.nlm.nih.gov/pmc/articles/PMC2742466/

International Olympic Committee (2017). *IOC Medical Commission position stand on the Female Athlete Triad.* Retrieved July 26, 2017 from https://stillmed.olympic.org/media/Document%20Library/OlympicOrg/IOC/Who-We-Are/Commissions/Medical-and-Scientific-Commission/EN-Position-Stand-on-the-Female-Athlete-Triad.pdf#_ga=2.131591631.1902406479.1501100002-783544667.1501100002

International Society for the Study of Trauma and Dissociation. (2004-2015). *What is dissociation?* For Students & Emerging Professionals, Dissociation FAQ's, Retrieved June 30, 2017 from http://www.isst-d.org/default.asp?contentID=76#diss

International Society for the Study of Trauma and Dissociation. (2004-2015). *Home page.* Available: http://www.isst-d.org/

Jacobson, H. L., Hall, M. E. L., Anderson, T. L., & Willingham, M. M. (2016). Temple or prison: Religious beliefs and attitudes toward the body. *Journal of Religion and Health, 55*(6), 2154-2173. Abstract. Retrieved June 6, 2017 from https://link.springer.com/article/10.1007/s10943-016-0266-z

Jaffe, M. L. (1998). *Adolescence.* New York: Wiley.

James, A., & Wells, A. (2003). Religion and mental health: Towards a cognitive-behavioral framework. *British Journal of Health Psychology, 8,* 359-376.

Jantz, G. L. (2010). *Hope, help & healing for eating disorders: A whole-person approach to treatment of anorexia, bulimia, and disordered eating.* Colorado Springs: Waterbrook Press.

Jantz, G. L. (2014, February 24). *How the 5 major types of abuse link to eating disorders.* The Center: A Place of Hope (2017). Retrieved March 20, 2017 from https://www.aplaceofhope.com/five-major-types-of-abuse-link-to-eating-disorders/

Jantz, G. L. (2016, June 25). *Helping children make healthy choices with technology.* Retrieved May 19, 2017 from http://www.drgregoryjantz.com/helping-children-make-healthy-choices-with-technology/

Jantz, G. L. (Speaker). (2016). *Eating disorders and whole person care.* (AACC Christian Counseling Best Practice Series Eating Disorders 2.0 103). Forest, VA: Light University.

Jenkins, K. (2016, December 1), *No butts about it, sitting less is beneficial in diabetes.* Retrieved May 14, 1017 from http://www.medscape.com/viewarticle/872604

Jeppson, J. E., Richards, P. S., Hardman, R. K., & Granley, H. M. (2003). Binge and purge processes in bulimia nervosa: A qualitative investigation. *Eating Disorders, 11*(2), 115-128.

Johnson, C., Powers, P. S., & Dick, R. (1999). Athletes and eating disorders: the National Collegiate Athletic Association study. *International Journal of Eating Disorders, 26*(2), 179-188.

Jortberg, B. T., Rosen, R., Roth, S., Casias, L., Dickinson, M., Coombs, L., et al. (2016). The Fit Family Challenge: A primary care childhood obesity pilot intervention. *Journal of the American Board of Family Medicine, 29*(4), 434-443.

Joy, E., Kussman, A., & Nattiv, A. (2016). 2016 Update on eating disorders in athletes: A comprehensive narrative review with a focus on clinical assessment and management. *British Journal of Sports Medicine, 50*(3), 154-162. Retrieved May 18, 2017 from http://www.medscape.com/viewarticle/857680

Kanel, K. (2007). *A guide to crisis intervention* (3rd ed.). Belmont, CA: Thomson.

Kaye, W. H., Nagata, T., Weltzin, T. E., George Hsu, L. K., Sokol, M. S., McConaha, C., et al. (2001). Double-blind placebo-controlled administration of restricting- and restricting-purging-type anorexia nervosa. *Biological Psychiatry: A Journal of Psychiatric Neuroscience and Therapeutics, 49* (7), 644-652.

Kelley, G. A., & Kelley, K. S. (2015). Evidential value that exercise Improves BMI *z*-Score in Overweight and Obese Children and Adolescents. *BioMed Research International.* Retrieved May 5, 2017 from https://www.ncbi.nlm.nih.gov/pmc/articles/PMC4609764/

Kenney, E. L., & Gortmaker, S. L. (2017, March). United States adolescents' television, computer, videogame, smartphone, and tablet use: Associations with sugary drinks, sleep, physical activity, and obesity. *Journal of Pediatrics, 182*, 144-149.

Kelty Eating Disorders. (2017). *Disordered eating.* Retrieved April 13, 2017 from https://keltyeatingdisorders.ca/types-of-disorders/disordered-eating/

Kimmons, J., Gillespie, C., Seymour, J., Serdula, M., & Blanck, H, M. (2009) Fruit and vegetable intake among adolescents and adults in the United States: percentage meeting individualized recommendations. *Medscape Journal of Medicine, 11*(1), 26. Abstract. Retrieved May 31, 2017 from https://www.ncbi.nlm.nih.gov/pubmed/19295947

Kinder, B. N. (1997). Eating disorders. In S. M. Turner & Hersen (Eds.), *Adult psychopathology and diagnosis* (3rd ed.) (pp. 465-482). New York: Wiley.

Kinzl, J. F., Twaweger, C., Guenther, V., & Biehl, W. (1994). Family background and sexual abuse associated with eating disorders. *American Journal of Psychiatry, 151* (8), 1127-1131.

Kirby, J. (2004). *Dieting for dummies* (2nd ed.). Indianapolis: Wiley.

Klass, K. (2015, June 8). Men and body image: 'They just want to work out'. *Montgomery Advertiser.* Retrieved June 19, 2017 from http://www.montgomeryadvertiser.com/story/life/2015/06/08/men-body-image-just-want-work/28708089/

Klimek, A. M. (n.d.). *Preventing relapse of eating disorders.* Retrieved June 9, 2017 from https://www.eatingdisorderhope.com/information/eating-disorder/preventing-relapse-of-eating-disorders

Koenig, K. (2017, June 29). *Hyperarousal and dissociation and emotional eating.* Retrieved June 30, 2017 from https://www.karenrkoenig.com/blog/hyperarousal-and-dissociation-and-emotional-eating

Kozlowski, E. (2013). *Can Christians practice mindfulness?* Retrieved October 13, 2017 from https://www.huffingtonpost.com/eden-kozlowski/mindfulness-and-religion_b_3224505.html

Koman, S., & Hanson-Mayer, G. (2015). *Athletes more susceptible to eating disorders.* Retrieved April 4, 2017 from https://www.waldeneatingdisorders.com/athletes-more-susceptible-to-eating-disorders/

Komosky, B. (n.d.). *6 Keys to maintaining eating disorder recovery.* Walden Eating Disorders Treatment. Retrieved May 16, 2017 from http://www.waldeneatingdisorders.com/6-keys-to-maintaining-eating-disorder-recovery/

Kratina, K., King, N. L., & Hayes, D. (1996, 1999, 2002). *Moving away from diets: New ways to heal eating problems & exercise resistance.* Lake Dallas, TX: Helm.

Kubetin, S. K. (2001, August 15). Eating disorders in high school. *OB/GYN News.* Available: https://www.highbeam.com/doc/1G1-78050833.html

LaFleur, E. (2017, June 10). *I've heard that breast-feeding promotes weight loss. Is that true?* Mayo Clinic. Retrieved July 15, 2017 from http://www.mayoclinic.org/healthy-lifestyle/infant-and-toddler-health/expert-answers/breastfeeding-and-weight-loss/faq-20094993

Lamoureux, M. M., & Bottorff, J. L. (2005). "Becoming the real me": Recovering from anorexia nervosa. *Health Care for Women International, 26*(2), 170-188.

Larkin, J., Rice, C., & Russell, V. (1999). Sexual harassment and the prevention of eating disorders: Educating young women. In N. Piran, M. P. Levine, & C. Steiner-Adair (Eds.), *Preventing eating disorders: A handbook of interventions and special challenges* (pp. 194-207), Ann Arbor: Taylor & Francis.

Levenkron, S. (1998). *Cutting: Understanding and overcoming self-mutilation.* New York, NY: Lion's Crown.

Levine, M. P., & Harrison, K. (2008). Effects of media on eating disorders and body image. In J. Bryant & M. B. Oliver (Eds.), *Media Effects: Advances in Theory and Research* (3rd ed., pp. 490-516). New York, NY: Taylor & Francis.

Levine, M. P., & Levine, R. (2006, Spring). The hunger for unconditional love. *Eating Disorders Today, 4,* 1, 14.

Levine, M. P., & Maine, M. (2002). *Ten things parents can do to prevent eating disorders.* Retrieved April 6, 2017 from http://cedd.org.au/wordpress/wp-content/uploads/2014/09/10-things-Parents-Can-Do-To-Prevent-Eating-Disorders1.pdf

Levine, M. P., & Smolak, L. (2006). *The prevention of eating problems and eating disorders: Theory, research, and practice.* Mahwah, NJ: Lawrence Erlbaum Associates, Publishers.

Levine, M., & Smolak, L. (2012). *The role of the educator: Some "don'ts" for educators and others concerned about a person with an eating disorder.* Retrieved April 3, 2017 from https://www.nationaleatingdisorders.org/sites/default/files/ResourceHandouts/SomeDontsForEducators.pdf

Li, R., Jewell, S., & Grummer-Strawn, L. (2003). Maternal obesity and breast-feeding practices. *American Journal of Clinical Nutrition, 77*(4), 931–936.

Life Recovery. (2017). *Home page.* Retrieved June 1, 2017 from http://liferecoverygroups.com/

Lobue, A., & Marcus, M. (1999). *The don't diet live-it workbook: Healing food, weight & body issues.* Carlsbad, CA: Gurze.

Locker, R. & Meyer, H. (2016, April 27). Haslam signs bill giving therapists protections [Electronic version]. In *The Tennessean.* Retrieved May 10, 2016, from http://www.tennessean.com/story/news/politics/2016/04/27/haslam-signs-controversial-bill-giving-therapists-protections/83509448/

Lord, V. M., Reiboldt, W., Gonitzke, D., Parker, E., & Peterson, C. (2016). Experiences of recovery in binge-eating disorder: a qualitative approach using online message boards. *Eating and Weight Disorders-Studies on Anorexia, Bulimia and Obesity*, 1-11.

Luftman, S., Marciano, E. (Producers), & Marciano, E. (Director). (1994). *When food becomes an obsession: Overcoming eating disorders* [Motion Picture]. United States: Hourglass.

Luftman, S., Marciano, E. (Producers), & Marciano, E. (Director). (1995). *Beyond the looking glass: Self esteem & body image* [Motion Picture]. United States: Hourglass.

Lumeng, J. C., Somashekar, D., Appugliese, D., Kaciroti, N., Corwyn, R. F., & Bradley, R. H. (2007). Shorter sleep duration is associated with increased risk for being overweight at ages 9 to 12 years. *Pediatrics, 120*(5), 1020-1029.

Ma. Y, He, F. J., Yin, Y., Hashem, K. M., & MacGregor, G. A. (2016). Gradual reduction of sugar in soft drinks without substitution as a strategy to reduce overweight, obesity, and type 2 diabetes: A modelling study. *The Lancet Diabetes & Endocrinology, 4*(2), 105-114. Summary retrieved May 14, 2017 from http://www.thelancet.com/journals/landia/article/PIIS2213-8587(15)00477-5/fulltext

Madden, M., Lenhart, A., Duggan, M., Cortesi, S., & Gasser, U. (2013, March 13). *Teens and technology 2013*. Retrieved May 5, 2017 from http://www.pewinternet.org/2013/03/13/main-findings-5/

Magee, C., Caputi, P., & Iverson, D. (2014). Lack of sleep could increase obesity in children and too much television could be partly to blame. *Acta Paediatrica, 103*(1), e27-e31.

Magee, L., & Hale, L. (2012). Longitudinal associations between sleep duration and subsequent weight gain: A systematic review. *Sleep Medicine Reviews, 16*(3), 231–241. Retrieved June 3, 2017 from https://www.ncbi.nlm.nih.gov/pmc/articles/PMC3202683/

Mandelbaum, B. R. (2015, October 1). *Doctors aren't doing enough to get patients to exercise.* Retrieved May 14, 2017 from http://www.medscape.com/viewarticle/851693

Matheson, H. & Crawford-Wright, A. (2000). An examination of eating disorder profiles in student obligatory and non-obligatory exercisers. *Journal of Sport Behavior, 23*, 42-50.

Mariani, M. (2016, June 23). *How pro-anorexia websites exacerbate the eating disorder epidemic.* Retrieved May 6, 2017 from http://www.newsweek.com/2016/07/01/pro-ana-websites-anorexia-nervosa-473433.html

Martin, M. A., Frisco, M.L., & May, A. L. (2009). Gender and race/ethnic differences in inaccurate weight perceptions among U.S. adolescents. *Women's Health Issues*; *19*, 292–299.

Martz, D. M. & Bazzini, D. G. (1999). Eating disorders prevention programming may be failing: Evaluation of 2 one-shot programs. *Journal of College Student Development, 40*, 32-42.

Matkovic, V., Jelic, T., Wardlaw, G. M., et al. (1994). Timing of peak bone mass in Caucasian females and its implication for the prevention of osteoporosis. Inference from a cross-sectional model. *Journal of Clinical Investigation, 93*(2), 799–808.

Matthews, D. A. (1998). *The faith factor: Proof of the healing power of prayer.* New York: Viking.

May, A. L., Kim, J. Y., McHale, S.M., & Crouter, C. (2006). Parent-adolescent relationships and the development of weight concerns from early to late adolescence. *International Journal of Eating Disorders, 39*(8), 729-740. Abstract. Retrieved June 22, 2017 from https://www.ncbi.nlm.nih.gov/pubmed/16927386

Mayo Clinic Staff. (2014). *Sleep-related eating disorder.* Retrieved April 20, 2017 from http://www.mayoclinic.org/diseases-conditions/sleep-related-eating-disorder/care-at-mayo-clinic/why-choose-mayo-clinic/con-20037290

Mayo Clinic Staff. (2015a). *Obesity Prevention.* Retrieved April 26, 2017 from http://www.mayoclinic.org/diseases-conditions/obesity/basics/prevention/con-20014834

Mayo Clinic Staff. (2015b). *Weight loss after pregnancy: Reclaiming your body.* Retrieved July 15, 2017 from http://www.mayoclinic.org/healthy-lifestyle/labor-and-delivery/in-depth/weight-loss-after-pregnancy/art-20047813

Mayo Clinic Staff. (2016a). *Anorexia nervosa.* Retrieved May 28, 2017 from http://www.mayoclinic.org/diseases-conditions/anorexia/diagnosis-treatment/treatment/txc-20179528

Mayo Clinic Staff (2016b). *Bulimia nervosa.* Retrieved May 28, 2017 from *http://www.mayoclinic.org/diseases-conditions/bulimia/diagnosis-treatment/treatment/txc-20179842*

Mayo Clinic Staff (2016c). *Klinefelter syndrome.* Retrieved May 10, 2016, from http://www.mayoclinic.org/diseases-conditions/klinefelter-syndrome/basics/definition/con-20033637

Mayo Clinic Staff (2016d). *Pyramid or plate? Explore healthy eating options.* Retrieved April 17, 2017 from http://www.mayoclinic.org/healthy-lifestyle/nutrition-and-healthy-eating/in-depth/healthy-eating-plan/art-20044905

Mayo Clinic Staff. (2016e,). *Vegetarian: How to get the best nutrition.* Retrieved April 19, 2017 from http://www.mayoclinic.org/healthy-lifestyle/nutrition-and-healthy-eating/in-depth/vegetarian-diet/art-20046446

Mayo Clinic Staff. (2017a). *Mediterranean diet: A heart-healthy eating plan.* Retrieved April 17, 2017 from http://www.mayoclinic.org/healthy-lifestyle/nutrition-and-healthy-eating/in-depth/mediterranean-diet/art-20047801

Mayo Clinic Staff. (2017b) *Prader-Willi syndrome: Symptoms and causes.* Retrieved April 21, 2017 from http://www.mayoclinic.org/diseases-conditions/prader-willi-syndrome/symptoms-causes/dxc-20316377

McGraw, P. (2003). *The ultimate weight solution: The 7 keys to weight loss freedom.* New York: Free Press.

Miller, W. C. (2003). Emotional distress and weight-related issues. *Healthy Weight Journal, 17*(6), 82-85.

Minirth, F. B., & Meier, P. D. (Speakers). (1991). *Eating disorders: Causes, symptoms, and treatment from a clinical and spiritual perspective* [Videotape]. United States: Christian Family Video.

Minirth, F., Meier, P., Hemfelt, R., Sneed, S., & Hawkins, D. (1990). *Love hunger.* Nashville: Thomas Nelson.

Ministry Tools Resource Center. (2010, June 24). *So, you were asked to be a health ministry coordinator!* Retrieved May 30, 2017 from https://mintools.com/blog/health-ministry.htm

MinistrySafe. (2016). *The safety system.* Retrieved June 27, 2017 from https://ministrysafe.com/the-safety-system/

Mintle, L. (Speaker). (2016). *Introduction to eating disorders: Risk factors, etiology, and assessment* (AACC Christian Counseling Best Practice Series Eating Disorders 2.0 101). Forest, VA: Light University.

Mitchison, D., & Mond, J. (2015). Epidemiology of eating disorders, eating disordered behavior, and body image disturbance in males: a narrative review. *Journal of Eating Disorders, 3*, 20. PDF retrieved June 18, 2017 from https://jeatdisord.biomedcentral.com/articles/10.1186/s40337-015-0058-y

Mond, J. M., Mitchison, D., & Hay, P. (2014). Eating Disordered in Men: Prevalence, impairment of quality of life, and implications for prevention and health promotion. In L. Cohn & R. Lemberg (Eds.), *Current findings on males with eating disorders* (p. 195). New York, NY: Taylor & Francis.

Moore, E. (2013, March 27). *Are you overweight or obese?* Retrieved April 22, 2017 from http://blackdoctor.org/27050/the-difference-between-overweight-and-obese__trashed/

Morgan, M., Shanahan, J, & Signorielli, N. (2008). In J. Bryant & M. B. Oliver (Eds.), *Media Effects: Advances in Theory and Research* (3rd ed., pp. 34- 49). New York, NY: Taylor & Francis.

Morgan, R. (2002, September 27). The men in the mirror. *Chronicle of Higher Education, 49*(5), A53-A54.

Moriarty, D. & Moriarty, M. (1993). *Sociocultural influences in eating disorders: shape, super woman and sport.* Paper presented at the Annual Meeting of the Canadian Association for Health, Physical Education and Recreation. Retrieved April 9, 2017 from https://archive.org/stream/ERIC_ED365655/ERIC_ED365655_djvu.txt

Moritz, G. J. (2013). Creating and sustaining a health and wellness ministry within the local church (Doctoral Dissertation, Liberty University Baptist Theological Seminary, 2013). Retrieved May 28, 2017 from http://digitalcommons.liberty.edu/cgi/viewcontent.cgi?article=1689&context=doctoral

Moulding, N. (2015). "It Wasn't About Being Slim" Understanding Eating Disorders in the Context of Abuse. *Violence Against Women, 21*(12), 1456-1480.

Muhlheim, L. (2017). *Relapse prevention plan.* Retrieved June 9, 2017 from http://www.mirror-mirror.org/relplan.htm

Murray, C., & Waller, G. (2002). Reported sexual abuse and bulimic psychopathology among nonclinical women: The mediating role of shame. International Journal of Eating Disorders, 32, 186-191.

Myers, J. E., & Sweeney, T. J. (Eds.). (2005a). *Counseling for wellness: Theory, research, and practice.* Alexandria, VA: American Counseling Association.

Myers, J. E., & Sweeney, T. J. (2005b). *Manual for the five factor wellness inventory (5F-Wel) Adult, teenage, elementary school versions.* Greensboro, NC: Author.

Myers, J. E., Sweeney, T. J., & Witmer, J. M. (2000). The wheel of wellness counseling for wellness: A holistic model for treatment planning. *Journal of Counseling and Development, 78*(3), 251-266.

Nash, J. D. (1999). *Binge no more: Your guide to overcoming disordered eating.* Oakland: New Harbinger.

Natenshon, A. (n.d.a). *Invest in your child's self-esteem.* Retrieved April 6, 2017 from https://www.edreferral.com/children-adolescents

Natenshon, A. (n.d.b). *When very young kids have eating disorders.* Retrieved May 7, 2017 from https://www.edreferral.com/children-adolescents

National Association for Males with Eating Disorders. (2017). *Home page.* Available: http://namedinc.org/

National Center for Health Statistics. (2017). *Prevalence of overweight and obesity among adults: United States, 2003-2004.* Retrieved March 22, 2017 from https://www.cdc.gov/nchs/data/hestat/overweight/overweight_adult_03.htm

National Eating Disorder Information Centre. (2014a). *Home page.* Available: http://nedic.ca/

National Eating Disorder Information Centre. (2014b). *Prevention & health promotion.* Retrieved April 3, 2017 from http://nedic.ca/give-get-help/prevention-health-promotion#edaw

National Eating Disorder Information Centre. (2014c). *Pro-eating disorder websites.* Retrieved May 5, 2017 from http://nedic.ca/know-facts/pro-eating-disorder-websites

National Eating Disorder Information Centre. (2014d). *What we have learned about primary prevention of food and weight preoccupation.* Retrieved May 5, 2017 from http://nedic.ca/what-we-have-learned-about-primary-prevention-food-and-weight-preoccupation

National Eating Disorders Association. (2005). *Know dieting: Risks and reasons to stop.* Retrieved March 22, 2017 from https://uhs.berkeley.edu/sites/default/files/bewell_nodieting.pdf

National Eating Disorders Association. (2013). *Eating disorders on the college campus* [Brochure]. Retrieved April 8, 2017 from https://www.nationaleatingdisorders.org/sites/default/files/CollegeSurvey/CollegiateSurveyProject.pdf

National Eating Disorders Association. (2016a). *Athletes and eating disorders.* Retrieved April 4, 2017 from https://www.nationaleatingdisorders.org/athletes-and-eating-disorders

National Eating Disorders Association. (2016b). *Dental complications of eating disorders.* Retrieved March 22, 2017 from https://www.nationaleatingdisorders.org/dental-complications-eating-disorders

National Eating Disorders Association. (2016c). *Eating disorders in LGBT populations.* Retrieved June 19, 2017 from https://www.nationaleatingdisorders.org/eating-disorders-lgbt-populations

National Eating Disorders Association. (2016d). *Get the facts on eating disorders: Dieting and the drive for thinness.* Retrieved May 4, 2017 from https://www.nationaleatingdisorders.org/get-facts-eating-disorders

National Eating Disorders Association. (2016e). *Home page.* Available: https://www.nationaleatingdisorders.org/

National Eating Disorders Association. (2016f). *Media, body image, and eating disorders?* Retrieved March 20, 2017 from https://www.nationaleatingdisorders.org/media-body-image-and-eating-disorders

National Eating Disorders Association. (2016g). *Meeting with and referring students who may have eating disorders.* Retrieved April 3, 2017 from https://www.nationaleatingdisorders.org/learn/help/educators/meeting-with-students

National Eating Disorders Association. (2016h). *Slips, lapses and relapses.* Retrieved June 9, 2017 from https://www.nationaleatingdisorders.org/slips-lapses-and-relapses

National Eating Disorders Association. (2016i). *What is body image?* Retrieved March 20, 2017 from https://www.nationaleatingdisorders.org/what-body-image

National Eating Disorders Collaboration. (2012a). *Eating disorders: Awareness, prevention and early intervention: In the community: Programs and resources.* Retrieved April 11, 2017 from http://www.nedc.com.au/resource/68/full-of-ourselves-a-wellness-program-to-advance-girl-power-health-and-leadership?page=85

National Eating Disorders Collaboration. (2012b). *Home page.* Available: http://www.nedc.com.au/

National Eating Disorders Collaboration. (2017, February 22). *Eating disorders in males.* Retrieved April 12, 2017 from http://www.nedc.com.au/eating-disorders-in-males

National Eating Disorders Collaboration. (n.d.). *NEDC Fact Sheet – Eating disorders in males.* Retrieved April 12, 2017 from http://www.nedc.com.au/eating-disorders-in-males

National Fragile X Foundation. (1998-2017). *Fragile X syndrome.* Retrieved April 25, 2017 from
https://fragilex.org/fragile-x/fragile-x-syndrome/

National Institute of Diabetes and Digestive and Kidney Diseases
Health Information Center. (2012, October). *Overweight & obesity statistics.* Retrieved April 22, 2017
from https://www.niddk.nih.gov/health-information/health-statistics/overweight-obesity

National Institutes of Health. (1998, September). Clinical guidelines on the identification, evaluation,
and treatment of overweight and obesity in adults: The evidence report. National Heart, Lung,
and Blood Institute; NIH Publication No. 98–4083. Available online:
https://www.nhlbi.nih.gov/health-pro/guidelines/archive/clinical-guidelines-obesity-adults-
evidence-report

National Institutes of Health. (2017a, February 23). *Overweight and obesity.* Retrieved April 22, 2017 from
https://www.nhlbi.nih.gov/health/health-topics/topics/obe#

National Institutes of Health. (2017b, February 23). *Overweight and obesity: Causes.* Retrieved April 24, 2017
from https://www.nhlbi.nih.gov/health/health-topics/topics/obe/causes

National Organization for Rare Disorders. (2016). *Borjeson-Forssman-Lehman syndrome.* Retrieved April 25,
2017 from https://rarediseases.org/rare-diseases/borjeson-forssman-lehman-syndrome/

Nattiv, A., Loucks, A. B., Manore, M. M. et al. (2007). American College of Sports Medicine position stand: The
female athlete triad. *Medicine and Science in Sports and Exercise, 39*(10), 1867–1882. Abstract.
Retrieved July 26, 2017 from https://www.ncbi.nlm.nih.gov/pubmed/17909417

Nazarene Safe (2017). *Home page.* Available: http://nazarenesafe.org/

Neumark-Sztainer, D. (2005). *I'm, Like, SO Fat!: Helping your teen make healthy choices about eating and
exercise in a weight-obsessed world.* .New York: Guilford.

Neumark-Sztainer, D. (2009). Preventing obesity and eating disorders in adolescents: What can health care
providers do? *Journal of Adolescent Health, 44*(3), 206-213.

Neumark-Sztainer, D., & Hannan, P. (2001). Weight-related behaviors among adolescent girls and boys: A
national survey. *Archives of Pediatric and Adolescent Medicine, 154,* 569-577.

Neumark-Sztainer, D., Story, M., Hannan, P. J., Beuhring, T., & Resnick, M. D. (2000). Disordered eating among
adolescents: Associations with sexual/physical abuse and other familial/psychosocial factors.
International Journal of Eating Disorders, 28(3), 249-258.

New Life Ministries. (2017a). *Living Light Intensive Workshop.* Retrieved June 1, 2017 from
http://newlife.com/workshops/living-light/

New Life Ministries. (2017b). *Meet the Hosts.* Retrieved June 1, 2017 from http://newlife.com/broadcasts/meet-
the-hosts/

Nichols, M. P., & Schwartz, R. C. (2001). *The essentials of family therapy.* Boston: Allyn and Bacon.

Nielsen, L. (2000, September). Black undergraduate and white undergraduate eating disorders and related
attitudes. *College Student Journal, 34*(3), 353.

Nordqvist, J. (2013, May 14). *Sexually harassed men undergo extreme measures to control weight.* Retrieved
June 20, 2017 from http://www.mideastclinics.com/healthNews/16550/HYI/Sexually-Harassed-Men-
Undergo-Extreme-Measures-To-Control-Weight.html

O'Brien, P.E., Sawyer, S. M., Laurie, C., Brown, W. A., Skinner, S., Veit, F. et al., (2010). Laparoscopic adjustable gastric banding in severely obese adolescents: A randomized trial. *JAMA, 303*(6), 519-526. doi:10.1001/jama.2010.81.

O'Dea, J. (2002). The new self-esteem approach for the prevention of body image and eating problems in children and adolescents. *Healthy Weight Journal, 16*, 89-93.

Ogden, C. L., Carroll, M. D., Fryar, C. D., & Flegal, K. M. (2015, November). *Prevalence of obesity among adults and youth: United States, 2011-2014.* CDC National Center for Health Statistics data brief 219. Retrieved April 23, 2017 from https://www.cdc.gov/obesity/data/adult.html

Oken, E., Taveras, E. M., Kleinman, K. P., Rich-Edwards, J. W., & Gillman, M. W. (2007). Gestational weight gain and child adiposity at age 3 years.*American Journal of Obstetrics and Gynecology, 196*(4), 322.e1–322.e8. http://doi.org/10.1016/j.ajog.2006.11.027

Olbers, T., Beamish, A. J. Gronowitz, E., Flodmark, C. E., Dahlgren, J., Bruze, G. et al. (2017, March). Laparoscopic Roux-en-Y gastric bypass in adolescents with severe obesity (AMOS): a prospective, 5-year, Swedish nationwide study. *The Lancet Diabetes & Endocrinology, 5*(3), 174-183.

O'Meara, A. (2015, November 7). *The percentage of people who regain weight after rapid weight loss and the risks of doing so.* Retrieved March 19, 2017 from http://www.livestrong.com/article/438395-the-percentage-of-people-who-regain-weight-after-rapid-weight-loss-risks/

Orbitello, B., Ciano, R., Corsaro, M., Rocco, P. L., Taboga, C., Tonutti, L., et al. (2006). The EAT-26 as screening instrument for clinical nutrition unit attenders. *International Journal of Obesity, 30*, 977-981.

Orgeron (aka, Owens), P. K. (2016). *We survived sexual abuse! You can too! Personal stories of sexual abuse survivors with information about sexual abuse prevention, effects, and recovery.* Madison, TN: ABC's Ministries.

Orgeron, P. K. (2017). *Food as an idol: Finding freedom from disordered eating.* Nashville, TN: ABC's Ministries.

Owens (aka, Orgeron), P. K. (2001). *Counseling sexuality: A Christian perspective.* Unpublished manuscript. Morehead State University at Morehead, KY.

Owens (aka, Orgeron), P. K. (2002). *Eating disorders: Etiology, treatment, and prevention.* Unpublished manuscript. Morehead State University at Morehead, KY.

Owens (aka, Orgeron), P. K. (2003a). *Disordered eating in higher educations students: The role of student personnel in the prevention of disordered eating.* Unpublished manuscript. Morehead State University at Morehead, KY.

Owens (aka, Orgeron), P. K. (2003b). *Food as a drug: The addictions model of weight and disordered eating.* Unpublished manuscript. Morehead State University at Morehead, KY.

Owens, (aka, Orgeron), P. K. (2004a). *Linking sexual abuse and disordered eating: Etiology, treatment, and prevention.* Unpublished manuscript. Liberty University at Lynchburg, VA.

Owens (aka, Orgeron), P. K. (2004b). *The solution to disordered eating: Do diets work?* Unpublished manuscript.

Owens (aka, Orgeron), P.K. (2008). *Disordered eating in adolescents: Classifications, etiology, treatment, and prevention.* Unpublished manuscript. Morehead State University at Morehead, KY.

Owens (aka, Orgeron), P. K. (2009). *Exploration linking self-reported disordered eating and wellness in undergraduate health students.* Abstract of applied project for education specialist degree. Morehead State University at Morehead, KY. Available: https://eric.ed.gov/?id=ED532166

Ozier, A. D., Henry, B. W., & American Dietetic Association (2011, August). Position of the American Dietetic Association: Nutrition intervention in the treatment of eating disorders. *Journal of the American Dietetic Association,* 111(8), 1236-1241.

Panagiotopoulos, C. (2000). Electrocardiographic findings in adolescents with eating disorders. *Pediatrics, 105*(5), 1100-1105.

Parry, N. M. (2017, March 7). *Maternal obesity may increase child's risk for cerebral palsy.* Retrieved June 11, 2017 from http://www.medscape.com/viewarticle/876820

Patel, S. R., & Hu, F. B. (2008). Short sleep duration and weight gain: a systematic review. *Obesity (Silver Spring, Md.), 16*(3), 643–653. http://doi.org/10.1038/oby.2007.118

Patton, G. C. (1999). Onset of adolescent eating disorders: population based cohort study over 3 years. *British Medical Journal.* 318, 765-768. Available: https://www.researchgate.net/publication/13207761_Patton_GC_Selzer_R_Coffey_C_Carlin_JB_Wolfe_R_Onset_of_adolescent_eating_disorders_population_based_cohort_study_over_3_years_BMJ_318_765 -768

Pauli, D., Aebi, M., Metzke, C. W., & Steinhausen, H. C. (2017). Motivation to change, coping, and self-esteem in adolescent anorexia nervosa: A validation study of the Anorexia Nervosa Stages of Change Questionnaire (ANSOCQ). *Journal of Eating Disorders, 5,* 1-11. Retrieved May 19, 2017 from https://www.researchgate.net/publication/316170739_Motivation_to_change_coping_and_self-esteem_in_adolescent_anorexia_nervosa_A_validation_study_of_the_Anorexia_Nervosa_Stages_of_Change_Questionnaire_ANSOCQ

Paxton, S. J. (1999). Peer relations, body image, and disordered eating in adolescent girls: Implications for prevention. In N. Piran, M. P. Levine, & C. Steiner-Adair (Eds.), *Preventing eating disorders: A handbook of interventions and special challenges* (pp. 134-147), Ann Arbor: Taylor & Francis.

Pedersen, T. (2015). Exercise a treatment for eating disorders?. *Psych Central.* Retrieved on March 25, 2017, from https://psychcentral.com/news/2011/01/15/exercise-a-treatment-for-eating-disorders/22646.html

Pete Walker, M.A., MFT (2017). *Home page.* Available: http://pete-walker.com/

petechiae. (n.d.). *Dictionary.com unabridged.* Retrieved March 28, 2017 from Dictionary.com websitehttp://www.dictionary.com/browse/petechiae

Peterson, J., Atwood, J. R., & Yates, B. (2002). Key elements for church-based health promotion programs: Outcome-based literature review. *Public Health Nursing, 19*(6), 401-411. Abstract. Retrieved May 29, 2017 from http://onlinelibrary.wiley.com/doi/10.1046/j.1525-1446.2002.19602.x/full

Pew Research Center. (2017). *Religious Landscape Study.* Retrieved May 30, 2017 from http://www.pewforum.org/religious-landscape-study/

Phelps, L., Dempsey, M., Sapia, J., & Nelson, L. (1999). The efficacy of a school-based eating disorder prevention program: Building physical self-esteem and personal competencies. In N. Piran, M. P. Levine, & C. Steiner-Adair (Eds.), *Preventing eating disorders: A handbook of interventions and special challenges* (pp. 163-174). Ann Arbor: Taylor & Francis.

Phillips, D. (2016). *Nearly 4% of all-cause mortality linked to excess sitting.* Retrieved May 15, 2017 from http://www.medscape.com/viewarticle/861316

Piper, J. (2015, December 17). *Four signs food has become an idol.* Retrieved March 15, 2017 from http://www.desiringgod.org/interviews/four-signs-food-has-become-an-idol

Piran, N., Levine, M. P., & Steiner-Adair, C. (1999). *Preventing eating disorders: A handbook of interventions and special challenges.* Ann Arbor: Taylor & Francis.

Pitman, K. R. (2016). *How to heal the emotional roots of food compulsions.* Retrieved March 24, 2017 from https://growinghumankindness.com/heal-emotional-roots-eating-disorder/

Pope, H. G., Jr., Phillips, K. A., & Olivardia, R. (2000). *The Adonis complex: How to identify, treat, and prevent body obsession in men and boys.* New York: Simon & Schuster.

Powers, S. K., & Dodd, S. L. (2003). *Total fitness and wellness* (3rd ed.). San Francisco: Benjamin Cummings.

PPE Coalition for Youth Sports Health & Safety. (2010, May 13). Athletes, physicians urge adoption of new medical screening tool. Press Release. Retrieved July 28, 2017 from https://www.aap.org/en-us/about-the-aap/Committees-Councils-Sections/Council-on-sports-medicine-and-fitness/Documents/Media-Alert-Athletes-Physicians-Urge-Adoption-of-New-Medical-tool.pdf

Prader-Willi Syndrome Association (USA). (2016a). *About Prader-Willi syndrome.* Retrieved April 21, 2017 from http://www.pwsausa.org/about-pws/

Prader-Willi Syndrome Association (USA). (2016b). *Home page.* Available: http://www.pwsausa.org/

Premier Life. (2014). *The church and eating disorders.* Retrieved May 29, 2017 from https://www.premierlife.org.uk/Health/Mental-Health/Eating-Disorders/The-Church-and-eating-disorders

Puhl, R. M. (2017, May 11). *Weighing words when talking to teens about body weight.* Retrieved May 11, 2017 from http://www.medscape.com/viewarticle/879598

Rabinor, J. R. (2002). *A starving madness: Tales of hunger, hope & healing in psychotherapy.* Carlsbad, CA: Gurze.

Raevuori, A., Keski-Rahkonen, A. K., & Hoek, H. W. (2014). A review of eating disorders in males. *Current Opinion in Psychiatry, 27*(6), 426-430. Retrieved June 16, 2017 from http://www.medscape.com/viewarticle/832375

Raj, M., & Kumar, R. K. (2010, November) Obesity in children & adolescents. *Indian Journal of Medical Research, 132*(5), 598-607.

Rapaport, L. (2015). *Half of U.S. women are overweight during pregnancy.* Retrieved June 11, 2017 from http://www.medscape.com/viewarticle/847322

Ray, S. L. (2004). Eating disorders in adolescent males. *Professional School Counseling, 8*(1), 98-101.

Rayle, A. D., & Myers, J. E. (2004). Counseling adolescents toward wellness: The roles of ethnic identity, acculturation, and mattering. *Professional School Counseling, 8*(1), 81-90.

Raymond, A. (2017, May 5). *How to know if it's time to return to exercise.* Retrieved May 16, 2017 from http://www.empoweredeatingblog.com/eating-disorder-recovery/how-to-know-if-its-time-to-return-to-exercise/

Real, T. (1997). *I don't want to talk about it: Overcoming the secret legacy of male depression,* New York, NY: Scribner.

Reel, J. J. (2013). *Eating disorders: An encyclopedia of causes, treatment, and prevention.* Santa Barbara, CA: ABC-CLIO, LLC.

Regan, J. (2013, January 7). *One pound of fat versus one pound of muscle – clearing up the misconceptions.* Retrieved April 22, 2017 from https://bamboocorefitness.com/one-pound-of-fat-versus-one-pound-of-muscle-clearing-up-the-misconception/

Regard, M., & Landis, T. (1997). "Gourmand syndrome": eating passion associated with right anterior lesions. *Neurology, 48*(5), 1185-1190. Abstract retrieved April 21, 2017 from https://www.ncbi.nlm.nih.gov/pubmed/9153440

Remuda Ranch. (2014a). *The effects of anorexia and bulimia on your oral health.* Retrieved March 22, 2017 from https://www.remudaranch.com/blog/item/21-eatingdisordersteeth

Remuda Ranch. (2014b). *Equine therapy and eating disorders.* Retrieved March 27, 2017 from https://www.remudaranch.com/blog/item/26-equine-therapy-and-eating-disorders

Remuda Ranch. (2016). *Horses are helping patients overcome eating disorders.* Retrieved March 27, 2017 from https://www.remudaranch.com/blog/item/143-horses-are-helping-patients-overcome-eating-disorders

Remuda Ranch. (2017a). *EAGALA.* Retrieved March 27, 2017 from https://www.remudaranch.com/about/types-of-therapy/eagala

Remuda Ranch. (2017b). *Expressive arts therapy.* Retrieved March 27, 2017 from https://www.remudaranch.com/about/types-of-therapy/expressive-arts-therapy

Resnicow, K., Campbell, M. K., Carr, C., McCarty, F., Wang, T., Periasamy, S. et al. (2004). Body and soul: A dietary intervention conducted through African-American churches. *American Journal of Preventive Medicine, 27*(2), 97-105. Abstract. Retrieved May 30, 2017 from http://www.ajpmonline.org/article/S0749-3797(04)00085-6/abstract

Reynolds, S. (2009). *Bod 4 God: The four keys to weight loss.* Ventura, CA: Regal.

Reynolds, S. (2012). *Get off the Couch: 6 Motivators for Health.* Ventura, CA: Regal.

Reynolds, S. (2016). *Bod4God: Twelve weeks to lasting weight loss.* Grand Rapids, MI: Revell.

Rieger, E., Touyz, S. W., & Beumont, P. J. V. (2002). The Anorexia Nervosa Stages of Change Questionnaire (ANSOCQ): Information regarding its psychometric properties. *International Journal of Eating Disorders, 32*(1), 24-38.

Robbins, D. A. (1990-2017). *Breaking spiritual strongholds.* Retrieved May 24, 2017 from http://victorious.org/pub/breaking-strongholds-141

Roenneberg, T., Allebrandt, K. V., Merrow, M., Vetter, C. (2012). Social jetlag and obesity. *Current Biology, 22*, 939-943. Retrieved June 5, 2017 from http://www.cell.com/current-biology/fulltext/S0960-9822(12)00325-9?_returnURL=http%3A%2F%2Flinkinghub.elsevier.com%2Fretrieve%2Fpii%2FS0960982212003259%3Fshowall%3Dtrue

Rollin, J. (2017, May 9). You don't have to try to 'get your body back'. *The Huffington Post.* Retrieved May 16, 2017 from http://www.huffingtonpost.com/entry/5911f861e4b0e3bb894d5aea

Rorty, M., & Yager, J. (1996). Speculations on the role of childhood abuse in the development of eating disorders among women. In M. F. Schwartz & L. Cohn (Eds.), Sexual abuse and eating disorders (pp. 23-35). Bristol, PA: Brunner/Mazel.

Rosenfeld, S. (2017, May 5). *Why group?* Retrieved May 16, 2017 from http://www.oliverpyattcenters.com/why-group/

Rosettie, K. L., Micha, R., Penalvo, J. L., Cudhea, F., & Mozaffarian, D. (2017, March 8). *The impact of school food environment policies on child dietary intake and BMI and future cardiometabolic outcomes in the United States,* Abstract. Retrieved May 16, 2017 from http://www.abstractsonline.com/pp8/#!/4299/presentation/2468

Roth, K., Kriemler, S., Lehmacher, W., Ruf, K. C., Graf, C., & Hebestreit, H. (2015). Effects of a physical activity intervention in preschool children. *Medicine and Science in Sports and Exercise, 47*(12). Retrieved May 15, 2017 from http://www.medscape.com/viewarticle/855630_1

Rothkopf, A. C., & John, R. M. (2014). Understanding disorders of sexual development. *Journal of Pediatric Nursing, 29*(5), e23-e34. Available: http://dx.doi.org/10.1016/j.pedn.2014.04.002.

Rubenstein, G. (2010, February 18). Boys and body image: Eating disorders don't discriminate. *Edutopia.* Retrieved June 22, 2017 from https://www.edutopia.org/boys-eating-disorders

Rubin, J. S. (2004). *The Maker's Diet.* New York: Penguin.

Ruiz, J. R., Labayen, I., Ortega, F. B., Legry, V., Moreno, L. A., Dallongeville, J. et al. (2010). Attenuation of the effect of the FTO rs9939609 Polymorphism on total and central body fat by physical activity in adolescents. *Archives of Pediatrics & Adolescent Medicine, 164*(4), 328-333. Retrieved May 5, 2017 from http://jamanetwork.com/journals/jamapediatrics/fullarticle/383015

Russell-Mayhew, S. (2005). Betwixt and be'tween: Puberty and body image. *Eating Disorders Recovery Today, 3(2)*. Retrieved May 7, 2017 from http://www.eatingdisordersrecoverytoday.com/betwixt-and-between-puberty-and-body-image/

Russell-Mayhew, S., Arthur, N., & Ewashen, C. (2007). Targeting students, teachers and parents in a wellness-based prevention program in schools. *Eating Disorders: The Journal of Treatment & Prevention, 15*(2), 159-181. Abstract retrieved April 12, 2017 from https://www.ncbi.nlm.nih.gov/pubmed/17454075

Rutters, F. (2015). Stress, sleep and social jetlag: The obesity epidemic's psychosocial side. Medscape. Retrieved June 3, 2017 from http://www.medscape.com/viewarticle/852558

Rutters, F., Gerver, W. J., Nieuwenhuizen, A. G., Verhoef, S. P., & Westerterp-Plantenga, M. S. (2010). Sleep duration and body-weight development during puberty in a Dutch children cohort. *International Journal of Obesity* (London), 34, 1508-1514.

Rutters, F., Lemmens, S. G., Adam, T. C. et al. (2014). Is social jetlag associated with an adverse endocrine, behavioral, and cardiovascular risk profile? *Journal of Biological Rhythms, 29,* 377-383. Abstract. Retrieved June 5, 2017 from https://www.ncbi.nlm.nih.gov/pubmed/25252710

Rutters, F., Nieuwenhuizen, A. G., Lemmens, S. G., Born, J. M., & Westerterp-Plantenga, M. S. (2009) Acute stress-related changes in eating in the absence of hunger. *Obesity* (Silver Spring), *17,* 72-77.

Ryder, G. E. (2011, October 27). Is church making you fat? Research suggests the religious are more likely to put on pounds. *The Christian Post.* Retrieved May 29, 2017 from http://www.christianpost.com/news/is-Church-making-you-fat-research-suggests-thereligious-are-more-likely-to-put-on-pounds-59527/#HXzlTpDW1TwB8pQm.99

Saber, A. A. (2016, June 15). *Bariatric Surgery.* Retrieved May 11, 2017 from http://emedicine.medscape.com/article/197081-overview

SAMHSA. (2014). *SAMHSA's Concept of Trauma and Guidance for a Trauma-Informed Approach.* (14-4884). Rockville, MD: U.S. Department of Health and Human Services.

Sanci, L, Coffey, C., Olsson, C., Reid, S., Carlin, J. B., & Patton, G. (2008, March). Childhood sexual abuse and eating disorders in females: findings from the Victorian Adolescent Health Cohort Study. *Archives of Pediatrics & Adolescent Medicine, 162*(3), 261-267.

Sands, S. H. (2000). Self Psychology Therapy. In A. Freeman (Series Ed.), K. J. Miller, & J. S. Mizes (Vol. Eds.). Springer series on comparative treatments for psychological disorders: *Comparative treatments for eating disorders (pp. 182-206).* New York: Springer.

Sassi, F. (2016). Taxing sugar, Editorials. *BMJ.* Retrieved May 17, 2017 from http://www.bmj.com/content/352/bmj.h6904

Schoemaker, C., Smit, F., Bijl, R. V., & Vollebergh, W. A. M. (2002). Bulimia nervosa following psychological and multiple child abuse: Support for the self-medication hypothesis in a population-based cohort study. *International Journal of Eating Disorders, 32*, 381-388.

Schooler, D., & Ward, M. (2006). Average Joes: Men's relationships with media, real bodies, and sexuality. *Psychology of Men & Masculinity, 7*(1), 27-41.

Schwartz, M. F., & Cohn, L. (1996). *Sexual abuse and eating disorders.* Bristol, PA: Brunner/Mazel.

Schwartz, M. F., & Gay, P. (1996). Physical and sexual abuse and neglect and eating disorder symptoms. In M. F. Schwartz & L. Cohn (Eds.), *Sexual abuse and eating disorders* (pp. 91-108). Bristol, PA: Brunner/Mazel.

Schwarz, S. M. (2016, March 29). *Obesity in Children.* Retrieved May 11, 2017 from http://emedicine.medscape.com/article/985333-overview#a5

Sebire, N. J., Jolly, M., Harris, J. P., Wadsworth, J., Joffe, M., Beard, R. W. et al. (2001). Maternal obesity and pregnancy outcome: a study of 287,213 pregnancies in London. *International Journal of Obesity, 25*(8), 1175–1182.

Segal, M. (Editor), (2015) .*Killjoys: The seven deadly sins.* Minneapolis, MN: Desiring God.

Sesan, R. Peer education: A creative resource for the eating disordered college student. In L. C. Whitaker & W. N. Davis (Eds.). *The bulimic college student: Evaluation, treatment, and prevention* (pp. 221-240). New York: Haworth Press.

Shamblin, G. (1997). *The weigh down diet.* New York: Doubleday.

Sharp, M.D., Nindle, C. Westphal, K. A., Friedl, K. E., (1994). The physical performance of female army basic trainees who pass and fail the army body weight and percent fat standards. In F. Aghazadeh (Ed.). *Advances in industrial ergonomics and safety VI. (pp. 743-750).*

Simmons, D. Jelsma, J. G. M, Galjaard, S., Devlieger, R. Assche, A. V., Jans, G. et al. (2015, June). Results from a European multicenter randomized trial of physical activity and/or healthy eating to reduce the risk of gestational diabetes mellitus (GDM): The DALI lifestyle pilot. *Diabetes Care,* PDF retrieved June 12, 2017 from http://care.diabetesjournals.org/content/early/2015/06/18/dc15-0360

Siqueira, L. M., & Diaz, A. (2004). Fostering resilience in adolescent females. *The Mount Sinai Journal of Medicine, 71*, 148-154.

Smolak, L., & Murnen, S. K. (2002). A meta-analytic examination of the relationship between child sexual abuse and eating disorders. *International Journal of Eating Disorders, 31*, 136-150.

Smolak, L. (2011). Body image development in childhood. In T. Cash & L. Smolak (Eds.), *Body image: A handbook of science, practice, and prevention* (2nd ed.). New York: Guilford.

Solomon, A. (2017, July 6). *5 tips for supporting a loved one with an eating Disorder and PTSD.* National Eating Disorders Association. Retrieved July 11, 2017 from https://www.nationaleatingdisorders.org/blog/tips-for-supporting-loved-one-ptsd-eating-disorder

somatization. (n.d.). *The American Heritage® science dictionary.* Retrieved March 28, 2017 from Dictionary.com website http://www.dictionary.com/browse/somatization

Stanford Children's Health. (2017). *Obesity in adolescents.* Retrieved May 9, 2017 from http://www.stanfordchildrens.org/en/topic/default?id=obesity-in-adolescents-90-P01627

Steiner-Adair, C., & Sjostrom, L. (2006). *Full of ourselves: A wellness program to advance girl power, health, and leadership.* New York: Teachers College Press.

Stellato, K. (2015). *Binge eating disorder: Nutrition therapy.* Retrieved April 20, 2017 from http://www.waldenbehavioralcare.com/pdfs/BingeEatingDisorder-NutritionTherapy.pdf

Stochholm, K., Bojesen, A., Jensen, A. S., Juul, S., & Gravholt, C. H. (2012, February 22). Criminality in men with Klinefelter's syndrome and XYY syndrome: a cohort study. *BMJ Open, 2*(1). Retrieved May 10, 2016, from http://bmjopen.bmj.com/content/2/1/e000650.full

Stock, S., Miranda, C., Evans, S., Plessis, S. Ridley, J., Yeh, S. et al. (2007, October). Healthy Buddies: A novel, peer-led health promotion program for the prevention of obesity and eating disorders in children in elementary school. Abstract, *Pediatrics, 120*(4). Retrieved May 12, 2017 from http://pediatrics.aappublications.org/content/120/4/e1059.short

Stonebriar Psychiatric Services. (n.d.a). *About our Medical Director, board certified in psychiatry, Dr. Tharp ....* Retrieved July 1, 2017 from http://www.stonebriarps.com/DrTharp.html

Stonebriar Psychiatric Services. (n.d.b). *Home page.* Available: http://www.stonebriarps.com/Home.html

Stothard, K. J., Tennant, P. W., Bell, R., Rankin, J. (2009) Maternal overweight and obesity and the risk of congenital anomalies: a systematic review and meta-analysis. *JAMA , 301*(6), 636–650. doi:10.1001/jama.2009.113.

Strange, C. J. (2006). *Can fad diets work?* Retrieved April 19, 2017 from http://www.webmd.com/diet/features/can-fad-diets-work#1

Striegel-Moore, R. G., Dohm, F. A., Pike, K. M., Wilfley, D. E., & Fairburn, C. G. (2002). Abuse, bullying, and discrimination as risk factors for binge eating disorder. *American Journal of Psychiatry, 159*, 1902-1907.

Strother, E, Lemberg, R., Stanford, S. C., & Turberville, D. (2014). Eating disorders in men underdiagnosed, undertreated, misunderstood. In L. Cohn & R. Lemberg (Eds.), *Current findings on males with eating disorders* (pp. 13-22). New York, NY: Taylor & Francis.

Sundgot-Borgen, J. (1993). Prevalence of eating disorders in elite female athletes. *International Journal of Sport Nutrition, 3*(1), 29-40.

Sundgot-Borgen, J., & Torstveit, M. K. (2004). Prevalence of eating disorders in elite athletes is higher than in the general population. *Clinical Journal of Sport Medicine, 14*(1), 25-32. Retrieved June 12, 2017 from https://www.ncbi.nlm.nih.gov/pubmed/14712163

Taheri, S., Lin, L., Austin, D., Young, T., & Mignot, E. (2004). Short sleep duration is associated with reduced leptin, elevated ghrelin, and increased body mass index. *PLoS Med, 1*(3), e62. Retrieved June 3, 2017 from https://scholar.google.com/scholar?cluster=2160655641303461011&hl=en&as_sdt=0,43

Talamayan, K. S., Springer, A.E., Kelder ,SH, Gorospe, E. C. &, Joye, K.A. (2006). Prevalence of overweight misperception and weight control behaviors among normal weight adolescents in the United States. *Scientific World Journal,* 2006(6), 365–373.

Taveras, E. M., Rifas-Shiman, S. L., Oken, E., Gunderson, E. P., & Gillman, M. W. (2008). Short sleep duration in infancy and risk of childhood overweight. *Archives of pediatrics & adolescent medicine, 162*(4), 305-311.

Taylor, S. R., & Taylor, D. S. (2015). Management of adolescent obesity. *U. S. Pharmacist, 40*(5), 35-38. Retrieved May 12, 2017 from http://www.medscape.com/viewarticle/845873

Tharp, D. T. (2006a). Anorexia. *Stonebriar PsychiatricService News & Views, 2*(11). Retrieved March 28, 2017 from http://www.stonebriarps.com/files/August_2006_Anorexia.pdf

Tharp, D. T. (2006b). Binge eating disorder. *Stonebriar Psychiatric Service News & Views, 2*(11). Retrieved March 28, 2017 from http://www.stonebriarps.com/files/November_2006_Binge_Eating.pdf

The Center – A Place of Hope. (2017). *Male eating disorders.* Retrieved June 15, 2017 from https://www.aplaceofhope.com/our-programs/eating-disorders/male-eating-disorders/

The Daniel Plan. (2013). *Home page.* Available: https://danielplan.com/start/about-us/what-is-the-plan/

The Daniel Plan Store. (2017). *Home page.* Available: http://store.danielplan.com/

The Emily Program Foundation. (2017, May 18). *Fitness trackers and disordered eating.* Retrieved June 12, 2017 from https://www.emilyprogram.com/blog/fitness-trackers-and-disordered-eating

The Gale Group. (2002). Cohen syndrome. In *Gale Encyclopedia of Genetic Disorders.* Retrieved April 25, 2017 from Encyclopedia.com: http://www.encyclopedia.com/science/encyclopedias-almanacs-transcripts-and-maps/cohen-syndrome-0

The Healthy Teen Project. (2015). *Adolescent Eating Disorders such as anorexia, bulimia, and binge eating disorders are treatable.* Retrieved May 8, 2017 from http://www.healthyteenproject.com/adolescent-eating-disorders-ca

The Renfrew Center Foundation for Eating Disorders. (n.d.a). *Learning the basics: An introduction to eating disorders & body image issues.* [Brochure]. Retrieved April 4, 2017 from http://renfrewcenter.com/resources/educational-materials/brochures

The Renfrew Center Foundation for Eating Disorders. (n.d.b). *10 Things coaches & trainers can do to help prevent eating disorders in their athletes.* Retrieved June 12, 2017 from http://renfrewcenter.com/sites/default/files/10%20Things%20Coaches%20Can%20Do%20To%20Help%20Prevent%20Eating%20Disorders%20in%20Athletes.pdf

The Renfrew Center Foundation for Eating Disorders. (2017a). *Steps to help professionals make a difference in schools.* Retrieved April 3, 2017 from http://renfrewcenter.com/resources/for-schools

The Renfrew Center Foundation for Eating Disorders. (2017b). *Ten things coaches & trainers can do to help prevent eating disorders in their athletes.* Retrieved April 3, 2017 from http://renfrewcenter.com/resources/for-schools

The Something Fishy Website on Eating Disorders. (1998-2017). *Types of treatment.* Retrieved March 27, 2017 from http://www.something-fishy.org/reach/treatmenttypes.php

The Spiritual War. (n.d.). Retrieved May 23, 2017 from http://www.truthnet.org/Spiritual-warfare/1SpiritualWarfare/Spiritual-warfare.htm

Thompson, C., Muhlheim, L., & Farrar, T. (1997/2014). *Set point theory.* (Rev. ed.) Retrieved March 21, 2017 from http://www.mirror-mirror.org/set.htm

Thunberg, K. C. (1992). The Relationship between sexual abuse and eating problems (Doctoral dissertation, Hofstra University, 1992). *Dissertation Abstracts International, 53 (03)*, 762A.

Todd, A. (2017, April 3). *Oklahoma church supports healthy lifestyle.* Retrieved May 30, 2017 from http://disciples.org/congregations/oklahoma-church-supports-healthy-lifestyle/

Treasure, J. L., Schmidt, U. H., & Troop, N. A. (2000). Cognitive analytic therapy and the transtheoretical framework. In A. Freeman (Series Ed.), K. J. Miller, & J. S. Mizes (Vol. Eds.). Springer series on comparative treatments for psychological disorders. *Comparative treatments for eating disorders (pp. 283-308).* New York: Springer.

Trinity Health Weight Loss. (2011). *Transforming the body, mind, & spirit: Rom. 12:1.* Retrieved June 1, 2017 from http://www.trinityhealthweightloss.com/life.asp

Tripp, M. M., & Petrie, T. A. (2001). Sexual abuse and eating disorders: A test of a conceptual model. *Sex Roles: A Journal of Research.* 44(1), 17-32

Trockel, M. T., Barnes, M. D., & Egget, D. L. (2000). Health-related variables and academic performance among first-year college students: Implications for sleep and other behaviors. *Journal of American College Health, 49*, 125-131.

Tucker, M. E. (2015). *TV watching and feeling unsafe at school up childhood obesity.* Retrieved May 15, 2017 from http://www.medscape.com/viewarticle/844206

Tucker, M. E. (2016). *Call to reduce sugar in drinks, cutting obesity, diabetes rates.* Retrieved May 16, 2017 from http://www.medscape.com/viewarticle/856852

Turner, S. M., & Hersen, M. (1997). *Adult Psychopathology and Diagnosis* (3rd ed.). New York: Wiley.

Uher, R., & Treasure, J. (2005). Brain lesions and eating disorders. *Journal of Neurology, Neurosurgery & Psychiatry, 76*(6), 852-857. Retrieved April 21, 2017 from https://www.ncbi.nlm.nih.gov/pmc/articles/PMC1739667/

United States Department of Agriculture. (2017). *MyPlate: What is MyPlate?* Retrieved April 19, 2017 from https://www.choosemyplate.gov/

van den Berg, P., Wertheim, E.H., Thompson, J. K., & Paxton, S. J. (2002). Development of body image, eating disturbance, and general psychological functioning in adolescent females: A replication using covariance structure modeling in an Australian sample. *International Journal of Eating Disorders, 32*(1), 46-51.

Vandereycken, W. (2006, March/April). Media influences and body dissatisfaction in young women. *Eating Disorders Review, 17*, 5.

Vanderlinden, J., & Vandereycken, W. (1993). Dissociative experiences and trauma in eating disorders. *International Journal of Eating Disorders, 13*, 187-194.

Vesco, K. K., Dietz, P.M., Rizzo, J., Stevens, V.J., Perrin, N. A., Bachman, D. J., et al. (2009) Excessive gestational weight gain and postpartum weight retention among obese women. *Obstetrics & Gynecology, 114*(5), 1069–1075.

Victorian Centre of Excellence in Eating Disorders. (n.d.). *Anorexia Nervosa Stages of Change Questionnaire.* Retrieved May 19, 2017 from http://www.wales.nhs.uk/sitesplus/documents/866/ANSOCQ21.pdf

Villamor, E., Tedroff, K., Peterson, M., Johansson, S., Neovius, M., Petersson, G. et al. (2017). Association between maternal body mass index in early pregnancy and incidence of cerebral palsy. *JAMA. 317*(9), 925-936. Abstract. Retrieved June 11, 2017 from http://jamanetwork.com/journals/jama/article-abstract/2608220

Vine, M., Hargreaves, M. B., Briefel, R. R., & Orfield, C. (2013), Expanding the role of primary care in the prevention and treatment of childhood obesity: A review of clinic- and community-based recommendations and interventions. *Journal of Obesity.* Article ID 172035. Retrieved May 13, 2017 fromhttps://www.hindawi.com/journals/jobe/2013/172035/

Viner, R. M., Haines, M. M., Taylor, S. J. C., Head, J., Booy, R., & Stansfeld, S. (2006). Body mass, weight control behaviours, weight perception and emotional wellbeing in a multiethnic sample of early adolescents. *International Journal of Obesity, 30,* 1514–1521.

Winstead, N. S., & Willard, S. G. (2006). Gastrointestinal complaints in patients with eating disorders. *Journal of Clinical Gastroenterology; (8),* 678–682.

Vohs, K. D., Heatherton, T. F., & Herrin, M. (2001). Disordered eating and the transition to college: A prospective study. *International Journal of Eating Disorders, 29,* 280-288.

Vredevelt, P., Newman, D. Beverly, H., & Minirth, F. (1992). *The thin disguise: Overcoming and understanding anorexia and bulimia.* Nashville: Thomas Nelson.

Wade, T. D., & Lowes, J. (2002). Variables associated with disturbed eating habits and overvalued ideas about the personal implications of body shape and weight in a female adolescent population. *International Journal of Eating Disorders, 32*(1), 39-45.

Walden Center for Education and Research. (2015a). *Eating disorders among college students.* Retrieved April 8, 2017 from http://www.waldencenter.org/popular-searches/eating-disorders-among-college-students/

Walden Center for Education and Research. (2015b). *Teenage eating disorders.* Retrieved May 8, 2017 from http://www.waldencenter.org/popular-searches/teen-eating-disorders/

Walker, P. (2014). *Complex PTSD: From surviving to thriving.* Lafayette, CA: Azure Coyote.

Waller, G. (1993). Association of sexual abuse and borderline personality disorder in eating disordered women. *International Journal of Eating Disorders. 13,* 259-263.

Waller, G. (1991). Sexual abuse as a factor in eating disorders. *British Journal of Psychiatry. 159,* 664-671.

Wang, Y. C., Gortmaker, S. L., Sobol, A. M., & Kuntz, K. M. (2006, December). Estimating the energy gap among US children: A counterfactual approach. *Pediatrics, 118*(6). Available: http://pediatrics.aappublications.org/content/118/6

Wardle, J., Chida, Y., Gibson, E. L., Whitaker, K. L., & Steptoe, A. (2011). Stress and adiposity: A meta-analysis of longitudinal studies. *Obesity, 19,* 771-778.

Warren, R., Amen, D., & Hyman, M. (2013). *The Daniel Plan.* Grand Rapids, MI: Zondervan

Weaver, K., Wuest, J., & Ciliska, D. (2005). Understanding women's journey of recovering from anorexia nervosa. *Qualitative Health Research, 15*(2), 188-206.

WebMD. (2004). *Meet the Maker's Diet.* Retrieved June 2, 2017 from http://www.webmd.com/diet/features/meet-makers-diet#1

WebMD. (2005). *Pro-anorexia web sites: The thin web line.* Retrieved May 5, 2017 from http://www.webmd.com/mental-health/eating-disorders/anorexia-nervosa/features/pro-anorexia-web-sites-thin-web-line#1

WebMD. (2015). *10 ways to boost your metabolism* [Slideshow]. Retrieved May 10, 2017 from http://www.webmd.com/diet/ss/slideshow-boost-your-metabolism

WebMD. (2016). *Diets you should never try.* Retrieved April 17, 2017 from http://www.webmd.com/diet/ss/slideshow-bad-diets?ecd=wnl_wlw_041517&ctr=wnl-wlw-041517_nsl-ld-stry_1&mb=yAIkJ1tJLFoi092dPcLFzuHnVev1imbCKbr6f5nhQSE%3d#

WebMD Staff. (2017a). *Understanding anorexia - - Diagnosis and treatment.* Retrieved May 28, 2017 from http://www.webmd.com/mental-health/eating-disorders/anorexia-nervosa/understanding-anorexia-treatment

WebMD Staff.. (2017b). *Understanding bulimia: Treatment.* Retrieved May 28, 2017 from http://www.webmd.com/mental-health/eating-disorders/bulimia-nervosa/understanding-bulimia-treatment#1

Weiner, E. J., & Stephens, L. (1996). Sexual barrier weight: A new approach. In M. F. Schwartz & L. Cohn (Eds.), *Sexual abuse and eating disorders* (pp. 68-77). Bristol, PA: Brunner/Mazel.

Weiss, J. L., Malone, F. D., Emig, D., Ball, R. H., Nyberg, D. A., Comstock, C. H. et al. (2004). Obesity, obstetric complications and cesarean delivery rate–a population-based screening study. *American Journal of Obstetrics & Gynecology, 190*(4), 1091–1097.

Welles, C. (2017, June 12). *Severe eating disorders in men.* Retrieved June 27, 2017 from http://www.denverhealth.org/medical-services/acute-center-for-eating-disorders/acute-medical-mondays/article/severe-eating-disorders-in-men-47058

Weltzin, T. E., Cornella-Carlson, T., Fitzpatrick, M. E., Kennington, B., Bean, P., & Jefferies, C. (2014). Treatment issues and outcomes for males with eating disorders. In L. Cohn & R. Lemberg (Eds.), *Current findings on males with eating disorders* (pp. 151-167). New York, NY: Taylor & Francis.

Wennerstrand, A. L. (2002). *Dance/movement therapy in the treatment of eating and body image problems.* [On-line]. Available: https://www.edreferral.com/movement-therapy

Wertheim, E., Paxton, S., & Blaney, S. (2009). Body image in girls. In L. Smolak & J. K. Thompson (Eds.), *Body image, eating disorders, and obesity in youth: Assessment, prevention, and treatment* (2nd ed.) (pp. 47-76). Washington, D.C.: American Psychological Association.

Where do concerns about shape and weight come from? (2001, November/December). *Eating Disorders Review, 12*(6). Retrieved May 7, 2017 from http://eatingdisordersreview.com/where-do-concerns-about-shape-and-weight-come-from/

WikiHow. (n.d.). *How to deal with obesity.* Retrieved April 26, 2017 from http://www.wikihow.com/Deal-With-Obesity

Wikipedia, The Free Encyclopedia. (2016). *Bible Diet.* Retrieved June 2, 2017 from https://en.wikipedia.org/wiki/Bible_Diet

Wikipedia, The Free Encyclopedia. (2017a). *Body fat percentage.* Retrieved April 23, 2017 from https://en.wikipedia.org/wiki/Body_fat_percentage

Wikipedia, The Free Encyclopedia. (2017b). *Gender differences in suicide.* Retrieved June 27, 2017 from https://en.wikipedia.org/wiki/Gender_differences_in_suicide

Wikipedia, The Free Encyclopedia. (2017c). *Gourmand syndrome.* Retrieved April 21, 2017 from https://en.wikipedia.org/wiki/Gourmand_syndrome

Wikipedia, The Free Encyclopedia. (2017d). *Prader-Willi syndrome.* Retrieved April 21, 2017 from https://en.wikipedia.org/wiki/Prader%E2%80%93Willi_syndrome

Wikipedia, The Free Encyclopedia. (2017e). *Pro-ana.* Retrieved May 5, 2017 from https://en.wikipedia.org/wiki/Pro-ana

Williamson, D. A., & Netemeyer, S. B. (2000). Cognitive-behavior therapy. In A. Freeman (Series Ed.), K. J. Miller, & J. S. Mizes (Eds.). Springer series on comparative treatments for psychological disorders. *Comparative treatments for eating disorders (pp. 61-81).* New York: Springer.

Wilson, J. L, Peebles, R., Hardy, K. K., & Litt, I. F. (2006, December). Surfing for thinness: A pilot study of pro-eating disorder web site usage in adolescents with eating disorders. *Pediatrics, 118* (6), 1635–1643.

Winter, D., & Lemberg, R. (2014, October 1). *Overcoming Male Eating Disorders.* Retrieved June 19, 2017 from https://www.edcatalogue.com/overcoming-male-eating-disorder-shame/

Wonderlich, A. L., Ackard, D. M., & Henderson, J. B. (2005). Childhood beauty pageant contestants: Association with adult disordered eating and mental health. *Eating Disorders, 13,* 291-301.

Wonderlich, S. A., Peterson, C. B., Mitchell, J. E., & Crow, S. J. (2000). Integrative cognitive therapy for bulimic behavior. In A. Freeman (Series Ed.), K. J. Miller, & J. S. Mizes (Vol. Eds.). Springer series on comparative treatments for psychological disorders. *Comparative treatments for eating disorders (pp. 258-282).* New York: Springer.

Wong, M. S., Jones-Smith, J. C., Colantuoni, E., Thorpe, R. J. Jr., Bleich, S. N., & Chan, K. S. (2017). The longitudinal association between early childhood obesity and fathers' involvement in caregiving and decision-making. *Obesity.* PDF file retrieved June 27,2017 from http://onlinelibrary.wiley.com/doi/10.1002/oby.21902/full

Wikipedia, The Free Encyclopedia. (2017d). *Thought stopping.* Retrieved October 11, 2017 from https://en.wikipedia.org/wiki/Thought_stopping

World Health Organization. (2004). *Prevention of mental disorders: Effective interventions and policy options.* Summary Report. Retrieved March 30, 2017 from http://www.who.int/mental_health/evidence/en/prevention_of_mental_disorders_sr.pdf

World Health Organization. (2012). *Population-based approaches to childhood obesity prevention.* Retrieved May 12, 2017 from http://www.who.int/dietphysicalactivity/childhood/approaches/en/

World Health Organization. (2016). *Obesity and overweight.* Media centre fact sheets. Retrieved April 22, 2017 from http://www.who.int/mediacentre/factsheets/fs311/en/

Worthington, E. L., Jr., Mazzeo, S. E., & Kliewer, W. L. (2002). Addictive and eating disorders, unforgiveness and forgiveness. *Journal of Psychology and Christianity, 21*(3), 257-261.

Yang, K., Turk, M.T., Allison, V. L., James, K. A., & Cjasems, E. (2014). Body mass index self-perception and weight management behaviors during late adolescence. *Journal of School Health, 84,* 654-660.

Yun, K. (n.d.). *Multiple regression analysis of body fat percent and B.M.I. (Body Mass Index)*. Retrieved April 22, 2017 from https://rpubs.com/KyungYun/64367

Zagorsky, J. L., & Smith, P. K. (2011). *The freshman 15: A critical time for obesity intervention or media myth?* [Abstract]. Retrieved April 9, 2017 from http://onlinelibrary.wiley.com/doi/10.1111/j.1540-6237.2011.00823.x/full

Zeller, M. H., Noll, J. G., Sarwer, D. B., Reiter-Purtill, J., Rofey, D. L., Baughcum, A. E. et al. (2015). Child maltreatment and the adolescent patient with severe obesity: Implications for clinical care. *Journal of Pediatric Psychology, 40*(7), 640-648.

Zelman, K. M. (2016). *The Mayo Clinic Diet*. Retrieved April 20, 2017 from http://www.webmd.com/diet/features/the-mayo-clinic-diet#1

Zerbe, K. J. (1995). *The body betrayed: A deeper understanding of women, eating disorders, and treatment.* Carlsbad, CA: Gurze.

***

Appendixes

Appendix A

Scriptures Related to Gluttony
(By Book Order)

Numbers 11:4-9 – "⁴ Now the mixed multitude who were among them yielded to intense craving; so the children of Israel also wept again and said: "Who will give us meat to eat? ⁵ We remember the fish which we ate freely in Egypt, the cucumbers, the melons, the leeks, the onions, and the garlic; ⁶ but now our whole being *is* dried up; *there is* nothing at all except this manna *before* our eyes!" ⁷ Now the manna *was* like coriander seed, and its color like the color of bdellium. ⁸ The people went about and gathered *it,* ground *it* on millstones or beat *it* in the mortar, cooked *it* in pans, and made cakes of it; and its taste was like the taste of pastry prepared with oil. ⁹ And when the dew fell on the camp in the night, the manna fell on it.

Deuteronomy 21:20 – "And they shall say to the elders of his city, 'This son of ours is stubborn and rebellious; he will not obey our voice; he is a glutton and a drunkard.'"

Psalms 78:18 – "And they tested God in their heart
By asking for the food of their fancy."

Proverbs 23:2 – "And put a knife to your throat
If you *are* a man given to appetite."

Proverbs 23:20-21 – "²⁰ Do not mix with winebibbers,
Or with gluttonous eaters of meat; ²¹ For the drunkard and the glutton will come to poverty, And drowsiness will clothe *a man* with rags."

Proverbs 28:7 – "Whoever keeps the law *is* a discerning son, But a companion of gluttons shames his father."

Proverbs 25:16 – "Have you found honey? Eat only as much as you need, Lest you be filled with it and vomit."

Romans 13:14 – "But put on the Lord Jesus Christ, and make no provision for the flesh, to *fulfill its* lusts."

Romans 14:14-23 – "¹⁴ I know and am convinced by the Lord Jesus that *there is* nothing unclean of itself; but to him who considers anything to be unclean, to him *it is* unclean. ¹⁵ Yet if your brother is grieved because of *your* food, you are no longer walking in love. Do not destroy with your food the one for whom Christ died. [16] Therefore do not let your good be spoken of as evil; [17] for the kingdom of God is not eating and drinking, but righteousness and peace and joy in the Holy Spirit. [18] For he who serves Christ in these things[a] *is* acceptable to God and approved by men.

[19] Therefore let us pursue the things *which make* for peace and the things by which one may edify another. [20] Do not destroy the work of God for the sake of food. All things indeed *are* pure, but *it is* evil for the man who eats with offense. [21] *It is* good neither to eat meat nor drink wine nor *do anything* by which your brother stumbles or is offended or is made weak.[b] [22] Do you have faith?[c] Have *it* to yourself before God. Happy *is* he who does not condemn himself in what he approves. [23] But he who doubts is condemned if he eats, because *he does* not *eat* from faith; for whatever *is* not from faith is sin. [d]"

1 Corinthians 3:16-17 – "[16] Do you not know that you are the temple of God and *that* the Spirit of God dwells in you? [17] If anyone defiles the temple of God, God will destroy him. For the temple of God is holy, which *temple* you are."

1 Corinthians 6:12-13 – "[12] All things are lawful for me, but all things are not helpful. All things are lawful for me, but I will not be brought under the power of any. [13] Foods for the stomach and the stomach for foods, but God will destroy both it and them."

1 Corinthians 6:19-20 – "[19] Or do you not know that your body is the temple of the Holy Spirit *who is* in you, whom you have from God, and you are not your own? [20] For you were bought at a price; therefore glorify God in your body[a] and in your spirit, which are God's."

1 Corinthians 10:31 – "Therefore, whether you eat or drink, or whatever you do, do all to the glory of God."

Galatians 5:16-26 – "[16] I say then: Walk in the Spirit, and you shall not fulfill the lust of the flesh. [17] For the flesh lusts against the Spirit, and the Spirit against the flesh; and these are contrary to one another, so that you do not do the things that you wish. [18] But if you are led by the Spirit, you are not under the law.

[19] Now the works of the flesh are evident, which are: adultery,[a] fornication, uncleanness, lewdness, [20] idolatry, sorcery, hatred, contentions, jealousies, outbursts of wrath, selfish ambitions, dissensions, heresies, [21] envy, murders,[b] drunkenness, revelries, and the like; of which I tell you beforehand, just as I also told *you* in time past, that those who practice such things will not inherit the kingdom of God.

[22] But the fruit of the Spirit is love, joy, peace, longsuffering, kindness, goodness, faithfulness, [23] gentleness, self-control. Against such there is no law. [24] And those *who are* Christ's have crucified the flesh with its passions and desires. [25] If we live in the Spirit, let us also walk in the Spirit. [26] Let us not become conceited, provoking one another, envying one another.

Philippians 3:18-19 – "[18] For many walk, of whom I have told you often, and now tell you even weeping, *that they are* the enemies of the cross of Christ:[19] whose end *is* destruction, whose god *is their* belly, and *whose* glory *is* in their shame—who set their mind on earthly things."

Colossians 3:17 – "And whatever you do in word or deed, *do* all in the name of the Lord Jesus, giving thanks to God the Father through Him."
***

Appendix B

Adaptive Function of Eating Disorder Symptoms

Comfort/Nurturance

Numbing

Distraction

Sedation

Energizer

Attention—Cry for Help

Rebellion

Discharge Anger

Identity and Self-Esteem

Maintain Helplessness

Control and Power

Predictability and Structure

Establishment of Psychological Space

Reenactment of Abuse (Repetition/Compulsion)

Self-Punishment or Punishment of the Body

Containment of Fragmentation

Dissociation with Intrusive Thoughts, Feelings, Images

Cleanse or Purify the Self

Attempt "to Disappear" (Anorexia)

Create Large Body for Protection

Create Small Body for Protection

Avoidance of Intimacy

Release Tension Built Up From Hypervigilance

Symptoms Prove "I am Bad" Instead of Blaming Abusers

***

Appendix C

Eating Attitudes Test
EAT©David M. Garner & Paul E. Garfinkel (1979), David M. Garner, et al., (1982)

SECTION A

1. Age:

2. Sex:

3. Education:

If currently enrolled in college/university, are you a:

Freshman   Sophomore   Junior   Senior Grad Student

If not enrolled in college/university, level of education completed:

Grade School   High School   College   Post College

4. Ethnic/Racial Group:

African American Asian American Caucasian Hispanic American Indian   Other

5. Do you participate in athletics at any of the following levels:

        Intramural   Inter-Collegiate   Recreational

SECTION B

Please check one response for each of the following statements.	Always	Usually	Often	Sometimes	Rarely	Never
1. Am terrified about being overweight						
2. Avoid eating when I am hungry						
3. Find myself preoccupied with food						
4. Have gone on eating binges where I feel I may not be able to stop						
5. Cut my food into small pieces						

6. Aware of the calorie content of foods I eat					
7. Particularly avoid food with a high carbohydrate content (bread, rice, potatoes, etc.)					
8. Feel that others would prefer if I ate more					
9. Vomit after I have eaten					
10. Feel extremely guilty after eating					
11. Am preoccupied with a desire to be thinner					
12. Think about burning up calories when I exercise					
13. Other people think I'm too thin					
14. Am preoccupied with the thought of having fat on my body					
15. Take longer than others to eat my meals					
16. Avoid foods with sugar in them					
17. Eat diet foods					
18. Feel that food controls my life					
19. Display self-control around food					
20. Feel that others pressure me to eat					

21. Give too much time and thought to food						
22. Feel uncomfortable after eating sweets						
23. Engage in dieting behavior						
24. Like my stomach to be empty						
25. Have the impulse to vomit after meals						
26. Enjoy trying new rich foods						

SECTION C

	Never	Less than 1 time a month	1 to 3 times a month	Once a week	2 to 6 times a week	Once a day	More than once a day
1. Gone on eating binges? (Eating a large amount of food while feeling out of control)							
2. Made yourself sick (vomited) to control your weight?							
3. Used laxatives to control your weight or shape?							
4. Exercised to lose or to control your weight?							

5. What is your current weight?

Pounds: _____

What is your current height?

_____ Feet _____ Inches

6. What is your highest weight ever?

_____Pounds   What year was that? _____

7. What is your lowest weight at your current height?

_____ Pounds   What is your desired weight? _____ Pounds

8. Have you ever been treated for an eating disorder? Yes or No

9. If you have been treated for an eating disorder, was it through a: (Check all that apply)

Counselor __ Medical doctor __ Nurse __ Psychiatrist __ Psychologist __ Nutritionist __ Support Group __

10. Have you ever thought of or attempted suicide? Yes or No

For Females:

11. Do you have regular menstrual periods? Yes or No

12. Have you ever lost your period for 3 months or more (not due to pregnancy)? Yes or No

13. Do you take oral contraceptives? Yes or No

***

Appendix D

Treatment Facilities Directory

Facility	Location/Contact
Alexian Brothers Behavioral Health Hospital	Hoffman Estates, Illinois 800-432-5005; 847-882-1600 Fax: 847-755-8060 http://www.alexianbrothershealth.org/abbhh
Cambridge Eating Disorder Center	Cambridge, MA 888-900-2332; 617-547-2255 Fax: 617-547-0003 http://www.eatingdisordercenter.org/contact-us.html
Canopy Cove	Tallahassee, FL 1-800-236-7524 https://www.canopycove.com/
Castlewood Treatment Center For Eating Disorders	Ballwin, MO 888-822-8938; 877-796-6303 http://www.castlewoodtc.com/
Center for Discovery	Los Alamitos, CA 866-482-3876 http://www.centerfordiscovery.com/index.html
The Center for Eating Disorders at Sheppard Pratt	Baltimore, Maryland 410-938-5252 https://eatingdisorder.org/
Children's Health Eating Disorder Services	Plano, TX 214-456-8899; Fax: 469-303-4095 https://www.childrens.com/specialties-services/specialty-centers-and-programs/psychiatry-and-psychology/conditions-and-programs/eating-disorders
Del Amo Hospital	Torrance, CA 800-533-5266; 310-530-1151 http://delamohospital.com/

The Eating Disorder Treatment Program at Children's Hospital Colorado	Denver, CO 720-777-6200 https://www.childrenscolorado.org/doctors-and-departments/departments/psych/programs/eating-disorders/
Eating Recovery Center	Denver, CO 877-711-1878; 877-736-2140 https://www.eatingrecoverycenter.com/
EDCare	3 Locations: 1. Denver, CO 2. Colorado Springs, CO 3. Merriam, KS 866-771-0861 http://eatingdisorder.care/
Green Mountain at Fox Run	Ludlow, Vermont **800-448-8106; 802-228-8885** https://www.fitwoman.com/
Healthy Teen Project	Los Altos, CA 650-941-2300; Fax: 650-941-2305 http://www.healthyteenproject.com/
Institute of Living	Hartford, CT 800-673-2411; 860-545-7200 https://instituteofliving.org/programs-services/eating-disorders-program
Laureate Psychiatric Clinic	Tulsa, OK 800-322-5173 https://www.saintfrancis.com/laureate-psychiatric-clinic/eatingdisorders/Pages/default.aspx
McCallum Place Eating Disorder Centers	2 Locations: St. Louis, Kansas City 800-828-8158 https://www.mccallumplace.com/
McLean Klarman Eating Disorders Center (KEDC) for young women ages 16 to 26.	Belmont, Massachusetts 800-333-0338 http://www.mcleanhospital.org/programs/klarman-eating-disorders-center
Mirasol	Tucson, AZ 1-888-520-1700 http://www.mirasol.net/
Montecatini	Carlsbad, CA 866-449-1669; 760-436-2657 http://www.montecatinieatingdisorder.com/
Promises Scottsdale	Scottsdale, AZ 888-349-3818; International: 1-520-391-4705 https://www.sundancecenter.com/what-we-treat/eating-disorders/
Reasons Disorder Center	Los Angeles, CA 800-235-5570 x290 http://reasonsedc.com/

Remuda Ranch at the Meadows (Females only)	Wickenburg, AZ Intake: 866-332-7381 (outside US: 928-668-1999) Other Inquiries: 800-445-1900 (outside US: 928-684-3926) https://www.remudaranch.com/
Renfrew Center	800-RENFREW (736-3739) http://renfrewcenter.com/
River Centre Clinic	Sylvania, Ohio 43560 877-212-5457 http://river-centre.org/
River Oaks Hospital	New Orleans, LA 800-366-1740 http://riveroakshospital.com/
Rogers Memorial Hospital Eating Disorder Center	Oconomowoc, WI 800-767-4411 https://rogersbh.org/what-we-treat/eating-disorders/eating-disorder-residential-services/eating-disorder-center
Rosewood Ranch	Locations: • Wickenburg, AZ • Santa Monica, CA 844-338-8475 https://www.rosewoodranch.com/
Sanford Eating Disorders and Weight Management Center	Locations: • Sioux Falls, SD • Fargo, ND • Bemidji, MN 800-437-4010; 701-234-2000 http://www.sanfordhealth.org/medical-services/eating-disorders
Shades of Hope	Buffalo Gap, TX 800-588-HOPE http://shadesofhope.com/
Sierra Tucson Eating Recovery Program	Tucson, AZ 800-842-4487; 855-693-7208 http://www.sierratucson.com/programs/eating-recovery/

Texas Health Behavioral Health Services	Multiple locations in Texas 682-236-6023 https://www.texashealth.org/behavioral-health/Pages/Services/Eating-Disorders.aspx
Torrance Memorial Hospital Eating Disorders Program	Torrance, CA 310-325-9110 http://www.torrancememorial.org/Medical_Services/Eating_Disorders_Program.aspx
University Medical Center of Princeton at Plainsboro – Center for Eating Disorders Care	Plainsboro, NJ 877-932-8935 http://www.princetonhcs.org/phcs-home/what-we-do/university-medical-center-of-princeton-at-plainsboro/what-we-do/clinical-centers-for-care/center-for-eating-disorders-care.aspx
Upstate New York Eating Disorder Service	Locations: • Elmira, NY • Liverpool, NY • Ithaca, NY • Vestal, NY 977-765-7866; 607-732-5646 Fax: 607-732-0373 http://unyed.com/
Veritas Collaborative	Locations: • Durham, NC • Richmond, VA 855-875-5812 919-908-9730 https://www.facebook.com/veritascollaborative/
Walden Eating Disorders Treatment	Main Campus: Waltham, MA Multiple locations in MA, CT, & GA 781-647-6727 http://www.waldeneatingdisorders.com/
Westwind Counselling and Eating Disorder Recovery Centre	Brandon Manitoba Canada 888-353-3372; 204-728-2499 http://westwind.mb.ca/

***

Appendix E

Reading Lists

READING FOR PROFESSIONALS:

Cumella, E. J., Eberly, M. C., & Wall, A. D. (2008). *Eating disorders: A handbook of Christian treatment*. Wickenburg, AZ: Remuda Ranch.

Haynos, A. F., Forman, E. M., & Lillis, J. (2016). *Mindfulness & acceptance for treating eating disorders & weight concerns: Evidence-based Interventions*. Oakland, CA: Context Press.

Herrin, M. & Larkin, M. (2013). *Nutrition counseling in the treatment of eating disorder* (2nd ed.). New York, NY: Taylor & Francis.

Koenig, K. R., & O'Mahoney, P. (2017). *Helping patients outsmart overeating: Psychological strategies for doctors and health care providers*. Lanham, MD: Rowman & Littlefield.

Murray, S., Anderson, L., & Cohn, L. (2017). *Innovations in family therapy for eating disorders: Novel treatment developments, patient insights, and the role of carers*. New York, NY: Taylor & Francis.

Piran, N., Levine, M. P., & Steiner-Adair, C. (2014, 1999). *Preventing eating disorders: A handbook of interventions and special challenges*. Ann Arbor: Taylor & Francis.

Walsh, B. T. (2015). *Handbook of assessment and treatment of eating disorders*. Arlington, VA: American Psychiatric Publishing.

Wonderlich, S. A., Peterson, C. B., & Smith, T. L. (2015). *Integrative cognitive-affective therapy for bulimia nervosa: A treatment manual*. New York, N. Y.: Guilford.

Wooldridge, T. (2016). *Understanding anorexia nervosa in males: An integrative approach*. New York, NY: Taylor & Francis

GENERAL/SELF-HELP

Andersen, A., Cohn, L., & Holbrook, T. (2000). *Making weight: Men's conflicts with food, weight, shape & appearance*. Carlsbad, CA: Gurze.

Anonymous (1989). *Take it off and keep it off: Based on the successful methods of Overeaters Anonymous*. Chicago: Contemporary.

Arterburn, S., & Lamphear, V. (1979, 1980, 1982). *Gentle eating workbook*. Nashville: Nelson.

Appendixes

Gaesser, G. A. (2002). *Big fat lies: The truth about your weight and your health* (Updated ed.). Carlsbad, CA: Gurze.

Gaesser, G. A., & Kratina, K. (2000). *Eating well, living well when you can't diet anymore: A guide to help you reach your personal health goal.* Parker, CO: Wheat Foods Council.

Glennon, W. (2000). *200 ways to raise a boy's emotional intelligence: An indispensable guide for parents, teachers, and other concerned caregivers.* Berkeley: Conari.

Greene, B. (2002), *Get with the program: Getting real about your health, weight, and emotional well-being.* New York: Simon & Schuster.

Hirschmann, J. R., & Munter, C. H. (1988). *Overcoming overeating.* New York: Ballantine.

Hirschmann, J. R., & Zaphiropoulos, L. (1993). *Preventing childhood eating problems: A practical, positive approach to raising children free of food & weight conflicts.* Carlsbad, CA: Gurze.

Homme, M. (1999). *Seeing yourself in God's image: Overcoming anorexia and bulimia.* Chattanooga: Turning Point.

Jantz, G. L. (1995, 2002, 2010). *Hope, help, and healing for eating disorders.* Colorado Springs: Waterbrook.

McGraw, P. C. (2003). *The ultimate weight solution: The 7 keys to weight loss freedom.* New York: Free Press.

Minirth, F. B.., Meier, P. D., Hemfelt, R., Sneed, S., & Hawkins, D. (1990). *Love hunger: Recovery from food addiction.* Nashville: Thomas Nelson.

Minirth, F. B.., Meier, P. D., Hemfelt, R., Sneed, S., & Hawkins, D. (2004). *Love hunger: Breaking free from food addiction.* Nashville: Thomas Nelson.

Roth, G. (1991). When food is love: Exploring the relationship between eating and intimacy. New York: Penguin.

Roth, G. (2003). *Breaking free from emotional eating.* New York: Penguin.

Shamblin, G. (2000). *Rise above: God can set you free from your weight problems forever.* Nashville: Nelson.

Shamblin, G. (1997). *The weigh down diet.* New York: Doubleday.

Skorusa, J. (2002). *Staying healthy God's way: Unlocking God's power for health, happiness, & prosperity.* Longwood, FL: Xulon.

Walker, P. (2014). *Complex PTSD: From surviving to thriving.* Lafayette, CA: Azure Coyote.

***

Appendix F

Web Sites

ABC's Ministries (2017). Disordered eating resources page. Available: http://abcsministriesnashville.com/DisorderedEatingResources.html

Academy for Eating Disorders (2017). *Home page.* Available: http://www.aedweb.org/index.php

Academy of Nutrition and Dietetics (2017). *Home page.* Available: http://www.eatright.org/

American Academy of Child and Adolescent Psychiatry (2017). *Home page.* Available: https://www.aacap.org/

American Association of Christian Counselors (2016). *Home page.* Available: http://www.aacc.net/

Anorexia Bulimia Care (2015). *Home page.* Available: http://www.anorexiabulimiacare.org.uk/

Beyond Hunger: Freedom from the Obsession with Food and Weight (2017). *Home page.* Available: http://beyondhunger.org/

BibleStudyTools.com (2014). *Home page.* Available: http://www.biblestudytools.com/

Bulimia.com (2016). *Home page.* Available: http://www.bulimia.com/

Canopy Cove Eating Disorder Treatment Center. *Home page.* Available: https://www.canopycove.com/

Celebrate Recovery (2015). *Home page.* Available: http://www.celebraterecovery.com/

Eating Disorder Hope (2017). *Home page.* Available: https://www.eatingdisorderhope.com/

Eating Disorder Referral & Information Center (2017). *Home page.* Available: https://www.edreferral.com/

Eating Disorders Mirror Mirror (2017). *Home page.* Available: http://www.mirror-mirror.org/

Eating Disorders Treatment Center at River Oaks Hospital (2017). *Home page.* [On-line]. Available: http://riveroakshospital.com/programs/the-eating-disorders-treatment-center/

FINDINGbalance. *Home page.* Available: http://www.findingbalance.com/

Focus on the Family (1997-2016). *Home page.* Available: http://www.focusonthefamily.com/

Gurze/Salucore Eating Disorders Resource Catalogue (2015). *Home page.* Available: http://www.edcatalogue.com/

Men get eating disorders too! (MGEDT) (2017). *Home page.* Available: http://mengetedstoo.co.uk/

Appendixes

Multi-Service Eating Disorders Association (MEDA) (2017). *Home page.* Available:
http://www.medainc.org/

National Alliance on Mental Illness (2017). *Home page.* Available: http://www.nami.org/

National Association for Males with Eating Disorders (NAMED) (2017). *Home page. Available:*
http://namedinc.org/

National Association of Anorexia Nervosa (ANAD) (2017). *Home page.* Available:
http://www.anad.org/

National Eating Disorder Information Centre (NEDIC) (2014). *Home page.* Available: http://nedic.ca/

National Eating Disorders Association (NEDA) (2016). *Home page.* Available:
https://www.nationaleatingdisorders.org/

New Life Ministries, Inc. (1999-2016). *Home page.* Available: http://newlife.com/

Pete Walker, M.A., MFT (2017). *Home page.* Available: http://pete-walker.com/

RehabCenter.net (2016). *Substance abuse and eating disorders: Two issues, one recovery.* Available:
http://www.rehabcenter.net/substance-abuse-and-eating-disorders/

Remuda Ranch Programs for Anorexia and Bulimia (2017). *Home page.* Available:
https://www.remudaranch.com/?flash=yes

The Center: A Place of Hope (2017). *Home page.* Available: https://www.aplaceofhope.com/

The Eating Disorders Victoria (2016). *Home page.* Available: https://www.eatingdisorders.org.au/

The National Eating Disorder Information Centre (2014). *Home page.* Available: http://www.nedic.ca/

The Renfrew Center Foundation (2017). *Home page.* Available: http://renfrewcenter.com/

The Something Fishy Website on Eating Disorders (1998-2017). *Home page.* Available:
http://www.something-fishy.org/

***

Appendix G

Support Group/Educational Curriculum

American Association of Christian Counselors (2001). *Healthy sexuality*. Forest, VA: Author

American Association of Christian Counselors (2007). *Fresh starts recovery series: Forgiveness: Getting beyond your pain & past*. Forest, VA: Author.

American Association of Christian Counselors (2008). *Breaking free*. Forest, VA: Light University.

American Association of Christian Counselors (2009). *Professional life coaching certificate training program: MLCH 101 Health & wellness coaching*. Forest, VA: Light University.

American Association of Christian Counselors (2013). *Food, Mood & Life Series: Eating Disorders Diagnosis and Treatment*. Forest, VA: Light University.

International Association of Eating Disorders Professionals Foundation (2017). Online institute for certification. Information available: http://www.iaedp.com/institute/

Kater, K. (2012). *Healthy bodies; Teaching kids what they need to know: A comprehensive curriculum to address body image, eating, fitness and weight concerns in today's challenging environment* (Volume 3) (2012). North St. Paul, MN: Body Image Health.

Laaser, M. (Speaker). (2003). *The Geneva series: course GSCO 501 Assessment & treatment of sexual addiction*. Forest, VA: American Association of Christian Counselors.

Lewis & Clark Graduate School of Education and Counseling (2017). *Continuing education eating disorders certificate*. Information available: https://graduate.lclark.edu/programs/continuing_education/certificates/eating_disorders/

Light University (2009). *Addiction & recovery*. Forest, VA: Author.

Light University (2013). *Food, mood & life series: Eating disorders: Diagnosis and treatment*. Forest, VA: Author.

McCubbrey, D. (2017). *Eating disorder intuitive therapy (EDIT)^{TM}: Eating disorder training & certification*. Information available: http://editcertified.com/

Mintle, L. (n. d.). *Courageous living series: You and your body: Understanding eating disorders*. Forest, VA: Light University.

National Centre for Eating Disorders (2012). Professional training courses in eating disorders, obesity & nutrition from NCFED. Information available: https://eating-disorders.org.uk/professional-training/

Appendixes

Sledge, T. (1992). *Making peace with your past: Help for adult children of dysfunctional families.* Nashville: LifeWay Press.

Woodley, J. (2008). *In the wildflowers.* Setauket, NY: Restoring the Heart Ministries, Inc.

***

The 12 Steps*

1. **We admitted that we were powerless over our problems and that our lives had become unmanageable.**
    "I know that nothing good lives in me...I want to do what is right, but I can't." – Romans 7:18, see also John 8: 31-36; Romans 7:14-25.

2. **We came to believe that a Power greater than ourselves could restore us to sanity.**
    "God is working in you, giving you the desire and the power to do what pleases him." – Philippians 2:13; see also Romans 4:6-8; Ephesians 1:6-8; Colossians 1:21-22; Hebrews 11:1-10.

3. **We made a decision to turn our wills and our lives over to the care of God.**
    "Dear brothers and sisters, I plead with you to give your bodies to God because of all he has done for you. Let them be a living and holy sacrifice–the kind he will find acceptable." – Romans 12:1; see also Matthew 11:28-30; Mark 10:14; James 4:7-10.

4. **We made a searching and fearless moral inventory of ourselves.**
    "Let us test and examine our ways. Let us turn back to the Lord." – Lamentations 3:40; see also Matthew 7:1-5; 2 Corinthians 7:8-10.

5. **We admitted to God, to ourselves, and to another human being the exact nature of our wrongs.**

    "Confess your sins to each other and pray for each other so that you may be healed." – James 5:16; see also Psalms 32:1-5; 51:1-3; 1 John 1:2-6.

6. **We were entirely ready to have God remove these defects of character.**
    "Humble yourselves before the Lord, and he will lift you up in honor." – James 4:10; see also Romans 6:5-11; Philippians 3:12-14.

7. **We humbly asked God to remove our shortcomings.**
    "If we confess our sins to him, he is faithful and just to forgive us our sins and to cleanse us from all wickedness." – 1 John 1:9; see also Luke 18:9-14; 1 John 5:13-15.

The 12 Steps Continued

8. **We made a list of all persons we had harmed and became willing to make amends to them all.**
   "Do to others as you would like them to do to you." – Luke 6:31; see also Colossians 3:12-15; 1 John 3:10-20.

9. **We made direct amends to such people wherever possible, except when to do so would injure them or others.**
   "If you are presenting a sacrifice at the altar and...someone has something against you, leave your sacrifice there at the altar. Go and be reconciled to that person. Then come and offer your sacrifice to God." – Matthew 5:23; see also Luke 19:1-10; 1 Peter 2:21-25.

10. **We continued to take personal inventory, and when we were wrong, promptly admitted it.**
    "If you think you are standing strong, be careful not to fall." – 1 Corinthians 10:12; see also Romans 5:3-6; 2 Timothy 2:1-7; 1 John 1:8-10.

11. **We sought through prayer and meditation to improve our conscious contact with God, praying only for knowledge of his will for us and the power to carry it out.**
    "Devote yourselves to prayer with an alert mind and a thankful heart." – Colossians 4:2; see also Isaiah 40:28-31; 1 Timothy 4:7-8.

12. **Having had a spiritual awakening as a result of these steps, we tried to carry this message to others, and to practice these principles in all our affairs.**
    "Dear brothers and sisters, if another believer is overcome by some sin, you who are godly should gently and humbly help that person back onto the right path. And be careful not to fall into the same temptation yourself." – Galatians 6:1; see also Isaiah 61:1-3; Titus 3:3-7; 1 Peter 4:1-5.

*NOTE: The 12 Steps Retrieved June 2, 2017 from http://liferecoverygroups.com/the-12-steps/

***

The ABC's of Eating Well

*A*lways pray before eating.

*B*e thankful for God's provision.

*C*ommit to change for Christ.

*D*rink plenty of water.

*E*xercise too for good health!

*F*ruit is a must! : *F*ried Foods should be limited, if at all!

*G*et plenty of sleep and rest.

*H*ave healthy snacks available/with you when not at home.

*I*nvite your family to join you on your journey to eating well.

*J*oin a support group, if necessary.

*K*iss "dieting" goodbye.

*L*imit sweets and high-fat foods.

*M*eats should be lean and baked rather than fried.

*N*ever allow anyone to pressure you into eating.

*O*nly eat when you are physiologically hungry; stop when full.

*P*ermanent healthy lifestyle change is a key to eating well.

*Q*uit making excuses for being overweight and/or unhealthy.

*R*esist temptations to overeat, under eat, and to eat unhealthy.

*S*et positive examples to others regarding food and exercising

*T*ake your time eating; eat slowly.

*U*nderstand your body's signals for hunger and fullness.

*V*ictory over disordered eating comes through Jesus Christ alone.

*W*ellness: strive for it!

E*x*amine your motives. Are they healthy?

*Y*ou alone can make the choice to strive for wellness.

*Z*ip those wallets, purses, and those lips when being tempted.

***

E Continued

ABOUT THE AUTHOR

Pamela K. Orgeron, M.A., Ed.S., BCCC, ACLC, formerly Pamela K. Owens (1960-) was born in Ashland, KY. In 1986 she received a B.A. degree in Journalism-Public Relations from Marshall University, Huntington, WV. Also in 1986 Ms. Owens moved to Nashville, TN where she spent over 8 years employed with the Jean and Alexander Heard Library, Vanderbilt University. Before moving back to Kentucky in 2000, she also worked for Harris Publishing and Thomas Nelson Publishers. Ms. Owens received both an M.A. (2003) and an Ed.S. (2009) degree in Adult & Higher Education, Counseling Specialization from Morehead State University, Morehead, KY. Ms. Owens moved back to Nashville in 2009. Since then she has received an Advanced Diploma in Biblical Counseling from Light University and became a Board Certified Christian Counselor and a Board Certified Advanced Christian Life Coach. In 2010 she married Milton J. Orgeron. She and Milton are General Partners in *ABC's* Ministries, and are members of The Donelson Fellowship Freewill Baptist Church, Nashville, TN. Mrs. Orgeron also is a certified writer with the Institute of Children's Literature, West Redding, Connecticut. She also is a member of the American Association of Christian Counselors, the International Christian Coaching Association, and the Christian Association of Psychological Studies.

Pamela K. Orgeron

Contact Information

Pamela K. Orgeron, M.A., Ed.S., BCCC, ACLC
Christian Author, Counselor, & Life Coach
General Partner, ABC's Ministries
For more information about ABC's Ministries:
Visit the Website:
https://abcsministries.wordpress.com/

Pam also may be reached through the following:
https://www.facebook.com/AttnPamatABCsMinistries/
https://www.linkedin.com/in/pamela-orgeron-57873045/

www.ingramcontent.com/pod-product-compliance
Lightning Source LLC
Chambersburg PA
CBHW080556030426
42336CB00019B/3208